NEW WORLDS

The Great Voyages of Discovery 1400–1600

RONALD H. FRITZE

SUTTON PUBLISHING

First published in the United Kingdom in 2002 by
Sutton Publishing Limited · Phoenix Mill
Thrupp · Stroud · Gloucestershire · GL5 2BU

British Library Cataloguing in Publication Data
A catalogue record for this book is available from the British Library.

ISBN 0-7509-2346-6

Endpapers, front: The departure of Christopher Columbus from Palos, Spain. (Giraudon/Art Resource, NY); *rear: The Fountain of Youth* by Jacquerio Giacomo. (Scala/Art Resource, NY)

For Twylia

Typeset in 11/15 pt New Baskerville.
Typesetting and origination by
Sutton Publishing Limited.
Printed and bound in England by
J.H. Haynes & Co. Ltd, Sparkford.

We hope, with the help of God, that the great trade which now enriches the Moors of those parts, through whose hands it passes without the intervention of other persons or peoples, shall, in consequence of our regulations [i.e., Portugal's in the Indian Ocean trade] be diverted to the natives and ships of our own kingdom, so that henceforth all Christendom, in this part of Europe, shall be able, in large measure, to provide itself with those spices and precious stones. This, with the help of God, who in His mercy thus ordained it, shall cause our designs and intentions to be pushed with more ardour the war upon the Moors of the territories conquered by us in these parts, which your Highnesses are so firmly resolved upon, and in which we are equally zealous.

King Manuel of Portugal to Fernando and Isabel, July 1499[1]

Even though the ancestors of these Indians must have known our holy Catholic faith, the people have forgotten it. So it was a great service their Catholic majesties did for God, discovering the Indies. Our nation acquired enormous merit by finding these provinces and kingdoms full of lost souls and idolaters, owing to the diligence of the admiral Christopher Columbus, in company with him and under his guidance. Thus in these countries so far from Europe, where Hell swallowed so many millions of souls, the sacred Passion and the commandments of God and the Catholic Church were reintroduced and cultivated; idolatries and diabolical sacrifices and rites devoted to Satan for centuries ceased; and the practice of abominable crimes and sins against nature were forgotten.

Gonzalo Fernández de Oviedo[2]

I must insist that by all I have seen and heard and read, never did any man or vassal do such great service to his lord or king as Christopher Columbus to the Castilian crown. As a king may grant a city or town, a dukedom or principality, even a kingdom to whomever he wishes to exhalt, this famous sailor and admiral Columbus gave Castile a world full of kingdoms from which untold and priceless treasure of gold and silver, emeralds and pearls, flow to Spain.

Gonzalo Fernández de Oviedo[3]

Everything that has happened since the marvellous discovery of the Americas – from the short-lived initial attempts of the Spanish to settle there, right down to the present day – has been so extraordinary that the whole story remains quite incredible to anyone who has not experienced it at first hand. It seems, indeed, to overshadow all the deeds of famous men of the past, no matter how heroic, and to silence all talk of other wonders of the world. Prominent amid the aspects of this story which have caught the imagination are the massacres of innocent peoples, the atrocities committed against them and, among other horrific excesses, the ways in which towns, provinces, and whole kingdoms have been entirely cleared of their native inhabitants.

Bartolomé de Las Casas[4]

You must know that you are now in India, the abode of a diversity of peoples who prosper and grow rich on their gleaming gold and precious stones, their cinnamon and spices. This country where you have now made harbour is called Malabar.

The Moor Monsaide to the Portuguese of Vasco da Gama.[5]

Columbus did not find out America by chance, but God directed him at that time to discover it: it was contingent to him, but necessary to God; he reveals and conceals, to whom and when he will.

Robert Burton[6]

The reformation was preceded by the discovery of America, as if the Almighty graciously meant to open a sanctuary to the persecuted in future years, when home should afford neither friendship nor safety.

Thomas Paine[7]

The discovery of America, the rounding of the Cape, opened up fresh ground for the rising bourgeoisie. The East Indian and Chinese markets, the colonization of America, trade with the colonies, the increase in the means of exchange, and in commodities generally, gave to commerce, to navigation, to industry, an impulse never before known, and thereby, to the revolutionary element in the tottering feudal society, a rapid development.

Karl Marx and Friedrich Engels[8]

If the discovery of America was the occasion of the greatest outburst of reckless cruelty and greed known to history we may say this at least for it, that the gold of Mexico and Peru, unlike the gold of alchemists, was really there, palpable, yet, as ever, the most elusive of the Fata Morgana that lure men away from their homes, as a moment of reflection will convince anyone. For nothing is more certain than that there will never be enough gold to go around, as the Conquistadors found out by experience.

Joseph Conrad[9]

CONTENTS

PREFACE

They've found in Portugal since then [the time of Pliny and Strabo]
And in Hispania naked men
And sparkling gold and islands too
Whereof no mortal ever knew

Sebastian Brant, *Ship of Fools* (1494)[1]

The age of exploration during the fifteenth and sixteenth centuries has always exercised a fascination for the peoples of Europe and those of European ancestry. This period, particularly after 1492, was a time of bewildering change and intense excitement for Europeans. Much geographical knowledge that had been ill understood by Europeans, or even completely unknown to them, appeared more clear. The broad outline of the earth and its many peoples stood revealed for the first time in human history. Only the northern waters and coastlines of the Pacific Ocean and the vastness of the deep South Pacific remained largely unexplored. Otherwise Africa, the Americas and Asia were all opened to direct contact and trade with Europe. In the Americas and parts of Africa and Asia, contact would be transformed into conquest when strong land powers were not present to curb European aggression. Thanks to the efforts, the perseverance and the courage of Prince Henry of Portugal, King João II, Christopher Columbus, John Cabot, Vasco da Gama and many others the world had become one. That geographical unification of the peoples of the earth is one of the most significant events in all history both for good and for ill.

This book's purpose is to tell the story of European exploration from about 1400 to about 1600. It is a story that has been told many times before and it will be told many more times in the future. Now, at the beginning of the new millennium, is a particularly good time to retell the story of the age of exploration once more. The 1990s contained several important historical anniversaries that were intimately connected to the age of exploration – the 500th anniversaries of Christopher Columbus's first western voyage, John Cabot's voyage and the voyage of Vasco da Gama. Columbus's quincentenary was the biggest and most publicized event of these three and as a consequence also drew the most attention and controversy.[2] All three anniversaries prompted much new and excellent historical research. Biographies, historical surveys, specialized monographs and editions of primary sources all appeared in great numbers. Although much of these historical works dealt directly with Columbus, Cabot or Gama, many of the new works dealt with other topics generally or specifically connected to the age of exploration. This book has attempted to incorporate as much of that new scholarship into its narrative as possible. Of necessity this book is Eurocentric and in particular it concentrates on the accomplishments of Portugal and Spain. It would have taken a much longer book to also present the perspectives of the Africans, the Native Americans and the Asians who were directly affected by European contact.

In the spelling of personal names, the most familiar English form has been used for Columbus, Cabot, Magellan and other well-known explorers or historical personages. Otherwise the proper form of the person's name in their own native language has been used. The terms 'New World' and 'American Indian' have been avoided, while the Americas and Native Americans have been used in their place whenever possible.

ACKNOWLEDGEMENTS

The approach of the quincentenary of Christopher Columbus started the chain of events that led to the writing of this book. It rekindled a boyhood interest in the age of exploration and prompted the development of a special topics class while the author was teaching at Lamar University. A course on Columbus and the age of exploration seemed a natural educational opportunity as 1992 approached and it was for both teacher and students. Preparations for the course and intensive reading about the age of discovery sparked the idea for a book. One book led to another and another and now I am finishing the third that has been inspired by Columbus's 500th anniversary. A quote from Gibbon concerning his thoughts on the completion of the *Decline and Fall of the Roman Empire* captures my own feelings about finishing this book, however minor it may be in comparison: 'My pride was soon humbled, and a sober melancholy was spread over my mind, by the idea that I had taken an everlasting leave of an old and agreeable companion.'[1]

Writing this book and the others would not have been possible without the academic home that Lamar University provided for me for seventeen years between 1984 and 2001. Since July 2001, I have taken up a new position at the University of Central Arkansas. Both institutions promote scholarship by their faculty and deserve to be praised for providing that support. The staff of both the Gray Library at Lamar and the Torreyson Library at UCA are efficient and always ready to help. Their interlibrary loan facilities have been indispensable for my work. Two colleagues and dear friends at Lamar University deserve special recognition. Professor Christine Bridges-Esser of the English and Foreign Languages department and Professor Larry Allen of the Economics department read and commented on every chapter of this book. Their careful reading made it better. Any errors and infelicities remaining in this book are all my responsibility. My good friend Professor Jeremy Black of the University of Exeter was instrumental in getting this book contracted with Sutton Publishing. Anyone who knows Jeremy is aware of his vast professional generosity to colleagues. They will also recognize his intelligence and the simple and congenial pleasure of his company. The number of books he has helped get into print would make a substantial library on their own. The staff at Sutton Publishing have also been a joy to work with on this project. My commissioning editor Christopher Feeney stands out for his upbeat approach and his firm patience with an author who missed a deadline by about the same margin that Columbus missed reaching Asia. Alison Flowers, the copy editor for this book, has also been a complete pleasure to work with as the manuscript has gone through the process of preparation for publication. I also owe a very big thank you to David Bowie of the Archives Department of the University of Central Arkansas. He has worked with me to find and digitalize all the black and white illustrations used in this book. His generosity with his time and technical skills is greatly appreciated and has enhanced this book. Finally I want to thank my wife Twylia for her love and support and for simply tolerating my sitting in the study working on a book. Her forbearance in this matter is particularly notable since in our own personal history she takes the role of William Henry, Duke of Gloucester to my Edward Gibbon. Be that as it may, without her around to share life with, none of it would be quite so good.

CHRONOLOGY

982	Erik the Red visits Greenland.
986	Bjarni Herjolfson sights North America while sailing to Greenland.
c. **1001**	Leif Ericsson sails to North America.
1095	Beginning of the First Crusade.
1237–42	Batu Khan and Mongol armies raid Eastern Europe.
1245–7	John of Plano Carpini's journeys to the Mongols.
1253–5	William of Rubruck visits Mongol capital of Karakorum.
1260–9	Nicolo and Maffeo Polo travel to China.
1271–95	Marco Polo's travels in China.
1291	Mameluke Turks capture Acre, the last Crusader stronghold in Palestine. Vivaldi brothers of Genoa attempt to sail to India either by circumnavigating Africa or crossing the Atlantic.
1312?	Lanzarote Malocello discovers Canary Islands.
1415	Portuguese capture Ceuta in North Africa.
1415–33	Various Portuguese voyages down the African coast to just short of Cape Bojador.
1419–25(?)	Discovery or rediscovery of Madeira by the Portuguese.
1427	Discovery or rediscovery of the Azores by the Portuguese.
1435	Gil Eanes manages to sail past Cape Bojador.
1451	Birth of Columbus.
1460	Death of Prince Henry the Navigator.
1479	Treaty of Alcaçovas.
1481	Portuguese build São Jorge de Mina on the Guinea coast.
1482–4	Voyage of Diogo Cão to Cape Santa Maria.
1485	Second voyage of Diogo Cão reaches Walvis Bay.
1487–8	Bartolomé Dias discovers Cape of Good Hope.
1492	**2 Jan.** Fall of Granada.
	3 Aug. Fleet of Columbus departs Palos.
	12 Oct. Columbus' fleet sights land in the Western Atlantic.
1493	**15 Mar.** Columbus arrives back at Palos.
1493–6	Columbus' second voyage to the Americas.
1494	**7 June.** Treaty of Tordesillas.
1497	**May–August.** John Cabot's voyage to Newfoundland.
1497–9	Vasco da Gama's first voyage to India.
1498	**18 May.** Vasco da Gama reaches India.

1498–1500	Columbus' third voyage to the Americas.
1498	**5 Aug.** Columbus lands on the South American mainland.
1499–1500	First voyage of Amerigo Vespucci to South America.
1500–1	Pedro Cabral's voyage to India.
	22 Apr. Pedro Cabral discovers Brazil for Portugal.
1501–2	Second voyage of Amerigo Vespucci to to South America.
1502–3	Vasco da Gama's second voyage to India.
1502–4	Columbus' fourth voyage to India.
1506	**20 May**. Death of Columbus.
1509	**3 Feb.** Battle of Diu.
1510	Albuquerque captures and defends Goa.
1511	Albuquerque captures Malacca.
1513	Balboa discovers the Pacific Ocean.
1515	Albuquerque captures Hormuz.
1517	Expedition of Francisco de Cordoba to the Yucatan.
1518	Expedition of Juan de Grijalva to the Yucatan and Mexico.
1519–21	Cortés' conquest of Mexico.
1519–22	Magellan's voyage of circumnavigation.
1524	**9 April.** Vasco da Gama sails to India on his third voyage.
	24 Dec. Death of Gama in India.
1424–5	Pizarro's first voyage in search of Peru.
1526–8	Pizarro's second voyage in search of Peru.
1530–3	Pizarro's third voyage to Peru and the conquest of Peru.
1534	Jacques Cartier's first voyage to North America.
1535–6	Jacques Cartier's second voyage to North America.
1536–7	Quesada explores and conquers Columbia and the Chibchas.
1539–43	De Soto's expedition to explore and to conquer La Florida.
1540–2	Coronado's expedition into the lands north of Mexico.
1541–2	Francisco de Orellana's voyage down the Amazon River.
1541–3	Third voyage of Cartier to North America and the voyage of Roberval.
1562	Jean Ribaut attempts first French settlement at Port Royal.
	John Hawkins' first slaving expedition to the West Indies.
1564	Second French attempt to establish a North American settlement.
	John Hawkins' second slaving expedition to the West Indies.
1565	Spanish forces destroy the French settlements in the Florida region.
1567–8	John Hawkins' third slaving voyage to the West Indies.
1577–80	Drake's voyage of circumnavigation.
1584–90	Sir Walter Ralegh's Roanoke Colony.
1595	**May–June.** Ralegh's first voyage to Guiana.
1617–18	Ralegh's second voyage to Guiana.

CHAPTER ONE

WORLD VIEWS BEFORE THE AGE OF EXPLORATION

The discovery of the New World marks the end of fabulous geography.
Joseph Conrad (1925)[1]

The age of exploration (1400–1600) opened up the geographical and cultural horizons of Europeans along with the rest of the world in an unprecedented and permanent way. The Greek and Roman merchants travelling to India and China during the era of the Hellenistic Kingdoms and the Roman Empire, the medieval Norse settlers of Vinland in North America in about the year 1000, Marco Polo and his contemporary merchants and missionaries travelling through thirteenth-century Asia, Ibn Battuta's years of journeying through the Islamic lands of Africa, Europe and Asia in the fourteenth century and the Ming Chinese voyages into the Indian Ocean during the early fifteenth century all opened their respective society's geographical horizons, but only temporarily. Geographical scope and apparent permanence are what set the accomplishments of the age of exploration apart from those of any other era of travel and discovery. To understand the enormous impact of the explorations made during this period, it is crucial to try to see the world through the eyes of Europeans in about the year 1400. What did they know about the world's geography and its peoples? That knowledge, or, as was sometimes the case, that misinformation, guided where they thought they were going and what they would find when they ventured out from Europe. It also tempered how they interpreted and processed their impressions of the new peoples, plants, animals and places that they encountered in the course of their journeys. This chapter will look out from Europe at what its inhabitants thought about the geographical and cosmographical nature of the world, the continents of Asia and Africa and the Atlantic Ocean.

ANCIENT AND MEDIEVAL COSMOGRAPHY AND CLIMATOLOGY

The cosmographical and geographical concepts of Europeans in 1400 were more limited and much more highly circumscribed when compared with those of people living in the twenty-first century some 600 years in the future. Fifteenth-century people had a geocentric view of the universe which was also quite a finite place. They possessed no sense of a macrocosm of distant stars and galaxies. No telescope existed to reveal the seemingly infinite depths of outer space. Instead the sun, the moon, the known planets and the stars rotated around the earth on celestial tracks. All celestial

Fra Mauro's world map, 1459. This provides a view of European geographical knowledge on the eve of voyages of the 1490s. (Scala/Art Resource, NY)

objects were enclosed in a sphere beyond which lay God, Heaven and the infinite. Knowledge of the microcosm did not exist either. Just as there were no telescopes, there were also no microscopes. The existence of bacteria and other microscopic organisms remained unsuspected. But these gaps in the medieval world view had no practical impact on humanity's ability to engage in exploration and travel.

It is important for students of history to avoid taking a condescending attitude towards the people who lived in the past. Modern people are not any more intelligent than their ancestors. Medieval people possessed systems of thought and knowledge that explained the world around them in a reasonably satisfactory and useful manner. In many ways, for their needs, the cosmographic theories of the ancient and medieval worlds served their users just as well as most scientific theories benefit people living in the modern age.

One aspect of late medieval cosmography that has been the subject of highly inaccurate impressions by modern popular culture is the question of the sphericity of the earth and the contributions of Christopher Columbus to that idea.[2] Thanks to the writings of the American Washington Irving (1783–1859), the mistaken notion arose that medieval people, both the highly educated and the uneducated, believed that the earth was flat. Then in the late fifteenth century the enlightened Christopher Columbus appeared and changed all that by arguing that the earth was round and proved it by his successful voyages. Nothing could be further from the truth. Knowledge of the sphericity of the earth goes back to the Pythagorean scholars of the fifth-century BC in Greek Asia Minor.[3] While there were a few ambiguous spots in the centuries immediately following the fall of the Western Roman Empire in AD 476, educated Europeans continued to reject belief in a flat earth from the classical era of the Greeks and Romans onward. Only Cosmas Indicopleustes, a mid-sixth-century merchant turned monk and cosmographer, attempted to argue, albeit somewhat confusedly, for a flat earth. His book *Christian Topography*, however, failed to convince any educated European of the early Middle Ages.[4] Both Bishop Isidore of Seville (*c.* 560–636) and the Venerable Bede (*c.* 673–735) have been mistakenly considered adherents of the flat-earth theory but careful examination of their writings show them to be followers of the prevailing spherical-earth theory. Such greats of medieval thought as St Augustine of Hippo (354–430), Albertus Magnus (1206–80) and Roger Bacon (*c.* 1213–91) in their writings all accepted the sphericity of the earth as common knowledge among the educated and so obvious a fact as to not require any proof. Nor did informed people living in fifteenth-century Europe question the sphericity of the earth.

The geographical question that had been debated without resolution since the Hellenistic and Imperial Roman eras concerned the size of the earth's sphere. Just how big was the circumference of the earth? No one knew for certain because the ancient and medieval technology available for making precise measurements of time and distance was not adequate for such a task. Several ingenious methods for measuring the earth's circumference were developed by scholars of the ancient world but they had produced significantly different figures. Erastothenes (b. 280 BC), the librarian of the Alexandrian Library, calculated that the earth was 250,000 stadia in circumference, which was a measure that came fairly close to being the equivalent of the earth's true circumference of 24,902 miles. Later Marinus of Tyre (fl. AD 100) revised and lowered Erastothenes' figures when he estimated that the earth's circumference was actually 180,000 stadia or about 18,000 miles. Unfortunately for the future quality of geographical knowledge through the Middle Ages, Marinus's calculation found favour with Claudius Ptolemy, who lived in the second century AD and was considered the greatest cosmographer and geographer of the ancient world.[5] Ptolemy's prestige among medieval European scholars meant the Marinus of Tyre's figure for the size of the earth was the one most commonly accepted by fifteenth-century geographers, including Columbus. But Marinus of Tyre's earth was approximately 25 per cent too small. For people arguing for the feasibility of a western voyage across the Atlantic to Asia, such as Paolo Toscanelli del Pozzo and Christopher Columbus, Marinus's small earth was a good thing. His figure for the circumference of the earth brought Asia and Europe about 6,000 miles closer together than the one calculated by Erastothenes. An ocean voyage that was 6,000 miles shorter was a more feasible enterprise given the limitations of fifteenth-century sailing vessels.

The zonal theory of climate formed a logical outgrowth of the concept of the earth as a sphere.[6] Parmenides (fl. 450 BC), an early Greek scholar, divided the earth into five sections of climate. His theory of climatic zones was based on the simple observation that in the northern hemisphere, lands to the south tended to be warmer than lands in northern regions. Frigid zones were located at the northern and southern poles, while along the equator lay the torrid zone that divided the earth. All three of these regions were considered uninhabitable and even impassable by normal human beings. In between them were the northern and southern temperate sectors which were potentially habitable. The great Aristotle adopted the zonal theory and thanks to his great authority, the concept entered the scientific lore of both European and Islamic civilization where echoes of it have persisted into modern times.

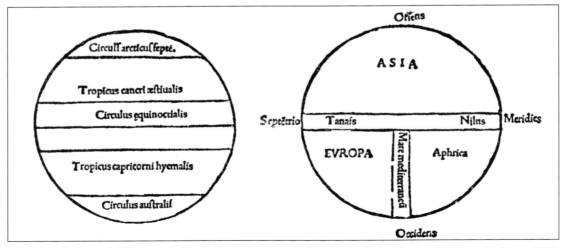

T-O Map of the world. From A.E. Nordenskiöld, *Facsimile-Atlas to the Early History of Cartography* (rprt. 1889, New York, Dover, 1973), p. 38.

Of special interest to the history of exploration was the idea that the torrid zone of the equator was uninhabitable and, in fact, was impossible to cross. The intense heat of this area would kill anyone foolhardy enough to try and cross it. Even the waters of the seas in the torrid zone were thought to be hot enough to be perpetually boiling. Such views had an inhibiting effect on people's desire to travel south and would bedevil Prince Henry the Navigator's early efforts to explore the West African coast. Equally fascinating is that the belief in the deadliness of the torrid zone persisted even after well-known western travellers, such as Marco Polo, had crossed the equator and survived. José de Acosta (1539/40–1600), a Spanish Jesuit scholar and missionary, commented on the fallacy of continuing to believe in the deadly temperatures of the torrid zone when practical experience had shown that it was not true. He recalled in his book *The Natural and Moral History of the Indies* how during his voyage from Spain to the Americas, cool temperatures at sea had compelled him to don a coat as his ship was crossing the equatorial waters where the supposedly deadly torrid zone was located.[7] Acosta and others recognized that their direct physical experiences contradicted Aristotle's ideas about the deadly nature of the torrid zone. But in spite of that failure of Aristotelian ideas, they continued to be taught in schools and universities because the zonal theory of climate possessed some validity as a description of the various weather conditions.

THE THREE CONTINENTS

From ancient times, peoples of Europe and the Mediterranean world knew of the existence of only three continents – Africa, Asia and Europe. There were vague but persistent speculations about antipodal lands to the west or to the south that derived from the Greek scholar Crates of Mallos (fl. second century BC).[8] No one, however, had managed to visit these antipodal regions by 1400, at least as far as anyone among the educated elite of medieval Christendom knew. The idea that there were only three continents had become deeply ingrained in medieval European thinking. The three continents were each associated with one of Noah's sons – Ham (Africa), Shem (Asia) and Japeth (Europe). Some traditions also identified each of the Three Magi or Wisemen with one of the three continents.[9] Adding any new continents to such a world view would require a major revolution in geographical thinking, something that no one in the fifteenth century was prepared to undertake, especially since there was as yet no empirical evidence to support such a change in ideas.

Medieval European knowledge of Asia and Africa remained somewhat unclear and muddled throughout the centuries before 1500. A large portion of that information consisted of highly inaccurate lore that had been inherited from the Greeks and the Romans. Prior to the age of Alexander the Great (356–325 BC), Greek knowledge of Asia had been limited to the Assyrians and their successors the Persian Empire. Herodotus, the first Greek historian, and early geographers appear to have considered the Middle East region and a vaguely recognized India as the geographical limits of Asia. Awareness of the Far East and China was virtually non-existent, while the vast

World map based on Macrobius showing an equatorial ocean dividing the known world from the antipodes. From Justin Winsor, *Narrative and Critical History of America* (Boston, Houghton Mifflin, 1889), vol. 1, p. 10.

region of Siberia was included in the continent of Europe. By the time of the Roman Empire of the second century AD, when the great geographer Claudius Ptolemy lived, the western world had become conscious of China and both China and Siberia were classified as part of the vast continent of Asia.

Some ancient geographers went on to develop the unfortunate idea that Asia was even bigger than it actually was. Marinus of Tyre estimated that the Eurasian landmass extended for 225° from east to west at the latitude of Rhodes. In reality the distance from east to west along that latitude was actually 140°. Ptolemy rejected Martinus's extreme figure but still significantly overstated the size of the Eurasian landmass by estimating it to be 180° across. Most of that extra area was credited to a vague but vast Asia. A bigger Asia along with a smaller circumference of the earth combined to make the potential size of the unexplored Atlantic Ocean even smaller.[10] Advocates of a western oceanic voyage to Asia, particularly Columbus, were quick to adopt concepts of a small earth and big Asia into their cosmographies.

ASIA AND THE MARVELS OF THE EAST

Western knowledge of Asia was plagued from its beginnings by a highly inaccurate corpus of information known as the 'Marvels of the East', or the 'Wonders of the East'.[11] According to this body of geographical and cultural lore, India and East Asia were lands full of strange and astonishing peoples, plants, animals, places and things. Ctesias of Cnidos (fl. 405–398 BC), a physician to the Persian King Artaxerxes II, wrote a description of India based on second-hand accounts garnered from other travellers. It depicted India as a land of monstrous races, strange animals, exotic plants and fabulous riches. Alexander the Great's (356–323 BC) conquest of the Persian Empire and his brief invasion of the Indian subcontinent further stimulated Greek interest in India and any lands that lay beyond. Megasthenes (*c.* 350–290 BC) travelled to India as a Seleucid ambassador to the court of Candragupta, ruler of the Mauryan Empire. His account, called the *Indica*, while more accurate than Ctesias also contained tales of bizarre humans, weird beasts and other marvels. The association of tales of wonders and riches with India is not surprising. It is a vast land that is filled with remarkable and exotic things, or at least it would have appeared that way to the Greeks of the fourth century BC. Brahmans, yogis, Hindu gods and goddesses, cobras, elephants, tigers and banyan trees all must have appeared highly unusual, fearsome or wonderful to early Greek visitors. The traditional 'Marvels of the East' were merely an exaggerated account of the many unique and unfamiliar things that actually existed in India.

The accounts of Ctesias and Megasthenes also proved to be amazingly enduring in their impact in spite of, or perhaps because of, their inaccuracies. Pliny the Elder (AD 23–79) in his popular *Natural History* based the description of India and the East on Ctesias, Megasthenes or sources dependent on them. In contrast, other Roman geographers such as Strabo (b. *c.* 64 BC) and Claudius Ptolemy (fl. second century AD) expressed doubts about the reality or the accuracy of the so-called 'Marvels of the East'. But when the Western Roman Empire collapsed during the fifth century AD, it was Pliny's books that survived and remained popular among medieval scholars. The more accurate geographies of Strabo and Ptolemy either became lost or were only available in far fewer copies. As a result, Pliny's version of the 'Marvels of the East' dominated and became the mainstay of medieval geographical thought.

The survival of such sensationalized information about the East is rather amazing because the Hellenistic Greeks and the Romans traded regularly with India. (See pp. 25–8.) Caravans trudged along the Silk Road of Central Asia, while Greek and Roman ships learned to sail to India using the monsoon winds. Although the details were vague, the existence of China and its silk was well known by the time of Pliny the Elder. It was called 'Seres', 'Serica', or 'Sinae', all names that reflected its strong association with the highly prized commodity of silk. There are some reports of Romans and Han Chinese trying to establish direct contact between their two cultures but nothing of substance came of these efforts.[12] Instead the better information about the East faded from the memory of westerners with the decline and fall of the Western Roman Empire.

The early Christian writers of the Roman Empire and later medieval Christian scholars took the lore of the 'Marvels of the East' and both added to it and Christianized it. Fabulous and largely fictitious exploits of a Judaized or Christianized Alexander the Great joined the catalogue of eastern wonders.[13] By the time of the Crusades in the eleventh century, Europeans once again knew that China and other Far Eastern lands existed. Benjamin of Tudela's description of his travels during 1166–71 was the first book in medieval Western Europe to mention China or a route to China.[14] At about the same time during the era of the Crusades in the twelfth and thirteenth centuries, a legend arose concerning a powerful Christian ruler whose kingdom was located in Asia. It was hoped that this reader, who was called Prester

John, and his great armies would come to the aid of the beleaguered Crusaders in Palestine and destroy the forces of Islam. The German chronicler Otto of Freising recorded that Prince Raymond of Antioch sent Bishop Hugh of Jabala to seek assistance from Pope Eugenius III in Italy. A meeting took place on 18 November 1145 during which Bishop Hugh told the story of a great Asian ruler named John who was both a king and a priest, a descendant of the Three Magi and a foe of Islam.

In the opinion of most modern scholars, Hugh of Jabala's story about Prester John did not create the legend. Instead it was a response to a number of Prester John stories that were already circulating in European courts and centres of power. Speculation about Prester John rose to new heights in about 1165 when the *Letter of Prester John* to the Byzantine Emperor Manuel began to circulate throughout Europe. Originally written in Latin, it was quickly and widely translated into the various European vernaculars. Although a complete fraud probably produced by some mischievous monk, for several centuries many believed it to be a genuine document. The *Letter of Prester John* performed the function of unifying the various oral tales of Prester John in written form. Other authors added various bits of fantastical geographical lore to the *Letter* over the years of copying and recopying it.

Medieval Europeans developed elaborate descriptions of the land of Prester John which borrowed heavily from the classical traditions of the 'Marvels of the East' and the romances of Alexander the Great. As a king of India, Prester John was supposed to be incredibly wealthy especially because all travellers' lore associated Indian rulers with great riches. The *Letter of Prester John* claimed that his kingdom encompassed the Three Indias and contained seventy-two provinces each ruled by a king. Its boundaries were unmeasurable. Agriculturally the realm of Prester John was a land of milk and honey but it also produced valuable pepper. Its rivers were cornucopias of gold and jewels. The land also contained a huge desert referred to as the Sandy Sea. It consisted of great shifting dunes of sand, rivers of rocks and was inhabited by fish who lived in sand not water. Prester John's realm also housed the Terrestrial Paradise at its far eastern extremity. This included the four rivers of Paradise – the Tigris, the Euphrates, the Pison and the Gihon, all of which were also filled with gold and precious stones. Near the Terrestrial Paradise was the much-sought-after Fountain of Youth which some writers claimed accounted for Prester John's apparently extreme longevity. The *Letter* also claimed that Prester John was descended from the Magi who were supposedly converted to Christianity by St Thomas. This overall image of Prester John was further reinforced by the account of his kingdom contained in the fictional *Travels of Sir John Mandeville*. The Prester John legend also received powerful impetus from ill-understood rumours of monumental events that were taking place in Central and East Asia in the mid-twelfth century as a result of the Mongol conquests. During the fourteenth and fifteenth centuries, as Asia became better known to Europeans as a result of the travels of John of Plano Carpini, Marco Polo and the many other Christian diplomats, merchants and missionaries, the location of Prester John's kingdom shifted to Africa, specifically the Christian realm of Ethiopia.

The dramatic change of Prester John's location from Asia to Africa is not quite as sensational as it might seem to a modern person. Medieval Europeans counted Ethiopia as one of the Three Indias, with the other two lying in Asia. Portuguese explorers, diplomats and missionaries who visited Ethiopia in the fifteenth, sixteenth and early seventeenth centuries all called it the land of Prester John. They persisted in calling the Emperor of Ethiopia by the title of Prester John to the great confusion of the Ethiopians who had no knowledge of this. But as the Portuguese visited Ethiopia and came to know more about that land, they began to realize that it was not the realm of the legendary Prester John. From that point the story slowly faded from consideration as an account of a true and literal geographical place. During its heyday from the twelfth to the sixteenth century, the legend of Prester John added further embellishments to the traditional corpus of lore concerning the 'Marvels of the East'. The belief in Prester John provided a significant motivation for European explorations and missionary journeys into Asia and Africa. Medieval Christian scholars even had a ready explanation for why there were marvels in the eastern and southern lands but not in Christendom. According to William of Auvergne, who wrote in the early thirteenth century, Europe lacked wonders because it was Christian. The demons responsible for amazing phenomenons no longer resided in Europe. In heathen lands like India, however, demons still worked their magic and monsters, magic gems and strange plants still flourished.

The catalogue of marvels is long and various monstrous races of men formed a large section of it, of which there were two basic types.[15] First, there were peoples who practised odd or repellent customs, at least according to the standards of western civilization, but who were otherwise physically just like other human beings. Gymnosophists stood on one leg and worshipped the sun, while Bragmanni were eastern wise-men who went naked and lived in caves. Stories of the former were probably based on contacts with the sun-worshipping Parsees, while the latter group were obviously derived from meetings with members of the Brahmin caste of Hindu India. Tales of some version of the female warriors commonly known as Amazons are found throughout the world. These women either ruled their men or lived in societies where men were excluded except on temporary occasions when they were admitted into Amazon society for purposes of procreation. But apart from reversing traditional gender roles, Amazons were fully human in every other sense. The same observation applied to the Anthrophagi or man-eaters. Their aberrant custom was to make a meal out of their fellow human beings, particularly hapless travellers passing through the lands of the Anthrophagi. Cannibalism, a word that did not come into usage until after Columbus's encounter with the Caribs of the Americas, is a practice that is almost universally known and which is also almost universally attributed to some distant and/or disliked group.[16] Anthrophagi, like other grotesque races, lived at the edges of the known world. Anthrophagi could be human in appearance or they could be truly monstrous. The Cynocephali, or dog-headed people, were supposed to be cannibalistic as were several other races of unnatural humans. Columbus and the other explorers of the fifteenth and sixteenth centuries were travelling to the

A detail from a map of Arabia, East Africa, West India and Madagascar by Diego Homem, 1558. This section depicts Prester John seated on a throne. Medieval Europeans initially placed Prester John and his kingdom in East Asia but by the sixteenth century his location had shifted to Ethiopa. (Heritage Image Partnership)

geographical fringes of the earth, at least from their point of view. They were taught by a centuries-old accumulation of geographical and ethnographical lore to expect abnormally behaving humans in such regions. So it is not surprising that Columbus would return from his first voyage with reports of cannibals and Amazons.

The second basic type of monstrous race were those humans who were physically different or deformed in some significant manner. According to medieval scientific concepts, environments with extremes of heat and/or cold would produce malformed humans. The wastelands of the arctic and the deserts and jungles of Asia and Africa were all potential breeding grounds for monstrous humans. Giants and pygmies were a simple form of mutant humans, only extremes of size set them apart from the norm. Other physical deformities were more striking. The Cynocephali were people with dogs' heads and human bodies and were an especially common variety of monstrous human.[17] Many other cultures of Asia mention their existence, not just medieval Europeans. Besides their practice of cannibalism, another interesting and symbolic aspect of the lore of the Cynocephali claimed that they and the Amazons bred with each other. All male children of such unions were born dog-headed while all female children were fully human in appearance. The Cynocephalic fathers would raise the

Amazon warriors using prisoners for target practice while they prepare to roast them over a fire. Medieval scholars considered Amazons to be both an unnatural monstrous race and a deadly one. An old print from J.A. Zahm, *The Quest for El Dorado* (New York, Appleton, 1917), p. 66.

male babies while the Amazons raised any female offspring. Thus were the two groups able to maintain their separate existences while occasionally engaging in some symbiotic breeding for their mutual perpetuation.

Other common monstrous races included the Cyclopes who were one-eyed giants of a surly and solitary nature, as opposed to the Monoculi who were normal-sized humans possessing only one eye. Unipeds or Monocoli were a malformed race that only had one leg and moved about by hopping. According to the medieval Norse work *Eirik's Saga* during the expedition of Thorfinn Karlsefni to Vinland, or North America, in the early years of the eleventh century, a Uniped killed Thorvald Ericsson with an arrow and hopped away to safety as the astonished Norse looked on. *Eirik's Saga* dates to about 1250 in its written form and the appearance of the Uniped testifies to the ubiquity of monstrous race lore in medieval Europe. Even the isolated Icelanders knew about the different varieties of abnormal humans and expected to encounter them at the margins of the known world.[18] Another race, the Blemmyae, had no head and instead had their faces on their chests and there were several dozen other types of monstrous humans thought to inhabit the wilds of Africa, Asia and the northern regions.

For medieval Christians, the important considerations regarding these miscreated races concerned whether they had souls, could believe in God and could be saved. In other words, were they ultimately humans or animals? St Augustine of Hippo

Cynocephali or dog-headed men, one of the monstrous races most commonly discussed by medieval scholars. This print is based on the *Livre des Merveilles* and comes from the Yule-Cordier edition of *The Travels of Marco Polo* (rprt 1903, New York, Dover 1993), vol. 2, p. 311.

Blemyae or acephali, a monstrous race with no heads and faces in their chests. Medieval geographers commonly placed them on *mappae mundi*. Ralegh would later claim that some lived in the kingdom of Guiana. An old print from J.A. Zahm, *The Quest for El Dorado* (New York, Appleton, 1917), p. 176.

answered that question with a firm yes and he was not alone. Other medieval theologians, however, were not so sure. By the sixteenth century, a similar debate, involving the great evangelist of the Native Americans, Bartolomé de Las Casas, would deal with the question of the humanity of the native inhabitants of the Americas.

Belief in the existence of monstrous races remained strong in fifteenth-century Europe in spite of the failure of earlier medieval travellers like Marco Polo and William of Rubruck to sight any such beings. Of course the fictional Sir John Mandeville encountered a variety of grotesque races during his travels. But in spite of their never having taken place, his experiences were generally better accepted and considered more factual than Marco Polo's by the people of the later Middle Ages. As a result they ironically provided seeming confirmation of the existence of the mythical monstrous races.

Other Christianized 'Marvels of the East' included hordes of gold and precious gems, the Terrestrial Paradise and the Fountain of Youth. Medieval people regarded hot climates as the natural home for precious metals and gems, particularly in the beds of rivers. According to the 'Marvels of the East', India's rivers were full of diamonds, rubies, emeralds and sapphires. Stories about the powerful empire of Prester John repeated the same basic descriptions. According to the Bible, the Terrestrial Paradise lay somewhere to the East and later medieval *mappae mundi* placed it at the eastern-most shore of Asia. The four rivers of Paradise were said to be full of precious stones, and at least they were in the vicinity of Paradise. When they flowed through the realm of Prester John, they were still close to Paradise. The *Letter of Prester John* also mentioned a fountain of youth which when old people drank of its waters, they were transformed back to being healthy thirty-year-olds. This miraculous fountain was located in the Far East on an island close to the Terrestrial Paradise. Since Columbus and the other early explorers at first thought they had reached eastern-most Asia by sailing west across the Atlantic, it is not surprising that they would assume that they were near the Terrestrial Paradise and the Fountain of Youth.[19]

The vastness of Asia was intimidating to European travellers. Its mountain ranges and deserts were formidable but they could be crossed by determined merchants and traversed they were countless times. The Indian Ocean had its special navigational secrets but it was not as unpredictable as the turbulent Atlantic Ocean. What truly blocked sustained European contact with Asia was the various Islamic powers that lay astride the trade routes and who were not inclined to share the wealth of the international trade with European merchants if they could avoid it.[20] Only

The Fountain of Youth by Jacquerio Giacomo, fifteenth century. Medieval Europeans believed that a Fountain of Youth existed somewhere in the vastness of eastern Asia. (Scala/Art Resource, NY)

Paradise on Earth by Dieric Bouts (*c.* 1415–75). For Medieval Europeans the Garden of Eden was a literal place that was located at the eastern-most point of the landmass that formed the earth's three known continents. The streams coming out of the Fountain in the Garden formed the Four Rivers of Paradise. (Réunion des Musées Nationaux/Art Resource, NY)

the incursion of the Mongols temporarily broke the Islamic monopoly from about 1250 to 1350. But even when the trade routes to Asia lay open to European merchants during the Pax Mongolica (Mongol peace), the journey was long, expensive and highly dangerous. Such conditions did not deter the Polos, and nor did they deter many others who neglected to leave a written account of their adventures like Marco Polo.

AFRICA

Africa lay to the south of Europe and was an even greater mystery to Europeans. For the ancient Greeks the region of North Africa that was located west of Egypt was known as Libya. That name sometimes referred to the whole continent of Africa. South of Egypt was the land of Ethiopia, sometimes called Abyssinia. Ethiopia had long been the home of advanced civilizations and when the first Greek travellers reached that country in 665 BC they were apparently quite impressed by what they saw. According to Homer, the gods were particularly fond of the dark-skinned Ethiopians and visited them for festivals. The Homeric Greeks followed later by Herodotus both conflated the Ethiopians of Africa with the dark-skinned peoples of India. A mistaken assumption arose that Ethiopia and the Indian subcontinent were somehow geographically connected. Given this error, it is not surprising that the great geographer Claudius Ptolemy concluded that the Indian Ocean was a landlocked sea with a land-bridge between Ethiopia and India located to the south. It also explains why some ancient geographers considered Africa and India to be one continent. By the twelfth century AD, medieval Europeans were referring to Ethiopia as Middle India, while Asiatic India was divided into the northern portion known as Nearer India and the southern portion known as Further India.

The size and the shape of Africa remained a mystery to Europeans in 1400. Their ignorance was not surprising. North Africa had been under Islamic domination from the time of the Muslim conquests of the seventh and the eighth centuries. In spite of the mutual hostility between Muslims and Christians, trade took place. Gold, slaves and salt were for sale in the North African markets, all of which were products that had their origins further south into and across the dreaded Sahara.[21] The Sahara is a huge desert that presents a formidable barrier to contact between the Mediterranean coast of North Africa and the savannahs and jungles of tropical Africa. But while the desert obstacle was formidable, it was by no means impassable. Oases of various sizes are scattered across the expanse of the Sahara. Even in antiquity caravan routes criss-crossed the great desert and provided viable routes for goods and people travelling north and south. The Garamantes were an ancient desert people known to Herodotus. After 200 BC Nabataean Arabs introduced the dromedary camel into Africa and as their use spread westward across the Sahara, these reliable ships of the desert helped to open caravan routes across even the most desolate sandy parts.[22]

Europeans knew about the gold of West Africa and mysterious Ethiopia but they knew little else about the great continent of Africa. Hostile Muslims jealously guarded knowledge of and access to the caravan routes. The true size and shape of

Africa were unknown. Greek and Roman geographers assumed that Africa was considerably smaller than it actually was. They imagined a continent that had a southern coastline that went eastward from approximately the southern coast of West Africa over to the Horn of East Africa. The lands of the Congo River basin and southward did not exist for the peoples of the ancient Mediterranean. This erroneous idea of a much smaller Africa made it appear to be much more feasible to circumnavigate it. Theoretically, given these assumptions about the size and the shape of Africa, a voyage along the southern coast of the continent would not have been much longer than a voyage sailing along the Mediterranean coast of North Africa. There was even some ancient testimony that such a voyage of circumnavigation had actually been made. In his *History* Herodotus reported that Pharaoh Necho of Egypt (r. 609–593 BC) hired some Phoenician sailors and ships to attempt to sail around Africa. The Phoenicians sailed down the Red Sea and southward along the coast of East Africa. Three years later they reappeared in the Mediterranean Sea having successfully completed their circumnavigation of Africa. No one followed up their singular accomplishment. The length of the voyage indicated that sailing around the southern coast of Africa was considerably more difficult and time-consuming than sailing along the coast of North Africa. Although Herodotus reported the story of the Phoenicians' voyage, he expressed scepticism

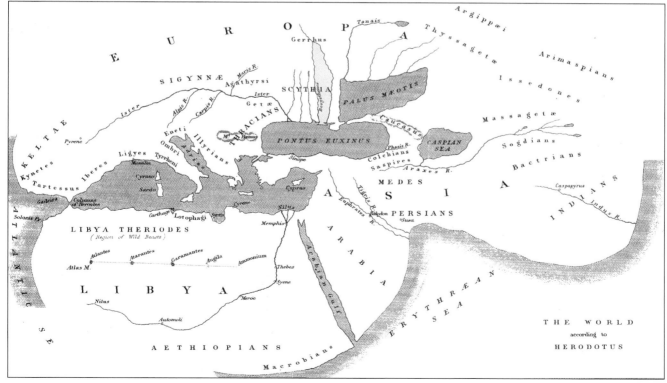

World map showing Herodotus's concept of geography. From E.H. Bunbury, *A History of Ancient Geography*, 2 vols, 2nd edn (rprt. 1883, New York, Dover, 1959), vol. 1, p. 173.

that the trip had even taken place, although a number of modern scholars have cautiously tended to accept the veracity of the story.

Other ancient attempts to circumnavigate Africa followed over the centuries but none came close to succeeding.[23] Still the tantalizing suggestion remained that such a voyage was geographically feasible and that remained in the consciousness of medieval Europeans. While this possibility of sailing around Africa and reaching India did not motivate Prince Henry the Navigator's initial efforts at African exploration, it did come to influence the succeeding Portuguese programme of African expeditions later in the fifteenth century. Ironically, just as the Portuguese were progressing down the west coast of Africa, theoretical geographical thought was shifting in a direction that was distinctly unfavourable to ideas about the possibility of circumnavigating Africa.

The ancient geographer Claudius Ptolemy believed that the Indian Ocean was a landlocked sea. According to his conception, Africa and Asia were linked together to the south of the Indian Ocean by a great landmass. If this situation was true, attempts to circumnavigate Africa to reach the Indian Ocean were doomed to failure. For most of the Middle Ages, however, Ptolemy's *Geography* was unknown and unavailable, unlike his astronomical writings. It was not until 1410 that a Latin translation of Ptolemy finally appeared in Western Europe and its diffusion was slow. There is no evidence that this Latin version of Ptolemy had reached Portugal by the time of the death of Prince Henry the Navigator in 1460.[24] Ptolemy's erroneous conclusions may have later given the Portuguese some cause to worry about their plans to sail around Africa to reach India but that worry would have been decisively dispelled by Bartolomé Dias's successful voyage down the West African coast and around the Cape of Good Hope to the Indian Ocean in 1487–8.

THE ATLANTIC OCEAN

To the west Europe was bounded by the Atlantic Ocean. Of the world's oceans, it is the stormiest and most turbulent. The Atlantic presented a formidable and dangerous challenge to the sailors of the ancient and medieval eras. Homeric Greeks thought it was part of the world-encircling River Ocean. Hellenistic Greeks and the Romans would have considered it to be a vast sea that separated them from Asia to the west. Medieval Arabs living in Islamic Spain and North Africa called it the Green Sea of Darkness and generally feared its storms, fogs and the monsters that supposedly lurked in its depths.

Prehistoric sailors along the coast of Western Europe were the first to travel on the turbulent waters of the Atlantic Ocean. Intrepid Phoenician seamen ventured from the Mediterranean Sea into the Atlantic well before 490 BC when the expeditions of Hanno and Himilco explored the Atlantic coasts of Africa and Europe. It appears that Phoenician ships also reached the Madeira and Azores Islands. The Greek Pytheas of Massilia circumnavigated the British Isles sometime between 325 and 300 BC. Roman ships sailed along the coast of Europe but they were not nearly as adventurous as the

Sir Walter Ralegh searching for El Dorado on the Orinoco River while fearsome monsters threaten, from a print by Theodore de Bry. From J.A. Zahm, *The Quest for El Dorado* (New York, Appleton, 1912), p. 157.

Carthaginians. The problem that Mediterranean sailors faced upon entering the Atlantic Ocean was that their galleys were not particularly suited for its rough waters.

After the Western Roman Empire fell in AD 476 knowledge of the Atlantic temporarily regressed. Irish monks were travelling regularly to Iceland well before 795. Shortly after daring Norse or Viking sailors from Scandinavia burst upon the Atlantic world. The first Viking raid occurred in 793.[25] Soon the Norse had ventured far into the Mediterranean Sea and deep into the interior of Russia. Eventually they made their way across the Atlantic to North America. The first Norse accidentally reached Iceland in 860. Permanent settlement began during the 870s. Other Norse ships sighted Greenland sometime between 900 and 930, although the first colony did not become established until 986. In that same year Bjarni Herjolfsson was blown to North America while on his way to join the first settlers on Greenland. Declining to go ashore on that unknown land he made his way instead to Greenland as quickly as he could. His discovery prompted Leif Ericsson to attempt a permanent settlement on Vinland, or North America, in 1001 or shortly thereafter. Historians have hotly debated the exact location of Vinland since the nineteenth century. Various speculations have identified

The Norse discovery of Greenland. From William Cullen Bryant, *A Popular History of the United States* (New York, Scribners, 1891), vol. 1, p. 35.

Vinland with sites anywhere from Florida to Labrador. Archaeological discoveries made in the 1970s have replaced speculation with hard evidence by uncovering a Norse settlement at L'Anse aux Meadows on Newfoundland. This site may even be Leif's actual camp. Leif's effort soon failed, as did several other later Norse attempts to colonize North America. The Norse possessed neither sufficient numbers nor the superior technology that would have enabled them to overcome the hostility of the indigenous inhabitants of Vinland. Later the Norse settlements scattered across the Atlantic withered as the climate turned cooler making the raising of cattle and crops less certain and rendering oceanic travel more dangerous. Sometime between 1450 and 1500 the last Norse settler on Greenland died.

Apart from the Norse, other medieval Europeans showed little interest in the vast ocean that formed the western boundary of their world. Medieval scholars accepted the sphericity of the earth. One of the implications of their awareness of the earth being round was that Asia lay on the opposite shore of the Atlantic Ocean from Europe. Aristotle, Seneca and Pliny had all speculated that India could be reached by means of a western voyage. Most medieval geographical thinkers, however, gave little time to such ideas. Their world view was restricted by centuries of regarding the Atlantic Ocean as the western-most rim of the world. Medieval world maps, or *mappae mundi*, contributed to that blinkered concept by placing Asia on the far eastern end of any flat map of the world while the Atlantic Ocean was placed on the far western end of the map with no apparent connection between them. It was a difficult conceptual framework to break out of, particularly since globe maps did not make their appearance until Martin Behaim constructed his globe in 1492. Without a sphere, it was difficult for a medieval scholar to picture the earth as a geographic whole. However, some medieval thinkers still managed to make the necessary conceptual break. Roger Bacon (*c.* 1214–*c.* 1294) in his *Opus Majus* discussed the ideas of Aristotle, Seneca and Pliny concerning the possibility of making a western voyage to Asia. He agreed that such a journey was possible. Thanks to the slow circulation of concepts in medieval Europe, Bacon's ideas had little impact until the beginning of the fifteenth century.[26]

Medieval Europeans did not simply view the Atlantic Ocean as a vast, watery void, possibly ending at the coast of Asia. Rather they filled it with mysterious islands that had occasionally been reached by legendary sailors. The ancient Irish *immrama* or voyage narratives told of Atlantic expeditions by Bran and Mael Dúin. That genre culminated in the popular Christianized *immrama* the *Navigatio Sancti Brendani*, composed between about 900 and 920. According to the *Navigatio,* toward the end of his life St Brendan (*c.* 486–575) undertook a seven-year oceanic voyage that visited many islands including the vast Land of Promise of the Saints. Some modern scholars have hypothesized that the historical St Brendan may actually have reached North America and that the *Navigatio* is a record of that voyage.[27] There is no convincing corroborating evidence to support that theory. Other legendary islands of the Atlantic

SIGURD STEPHANIUS, 1570.*

Sigurd Stephanius' map of 1570 showing the Norse discoveries in North America and depicting the Atlantic Ocean as an enclosed sea. From Justin Winsor, *Narrative and Critical History of America* (Boston, Houghton Mifflin, 1889), vol. 1, p. 130.

ft belua in mari que grece aspido delone dicit. lipido ul
Laune ñ aspido testudo. Ofew enim dicta. ob. secte
imminationem corporis. est eni siaio ille q̃ excepit

St Brendan the Navigator, thirteenth century, by an
unknown artist. A sixth-century Irish abbot,
St Brendan the Navigator supposedly sailed the
Atlantic Ocean and discovered western lands. In
this scene, he and his crew have mistakenly landed
on a giant fish. (Heritage Image Partnership)

included Avalon, the Isle of Brazil and Antillia among others. Antillia was by far the
most important to the history of geographical speculation, although it did not appear
on any European map until 1424 when the Venetian cartographer Zuane Pizzigano
placed it on his portolan sea chart. Many fifteenth-century Europeans thought Antillia
was the home of the legendary Seven Cities. The myth of the Seven Cities concerned
the story of how the Archbishop of Oporto and six other bishops along with their
Christian flocks had fled across the western Atlantic to escape the fury of the Islamic
conquest of Spain during the early eighth century. The refugees reached an island
about the size of Portugal and founded seven rich cities. During the fifteenth century
numerous tales of sightings or landings on the Isle of the Seven Cities or Antillia
circulated among the seafarers of Portugal and other countries. Both Toscanelli and
Columbus proposed to use Antillia as a way-station on their proposed voyages to Asia.[28]

Prior to the fifteenth century, the amazing thing is how little attention medieval
Europeans, apart from the Norse, paid to the Atlantic Ocean. For the most part, medieval
European voyages on the Atlantic were confined to routes hugging the coasts of Europe
and the British Isles. It was not until the fourteenth century that fishermen from England
and the German cities of the Hanseatic League began to visit the rich fishing grounds of
Iceland. At about the same time French and Basque sailors began to fish the region to
the south-west of Ireland. Such voyages allowed many different Europeans to develop the
experience and skills needed to sail the challenging and often deadly Atlantic Ocean.[29]
Prior to 1400, however, there was no serious or sustained efforts to reconnoitre or to cross
the great ocean that formed the western boundary of the medieval European world view.

CHAPTER TWO

TRADE AND CONTACT BETWEEN EUROPE, ASIA AND AFRICA BEFORE THE 1490s

According to what is said by the experienced pilots and mariners of those parts, there be 7,459 Islands in the waters [south of China] frequented by the said mariners. . . . And there is not one of those Islands but produces valuable and odorous woods like the lignoloe, aye and better too; and they produce also a great variety of spices. . . . In fact the riches of those Islands is something wonderful, whether in gold or precious stones, or in all manner of spicery; but they lie so far off from the main land that it is hard to get to them.

Marco Polo[1]

Venice was the Autocrat of Commerce; her mart was the great commercial centre, the distributing-house from whence the enormous trade of the Orient was spread abroad over the Western World.

Mark Twain (1869)[2]

Throughout much of human history, besides ever present curiosity, three things have motivated people to travel long distances – conquest, religion and trade.[3] Alexander the Great and his soldiers were not only the greatest conquerors of the ancient world, they also rank among its greatest travellers. Buddhism originated in India during the fifth or sixth century BC and spread to South-East Asia during the third century BC. It had reached China by the beginning of the Christian Era and entered Japan about 500 years later. Missionaries carried Buddhism's teachings throughout Asia while Buddhist pilgrims visited their religious homeland in India to acquire knowledge, relics and sacred texts to take back to their native lands. Christianity spread throughout the Roman Empire during the first three centuries AD until it became a legal religion in 313. It had taken definite root in Ethiopia by the fourth century with Christian communities appearing in India, Central Asia and East Asia by the seventh century. The first Christian missionaries visited all of those places much earlier than these dates, which mark the establishment of permanent Christian communities.[4] Islam spread more by means of conquest than by the proselytizing of its missionaries. Its founder Muhammad died in 632 and within 100 years of his death, the followers of Islam dominated the lands from the Iberian Peninsula along the south coast of the Mediterranean Sea all the way across the Middle East to the borders of China. After that date Islam continued to spread, albeit more slowly.[5] Long-distance trading had tended to provide a more steady motivation for travel and exploration than conquest or religion, although its manifestations have been far less dramatic.

Sea to the Gulf of Oman and turned north into the Persian Gulf where the trade goods were unloaded in the vicinity of modern Basra. From there caravans carried the Indian goods up the Tigris River to Seleucia. At that point the second route merged with the all-land route and headed toward the ports of Phoenicia, Antioch or Ephesus.

The third means by which Indian goods were transported to the Hellenistic Mediterranean was an all-water route and also originated in the ports of north-western India. After sailing across the Arabian Sea, however, instead of turning into the Persian Gulf, the Arab and Indian merchant ships coasted along the southern shore of Arabia and entered the mouth of the Red Sea at Aden. At that point the Indian goods were transferred to Greek ships from Ptolemaic Egypt, which sailed north to the Gulf of Suez. There the goods were put on caravans that carried them over to the Nile River valley and on to the great port of Alexandria. This trade was extremely lucrative and the Ptolemaic rulers of Egypt made it their policy to maintain a state monopoly over the trade in Indian goods. During the reigns of the early Ptolemies, they were in a good position to maintain their monopoly since they controlled not just the Red Sea route but also the ports of Phoenicia and Syria. Only Ephesus lay beyond their borders. In effect almost all Indian trade goods entering the Mediterranean passed through Ptolemaic hands except for those that travelled to Ephesus. That highly favourable commercial situation deteriorated drastically when the Seleucid Kingdom under Antiochus III the Great conquered Syria and Palestine, removing them from the Ptolemies in 200 BC. The defeat left the Ptolemies only in control of the Red Sea route, which was dominated from Aden to India by Arab and Indian middlemen who drove up prices and jealously excluded any Greeks, considering them as interlopers. On the other hand, some Indian merchants occasionally made their way up the Red Sea and all the way to the markets of Alexandria.

The traditional sea-way from the mouth of the Red Sea to India involved hugging the shore of southern Arabia. That route was safer than taking to the high seas especially for the flimsy Arab vessels which were both relatively small compared to other ancient sea craft and were built without nails. In 510 BC, the Greek Scylax sailed the coastal route on a mission for a Persian king who wanted to improve trade and communication between the various parts of his empire which included Egypt. No permanent changes in the nature of Indian Ocean trade followed from that voyage. Normally any Greek ship daring to follow that route faced a hostile coastline inhabited by resentful Arab traders with no tolerance for interlopers. That hostility made direct Greek voyages to India prohibitively hazardous. Then in about 120 BC, an Indian vessel ran aground on the western shore of the Red Sea. On it Ptolemaic officials found one surviving sailor who was just barely alive. His fellow shipmates had all died from their ordeals at sea and on the desolate coast. The Egyptians nursed the sailor back to health and he eventually learned the language of his hosts. Once he could make himself understood, the Indian mariner offered to pilot an Egyptian ship to India: once there they could make a fortune taking a cargo of Indian luxuries back to Egypt. The Indian's proposition appealed to King Ptolemy VIII Physkon (r. 146–116 BC), who organized an expedition.

Alexandria, Egypt. From William Cullen Bryant, *A Popular History of the United States* (New York, Scribners, 1891), vol. 1, p. 97.

He gave Eudoxus of Cyzicus command of the ship and with the Indian's help, the Greek–Egyptian vessel made a successful and lucrative round trip to India by sailing across the open waters of the Indian Ocean. Greek ships were built heavier and sturdier than Arab vessels and so could better withstand the turbulence and buffeting of a high-seas voyage.

Far more important, Eudoxus and his pilot, Hippalus, learned the secret of the monsoon winds as a result of this voyage. Climatic conditions involving the differences in the seasonal heating and cooling of the Asian landmass and the Indian Ocean create the monsoon winds. During the summer months the winds blow steadily from the south-west and are ideal for carrying a sailing ship from the mouth of the Red Sea across the Indian Ocean to the western coast of India. This summer monsoon can be violent with its winds often reaching gale force. The fragile dhows, the traditional coastal vessels of the Arabs, were not capable of surviving such weather conditions. During the winter months the course of the monsoon switches to the opposite direction. Blowing steadily from the north-west, the winter monsoon is gentle and so it could be and was used by the Arab dhows. Eudoxus's voyage opened up India to direct commercial contact with the Greeks of Egypt. It is not really accurate, however, to credit Eudoxus or Hippalus with discovering the monsoons. Indian vessels appear to have been using both winter and summer monsoons for quite some time while the

Arabs took advantage of the gentle winter monsoons to propel their ships. What Eudoxus and Hippalus did was to acquire that knowledge for the Mediterranean world and so open up the Indian Ocean to Greek shipping. It turned out to be a somewhat bitter accomplishment for Eudoxus. The greedy Ptolemaic government gobbled up most of the profits from his first voyage. When he made a second trip the same thing happened. Frustrated Eudoxus tried to avoid the Ptolemaic state monopoly over trade by attempting to circumnavigate Africa. Starting from the western Mediterranean and sailing through the Straits of Gibraltar, nothing came of Eudoxus's effort. Forced to turn back during his first attempt to sail around Africa, he disappeared during his second venture. Still, in spite of the somewhat stifling control of the Ptolemaic government, Greek ships began to make regular trading voyages to India.

Rome inherited this Indian Ocean trade when it added Egypt to its empire in 30 BC. But the Romans did more than maintain the existing commercial links with India, they greatly expanded the geographical scope of western trading interests into South and East Asia and also engaged in considerable diplomatic activity. An embassy from Ceylon, or as the ancient Greeks and Romans called it, Taprobane, visited Emperor Augustus in 26 BC. It was not a unique event. Other Indian powers sent ambassadors and diplomatic contacts were maintained between them and the Roman Empire through the reign of the Emperor Justinian (r. AD 527–65). Roman merchants regularly travelled to India and during the second and third centuries AD even reached China.

THE SILK ROAD

The fabled Silk Road between China and the West was coming into use at the same time or possibly even earlier than the high-seas trade route across the Indian Ocean. Beginning in about 800 BC, Chinese merchants carried goods to the nomadic Scythian tribes of Central Asia. Over time Chinese items, particularly the universally popular silk, worked their way into lands further and further west. Silk definitely prompted the growth of this trade route. It was a highly prized fabric in the ancient world. People wore it as clothing or used it in religious rituals as the archaeological evidence from various settlements in Central Asia shows. Eventually Chinese goods reached the Middle East and the Mediterranean world of the Hellenistic Greeks and the Roman Empire. Although the Mediterranean lands produced some silk from the cocoons of wild moths, 90 per cent of the silk they used was imported from China. It was a very popular fabric among rich Romans. By 100 BC records show that twelve caravans, each containing 100 or more people, travelled from China to the West every year. This so-called Silk Road had a dual function – to carry the luxury product of silk to the Mediterranean world and to carry more mundane trade goods to the steppe tribes that lived along its route.[11]

The Silk Road began in China at the city of Ch'ang-an and followed along the far western portion of the Great Wall. After passing through the town of An-his, several alternative routes took caravans around or through the fearsome Takla Makan desert. All of these roads eventually headed for the city of Kashgar on the western edge of the

Takla Makan. From there, the caravans moved on to the famed trading cities of Tashkent and Samarkand. At Samarkand the Silk Road merged with the all-land route between India and the Mediterranean world. Caravans from China could continue west to Seleucia (also known as Ctestisphon) with their final destination being the Mediterranean or Black Sea ports or they could turn south and cross the Hindu Kush mountains into India. It took about six months to travel from Peking to Samarkand.

The Silk Road passed through some of the world's most rugged mountains and harsh deserts. Predatory nomadic tribes occasionally attacked hapless caravans. Most groups, however, were more interested in obtaining trade goods and in gathering tolls or extorting protection money from the itinerant merchants. Obviously the Silk Road functioned best when great empires imposed order along substantial portions of its route. Not surprisingly, the heyday of the Silk Road was from 200 BC to AD 400 when the great empires of the Hellenistic Greeks and the Romans flourished in the West and the Qin and Han dynasties ruled China in the East. There is no evidence, however, that Roman and Chinese merchants or diplomats ever made direct contact along the Silk Road. The Parthians and later the Sassanid Persians whose empires straddled the great network of overland trade routes between East and West jealously guarded their position as middlemen and worked hard to prevent such a juncture.[12] The political and military power of these empires had seriously declined by about AD 400 and the traffic along the Silk Road slowed dramatically, although it never completely halted.[13]

Samarkand, one of the important cities located along the Silk Road. From the Yule-Cordier edition of *The Travels of Marco Polo* (rprt. 1903, New York, Dover, 1993), vol. 1, p. 184.

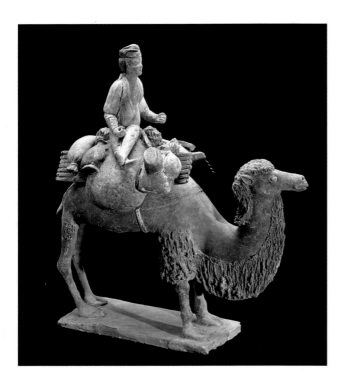

A terracotta figurine, Tang dynasty (618–906). Camels and riders like this one trudged back and forth along the Silk Road for centuries. (Réunion des Musées Nationaux/Art Resource, NY)

EAST–WEST TRADE BEFORE THE CRUSADES

The Byzantine or Eastern Roman Empire inherited the position of being the most important conduit of the East–West trade in luxury goods. Its capital of Constantinople also replaced decaying Rome as the principal market for Asian goods. Because of Constantinople's geographical position, the importance of the land routes of the Silk Road and the caravan roads from India increased. At the same time the sea routes from India through Egypt declined in their relative importance. The Byzantine government established a monopoly over the importation of silk from China during the fifth century. Shortly thereafter in 553 two Nestorian Christian monks smuggled the eggs of the silkworm out of China by concealing them in the hollow of a bamboo cane. They brought the eggs to Constantinople and from that point onward the production of domesticated silk spread through the Mediterranean world over the course of the next centuries. Western demand for silk was so high that imports from China continued, although the Chinese domination of silk production was broken. The same thing could not be said for Europe's growing demands for Asian spices and other luxuries.[14]

The problem with the Asian luxury trade for the European peoples was that they were located at the far end of a long and complicated network of trade routes. Goods passed from middleman to middleman, with a steady rise in prices occurring with each change of hands. Islam's rise to power during the seventh and eighth centuries and its conquest of Egypt, the Levant, Mesopotamia and Persia placed a powerful and

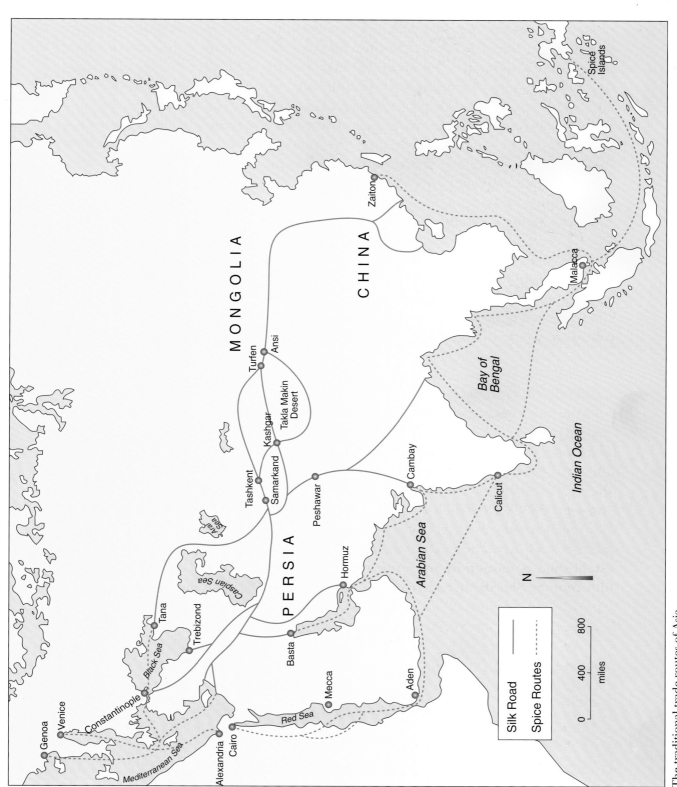

The traditional trade routes of Asia.

sometimes hostile middleman between the Europeans and the Asian spices they desired. Europeans faced the same problem with their trade with sub-Saharan Africa when Muslim forces conquered North Africa and took control of the caravan routes for gold and slaves. In this international network of trade, the Muslim lands functioned almost exclusively as middlemen and added little in the way of commodities to the flow of goods between East and West and between Europe and tropical West Africa. Trade goods passed through the Islamic lands or they were purchased by interested locals. Islamic merchants and governments grew rich from their fortuitous position in the network of trade routes but they did not contribute anything significant to the types or the amounts of the goods in circulation.[15]

In 969 the Fatimid rulers of Egypt broke away from the political control of the Abbasid Caliphs in Baghdad. They used their independence to re-establish Egypt's place as a major conduit for the spice trade between Asia and Europe by reopening the Red Sea and Indian Ocean trade route.[16] The flow of international commerce through the Middle East, particularly Egypt, also brought about the rise of various trading cities in southern France and Italy, most notably Venice and Genoa. These cities engaged in naval warfare against various Islamic powers from about 900 onward and quickly took over commercial shipping on the Mediterranean Sea. By 1000 the merchants of the Italian cities of Amalfi and Venice were carrying Asian spices to the rest of Europe. More than any other trading city, the Venetians developed very comfortable mercantile relations with the various Muslim powers.[17]

While the European trading cities aggressively scrambled to participate in the trading of Asian spices and luxuries, lulled by their geographically privileged position as middlemen, Muslim merchants rested on their economic laurels. Islamic

Venetian gallerys carried trade goods from the Near East to Europe. From Henry Eldridge Bourne and Elbert Jay Benton, *Introductory American History* (Boston, D.C. Heath, 1912), p. 136.

civilization showed slight interest in developing or promoting improvements in naval technology or maritime methods. Muslim merchants demonstrated no great curiosity or interest in the geographies or cultures of the lands around them. Marco Polo's account of Asia provided European merchants with far more accurate and useful information than was available to Muslim merchants of the late thirteenth century. Muslims also lacked the curiosity and the drive needed to engage in successful exploration.[18]

THE CRUSADES AND THE PAX MONGOLICA

The era of the Crusades (1096–1291) brought about cultural changes that significantly affected the international trade between the East and the West. When Crusaders visiting the Levant came into contact with Asian luxury goods on a more regular basis, they developed an even stronger taste and desire for those products than had existed previously. They took their tastes for Asian luxuries home with them and introduced others to the same goods. As a result European demand for spices and other exotic goods increased. The Crusades also embittered the peoples of the Islamic world against Christian Europe and so greatly increased the mutual hostility that had long existed between the two religions and civilizations. Christian fleets dominated the eastern Mediterranean from 1100 to 1291 and caused international trade to divert from Muslim Alexandria to the Christian-controlled ports of Tyre and Acre.[19]

While the Crusades changed the nature and the structure of the long-distance trade in Asian luxury goods, the establishment of the Mongol Empire during the early to mid-thirteenth century created an even greater impact. Genghis Khan forged the various Mongol tribes into a virtually unstoppable military machine. Under his leadership, Mongol forces overthrew the Qara Khitai Empire in 1218 and in 1219 destroyed the Khwarazmian Empire which sat astride the Silk Road. A Mongol raiding expedition under the command of the ferocious and highly effective general Subotai inflicted a nasty defeat on the army of Kiev in Russia at the Battle of Kalka River in 1223. The Mongol conquest of the Chin Empire in northern China began in 1211 but was not completed until 1234. Meanwhile, Genghis Khan died in 1227 but his empire lived on and continued to grow. From 1231 to 1236 Mongol forces devastated Persia and the Caucasus region. Then, in 1237, the Mongols returned to Russia under the leadership of Batu Khan and Subotai. By 1240 the ruthless invaders had captured Kiev and laid waste to the surrounding region. Turning on Central and Eastern Europe, the Mongol armies inflicted a series of defeats on German, Polish and Bohemian troops that culminated in the massive defeat of King Bela of Hungary at the Sajo River on 11 April 1241. An uncomprehending Europe lay open to further depredations when the death of the Great Khan Ogedei in the Mongolian homeland prompted the unstoppable Mongol armies to withdraw. Fortunately for the inhabitants of Central and Western Europe, the Mongols never returned, although much of Russia lay under the yoke of the Khanate of the Golden Horde for centuries.

A fifteenth-century map of
Constantinople by an unknown
cartographer. (Heritage Image
Partnership)

The central lands of Islam felt the next frightful strike of the Mongol lightning bolt.
In 1243 a Mongol army defeated the Seljuk Turks at the Battle of Kosedagh shattering
the large but rickety Seljuk Empire and bringing Anatolia under Mongol domination.
Even more fearsome was the Ilkhan Hulegu's conquest of southern Mesopotamia and
Syria between 1255 and 1260. Mongol troops took Baghdad in 1258 and proceeded to
execute the last Abbasid Caliph by sewing him up in a rug and having horses trample
him to death. Islam appeared to be on the verge of extinction to the wondering eyes
of the Crusaders as they gazed upon the destruction from their heavily fortified coastal
enclaves and castles. Christian speculation identified the Mongols as the subjects of
the legendary Christian monarch Prester John. The Pope and other Christian rulers
began to evaluate the Mongols as potential allies and converts rather than savage
marauders. But like Europe in 1241, Islam received a reprieve from utter ruin. The
Great Khan Mongke died in 1259 and the main Mongol armies in the Middle East
quickly headed off to the great rendezvous at the Mongol capital of Karakorum to
help elect his successor. In their absence, the Mamelukes of Egypt managed to defeat
the Mongol occupation force at Ain Jalut in 1260, a victory whose prime significance
lay in its psychological impact. It ended the Mongols' reputation for invincibility. The

Mongol conquests had reached their high point in the Middle East. Thereafter hostilities would periodically erupt between the Mongols and the Mamelukes in the decades that followed, while Crusaders and the Mongol Ilkhans of Persia sporadically courted each other as allies against Islam. No great results, either military or political, occurred as a consequence of these exertions.

The Mongol conquests and the Pax Mongolica that was established over much of Asia did have a significant commercial impact on the long-distance trade between Asia and Europe. For the first time in history Europeans established direct contact with the Far East, especially China. European geographical knowledge about Asia improved dramatically. Initially the Mongol conquests had disrupted the long-distance commercial network. Marauding armies made most travel along the caravan routes far too dangerous. Many of the fabled trading cities located along the Silk Road were mercilessly and devastatingly sacked. The damage transformed Samarkand into a mere shadow of its former greatness, while Balkh was destroyed so utterly that it was never re-occupied. Once the Mongols consolidated their power, international trade resumed. Now merchants could travel vast distances without danger or serious impediment because so many lands were under the strict rule of the Mongols.[20]

A sixteenth-century illustration showing Genghis Khan's troops storming Tangut fortress by an unknown artist. The armies of Genghiz Khan and his successors swept across Asia and parts of Europe to create a vast empire and the orderly conditions that long-distance traders needed. (Gulistan Imperial Library, Teheran/Art Resource, NY)

EUROPEAN TRAVELLERS IN ASIA

Diplomatic necessity tinged with missionary zeal motivated the first Western European visitors to the Mongol homelands.[21] Between 1245 and 1247 the Franciscan friar John of Plano Carpini travelled to the Great Khan of the Mongols as an envoy of Pope Innocent IV. Carpini's mission took two-and-a-half years and consisted of a round trip of 15,000 miles. Carpini described his travels: 'We feared we might be killed by the Tartars [i.e., the Mongols] or other peoples, or imprisoned for life, or afflicted with hunger, thirst, cold, heat, injuries, and exceeding great trials almost beyond our powers of endurance – all of which, with the exception of death and imprisonment for life, fell to our lot in various ways in a much greater degree than we had conceived beforehand.'[22] Diplomatically the mission

Soldiers of the First Crusade sighting Jerusalem for the first time. From Gustave Dore, *Dore's Illustrations of the Crusades* (New York, Dover Publications, 1997).

failed, but it did produce the first European description of Mongolia and China, Carpini's *History of the Mongols*.[23]

Other delegations visited the Mongols, although they were sponsored by King Louis IX of France not the papacy. Ascelinus of Lombardy reached the camp of the Mongol general Baiju at the Caspian Sea in 1247, while between 1249 and 1251 Andrew of Longemeau visited the Mongol regent Oghul Ghaimish at Lake Balkash. Neither mission proved successful, and on 7 May 1253 William of Rubruck set out from Constantinople on a third mission from Louis IX to the Great Khan at the Mongol capital of Karakorum. Travelling through Central Asia by means of the Mongol post-horse system, he arrived at Karakorum on 3 January 1254. Winter conditions made the latter part of his journey particularly harsh and his chronically drunk interpreter Abdullah added to the general unpleasantness of the situation. During his stay among the Mongols, William of Rubruck encountered various people from the many parts of Eurasia caught in the net of the Great Khan's empire, including Nestorian Christians, Russians and Chinese. The Great Khan Mongke expressed some interest in an alliance with the Christians even as the Mongol assaults on the Islamic heartlands were commencing. Ultimately, however, William of Rubruck's diplomatic efforts produced no tangible results. Even his narrative of his journey and his astute observations on Mongol culture were largely forgotten until the nineteenth century. Later the Nestorian clergyman Rabban Sauma would travel west between 1287 and 1288 on an ambassadorial mission to the papacy along with various Christian monarchs on the behalf of the Ilkhan Arghun of Persia, who was seeking to form a military alliance with the Christian powers against the Mamelukes of Egypt. Rabban holds the distinction of being the first person from China to visit the West but otherwise his mission, like those of Carpini and Rubruck, failed.[24] These results were typical, as disappointment and failure characterized the history of Mongol–Christian diplomacy in the mid- to later years of the thirteenth century. Distance, time and differing goals all worked to undermine the efforts of the two alien cultures to cooperate.

The Mongol conquests did not simply produce death and devastation. After the Pax Mongolica settled over much of Eurasia, Roman Catholic missionaries made their way to China and established a fleeting toehold in that distant land. John of Monte

Corvino, another Franciscan, travelled to China in 1289 on a diplomatic mission to Kublai Khan. He remained to found churches in Peking and other Chinese cities. Oderic of Pordenone and John of Marignolli on separate occasions visited Peking as missionaries for periods of several years at a time during the first half of the fourteenth century. Distance, lack of resources and the fall of the Mongol dynasty ruling China all combined to cause this Christian mission to wither after an apparently promising start.[25]

The Pax Mongolica also permitted direct trade to take place between Europe and China for the first time in history.[26] Unlike their Islamic counterparts, the European merchants involved in the long-distance trade in Asian luxury goods were intrepid, aggressive and willing to travel to foreign lands. They also surged ahead of the Muslims in their business methods, industrial technologies and the building and sailing of ships. Local autonomy and pride made the merchants of the Italian city-states adventurous and expansionistic. They also possessed political power which protected them from rapacious governments who might try to solve short-term financial problems by seizing their wealth. With such security, Italian merchants could plough their profits back into their businesses. In contrast, Muslim merchants spent

The Mongols were a nomadic people whose ability to move rapidly and with military ferocity allowed them to create a great empire across Eurasia. From the Yule-Cordier edition of *The Travels of Marco Polo* (rprt. 1903, New York, Dover 1993), vol. 1, p. 255.

their wealth on high living because they faced the chronic threat of confiscation by predatory governments such as the Mamelukes, who were always in need of more money to fuel their military establishments.[27]

On the eve of the Mongol conquests, Muslim Egypt and Christian Venice maintained a highly profitable monopoly over the international trade in spices and other Asian luxuries which they sold to the rest of Europe. Although prices for such goods steadily mounted, consumer demand also continued to grow. High prices for Asian luxuries did create frustration among consumers. Consequently the perennial quest to cut out the middleman resumed when the Pax Mongolica once more made increased use of the old Silk Road a possibility. European demand for silk also exceeded the local economy's ability to produce it. Consequently there was a ready market for Chinese silks in fourteenth-century Europe and a reasonably direct way to get them there.[28] Such trade opened cultural contacts so that Europeans of that time quickly knew more about China than ever before. They even knew more about China

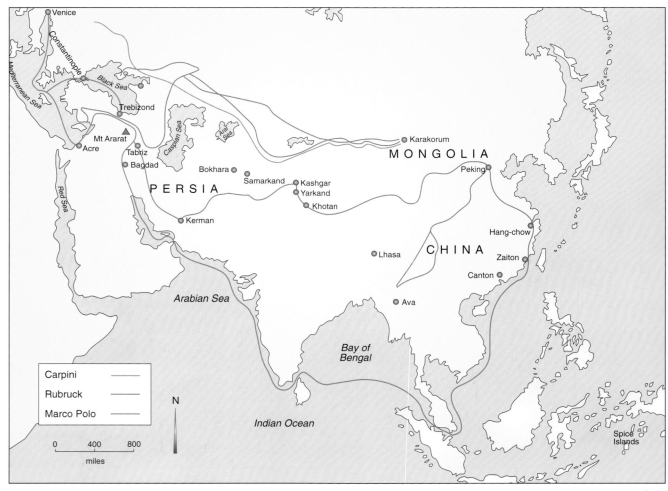

European travellers in Asia during the Pax Mongolica.

Odoric of Pordenone before Pope John XXII as he prepares to depart for China on a missionary journey. (Bibliothéque Nationale, Paris/Bridgeman Art Library)

than they did about India, a reversal of an ancient pattern. India, however, was not entirely ignored and Italian merchants visited that land in increasing numbers during the late thirteenth and the first half of the fourteenth centuries.[29]

The Genoese led the way in this new direct trade with China and India. At the same time, Venetians also reached China in large numbers including their most famous traveller, Marco Polo. European merchants in China, especially the Genoese, assisted the efforts of the Western Christian missionaries such as John of Monte Corvino. Missionary accounts treated the presence of other European traders as nothing exceptional. In the realm of fiction, the *Travels of Sir John Mandeville* mentioned that the Asian Christian potentate, Prester John, had a bodyguard of 10,000 Englishmen. While that statement was false and the book itself was largely fantasy, at the time readers widely believed it was a true account. Apparently the idea that significant numbers of Europeans went to visit and to live in Asian lands for years at a time was known by those who stayed behind in Europe to be a relatively frequent occurrence. With the famous exception of Marco Polo, neither the Venetian nor the Genoese merchants left any substantial records of their travels and business ventures in the various Asian lands or in Egypt. This odd and frustrating silence may be the result of the destruction and loss of many papers in the Venetian archives. It may also stem from an effort to protect trade secrets from potential competitors, a consideration that did not seem to bother Marco Polo.[30]

MARCO POLO

Marco Polo (1254?–1324) is possibly the most famous traveller in European history thanks to his book *Il Milione,* or as it is more commonly known *The Travels of Marco Polo.* Born in Venice in about 1254, Marco Polo belonged to a family of modestly prosperous merchants. His father Nicoló and his uncle Maffeo traded in Constantinople and the Black Sea region. In 1260 they decided to venture eastward and engage directly in trade with Central Asia. Journeying to Bulgar on the Volga River and then to Bukhara, they joined a diplomatic party travelling to the court of Kublai (r. 1254–91), the Great Khan of the Mongols. Their trip took a year but it proved very worthwhile. Kublai Khan showed a great interest in the West and in Christianity. He sent the Polos back home with one of his own envoys with a request that the Pope send 100 scholars to teach the Mongols about Christianity. He also asked the Pope for a gift of oil from the lamp burning in the Church of the Holy Sepulchre in Jerusalem. Shortly into their return journey, the Mongol emissary fell ill and had to drop out. The Polos pushed on by themselves and reached Acre in Palestine in April 1269 where they discovered that the old Pope had died and that papal elections were under way. Returning to Venice they learned that Nicoló's wife had died and his son Marco, now fifteen years old, was on the threshold of adulthood.

The Polos stayed in Venice for approximately two years waiting for the papal elections to be completed. As more and more time elapsed with no result, they decided to return to Kublai Khan lest he lose patience with them. Taking Marco with them, they proceeded to Acre in 1271 where they persuaded the papal legate Theobald of Piacenza to provide them with a gift of oil from the Church of the Holy Sepulchre. He also wrote letters for them to Kublai Khan explaining the reason for their delay and stating that the Polos had done their best to fulfil the Khan's wishes. The three Polos then departed for China. It was a false start for upon reaching Armenia they received a message from Theobald, who, in the meantime, had been elected Pope as Gregory X on 1 September 1271. He asked them to return to Acre where he assigned two Dominican friars to travel with them to the court of Kublai Khan as his ambassadors.

For a second time the Polos departed from Acre for the distant East. Wars raged along their route and the two Dominicans quickly grew fearful and discouraged, gave up their mission and turned back. The Polos, however, persevered and after three-and-a-half years of travel reached the Khan's summer palace at Shangtu. Their exact itinerary is unknown but they undoubtedly followed some variation of the caravan tracks that made up the old Silk Road. Kublai Khan greeted them joyfully and immediately developed a fondness for the young Marco. Marco quickly mastered the Mongol language and customs, eventually adding several other Asian languages to his repertoire. The Great Khan began giving the talented Marco various important responsibilities in the Mongol government.

Marco Polo worked for Kublai Khan for seventeen years, during which time he travelled through much of Asia and even (he claimed) served as the governor of the city of Yangzhou for three years. Shortly before his return to Venice, Marco went on a diplomatic mission to India. That Kublai Khan would so readily appoint a foreigner is not as surprising as it might at first appear. Kublai Khan and his Mongol warriors formed a tiny conquering minority who ruled over a vast subject population of Chinese. They did not trust the Chinese to serve in their administration and under the circumstances, the employing of foreigners as their government officials made sense.

Coming to China had been very lucrative for the Polos, but after seventeen years they grew homesick for Venice. After securing the reluctant permission of the ageing Kublai Khan, the Polos began their return home in 1292. This time they sailed from the Chinese port of Quanzhou to Java in the East Indies, on to India and through the Straits of Hormuz to the domains of the Ilkhans of Persia. Their journey took eighteen months. From Persia they travelled to Trebizond on the Black Sea coast of Asia Minor where they took passage on a ship and passed through Constantinople on their way to Venice. If the sixteenth-century historian of the age of discovery, Gian Battista Rasmusio, is to be believed, the Polos returned home seemingly empty handed in ragged Mongol garb so that, at first, no one recognized them. Once they settled into the family house, they changed into western attire and then ripped open the seams of their old Mongol clothing to reveal many hidden precious gems. Their many years in China had made them rich.

After returning to Venice, Marco Polo participated in one of Venice's many wars with Genoa and was captured in either 1296 or 1298. He shared his imprisonment

Genoa, 1481, by an unknown artist. (Museo Navale di Pegli, Genova/Art Resource, NY)

with a writer named Rustichello of Pisa and the two collaborated on a book about Marco's travels in Asia to pass the time. In 1299 Venice and Genoa made peace and Marco was able to return home where he married and raised a large family. He died in 1324 at about the age of seventy.

Marco Polo's book is his great legacy to the history of travel, exploration and geography. As the historian John Larner has written, 'Never before or since has one man [Marco Polo] given such an immense body of new geographical knowledge to the West.'[31] The quality of that knowledge about the Far East was also significantly better than anything available to the merchants and scholars of Islam.[32] Polo probably wrote his book from memory, although the medieval chronicler Jacopo di Acqui told how the captive Marco wrote to his father Nicoló asking him to send him his notes and other records of their travels. Just how much Rustichello embellished the account cannot be determined but he obviously enhanced it to a degree. *The Travels of Marco Polo* proved to be quite popular. Originally composed in a hybrid French–Italian dialect, it was quickly translated into Latin and many major European languages and dialects including French, Bohemian, Venetian, Catalan, Irish, Spanish and English.

The Travels of Marco Polo is not a travelogue describing his route and the adventures that befell him along the way. Instead the book begins with a brief prologue in the

An illustration from an early manuscript depticing Marco Polo departing from Venice on his way to fabled Cathay in 1271. (Mary Evans Picture Library)

form of an itinerary while the main body of the work is a country by country or region by region description of the lands and peoples of Asia. This sort of information is what would have been most useful to a European merchant wanting to do business in Central Asia and the Far East. Marco Polo visited some of the places he describes, but in other cases he merely reports stories he heard. Fact and fantasy are sometimes mingled. He provides recognizable descriptions of coal and paper money, and his account of the Old Man of the Mountain and his fanatical sect of Assassins is reasonably correct. The information about Japan is clearly second-hand, as Marco never visited that land. Standard European legends about Asian geography and ethnography also appear in his writing, including tales of Prester John and the missionary work of St Thomas in India.

Marco Polo's contemporaries found his stories of Cathay and other Asian lands engaging but sometimes unbelievable. Jacopo di Acqui in his chronicle mentioned that some people considered Polo to be an exaggerator, a liar or a spinner of tall tales. Interestingly, late medieval Europeans widely believed that the fictional Sir John Mandeville's journeys had actually taken place. Yet when compared to the

Chinese portrait of Kublai Khan. From the Yule-Cordier edition of *The Travels of Marco Polo* (rprt. 1903, New York, Dover 1993), vol. 1, p. 357.

sometimes outrageous material found in Mandeville's book, Marco Polo's account is quite tame. Some of his contemporaries even went so far as to assert that Marco never even made the long journey to China, an opinion echoed by some modern scholars, although most of the latter, however, believe that he did travel to China and that his book is largely based on his own experiences in Asia. The fact is, *The Travels of Marco Polo* supplied a relatively accurate survey of the many lands and peoples of Asia and was certainly far superior to the information previously available to medieval Europeans.

THE END OF THE PAX MONGOLICA AND THE REVIVAL OF ISLAM

The Crusades had increased Western Europeans' tastes for Asian luxury goods and the Pax Mongolica had served to allow them direct access to sources of those goods in Asia. Unfortunately for the European consumers, the conditions that made the Crusades and the Pax Mongolica possible were ending even as Marco Polo returned home from the court of Kublai Khan. Islamic civilization had experienced a period of weakness and political division during the early years of the Crusades. It was this situation that made European crusading possible. The appearance of the rampaging Mongol armies in the Middle East during the mid-thirteenth century had further weakened or destroyed some Muslim powers. But in the midst of Islam's darkest hour lay the seeds of a spectacular recovery. In 1250 the Turkish mercenaries known as the Mamelukes overthrew their masters, the Ayyubid dynasty of Egypt. Ten years later their forces defeated the Mongols at the hard-fought Battle of Ain Jalut near Nazareth. Meanwhile, growing fissures among the leadership of the Mongols provided an opportunity in 1261 for the Mameluke Sultan Baybars to make a mutually beneficial alliance with Berke Khan of the Golden Horde in Russia against the Mongol Ilkhans of Persia. In contrast the Ilkhans and the Crusader states of the Levant never managed to cooperate effectively against the Mamelukes. Mameluke armies began to reduce one Crusader stronghold after another in Palestine. An army belonging to the Ilkhans of Persia invaded Syria in 1281 and tried to relieve the Crusaders but the Mamelukes forced them to withdraw in the aftermath of the bloody Battle of Homs. The Mameluke assaults culminated in the fall of Acre in 1291 and with that traumatic defeat the last Crusader state on the mainland was swept away. The Mamelukes of

Egypt now controlled the terminuses of the caravan routes in the Levant and the Red Sea route to India. The old Fatimid monopoly over the spice trade had been restored and the Venetians were quick to resume their position as partners of the Mamelukes in the vast trading network of middlemen stretching to the Spice Islands.

Mongol control over China was also collapsing. Kublai Khan died in 1294 and was succeeded by his grandson Temur Oljaitu (1295–1307) who proved to be an effective ruler. Temur's successors, however, faced a deteriorating situation. Increasing disunity plagued the Mongols as they struggled to maintain their domination of the huge population of sullen and resentful Chinese. Epidemics swept China during 1353–4 as problems with famine grew, and these factors discredited Mongol rule in the eyes of the Chinese. Various centres of rebellion sprang up and the Mongols lacked the resources to suppress them. Most significantly in 1356 the Buddhist monk Chu Yuan-Cheng seized control of Nanking. By 1368 he had triumphed over both the Mongols and rival rebel leaders and founded the Ming (brilliant) dynasty which would rule China for the next 300 years. Unfortunately for Western merchants, the new Ming emperor wanted all foreigners out of China, not just the despised Mongols, and most of his subjects agreed with him. As a result both European trade and missionary activity came to a halt and China became closed to the West until the sixteenth century. Except for goods coming up the caravan routes from India the once flourishing overland trade routes of Central Asia were moribund. No new knowledge about China was added to the intellectual stores of the Europeans for some 150 years.

Marco Polo. From the Yule-Cordier edition of *The Travels of Marco Polo* (rprt. 1903, New York, Dover 1993), vol. 2, frontispiece.

Columbus's mental image of China or Cathay was derived from Marco Polo, a drastically obsolete source of information by the mid-fourteenth century.

European merchants faced another growing problem in Asia Minor. Mongol forces had smashed the Seljuk Turks at the Battle of Kosedagh and as a result temporarily controlled Anatolia. But as the Ilkhans' power diminished, Asia Minor became a cauldron of competing Turkish tribes and principalities. Ultimately successful in this competition were the Ottoman Turks. By 1362 they controlled north-west Asia Minor and substantial territories on the European side of the straits of the Dardanelles. From that point onward they had Constantinople, the last vestige of the Roman Empire, surrounded. They were in an excellent position to control the flow of trade between the

Sir John Mandeville, fifteenth century, by an unknown artist. The fictional Sir John is supposedly at work in his study. (Heritage Image Partnership)

Black Sea and the Mediterranean. In spite of European efforts, Ottoman power grew unstoppably and they expanded further into the Balkan peninsula. Tamerlane's crushing defeat and the capture of the Ottoman Sultan Bayazid at the Battle of Ankara in 1402 only caused a temporary halt in Ottoman expansion. It did preserve Constantinople from Turkish conquest for another fifty years but that was merely delaying the inevitable. That once great city was past any significant revival of its fortunes and was only living on borrowed time.

By the mid-fourteenth century two great Islamic powers controlled the trade routes to Asia, and China had closed itself to foreigners. European geographical horizons and commercial opportunities had not been so circumscribed for centuries. Trade with Asia did not end but it was now conducted at the whim of the Mamelukes and the Ottomans. Their rulers were not against trade and in fact encouraged it because they very much needed and desired the revenues it generated to support their voracious war machines. Ultimately, however, the Muslim rulers lacked a commercial vision that sought the capitalistic expansion of international trade to achieve greater volume of goods sold and profits. Their viewpoint was purely predatory. They sought to maximize revenues for the short term without reference to long-term consequences. Crippling confiscations of the wealth of Muslim merchants were a frequent occurrence in the Mameluke state. Such actions did not encourage Muslim merchants to consider the growth and survival of their enterprises unlike the more autonomous merchants of Europe. Muslim rulers drove up the prices of Asian luxuries to whatever level the market would bear.[33] Trade in Asian spices and other goods continued largely unabated but the Venetian–Mameluke monopoly and its accompanying high prices ultimately caused other Europeans to think more and more seriously about alternative routes to Asia and the Spice Islands.

THE TRANS-SAHARAN TRADE WITH WEST AFRICA

The gold of sub-Saharan West Africa played almost as important a role in the international commerce of late medieval Europe as the spices and the silks of Asia.

The trade in gold had existed for centuries before the coming of the Arabs into North Africa beginning in the late seventh century. The Arabs took over that trade and expanded it. The gold came from a mysterious land called Wangara which was probably located in the regions of Bambuk or Bure in tropical West Africa.[34] Wangaran miners painstakingly dug the gold out of pits in the earth in a debilitatingly hot climate. They then traded their hard-won gold for salt and other goods by means of the system of silent barter. Visiting merchants would lay out a pile of goods, primarily block salt from the Sahara, and withdraw. The timid but salt-starved Wangarans would come out of hiding and place an amount of gold next to the goods and disappear once more. Then the merchants would return. If satisfied with the amount of gold offered, they would take it and depart. Otherwise they would leave the gold and take away some of their trade goods. Eventually the two sides would reach a mutually satisfactory rate of exchange. All efforts to wrest the secret of the gold mines from the Wangarans failed and usually resulted in the Wangarans stopping the gold trade for greater or lesser periods of time. It always resumed because Wangara lacked and desperately needed the life-sustaining salt that the traders brought from the Saharan mines.[35] While the empires of Ghana and Mali both conquered Wangara, they never directly controlled its gold production. During the first half of the thirteenth century King Sudiata of Mali attempted to convert the pagan Wangarans to Islam only to precipitate a strike among the gold-miners for his trouble. He backed off from his religious policies and the flow of precious metal resumed.[36]

A bazaar in old Cairo, *c.* 1845. This image is a lithograph by Louis Haghe based on drawings made by D. Roberts. (Heritage Image Partnership)

The kings of Mali became wealthy thanks to the vast quantities of Wangaran gold that passed through their hands. Mansa Musa (1307/12–32/7) of Mali made a legendary pilgrimage to Mecca in 1324. His huge entourage, numbered at more than 15,000 people by one contemporary observer, spent prodigious amounts of gold along the way, especially in Cairo, the capital of the Mamelukes. The sheer amount of gold injected into the Cairene economy caused the value of that precious metal to remain depressed for over twelve years after Mansa Musa's visit.[37] Word of Mansa Musa's wealth quickly spread through the lands of Islam and of Europe. For Europeans, Mansa Musa became an emblem for the wealth to be found in sub-

Chinese junk. In the early fifteenth century the Chinese possessed a sophisticated ship-building technology which was allowed to fall into rapid decay prior to the arrival of the Europeans. William Cullen Bryant, *A Popular History of the United States* (New York, Scribners, 1891), vol. 1, p. 86.

Saharan Africa. In 1339, Angelino Dulcert, the Majorcan cartographer, placed a regal Mansa Musa on his map of Africa. He located the African king in the middle of the Sahara with the caption 'Rex Melly'. Similar depictions of Mansa Musa appeared on the maps of other European cartographers through the fourteenth and the fifteenth centuries.[38] An image of vast wealth beckoned for any European with the bravery and imagination to try and reach it. Economically, African gold provided the countries of Mameluke Egypt, North Africa and Mediterranean Europe with a very healthy supply of hard currency especially when compared with the Middle Eastern region of Islam beyond the domains of the Mamelukes. This gold served to stimulate the European economy and provided it with the liquidity that helped to propel it ahead of the economy of the Islamic Middle East.[39]

Geographically North Africa consisted of a habitable coastal strip. Various cities dotted its coastline and were supplied with food by their fertile immediate hinterlands. The entire region had adhered to Islam since the Arab conquest in the late seventh century. A range of mountains separated the fertile coastal plain from the vast and foreboding desert known as the Sahara which lay to the south. Although the Sahara was a harsh and even deadly environment, it was not impermeable to human travel nor was it totally uninhabitable. The indigenous inhabitants of the North African coastlands and the Saharan back country were a Caucasian people known as the Berbers. Some Berbers were sedentary city dwellers or farmers while others belonged to the nomadic tribes of the desert such as the Sanhaja or the fearsome Tuaregs. All of them had become heavily Arabized and Islamized in their culture and religion. To medieval Europeans they were the Moors, specifically they were Tawny Moors as opposed to the Black Moors who were black Africans who followed Islam.

The Sahara has been criss-crossed by caravan routes since ancient times. Many oases and wells are scattered through various parts of the desert and help to make travel possible. Nabataean Arabs introduced dromedary camels into the lands of the Sahara east of the Nile River during the last two centuries BC. From there the employment of that highly utilitarian animal rapidly spread westward. The arrival of the dromedary camel made the use of the western trans-Saharan caravan routes easier and safer.[40] This trade carried luxuries and manufactured goods of copper and iron from the Mediterranean world south to the Sudan, picking up salt along the way from the desert mines to sell to the salt-deprived Sahelians and Sudanese. In exchange, the

For Europeans of the fifteenth century, Cathay was a land of fantastic wealth and exotic luxuries. From William Cullen Bryant, *A Popular History of the United States* (New York, Scribners, 1891), vol. 1, p. 92.

peoples of sub-Saharan Africa provided gold and slaves for the caravans when they returned north. Hides, ivory and kola nuts were also important commodities carried by the north-bound caravans.[41] In the western Sahara, various cities, ancient Ghana, Walata and fabled Timbuktu, served as the principal southern terminuses of the caravan trade. The latter city dominated the southern end of the gold trade during the fifteenth century and was renowned for its wealth and sophistication.[42] Further east, cities such as Kano and Bornu by Lake Chad provided important entrepôts for caravans heading north across the eastern Sahara to Tripoli and Egypt. Along the North African coast, Tangier, Tunis, al Mahdiyyah, Bougie and Ceuta served as the northern destinations for the caravans.[43] Thousands of caravans crossed the Sahara over the centuries.

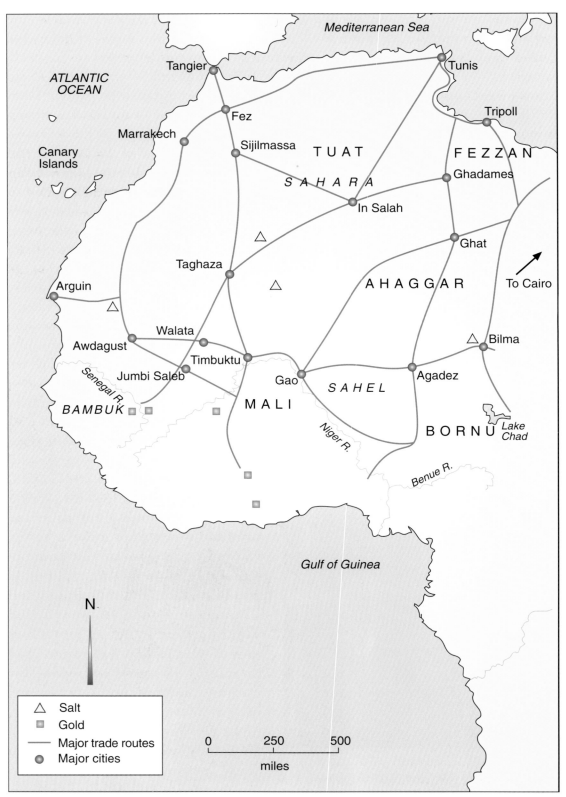

Trans-Saharan caravan routes.

Their journey was not an easy one, especially in the western Sahara where occasionally entire parties were lost due to lack of water or sandstorms. Expert desert navigators guided caravans across the trackless wastes more by the method of literally smelling the sands, which have different odours in various parts of the desert for those whose senses are attuned to it.[44]

From the point of view of Christian Europe the gold of sub-Saharan Africa represented a vital commodity. The black slaves brought north by the caravans were almost as economically important because they were used extensively in the burgeoning production of sugar on the plantations of the various Mediterranean islands and in Spain and Italy. In order to reach Europe African commodities had to pass through the hands of the Muslim merchants of the caravan routes and the North African ports. As middlemen the North African merchants caused prices to rise, a situation that the Europeans would have liked to avoid. As Muslims the North African merchants represented a despised creed and a centuries-old enemy to the Christians

Detail from a fifteenth-century map by Mecia de Villadeste depicting Mansa Musa, the legendary King of Mali, and hoards of gold. (Giraudon/Art Resource, NY)

of Mediterranean Europe. The Muslim merchants also jealously guarded their advantageous position in the trade network. Obviously they were quite happy to do business with the Venetians, the Genoese and the other Christian merchants but they were not about to allow Christian merchants to become directly involved with the lands south of the Sahara. A Florentine named Benedetto Dei supposedly made his way to Timbuktu in 1469 but it was a visit of no lasting significance.[45] The Muslims of North Africa continued to maintain their age-old monopoly over the trans-Saharan trade and by 1400 this was becoming increasingly irritating to the Portuguese. So galling was it that they decided to do something about it.

CHAPTER THREE

LATE MEDIEVAL EUROPEAN EXPLORATION OF THE ATLANTIC AND AFRICA BEFORE 1492

How vigilant and studious was the infante Dom Henrique, son of King John the first of blessed memory, in the exploration of the coast of Africa, and what he expended in the matter, continuing with this business with great glory and honour in God's name and praise to himself until his death . . . having already received great honour and profit as the fruits of his labours.

Damião de Goes (1566/7)[1]

Traditionally historians have located the original impetus for the European explorations of the world during the fifteenth and sixteenth centuries in a desire to acquire the precious spices of the Far East. While this played a big part in the vast geographical expansion of European influence, it was not the only or even the most powerful of the initial motivations. Various European explorers, traders and settlers began to venture onto the high seas of the Atlantic Ocean and down the west coast of Africa by the end of the thirteenth century. This geographical expansion was for the most part an extension of the trading activities that had been taking place in the western region of the Mediterranean Sea for some time.

The international trade of the western Mediterranean by the late thirteenth century had come to focus heavily on the trade in sugar, slaves and gold.[2] The Crusades had brought Europeans into close contact with sugar and they quickly developed a taste for the sweet condiment.[3] That taste grew and would eventually become a voracious appetite among Europeans of all classes by the late eighteenth and the nineteenth centuries. Unlike the various spices, sugar could be grown in many places throughout the Mediterranean basin. As a result during the fourteenth century, sugar plantations flourished on Sicily, in the Algarve and in Granada along with other places. Sugar production would spill into the Atlantic Ocean during the fifteenth century when it was discovered that it could be grown on Madeira and the Cape Verde Islands.

The slave trade predated the sugar trade by thousands of years but the two activities would quickly become intertwined because of sugar production's prodigious demands for labour. For centuries Christians had enslaved Muslim soldiers taken as prisoners of war and civilians kidnapped during raids or captured when cities were sacked. Muslims did the same thing to Christians. After a while, the religious distinction used in the slave trade became blurred. Christian merchants and consumers would buy slaves of any religion and so would the Muslims. Both European Christians and the Muslims of North Africa exhibited a special fondness for slaves from Black Africa.

Negro slaves represented the exotic and the unique to purchasers. As such they were considered status symbols and were highly prized as domestic servants in the very early stages of the Atlantic slave trade. Black slaves living in a white society stood out and this made it hard for them to run away, which was a definite advantage from the owner's point of view. Furthermore, popular assumptions credited Black Africans with being better workers. By the fourteenth century slavery was widely practised throughout the Mediterranean world. Demand for more slaves was growing and this prompted Europeans to enter the Atlantic seeking new sources of slaves in sub-Saharan Africa and the Canary Islands.

Finally the trade in West African gold supplied the economies of Muslim North Africa and the Christian Mediterranean with an important stimulus. Prosperity became closely linked to the gold coinage. Getting more and more gold into the economy and cutting out the North African middlemen provided a major motivation for the early exploration of Atlantic Africa.

Genoa dominated the trading world of the western Mediterranean but did not monopolize it. The Christian merchants of Provence and Aragon, along with Italian cities, also participated in that trade. During the era of the Crusades in the Middle East, Genoa acquired extensive business interests in the eastern Mediterranean. Acre and other parts of the Outremer had Genoese quarters as did Constantinople. Genoese trading colonies appeared along the shores of the Black Sea and the Genoese played a crucial role as middlemen in the slave trade between the Black Sea region and Egypt. The Pax Mongolica opened up additional trading opportunities all the way to China and India. The Battle of Ain Jalut in 1260 marked the zenith of Mongol power. From that point onward disunity grew among the Mongol khanates and a general decline began. At the same time the Mamelukes of Egypt led a resurgence of Islam. One after another the Crusader strongholds were taken by the Mamelukes culminating in the fall of Acre in 1291. This event caused Pope Nicholas IV to issue a boycott on trading with Islam by Christian merchants. The Genoese situation in the eastern Mediterranean and Black Sea would continue to deteriorate causing them to turn their attention back to the western Mediterranean and the Atlantic trade.[4]

LATE MEDIEVAL EUROPE AND THE CANARY ISLANDS

One of the first manifestations of Genoese interest in Atlantic exploration was the mysterious Vivaldi enterprise of 1291. A number of citizens of Genoa decided to pool their resources to outfit a substantial expedition to India. The fleet consisted of two galleys that were placed under the command of the brothers Ugolino and Vadino Vivaldi and supposedly equipped with supplies for ten years. Two members of the then new and vigorous Franciscan order also accompanied the galleys. Departing in May 1291, the fleet passed the Straits of Gibraltar and was last sighted at a place called Gozora. Some scholars have identified Gozora as Cape Nun and almost all agree that it was located somewhere between the Canary Islands and the beginnings of Black Africa. It may be that the Vivaldi brothers were the first Europeans to rediscover the Canaries in the post-Classical era.

Where the Vivaldis sailed after Gozora is uncertain. Their stated objective was to travel on the ocean to parts of India, which is a somewhat vague destination in light of European geographical concepts during the late thirteenth century. Most scholars feel that the Vivaldis intended to circumnavigate Africa while a minority suggest that they planned to sail west to Asia and so anticipated Columbus's first voyage by 200 years. Later fourteenth- and fifteenth-century reports of Vivaldi survivors and descendants in both West and East Africa tend to bolster the African route hypothesis, although the reliability of these accounts is questionable. Whichever route the Vivaldis took, their expedition marked the beginning of the European expansion into the Atlantic Ocean and along the coast of West Africa that ultimately led to Columbus's and da Gama's voyages.[5]

While the Vivaldis failed in their effort to develop a new trade route to Asia, the Italian presence in the Atlantic grew. Merchants of both Venice and Genoa journeyed through the Straits of Gibraltar carrying southern goods to England and the Low Countries and seeking to buy the wool and cloth products of those lands. They made various stops along the way and soon Genoese and Venetian communities appeared in the various important ports of call. The Genoese appear to have been particularly active in Portugal, where King Dinis (1279–1325) proved to be particularly welcoming to foreign merchants.[6] Some of the Genoese in Portugal even managed to enter the Portuguese aristocracy. Later Columbus would find significant support and employment from the Genoese merchant community in Portugal.

Sometime prior to 1340, the Genoese began to visit the Canary Islands or as they had been known since the Classical era, the Fortunate Isles. Although Europeans were aware of the existence of the Canaries, it was only in the vaguest manner. In 1300, European knowledge of the Canaries, which really did exist, was no more reliable than information about St Brendan's Isle which did not exist. A Genoese expedition under the leadership of Lanzarotto Malocello visited the Canaries in 1336 or earlier and gave his name to one of the islands. That voyage was followed by a joint expedition of Genoese, Florentines and Portuguese in 1341 who embarked from Lisbon intent on conquest. Visiting thirteen islands, they found six to be inhabited (actually seven of the Canary Islands were inhabited) by people who lived in houses and farmed. Overall the results of the venture were disappointing as the Canary Islands did not possess any significant wealth. At that point the Genoese and Portuguese quickly lost interest. It would not be revived until the 1420s under the guidance of Prince Henry the Navigator.[7]

Majorcans and Catalans quickly took up the task of exploring the Canary Islands. Both groups cooperated closely in the international trade of the western Mediterranean and were interested in expanding their activities into the Atlantic Ocean. Majorca was also the home of Ramon Llull's missionary school. Llull was a great advocate and promoter of peaceful missionary activity among heathens and the

point Castile had acquired a firm claim to the Canaries that was supported by permanent settlements, squalid as they might be. Within a few years Prince Henry the Navigator would attempt to revive Portugal's claims to the same islands and Europe's first colonial war would begin.

PORTUGAL, THE AVIS DYNASTY AND CEUTA

Shortly after Bethencourt and La Salle began their conquest of Lanzarote and Fuerteventura, another power re-entered the area of overseas expansion – Portugal. In 1400 Portugal would have appeared to the casual observer to be a somewhat unlikely candidate to become the trailblazer of European expansion in the fifteenth century. The small country possessed no great resources of wealth. Farming Portugal's rugged landscape was a relatively thankless task. No forest in Portugal contained large numbers of the types of trees that produced fine lumber for ships and buildings. The earth of Portugal did not yield up any appreciable amounts of precious metals. In terms of population, a number one resource for any pre-industrial society, the country was also deficient. With barely a million inhabitants, Portugal would eventually find itself hard-pressed to supply the manpower needed to maintain a world empire. Furthermore, although a monarch ruled Portugal, the kings of Portugal had to contend with a proud and unruly nobility that was quite ready to rebel at the slightest excuse. At the same time larger and more populous Castile lay to Portugal's east, chronically hostile and ever-ready to invade what the Castilian monarchs considered was a breakaway province of their kingdom. Given such circumstances, no practical-minded person in 1400 would have imagined that an imperial future on a global scale lay ahead for Portugal.

A more astute observer of the Portuguese situation in 1400, however, would have looked past the deficiencies and discovered that the solid foundations for overseas expansion actually existed in Portugal. While not particularly wealthy, Portugal was undergoing continued economic growth, and so was capable of supporting some overseas development. Close links had been nurtured with the Genoese, many of whom lived in Portugal and some of whom had even entered the Portuguese elite. The Genoese possessed

João I, king of Portugal and founder of the Avis dynasty. From J.P. Oliveira, *The Golden Age of Prince Henry the Navigator* (New York, Dutton, 1914).

centuries of experience of overseas trade and settlements. Finally, the Portuguese monarchs protected their native community of merchants and supported its enterprises. They wisely saw a definite link between the strength and the security of their realm and commercial prosperity.[14]

In 1405 the talented João I (1385–1433) ruled Portugal. He was the illegitimate son of Pedro I (r. 1357–67) and initially did not possess a serious claim to the throne. His father did secure his financial future by bestowing on him the lucrative position of Grand Master of the Order of Avis. When Pedro I died in 1367, his legitimate son Fernando I (r. 1367–83) succeeded him. Fernando I married Leonor Teles de Meneses and they produced a daughter named Beatriz in 1372. Through much of his reign Fernando I warred with Castile, unfortunately with little success. When Juan I of Castile invaded Portugal in 1381 a desperate Fernando I made a peace in 1382 which included the marriage of his daughter Beatriz to Juan I in 1383. The son of this

A fifteenth-century painting depicting the marriage of João I of Portugal and Philippa of Lancaster, the parents of Prince Henry the Navigator, in 1387. (Heritage Image Partnership)

dynastic union would rule both Portugal and Castile. At that point Fernando I died and Juan I saw a chance to unite the two kingdoms early. He secured the support of his mother-in-law Leonor Teles, the regent for Beatriz, in his efforts. The Portuguese people, however, had ideas of their own. The prospect of a dynastic union with despised Castile aroused a growing resistance. That Leonor Teles supported the Castilian pretensions only discredited the plan for union even further as she was held in general contempt for her notoriously immoral conduct at the Portuguese court. By 1384 the young João of Avis joined the rebellion and the Cortés at Coimbra elected him King of Portugal. As the new King of Portugal he quickly proved himself a better military commander than his half-brother Fernando I by decisively defeating the Castilian army of Juan I at the Battle of Aljubarrota in 1385. Because hostilities between Castile and Portugal continued, João I sought an alliance with the ambitious John of Gaunt of England in 1386. The resulting agreement is known as the Treaty of Windsor and included João I's marriage to Gaunt's daughter Philippa of Lancaster. From that point João I managed to secure his new dynasty of Avis and the independence of Portugal in spite of sporadic Castilian hostility along the border between the two nations.[15]

The marriage of João I and Philippa of Gaunt turned out to be very fertile. Although their first two children died in infancy, the remaining six children survived to adulthood. The oldest was Duarte, the future king, who was born in 1391. He was followed by Pedro in 1392, Henry in 1394, Isabel in 1397, João in 1400 and Fernando in 1402. During the lifetime of João I, his sons got along with each other. Duarte, the oldest and the heir to the throne, turned out to be a rather bookish, scholarly person. He may have felt somewhat intimidated by his extremely successful father and pressured by his ambitious and forceful younger brothers Pedro and Henry. Contemporary evidence strongly indicates that João I considered Henry to be his favourite son. That parental support would later help Henry to obtain the resources he needed to begin and to maintain his programme of Atlantic and African exploration.

João I's success against Castile finally brought Portugal peace and security in 1411. This, however, was a mixed blessing. Portugal's warlike nobles, including the King's sons, longed for a war to prove themselves as warriors and win their knighthoods in real battle rather than a tournament. The hard-won peace with Castile needed to be preserved and that left João I without any eligible enemies on Portugal's direct border. Instead he looked overseas for a place to employ his army. Because Portugal had a long and venerable history of crusading warfare against the Moors of Iberia and North Africa, a Moorish target seemed an excellent choice. The Moorish emirate of Granada was closest but Castile jealously regarded Granada as a prime target for a future Castilian reconquest for Christendom. A Portuguese attack there would threaten the fragile peace between the two realms. This forced João to look beyond Granada to the Muslim lands of North Africa. The Marinid kingdom of Fez in Morocco had entered into a state of decline that would lead to the disintegration of the central government's control as the fifteenth century proceeded. It was a situation that persuaded João I that it would be feasible for a Portuguese force to attack a Muslim port, capture it and hold it. In this way João I hoped to begin the reconquest of the once Christian lands of North Africa and free them from the domination of despised Islam. This action would also be considered a trespass by Castile. The Castilians claimed the exclusive right to reconquer all Muslim territories that had once formed the Visigothic kingdom of Spain. This included the ancient North African province of Maurentania which basically comprised the same territory as Morocco. In the case of Morocco, however, the Castilian claims were based on less firm legal ground while their own immediate military plans against the Moors remaining on the Iberian Peninsula were not threatened by any Portuguese actions in North Africa.

By 1412 João I and his council had decided to attack the Muslim city of Ceuta which lay across the strait from the stronghold of Gibraltar. Ceuta appeared to be a good choice. It was an important Mediterranean entrepôt for the trans-Saharan caravan

Troops boarding ships for Portugal's assault on Ceuta. From J.P. Oliveira, *The Golden Age of Prince Henry the Navigator* (New York, Dutton, 1914).

trade and the Portuguese hoped to insert themselves into that lucrative commerce by capturing Ceuta. The city also provided an important staging area for Muslim reinforcements and supplies on their way to relieve their beleaguered co-religionists in Granada. Its capture would actually benefit Castilian efforts to conquer Granada. Of domestic importance, the expedition against Ceuta would provide employment for the Portuguese soldiers who were idle as a result of the treaty with Castile of 1411. In addition the young princes would get a chance to win their knighthoods in battle. Portugal would also secure protection from raids by Muslim pirates based in Ceuta while the city would provide an excellent base for a continued Portuguese conquest of Morocco. Ultimately João I's fundamental reason for attacking Ceuta was the demands of chivalry and the need to wage a glorious war against the infidel.[16] Everyone would benefit from a successful expedition except the unfortunate Moors living in Ceuta.

João I finalized the decision to attack Ceuta in 1412. Although he publicly expressed initial scepticism over the plan when his treasurer João Afonso presented it in 1412, he may have been independently contemplating an assault on Ceuta as early as 1409. The King's advisors did not universally consider an attack on Ceuta to be a good idea and discussion of the policy was heated. Ultimately the King's view prevailed but this deliberation foreshadowed future debates over Portugal's explorations and overseas expansion. The policies that led to Portugal's establishment of a global empire of trade faced vigorous opposition every step of the way. No one should ever consider the foundation of Portugal's or Spain's overseas empires to be part of some inevitable and irresistible process of historical destiny. The Portuguese could have decided to stop at any time. The Ming dynasty of China's abandonment of both Zheng Ho's explorations of the Indian Ocean during the first half of the fifteenth century and the naval technology that made those voyages possible is a case in point.

João I began the massive process of gathering the men and the ships needed for a successful assault on Ceuta. Some chronicles claim that the Portuguese force consisted of over 200 vessels and 50,000 men. More reliable contemporary reports, though place the number of ships at about 120 with 19,000 soldiers sailing on them.[17] It was impossible for João I to keep the massing of so many troops a secret. He did, though, succeed in keeping its ultimate destination a surprise. Apprehension about the objective of João I's preparation was rife throughout the lands of the western Mediterranean and the Atlantic seaboard, both Christian and Muslim. Was a place in Castile the target, or Granada, or Aragon, or North Africa, or Sicily or France? Even ports in the Low Countries feared a possible attack. While this uncertain situation raised international tensions, it also served to keep the Moroccans and the garrison of Ceuta off-balance and unprepared.

The Portuguese fleet sailed from the Tagus River on 25 July 1415 and reached Lagos on the 27th. After taking on more supplies and making more preparations, the fleet embarked once more. The crossing proved difficult and unfavourable winds caused the fleet to overshoot Ceuta. That problem turned out to be a big asset to the Portuguese because it convinced the Moors that Ceuta was not the target and they relaxed their defensive work. So when the Portuguese fleet reappeared on 20 August the Moorish garrison of Ceuta was taken by surprise with no hope of timely relief from other Moorish forces. The Portuguese stormed the city on 21 August. In the fighting Prince Henry acquitted himself bravely. Recognizing that continued resistance was futile, the Moorish garrison abandoned the city and many of the Muslim residents followed them. Afterwards, the victors sacked the hapless port and on 25 August, João I's three sons – Duarte, Pedro and Henry – were all knighted. As military operations go, especially medieval ones, the capture of Ceuta was a great success, particularly because it was accomplished in a brief amount of time with minimal loss of life.[18]

With the taking of Ceuta, Portugal had its first overseas possession and its first victory at the start of its almost 200-year long quixotic quest to conquer Morocco. Not everyone, however, viewed the success at Ceuta as the beginning of something of long-term importance. Many Portuguese thought that the occupation of Ceuta would prove too expensive in comparison to any benefits it produced. Given Portugal's meagre base of resources, occupying Ceuta was an expensive luxury that the little kingdom could ill afford. While many Portuguese may have agreed with João I's chivalric motivations for attacking Ceuta, they expected that he would abandon it after subjecting the city to a profitable pillaging. Instead the King ordered the city to be garrisoned and appointed a governor to rule over it. In establishing this expansionist policy João I enjoyed the enthusiastic support of his third and favourite son Henry, a Crusader and knight errant to his core.[19]

Unfortunately for João I, the naysayers proved to be right about the true worth of Ceuta. The city's defence required an expensive garrison of over 2,500 troops. Such a standing force represented a major burden to the finances of a small country like Portugal. Muslim counter-attacks in 1418 and 1419 necessitated Portugal sending relief expeditions, which cost the country an even greater amount of money. Even more disappointing, the Muslim merchants involved with the sub-Saharan caravan trade were easily able to relocate to alternative Mediterranean ports when Ceuta fell into the hands of the Christians. Portugal ended up in possession of an empty shell with no commercial value.[20] In spite of such difficulties, both King João I and Prince Henry remained determined to continue holding Ceuta in spite of the widespread opposition to this in Portugal. After a few years the opponents of the policy came to include the Crown Prince Duarte and Prince Pedro. Commerical and financial considerations never loomed too large in the accounting of such inveterate knights errant and Crusaders as João I and Prince Henry. For them, further conquests in Morocco were the proper use of Portugal's resources.[21]

The expedition against Ceuta and its aftermath of continued military forays against Morocco brought the young Prince Henry into the foreground of world history. After recklessly participating in the storming of Ceuta and vigorously supporting his father's decision to occupy the town, Henry received his reward on 18 February 1416 in the form of an appointment as the royal administrator over Ceuta and its defences. That office gave him the first source of the revenue he would need to pursue his own crusading and evangelizing goals. For English-speaking people, Prince Henry is the man commonly known by the title of 'The Navigator', an appellation bestowed on him by the nineteenth-century historian Richard Henry Major and others. Traditionally historians from the sixteenth to the twentieth century have portrayed Henry as a precocious genius and innovator who established and oversaw a programme of systematic exploration based on the most up-to-date scientific knowledge and techniques. The existence of his school of navigation and cartographic studies at Sagres has been shown to be a myth. Some of the more teleological accounts even credit Prince Henry with the origination of Portugal's scheme to circumnavigate Africa to reach the spice marts of Asia.[22]

Prince Henry was the third son of João I and Philippa, the daughter of John of Gaunt, which made him half English, or at least English to the extent that any member of the Plantagenet line was actually English. Queen Philippa appears to have been close to her children and probably passed the traditional chivalric values of the Plantagenets to them. Henry revered and loved his warrior father. The two men were kindred spirits in their love of knightly warfare and crusading, which forged a bond between them that helped to make Prince Henry his father's preferred son.

Little detailed information has survived about Prince Henry's youth. His parents provided him with an excellent humanistic education and he showed interest in and talent for the study of cosmography and cartography.[23] Gomes Eannes de Azurara, Henry's admiring chronicler, described him as a large, strongly built man with fair hair that had darkened with age and exposure. His face habitually wore an expression that 'inspired fear in those who did not know him'. He carried himself with dignity, was soft-spoken and appeared to have excited love and admiration from those close to him. Like his brothers Duarte and Pedro, Henry demonstrated a natural intelligence although he was not bookish to the same degree as Duarte or even Pedro. He showed wisdom and discretion in his actions, in so far as those qualities accorded with his wholehearted acceptance of the values of chivalry and crusading. Such values left him constantly in debt but this sort of profligate activity was greatly admired by the fifteenth-century Portuguese elite.[24] Henry's indebtedness stemmed from his expenditures on crusading and exploration. In terms of his personal behaviour, he was conventionally pious and rather abstemious. Azurara claimed, 'I know not how to find any prince so Catholic and religious [as Henry] that I could say as much of him.'[25] He remained a virgin throughout his lifetime, a choice that must have caused as much incomprehension among his contemporaries at the sexually indulgent Portuguese court as it would among many people half a millennium later. Never one to indulge heavily in drinking wine, later in life Henry began to abstain from wine completely and took constantly to wearing a hairshirt under his clothing.[26] In all of these things, Prince Henry was very much a man of the later Middle Ages. Henry's medieval nature determined the formulation and the conduct of his programme of Atlantic and African exploration. His plans did not have their origin in any precocious scientific spirit that he supposedly possessed because, in fact, he had no such tendencies.

Azurara identified six reasons that motivated Prince Henry to promote his exploration of the Atlantic islands and what he knew as Guinea, i.e., coastal West Africa. Curiosity provided the first reason – Henry wanted to know what lay beyond the fabled and fearsome Cape Bojador. After that, economics drove his actions. He wanted to find other Christians and take up trade with them. Crusading strategy formed his third motivation. He needed to determine the extent of Islam's power in West Africa. How far south did it extend? Directly connected to this third goal was Henry's fourth spur, the desire to find African Christians and to enlist their aid in the European Crusade against Islam. Africa also contained heathens who needed conversion to Christianity and that formed the fifth motivation. Finally, the sixth and most important reason for Henry's African enterprise was one completely alien to the values of scientific enquiry – it was his astrological destiny. As Azurara put it, 'over and above these five reasons I have a sixth that would seem to be the root form which all the others proceeded: this is the inclination of the heavenly wheels'.[27] Henry's horoscope, which had been cast when he was quite young, predicted that he would 'toil at high and mighty conquests, especially in seeking out things that were hidden from other men and secret'.[28] It was a prediction that he took quite seriously. The Prince placed great faith in the efficacy of astrology and used his horoscope as a road map for his life. His horoscope predicted that Henry would be a conqueror and an explorer and those are the activities that he pursued through his adult life.[29] Duarte Pacheco, writing at the beginning of the sixteenth century, credited Henry's inspiration to be an explorer to a more conventional and pious source, a dream sent from God. Supposedly, one night a revelation came to Prince Henry that he would perform a great service to God by discovering Ethiopia and other unknown lands in Africa. His find would bring many of the Africans to the Christian faith and eternal salvation. Trade between Portugal and Africa would result in gold and other valuable trade goods flowing into Portugal making his country rich. Portugal's new wealth would in turn allow its King and his people to make war on the Muslim enemies of the Christian Church.[30] Whether Prince Henry literally had such a dream or not, visions of evangelizing the heathen, acquisition of vast new wealth and Crusades against the Muslims inspired the future explorations of many Portuguese during the fifteenth century along with diverse other people including Christopher Columbus.

For Prince Henry, the capture of Ceuta in 1415 marked merely the beginning of his astrologically anticipated career as a conqueror. All of the disintegrating kingdom of Fez in Morocco lay open for further conquest as did the Canary Islands, which largely remained outside European control in spite of the efforts of Bethencourt and his comrades-in-arms. In 1420 King João I greatly added to his son's resources by obtaining for him a papal appointment as administrator general of the rich Order of Christ. The Prince would use its revenues to support his Atlantic and African ventures and his Moroccan acquisitions.[31] Portugal's overseas policy involved the continued occupation of Ceuta while merchants and raiders advanced further and further down the Moroccan coast toward unknown lands and beyond. This policy was favoured by many segments of Portuguese society – merchants, would-be pirates, zealous Crusaders and adventurous spirits. Opposition to overseas expansion was also present and would continue to exist up to and well after Vasco da Gama's first voyage to India. Still it was Prince Henry who most consistently promoted and supported African expansion.[32]

TECHNOLOGY AND EXPLORATION – NAVIGATION, CARTOGRAPHY AND SHIPS

Some histories of the early modern expansion of Europe have tended to place a large emphasis on scientific and technological advances in navigation and cartography making it all possible. With the crucial exceptions of important innovations in ship design and naval armaments that is not really true. Navigational techniques used during the fifteenth century showed little change from how Europeans of earlier centuries had navigated their sea-going vessels. Prior to the beginning of the age of exploration, European ships, except for the Norse, had been confined to the waters of the Mediterranean Sea or had hugged the Atlantic coast of Europe and North Africa. The possibility for true navigation, defined as 'the art of taking ships from one place to another out of sight of land' was non-existent.[33] Overseas expansion, however, necessitated that Europeans make high-seas voyages with long periods of time out of the sight of land. The Portuguese mariners of Prince Henry the Navigator led the way in sailing the high seas but it would not be until late in the fifteenth century, well after the death of Prince Henry, that they consistently began to use techniques of true navigation.

Initially Portuguese seamen employed fairly primitive techniques. They used the compass to find direction, estimated latitudes to help place their location, studied any available maps and charts to guide their course and utilized a lead to take soundings of the water's depth.[34] The introduction of more precise astronomical instruments to determine latitude during a sea voyage did not become widespread until late in the fifteenth century. The earliest mention of a Portuguese ship using a navigational instrument comes from 1460 when the sea-captain Diogo Gomes reported operating a quadrant to determine his

Astrolabe of the great astronomer Regiomontanus. From Justin Winsor, *Narrative and Critical History of America* (Boston, Houghton Mifflin, 1886), vol. 2, p. 96.

latitude during a voyage to the Guinea Coast. Some historians also doubt the accuracy of his account.[35] More complex navigational instruments did not necessarily lead to more precise measurements of latitude. Imperfect conditions caused by seaboard motion, the complicated mathematical calculations needed to complete successfully the measurement of latitude and the lack of detailed tables of astronomical observations all worked to make the new techniques of astronomical navigation very unreliable during the late fifteenth century and well into the sixteenth century.[36] Equally important, the measurement of longitude remained completely elusive until the development of an accurate and reliable marine chronometer in the later eighteenth century. This inability to determine east–west location necessitated the use of dead-reckoning sailing by the mariners of the age of exploration. The technique of dead-reckoning consisted of a ship's captain estimating his location by calculating how far the ship had travelled east or west in a day. The captain did this by keeping records of the ship's speed and direction and then plotting that information on a nautical chart. While many sailors of the early modern era, most famously Christopher Columbus, were astonishingly accurate dead-reckoning navigators, it was still an imprecise art of navigation rather than the exact science that astronomical navigation would eventually become.[37]

During the last decades of the fifteenth century, the Portuguese developed better astronomical navigational techniques in response to the necessity of making high-seas voyages. Initially their results were imperfect but they improved over time as detailed astronomical tables appeared and systematic surveys of the newly explored African coasts were made.[38] Other nations followed the Portuguese's lead as they in turn began sailing the high seas, but in spite of notable improvements, throughout the sixteenth century astronomical navigation remained a flawed craft with immense potential for endangering ships and sailors when errors occurred.

During the Middle Ages, there were basically two types of maps available – the *mappa mundi* and the portolan chart. The term *mappa mundi* could refer to any map of the world and they depicted many different types of information along with much symbolism.[39] Patterns of the number four were repeated over and over again – winds, rivers of Paradise, climates and corners of the earth. The Ebstorf *mappa mundi* showed the earth as the body of Christ. Other images emphasized the correspondence between Noah's three sons and the three known continents – Shem and Asia, Ham and Africa and Japheth and Europe. Marvels and wonders also appeared liberally on many *mappae mundi* including the stock features of freakish animals, monstrous races of people, Prester John, the Terrestrial Paradise and the land of the imprisoned Gog and Magog. *Mappae mundi* were not, however, merely works of symbol and fiction. Large amounts of accurate historical and geographical information frequently appeared on them or were added to existing *mappae mundi* as new details became available in Europe.

Mappae mundi can be classified into four basic categories: tripartite, zonal, quadripartite and transitional. Tripartite *mappae mundi* show the world as the three continents of Africa, Asia and Europe surrounded by the River Ocean. The three continents are separated from each other by the Don River, the Nile River and the Mediterranean Sea. Generally these *mappae mundi* were oriented to the east rather than the north, like modern maps. Some tripartite maps were schematic, i.e., they were presented as geometrical forms based on the shapes of a T being placed inside an O. Hence these schematic maps are known as T-O maps. Other tripartite maps were non-schematic in that they arranged the three continents in a T-O pattern although they also attempted to depict accurate historical and geographical information. Both the famous Hereford and Ebstorf *mappae mundi* are non-schematic tripartite maps.

Zonal *mappae mundi* divided the earth into five or seven zones of climate. There was an uninhabited northern, frigid zone, one or two inhabited northern, temperate zones, an uninhabited torrid zone along the equator, one or two possibly inhabited, southern, temperate zones and an uninhabited, southern, frigid zone. Zonal maps were always oriented to the north. Purely zonal maps were always very schematic in their presentation.

Quadripartite *mappae mundi* combined features of both tripartite and zonal maps. They depicted climate zones and the three known continents, sometimes in a T-O configuration. They added a fourth unknown landmass in the southern hemisphere that was sometimes labelled the antipodes and occasionally called the antichthones.

Finally, the transitional *mappae mundi* of the fourteenth and fifteenth centuries mark a shift away from the other types, being largely depictions of symbolism and religious cosmography, towards being truly accurate geographical representations. Transitional *mappae mundi* centre on a reasonably accurate map of the Mediterranean Sea/Black Sea basin but as they move away from that point, they become more vague, more inaccurate and more symbolic. The influences of portolan charts are evident in the precise presentation of the greater Mediterranean region. In some transitional *mappae mundi*, the influence of Claudius Ptolemy's recently discovered *Geography* is also quite apparent, particularly when the error of depicting the Indian Ocean as a landlocked sea appears. The Catalan Atlas, the controversial Vinland Map and the world map of Paulo Pozzo Toscanelli are all examples of the transitional type of *mappae mundi*. From the late fifteenth century *mappae mundi* faded from use as they were replaced by world maps that attempted to portray geographical knowledge in the most accurate way possible.

Medieval *mappae mundi* were not intended to be used as guides for navigation and travel. Instead, they presented the world and its history in a way that helped believers to understand Christian cosmography. In this role they deeply influenced the geographical and ethnographical expectations of medieval merchants and pilgrims as they travelled to other lands. It is also important to remember that the vast majority of *mappae mundi* depicted the earth as spherical even though they were drawn on a flat, two-dimensional surface. Medieval scholars produced the *mappae mundi* and among medieval scholars the belief in a spherical earth was almost universal.

Portolan charts were medieval nautical maps that were used in conjunction with dead-reckoning sailing to navigate the Mediterranean Sea and the west coast of

Europe.[40] The first surviving portolan charts date to 1270. Centring on the Mediterranean and Black Sea regions, these maps exhibit a great and obvious improvement in geographical accuracy compared to what preceded them. As the portolan charts moved beyond the Mediterranean and the west coast of Europe, their accuracy blurred and faded. Many of the surviving copies of portolan charts appear to have been the possessions of rulers or scholars since they are heavily decorated and annotated. These embellished portolan charts, however, were clearly derived from other working portolan charts that were used by seamen for practical navigation.

Portolan charts originated from the information found in portolans (or rutters), which were names for books of sailing directions used by seafarers in the Mediterranean Sea. The name portolan had its origin in the Latin word *portus*, port, since the portolans gave the directions needed to sail from one port to another. The early history of portolan charts is obscure and controversial. The oldest surviving of these documents are virtually fully developed and represent an apparently major and sudden leap in cartographic accuracy. No evidence of any evolutionary or historical progress has survived. As a result, there are many conflicting theories about the origins of the portolan chart. Some historians claim that they are based on lost ancient cartographic prototypes which go back variously to the Phoenicians, the Carthaginians, the Greeks or the Romans. It has even been suggested, although not widely accepted, that the portolan charts were based on information handed down from an ancient ice-age super-civilization or extra-terrestrial visitors. Other scholars suggest a medieval source for them. They submit that portolan charts originated as the result of people combining the use of the traditional portolan, i.e., detailed sailing directions, with the use of the compass to navigate. The new technology of the compass would have made it possible to compose more accurate maps. Since compasses were introduced in Europe in about 1200 and the earliest portolan charts date to 1270, a sudden medieval origin becomes explicable. The lack of preliminary versions of portolan charts is attributable to the fact that they were intended to be practical navigational tools. Sailors used them on voyages until they were worn out or were lost at sea. The old ones were thrown away and replaced with new ones. As a result, the fancy, decorative versions of portolan charts have survived in disproportionate numbers because they were valued *object d'art* and did not have to suffer the rigours of going to sea.

Portolan charts provided accurate information for ships operating in the Mediterranean Sea, the Black Sea and the west coast of Europe. Coastlines were truly drawn and ports were placed correctly, while promontories, reefs and shoals were clearly indicated. Various colour codings were used to show the relative importance of various ports and geographical features. The most distinctive features of a portolan chart were the rhumb lines which formed a complex web that was an aid to dead-reckoning navigation. Each set of rhumb lines was based on a circle. They radiated out from the centre of the circle in thirty-two different directions based on the wind rose with its eight major winds and the accompanying half and quarter wind directions.

Navigators used the lines to help determine the distance and the direction that their ship travelled. It was a system that worked surprisingly well. Christopher Columbus was an excellent dead-reckoning navigator. With the coming of the sixteenth century and the vast increase in geographical information from the numerous European voyages of exploration, new cartographic techniques were needed. The Portuguese conducted surveys of the recently explored coasts and compiled detailed sailing directions to guide their ships to Africa and Asia. They also began to produce more accurate maps that functioned better than the traditional portolan charts. Cartographers followed their lead and developed grid systems of coordinated lines of latitude and longitude with the most notable and useful being that of Gerard Mercator. As a result of these new techniques of mapping, portolan charts were gradually rendered obsolete and were abandoned by sailors. They were replaced by increasingly more sophisticated and practical maps that culminated in Mercator's famous projection which greatly eased the problems of navigation.

The truly significant innovations and advancements in navigation and cartography all occurred well after the process of overseas expansion by the Portuguese had been under way for some time. Technological progress did, however, play a role in allowing the exploration to get started. It was in the area of shipbuilding and design that technological innovations made overseas exploration possible. Prior to the fifteenth century, Europeans had employed two basic types of sea-going vessels. Mediterranean galleys had been around for thousands of years. While well suited to the relatively calm Mediterranean Sea, they were not appropriate for long voyages or for the rugged conditions of high-seas sailing on the Atlantic Ocean. Galleys required sizeable crews of rowers to man the banks of oars. Such large numbers of people on a ship would quickly consume the available provisions during long voyages out of the sight of land or along barren shores where reprovisioning was impossible. Mediterranean galleys also were not built to withstand for long the rough seas and powerful storms of the Atlantic. To sail on those seas, the countries of Atlantic Europe used the ship known as the cog. This clumsy craft had a squatty hull that could withstand the stresses and strains of heavy seas and a large capacity for carrying cargo. The problem was that they were not easily manoeuvrable and possessed a relatively deep draught which meant that they were not good ships to sail along an unfamiliar coast with unknown shallows and reefs. Cogs employed square-shaped sails as their primary source of locomotion. Their square rigging made them very dependent on favourable winds coming from the right direction. Sailing a cog down the frequently shallow coast of north-west Africa was a hazardous enterprise. If a cog managed to reach the Canary Islands safely, it faced contrary prevailing winds when it tried to make its way back home. Given the limitations of both galleys and cogs, European oceanic expansion remained severely hampered until the early decades of the fifteenth century.

The Portuguese managed to get around the constraints of galleys and cogs when they began to employ the new type of sailing ship known as the caravel. Combining elements of the Mediterranean and the Atlantic shipbuilding traditions, the first

Sailing ships from the age of exploration with square and lateen rigging. From Charles Kendall Adams and William P. Trent, *A History of the United States* (Boston, Allyn & Bacon, 1909), p. 10.

caravels were simple fishing boats that operated in the coastal waters of the Iberian Peninsula. The physical attributes of the caravels made them ideally suited to exploring the coast of West Africa. Their slim hulls and axial rudders made them easy to steer in the frequently tight conditions of coastal waters and estuaries. Possessing a shallow draught, caravels could sail on waters that were not very deep, a great asset when a ship was operating along an uncharted coast. Most importantly, the Portuguese equipped their caravels with large, triangular sails which they mounted on an extremely long boom. These sails were known as a lateen rig and allowed caravels to sail extremely close to the wind. This characteristic meant that they could take advantage of winds from a larger range of directions. Portuguese caravels could cruise down the coast of north-west Africa and then make their way back in the face of adverse prevailing winds by periodic adjustments of their course and sails through tacking. Caravels rigged with lateen sails were called *caravela latina* by the Portuguese. The intrepid Italian seamen Alvise Cadamosto paid tribute to the qualities of the Portuguese caravel when he wrote, 'The caravels of Portogallo [Portugal] being the best ships that sailed the seas and being well furnished with every necessity, he [Prince Henry] considered it possible for them successfully to sail everywhere.'[41] Their special sailing attributes helped make the Portuguese exploration of the African coast possible as well as the early Spanish voyages to the Americas.

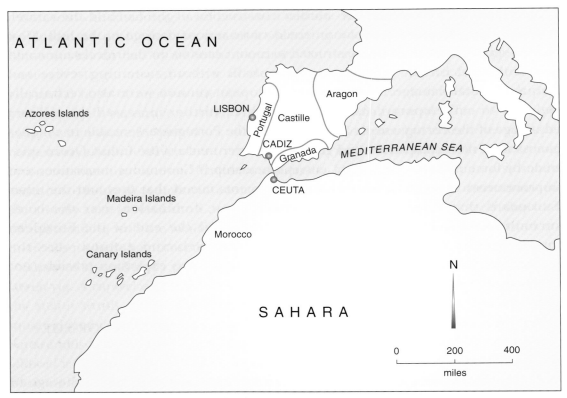

The Iberian Peninsula and the Atlantic islands.

Prince Henry's ambitions. Unfortunately for Prince Henry, these same islands were also difficult to conquer. The natives resisted with fierce determination and although they only possessed stone-age weapons, they used the rugged terrain of the mountainous western Canary Islands to great advantage. In 1424 Prince Henry sent an expedition to seize Grand Canary which resulted in an embarrassing repulse for the Portuguese.

Defeat, however, left Prince Henry undaunted; instead of being discouraged, gaining control of the Canaries almost became an obsession for him. Portuguese raiders, as well as other Europeans, descended on the Canaries for slaves which slowly reduced the manpower available to the natives for continued resistance. Meanwhile, Prince Henry slowly gathered his resources for another assault on the Canaries. When the preparations were completed, he sent a fleet against Tenerife in 1434. Although the Portuguese managed to take 400 prisoners, they failed to break the native resistance. Later, when the Portuguese attacked Gomera, they also managed to cultivate allies among some of the feuding native clans. Some Gomerans even joined the Portuguese in slave raids against La Palma. But in spite of such assistance and the exploitation of the divisions among the natives of the Canaries, the Portuguese had failed to conquer either Gomera or La Palma by 1446. At that time Henry shifted from trying to take the native-controlled islands to seizing those already in European hands.[48]

In 1448 Maciot de Bethencourt ceded his rights of lordship on Lanzarote to Prince Henry. Bethencourt only possessed a claim to part of the island but Henry asserted that the agreement gave him lordship over all the Canaries. The Castilians refused to accept the agreement as valid and maintained that they had the best claim to the Canaries. Prince Henry and the Portuguese moved in anyway. Initially the existing European settlers accepted Prince Henry's rule but his officials soon proved to be oppressive and incompetent. The residents of Lanzarote drove them out in 1450 and the Portuguese bids to reassert their control later that year and in 1451 both failed. Castilian forces also opposed the Portuguese attempt to conquer Lanzarote. The resulting conflict between Portugal and Castile was Europe's first colonial war. It ended with a marriage treaty between the two countries in 1454.[49] Prince Henry was left with nothing to show for his obsessive efforts to gain control of the Canaries. He possessed insufficient military resources to prevail over either the Canarians or the Castilians and what he did have, he used poorly.[50] The Portuguese–Castilian rivalry over the Canaries did not end there either. It erupted again during the succession war between Portugal and Castile from 1475 to 1479. In that conflict, Castile emerged victorious in March 1476 at Toro, the one major land battle on the Iberian Peninsula. The naval war in the Canaries went in favour of Portugal as her navy defeated all of the Castilian fleets sent to the islands between 1476 and 1480.[51] The Treaty of Alcaçovas ended that war and gave Castile clear title to the Canaries, while giving Portugal a sure monopoly over the lucrative trade with the Guinea Coast of West Africa.

Prince Henry's efforts to claim and to settle the Madeira Islands for Portugal were far more successful that his activities in the Canaries.[52] Europeans had known about the Madeiras since 1351, when they first appeared on the Medici Atlas. Genoese sailors in the service of Portugal discovered them, probably in the course of a return trip from the Canaries. Both islands, Porto Santo and Madeira, were uninhabited with rugged terrain. Madeira (meaning wood) was heavily forested. João Gonçalvas Zarco and Tristão Vaz Teixeira, both members of Prince Henry's household, supposedly came to Madeira between 1418 and 1425. But it appears that a truly permanent settlement was not established until the mid-1430s or later. Turbulent nobles and knights made Madeiran society violent and unpredictable.[53] The early settlers got off to a bad start. They attempted to clear some of Madeira's densely wooded land by burning off the trees in the region of Funchal. The fire raged out of its makers' control and forced people to take refuge in streams and in the sea where they spent two days and nights waiting for the fire to burn itself out. Claims that the conflagration swept the entire island were obviously exaggerated. Many trees remained while a large amount of land had been cleared for cultivation.[54] The settlers planted grapes and in a short time they were shipping a quality wine and excellent timber for building and furniture to Portugal at low prices. Both commodities greatly improved Portuguese daily life.[55] Sugar production began on Madeira in 1452 with canes brought from Sicily with capital provided by Genoese financiers. It quickly proved a lucrative enterprise and remained the mainstay of the Madeiran economy until the seventeenth century. The success of the Madeiran sugar industry encouraged the spread of sugar cultivation to the Azores, the Cape Verdes and Brazil as the Portuguese came to settle them. Sugar production's demand for labour also provided a ready market for slaves taken from the Canaries or West Africa.[56]

Prince Henry began the settlement of Porto Santo with a grant to Bartolomé Perestrello in 1446. Unlike Madeira, Porto Santo did not develop into a farming community. Once again the early residents made a mistake that turned out to have huge environmental consequences. They introduced rabbits to the island which lacked natural predators. Soon the rabbits multiplied to the extent that they rendered farming and gardening impossible. The Portuguese abandoned the island but later returned. Initially they were limited to raising livestock but eventually they brought the rabbit population under control and some agricultural work took place.[57] Overall, the settlement of the Madeiras proved to be a success and Prince Henry as lord of the islands benefited significantly from the large revenues that they produced.

Europeans knew of the existence of the Azores by 1375 when Abraham Cresques first depicted them on his Catalan Atlas. Nothing, however, came of that discovery until Diogo de Silves of Portugal came across the Azores again in 1427.[58] Whether Silves purposefully sailed to the Azores or reached them through the chance vagaries of winds is not certain. In 1431 or 1432 Prince Henry had domestic animals placed on the uninhabited islands to provide resupply for future Portuguese ships visiting the islands. Henry's brother the Regent Pedro gave him the right to colonize the Azores in 1439. Like the Madeira Islands, the settlers on the Azores were a rough and ready lot. Their remoteness and general undesirability meant that convicts and foreigners were among the early residents.[59] The islands possessed fertile soil and were well watered. Initially the Portuguese tried to grow sugar cane but grain crops ultimately proved far more viable in view of the somewhat cool climate. Unfortunately for the settlers of the Azores, wheat, sheep and cattle were not the sort of commodities that produced great wealth. Instead the Azores came to serve as a rest-stop for picking up fresh provisions by ships returning from the Americas.[60] They also provided a jumping-off point for Portugal's continuing efforts to explore the Atlantic Ocean during the second half of the fifteenth century. Diogo de Teive's discovery in 1452 of Flores and Corvo, the western-most of the Azores, marks a first step in that enterprise.[61] With the Azores, Prince Henry had established another successful colony on some far Atlantic islands that would prove valuable to Portugal over the years.

Portugal's final island settlements during the fifteenth century were the Cape Verde Islands. Portuguese explorers came across this group sometime during the late 1450s up to 1460. Like the Madeiras and the Azores, the Cape Verdes were uninhabited. King Afonso V granted Antonio di Noli and Diogo Afonso captaincies over the islands in 1462, which included the right to found settlements and these represented the first European colony in the tropics.[62] Potential settlers from Portugal found the Cape Verdes to be extremely unattractive with the result that Portuguese authorities were forced to rely on slave labour when they established

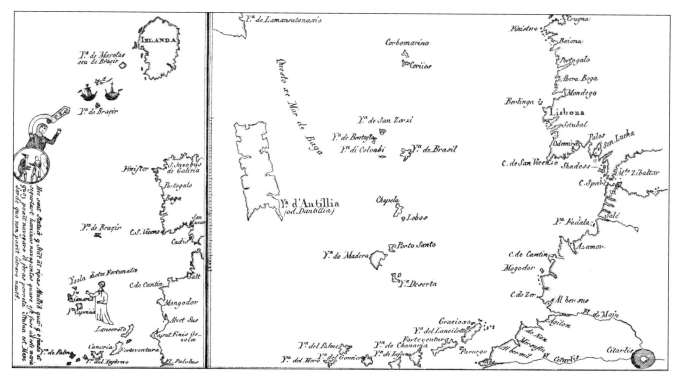

Andreas Blanco's map of 1436 showing the island of Antillia in the mid-Atlantic. From Justin Winsor, *Narrative and Critical History of America* (Boston, Houghton Mifflin, 1889), vol. 1, p. 54.

sugar plantations there. By 1500 Santiago remained the only permanent community in the Cape Verde group in spite of the success of growing sugar there.[63] While not founded by Prince Henry, Santiago was of the same type as those successful settlements that the Prince had begun on the Madeiras and the Azores. The work on these islands formed a model in miniature for the future European conquests and settlements in the Americas. These island communities formed a legacy of enterprise that Prince Henry and his fellow fifteenth-century Portuguese would have considered to be every bit as important as his African explorations.

The Portuguese discovery and settlement of the Madeiras and the Azores was not an isolated and accidental set of occurrences. Medieval Europeans believed that the Atlantic Ocean had islands scattered throughout it. When wandering mariners encountered the Madeiras and the Azores in the late fourteenth century, it was not so much a surprise as it was a fulfilment of their geographical expectations.[64] The belief that additional, undiscovered islands lay somewhere in the Atlantic's vastness continued into the fifteenth century and stimulated various Portuguese voyages of exploration. In 1424 the mythical island of Antillia first appeared on the map of Zuane Pizzigano. Antillia was a relatively large island which was apparently equal in size to Portugal itself. It was also the home of the Seven Cities of Gold, a group of wealthy settlements supposedly founded by refugees from the Muslim conquest of Iberia in the eighth century. When Diogo de Teive discovered Flores and Corvo, the western-most Azores, in 1452, he was actually looking for Antillia.[65] Other trips followed or at least were planned. In 1462 King Afonso V granted João Vogado the islands of Capraria and Lovo if he could find and settle them. Naturally Vogado failed because the islands did not exist. Some early twentieth-century Portuguese historians credit another Portuguese sailor named João Vaz Corte-Real with the discovery of America in 1472 possibly in the company of the Danes Didrik Pining and Hans Pothorst. The general community of professional historians, however, tend to doubt that any such voyage was ever planned let alone that it occurred or actually found something.[66]

The Portuguese King Afonso V continued to be interested in the exploration of the western Atlantic Ocean. In January 1474 he granted Fernão Teles the right to seek out and to settle on any Atlantic islands that he might find, provided they were not near the Guinea Coast of Africa. Afonso V extended the grant to Teles in November 1475 to include the Seven Cities and Antillia. But whether Teles ever sailed is unclear and even if he did, he found nothing. The same observation applies to the supposed voyage of Antonio Leme to Antillia in 1484.[67]

The voyage of Ferdinand Van Olmen was one of the better-documented fifteenth-century Portuguese voyages into the western Atlantic. Van Olmen was one of many Flemings who settled on Portugal's various Atlantic islands. Other variations of his name were Ferdinand Van den Olm and Fernão d'Ulmo by the Portuguese and Fernando de Olmos by the Spanish. He had done quite well in the Portuguese service and had become a knight of the royal court. When he settled on Terceira in the Azores he also acquired the captaincy of part of that island. By early 1486, Van Olmen was engaged in negotiations with King João II of Portugal for a voyage of discovery into the western Atlantic. João II confirmed their agreement by letters patent on 3 March which gave Van Olmen the right to make such a journey.

The single most important fact in Van Olmen's agreement with João II was that Van Olmen would pay for the expedition, not the King. Several years earlier Christopher Columbus had approached the Portuguese King with a similar plan but when he asked for royal financing, it was refused. João II was quite interested in the exploration of the western Atlantic but only on the cheap. Van Olmen's destination was the legendary Island of the Seven Cities, although no one knew if it was actually a single island, an island group or a continent. In exchange for his funding the voyage of discovery, Van Olmen would receive the rule of any lands he found and have full legal jurisdiction over them whether they were uninhabited or inhabited. If the natives proved hostile, Van Olmen would also command any fleet sent to conquer them. His title to any discoveries would also be hereditary and would pass to his heirs whether male or female.

Apparently Van Olmen could not afford personally to finance the entire expedition and so found a partner, João Afonso de Estreito of Funchal, Madeira. The two men reached an agreement on 12 June 1486 in which they would divide any lands they discovered in half. Estreito agreed immediately to supply Van Olmen with the sum of

6,000 reals. Basically Van Olmen would pay for the crews and Estreito would pay for the expedition's two ships. Each man would command one of the ships. João II confirmed their contract by royal decree on 24 July. He added the clause that Van Olmen would hold overall command for the first forty days after which Estreito would command until the expedition returned to Portugal. On any lands they discovered, the two men would exercise joint authority.

The Van Olmen/Estreito expedition was scheduled to depart from Terceira during March 1487. Martin Behaim, the famous German cartographer, was living on Fayal in the Madeiras at that time and was supposedly allowed to take passage on the voyage. He apparently did not exercise that privilege

Martin Behaim, explorer for Portugal, globe-maker and contemporary of Columbus. From Justin Winsor, *Narrative and Critical History of America* (Boston, Houghton Mifflin, 1886), vol. 2, p. 104.

since there is no indication of Van Olmen's route on Behaim's globe of 1492. Some scholars have speculated that Van Olmen never even sailed himself since no official documents have survived mentioning the voyage's aftermath. The general scholarly consensus, however, is that Van Olmen's expedition sailed but failed to make a landfall. Bartolomé de Las Casas mentioned the expedition as a fact in his *Historia de Indias*, although he never provided the further details that he promised his readers.

Ferdinand Van Olmen's expedition failed for two reasons. First, it started in March, which is a bad season for any relatively small sailing ship to attempt to cross the stormy North Atlantic. Second, it started from the Azores which are located at a latitude in which the prevailing winds do not favour western voyages. Like other Portuguese voyages departing from the Azores before and after him, Van Olmen took on virtually impossible sailing conditions and predictably did not succeed.

In spite of Van Olmen's failure, João II apparently retained his interest in western Atlantic voyages. When Columbus offered his services again in 1488 the King responded by inviting him to Portugal. Unfortunately for Columbus, Bartolomé Dias returned from the Cape of Good Hope in December of 1488 causing Portuguese interest in a western route to Asia to fade.

It was not until the end of the fifteenth century that Portuguese interest in the exploration of the western Atlantic revived. In October 1499 King Manuel granted a patent to João Fernandes Lavrador of Terceira in the Azores to seek out 'certain islands in our [the Portuguese] sphere of influence'. Sailing north Fernandes reached

Cape Farewell on Greenland which marked the rediscovery of that frigid land where the pathetic remnants of the forgotten Norse colonies had died out decades earlier. It was named Lavrador (farmer) after Fernandes, although the name migrated westward on maps to Canada when cartographers began calling Greenland by its original name again. Little came of Fernandes's discovery and when he returned to Terceira he learned the unpleasant news that in May 1500 King Manuel had granted Gaspar Corte-Real a patent of discovery very similar to his.[68]

Gaspar Corte-Real made his first voyage in the summer of 1500 and apparently reached Newfoundland, a seemingly more promising landfall that Fernandes's on Greenland. Of course, Gaspar Corte-Real was blithely unaware that John Cabot had preceded him in discovery by several years. When he returned to Portugal in the autumn of 1500 he began planning a new voyage to the north. In May 1501 Corte-Real departed with three ships and returned to Newfoundland. There the Portuguese proceeded to capture and to enslave fifty-seven Indians from the Beothuk tribe, continuing their bad habits from the Guinea Coast slave trade in Africa. Only two of the ships managed to return home in October. Gaspar Corte-Real's vessel continued to explore the coast and was never heard from again. Undeterred, in January 1502 King Manuel assigned Gaspar's patent to his older brother Miguel Corte-Real. Unfortunately for Miguel, his luck ran no better than his younger brother's. Sailing in May 1501, Miguel's ship was also lost with his entire crew. Although the patent for exploration remained in the Corte-Real family for another seventy years, no further northern voyages took place. Sailing west across the Atlantic Ocean from the Azores was just too difficult and dangerous. Except for some intrepid fishermen, the Portuguese abandoned trips in that direction.[69]

CAPE BOJADOR AND BEYOND

In 1420 European ships only made their way down the Atlantic coast of Africa as far as the Canary Islands or visited Moroccan ports along the way. Moorish vessels did not ply the Atlantic waters because there was no need for them to do so. The trans-Saharan caravan routes already worked very well for the Muslims and the continued use of those routes assured their monopoly over trade with sub-Saharan West Africa. Fantastic tales abounded about the dangers of sailing down the African coast. Ancient lore taught that the torrid zone along the equator was uninhabitable due to the intense heat and that the waters of its seas were boiling. Closer at hand on the Moroccan coast lay Cape Nun of which it was said, 'who passes never returns'.[70] Far more perilous was the point on the coast that the Portuguese initially called Cape Bojador. They were mistaken, it was actually Cape Juby. The real Cape Bojador was located further south and presented no substantial obstacle to navigation. Cape Bojador/Juby, on the other hand, embodied a true hazard to unwary sailing vessels attempting to pass it. Treacherous currents and winds threatened to thrust passing ships onto the shore if they failed to stay far enough out to sea. No obvious promontory warned approaching ships to head out to sea as they neared Cape Juby. Instead mists from the high surf obscured the range of vision further. Contrary winds and currents also prevented a vessel that had passed Cape Juby from returning the same way. Furthermore, as far as the Portuguese knew, 'beyond this Cape [Bojador/Juby] there is no race of men nor place of inhabitants: nor is the land less sandy than the deserts of Libya, where there is no water, no tree, no green herb'.[71] To the south supposedly lay an empty wasteland not worth visiting. Cumulatively all of these stories reinforced the European sailors' basic fear of the unknown, in itself a potent psychological barrier. It also appears that the Muslims of Morocco contributed to the climate of fear by doing all that they could to promote stories about the perils of Cape Bojador and beyond. They hoped to discourage Christian ships from interloping on their trans-Saharan caravan trade.[72]

The actual physical terrain along the African coastline from well before Cape Bojador down to near the Senegal River was forbidding. Climatic conditions that had created the Sahara made the Atlantic coast of north-west Africa equally dry and desolate. Few plants and animals could survive in such an environment which in turn meant that few people lived in these desiccated lands. Berbers or Sanjaha people inhabited this part of Africa. Most of them were nomads, but some were poor fishermen eking out a living from the sea. Initially the Portuguese thought the region was uninhabited, which was not surprising considering the sparse population. Given the land's poverty and seeming emptiness, many Portuguese believed it to be not worth visiting. It took someone with the vision and persistence of Prince Henry to see past the desert to the land of gold that lay beyond it.

The beginning of Prince Henry's African explorations are obscure. A big breakthrough occurred in 1434 when Gil Eannes, a squire of the prince's household, rounded Cape Bojador/Juby and successfully returned to Portugal to tell of it. According to Azurara's version of events, by 1433 Prince Henry had on fifteen different occasions in the past twelve years sent ships to attempt a passage of Cape Bojador. That meant that his programme of exploration had begun in about 1421. Unfortunately each time his fearful captains approached Cape Bojador, they lost their nerve and instead turned to trading or raiding along the Moroccan coast or to slaving in the Canary Islands. Gil Eannes, himself, had made one failed attempt to round Cape Bojador in a barque during 1433 and instead settled for taking captives on the nearby Canaries. Upon Eannes's return, Prince Henry asked him 'to strain every nerve' and take the same small vessel and try to round Cape Bojador yet again. Such a charge from Prince Henry represented an imperative to Eannes and meant that he needed to produce results rather than more excuses. And that is exactly what Eannes did. Successfully rounding the cape in 1434 he found an empty land but did manage to go on shore and pick a sprig of rosemary. With that voyage of the brave Gil Eannes, a major and stubborn psychological barrier to sailing further south on the African coast had been removed. Or had it?[73]

The Venetian Alvise de Cadamosto (1430–80?), who sailed to Africa for Prince Henry in the 1450s, told a different story about the origin of Prince Henry's

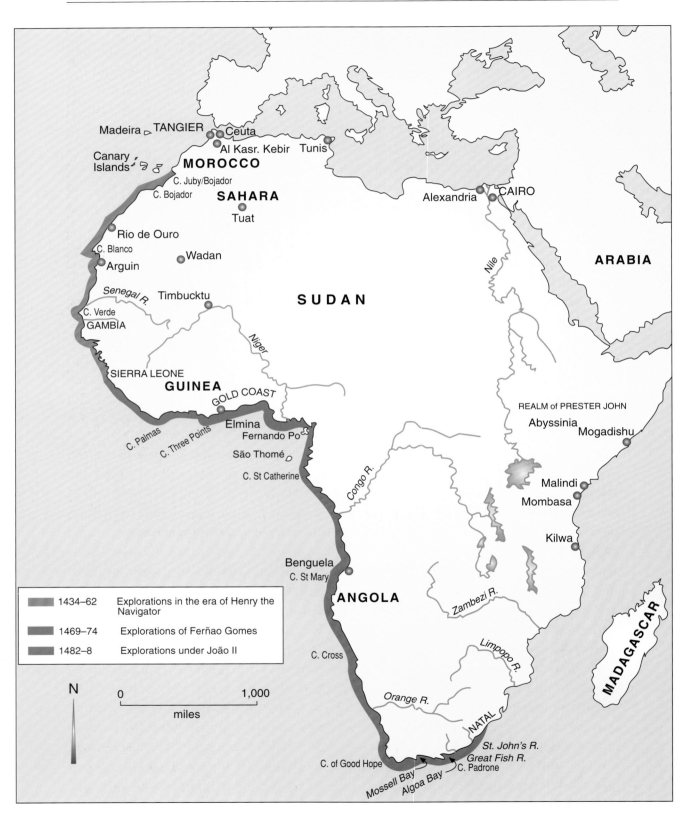

The Portuguese exploration of the African Coast.

programme of African exploration. Both King João I and Prince Henry waged continuous war on the Moorish kingdom of Fez. Sometime before 1433, as his death approached, the King secured a promise from his son Prince Henry that he would carry on their war against the Muslims. Duarte, the next King and Prince Henry's older brother, continued to support his brother's crusade against the Moors of Morocco. Portuguese raiders advanced further and further down the coast until they reached Cape Nun. There the last of the permanent settlements of the Moroccans ended. Prince Henry, however, wanted his ships to continue probing southward into the empty coastline until they once again reached lands with inhabitants. Each year Portuguese ships sailed 100 or 150 miles further south. After a few years they made contact with the nomadic Arabs, with the Azanagi branch of the Sanjaha and finally with the lands of the Negroes. In 1426 Fray Goncalvo Velho made his voyage to Terra Alta near Cape Bojador.[74] Cadamosto's

The fifteenth-century *Panel of the Infanta* by Nuno Goncalves from the St Vincent altarpiece. This scene depicts Prince Henry the Navigator and the future João II behind and to the far right of the central figure in red. (Giraudon/Art Resource, NY)

account takes some of the high drama out of Gil Eannes's achievement. At the same time, it also confirms the central role that Prince Henry played as the guiding spirit of Portugal's exploration of the African coast.

Prince Henry quickly followed up Gil Eannes's passage of Cape Bojador by sending Afonso Goncalves Baldaia and Gil Eannes past Cape Bojador for a second time in 1435. Sailing some 50 leagues south of the cape, the voyagers discovered human and camel tracks but no habitations.[75] The next year Baldaia sailed down the coast to the bay he mistakenly called Rio d'Ouro, thinking it was the fabled river of gold which led to the gold mines of West Africa. Baldaia landed two young men and their horses and instructed them to ride inland on a scouting expedition. Proceeding 7 leagues into the desolate land, the youths came upon a party of nineteen natives armed with the type of spears known as assegais. Being raised in the crusading milieu of implacable animosity toward Muslims, the two young Portuguese impetuously attacked. It was an inconclusive engagement. One youth suffered a wound as did one of the natives but neither side overcame the other.[76] At this point the Portuguese hoped to capture natives so that they could teach them their language and then use them as interpreters.[77] Soon after the Portuguese discovered a deserted village but never sighted any people. A frustrated Baldaia could not determine whether the locals were Muslims or simply heathens.[78] Actions like the youths' unprovoked attack on the band of native spearmen only served to arouse the fears and hostilities of the local inhabitants. They were also a harbinger of the type of relations that would all too frequently characterize Portuguese encounters with the various peoples of Africa and Asia.

It was at this point that Prince Henry's desire to conquer Morocco overshadowed his aspirations to explore Africa. In 1437 King Duarte organized an expedition against Tangier and placed Prince Henry in command. It turned into a humiliating defeat for the Portuguese. Moorish forces drove off the Portuguese and captured Prince Fernando, the youngest brother of King Duarte and Prince Henry. The Moroccans offered to return the young prince in exchange for the Portuguese handing Ceuta back to them. Initially Prince Henry agreed to the exchange, but later declined to carry out the bargain which enraged the Moroccans. As a result Prince Fernando found himself imprisoned under harsh conditions. He would languish in a Moroccan prison, unredeemed by his brothers until his early and inevitable death in 1443. Meanwhile, in 1438 King Duarte died leaving Portugal's affairs in a state of confusion that distracted Prince Henry from either further Moroccan conquests or African explorations for a while longer.[79]

SLAVES AND GOLD – THE PORTUGUESE REACH THE GUINEA COAST

By 1440 the situation in Portugal had settled enough for Prince Henry to resume African explorations. In that year he sent two caravels south, which is the first mention of this type of craft being used. On this voyage nothing of significance occurred. In 1441 the Prince sent Antão Goncalves down the coast in a small trading vessel to collect sea-wolf skins. In the course of this voyage he managed to capture a male and a female African at the Rio d'Ouro before being joined by Nuño Tristão. Goncalves's modest action marked the beginning of the Portuguese slave trade along the West African coast. As Azurara described it, 'for this deed of his [Goncalves], undertaken with so great boldness; for since he was the first who made booty in this conquest, he deserveth advantage over and above all others who in after time travailed in the matter'.[80] The two Portuguese parties came upon another group of natives and proceeded to attack them, killing four and capturing ten. At this point Goncalves returned to Portugal with his prisoners while Tristão sailed further south until he reached Cape Blanco. This expedition of Goncalves and Tristão revolutionized the Portuguese attitude toward the exploration of the West African coast. Instead of a wasteland devoid of any valuable products, the coastal lands were now seen as a source of valuable slaves. The Portuguese self-servingly justified this vile trade because besides enslaving the Africans, they also Christianized them, thus providing the Africans with priceless eternal salvation which made up for their enslavement.[81] In the sanctimonious words of Azurara, 'yet greater benefit [of the slave trade] was theirs [i.e., the slaves], for though their bodies were now brought into some subjection, that was a small matter in comparison of their souls, which would now possess true freedom forevermore'.[82] Portuguese slave raiders enthusiastically descended on the coast of West Africa. In 1443 Nuño Tristão made a new journey and reached Arguin Bay and continued to capture any natives who were either unable to flee or to mount an effective resistance. Up to this point the Portuguese had only encountered poor fishermen or desert nomads of Berber stock. A new phase occurred when Dinis Dias reached Cape Verde in 1444 and passed the desert zone into the more heavily populated lands of tropical Africa.[83]

At first the Portuguese viewed the reaching of black Africa as simply a richer hunting ground for their slaving activities. That, however, proved to be a major miscalculation. The black Africans were indeed numerous but they were also heavily armed and completely fearless in the face of Portuguese firearms and cannons. In 1445 or 1446 the intrepid Nuño Tristão and his crew came close to being wiped out by the inhabitants of the Geba River. Tristão and twenty-one men made their way up the river in two small boats. Arriving at some dwellings along the riverbank, they also came up against 12 native boats containing 70 or 80 warriors armed with bows and arrows. The native boats attacked and rained a shower of poisoned arrows down on the Portuguese. Prudently the Portuguese hastily fled back to their ship, which was moored at the river's mouth, with the angry natives in hot pursuit. By the time the Portuguese reached their ship, every one of them had been wounded by an arrow and the poison had already killed four of them. Still the Africans fiercely pressed their attack and forced the Portuguese to cut their anchor cables and abandon their boats. Before the Portuguese managed to head out to sea, two of the seven people who had remained on the ship had also been killed by arrows. Only five of Tristão's crew remained unwounded: the purser, a common seaman, an African interpreter and two boys who served as esquires. Two of the wounded men would manage to fight off the effects of the poison only after twenty days of illness. Everyone else, including Nuño Tristão, died from the poison. None of the survivors knew the art of navigation but the purser Airas Tinoco successfully managed to sail the ship back to Portugal.[84] It was a disastrous voyage but the tragedy of Nuño Tristão did not discourage the Portuguese from sailing to the Guinea Coast in search of trade.

By 1448 fifty-one Portuguese ships had sailed past Cape Bojador and had reached as far south as present-day Guinea-Bissau. At that point the Portuguese had kidnapped a total of 927 Africans and sold them as slaves. It was a minuscule number compared to the millions of people that would eventually be shipped out of Africa as slaves, but it was the beginning. Given the disastrous outcome of Nuño Tristão's last voyage, Prince Henry and the rest of the Portuguese quickly came to realize that they would have to change their approach to slaving in Africa. Some Portuguese from the very beginning of contact with sub-Saharan Africa had favoured peaceful trading for slaves instead of raiding. The black Africans had proven to be too numerous and too well armed for the Portuguese to continue to rely on military force to secure slaves. Bowing to necessity, in 1448 Prince Henry shifted to a policy of peaceful trading with the Africans.[85]

The period from 1448 until the death of Prince Henry was marked by continual growth in Portuguese trade with West Africa but only a modest further expansion of Portuguese exploration of the African coastline. In 1448 merchants from Lagos established a fort and a trading post on Arguin Island which gave the Portuguese their first permanent base in West Africa. Profits from the Guinea trade in gold and slaves were high, ranging from five to seven times the amount of capital invested. During the 1450s, between ten and twelve ships annually sailed from Portugal to the Guinea Coast to reap substantial riches that awaited them.[86]

From 1448 through most of the 1450s, Portuguese activity in West Africa basically focused on trade rather than sustained explorations further along the coastline. The expeditions that did take place were motivated by a desire to improve trading opportunities in the region and largely consisted of trips into the African interior. One example of this sort of activity was the journey of the Italian Antoine Malfante, who made his way to the important way-station of Tuat along the caravan routes. Another important visitor to West Africa was Alvise de Cadamosto, a Venetian who entered the service of Prince Henry. In 1455 he sailed for the Guinea Coast in a trading caravel outfitted by Prince Henry in exchange for a 50 per cent share of Cadamosto's profits. Proceeding south Cadamosto visited the Canary Islands, Arguin Island and finally reached the Senegal River, trading all along the route. After leaving the Senegal River, Cadamosto's ship joined forces with two other vessels, including one commanded by Antoniotto Uso di Mare, a Genoese also sailing in Prince Henry's service. Reaching the Gambia River, the Europeans attempted to travel up the river but encountered some hostility from the local inhabitants. After arranging a parley, the mystified Europeans asked the natives why they were so hostile when all that Cadamosto and his companions wanted was peaceful trade with them as had occurred on the Senegal. The wary natives rejected the Europeans' overtures unequivocally. In their opinion, any Africans who had traded with the Europeans' were bad people themselves. As Cadamosto related the conversation, the inhabitants of the Gambia, 'firmly believed that we Christians ate human flesh, and that we only sought negroes to eat them: that for their part they did not want our friendship on any terms but sought to slaughter us all'.[87] Such was the result of almost fifteen years of Portuguese slave-raiding and forcible kidnapping along the West African coast – a fear and loathing of the Europeans. Nothing the Europeans were willing to do or offer could change the Gambians' minds. Instead the Europeans had to fight their way back out to sea. After this adventure, it was sometime late in 1455 when Cadamosto returned to Portugal.

After spending only a brief time back in Portugal, Cadamosto sailed to the Guinea Coast of Africa for a second time in March 1456 in the company of Uso di Mare.[88] After travelling past the Canaries, a storm struck in the vicinity of Cape Verde and blew the Portuguese expedition out to sea. There Cadamosto sighted two islands that he named

Boavista and Santiago. This encounter and Cadamosto's published account of it has led some people to credit him with the discovery of the Cape Verde Islands. But just who really located the Cape Verde Islands and when they did it is unclear from the surviving records. The Portuguese trader and explorer Diogo Gomes claimed that he was the first person to find that island group. Other documents credit the discovery to Gomes's companion Antonio di Noli, another Genoese merchant/explorer in the service of Prince Henry.[89] Certainly in 1462 Antonio di Noli along with Diogo Afonso received captaincies from King Afonso granting them the right to establish settlements on the Cape Verde Islands. The one they founded on Santiago in the Cape Verde Islands was the first Portuguese settlement in the wet tropics.[90] It is possible that Diogo Gomes reached the Cape Verdes as early as 1456 and Antonio di Noli definitely discovered them no later than 1462. Cadamosto's account of his two voyages provides evidence that relations between the Portuguese and the black Africans were improving now that the Portuguese had abandoned slave-raiding for peaceful trading.

Diogo Gomes was a Portuguese citizen who sailed for Africa in the service of Prince Henry. In either 1456 or 1457 he made his way far up the Gambia River. As was the case with Cadamosto, Gomes encountered suspicion and hostility from some of the peoples he met but others were willing to negotiate and to trade with the Europeans. Travelling up the river to Cantor, he acquired much valuable information about the trade routes of Timbuktu and the trans-Sahara. He also learned about the configuration of the mountains in that region which created a watershed for some local rivers to flow east and others west. These details undermined the prevailing geographical theory among Europeans concerning the existence of a western branch of the Nile River that flowed through West Africa. This western Nile would have allowed Portuguese ships to sail up it all the way to Ethiopia and the realm of Prester John.[91] Gomes also learned that too much time spent in the African interior caused outbreaks of deadly diseases among his crew.

The flourishing trade in slaves and gold at Arguin, Senegal and even Gambia held a far greater attraction for the Portuguese ships sailing to West Africa than sustained investigations along the unexplored coast to the south. Prince Henry had neither the time nor the energy to devote to promoting exploration during most of the 1450s. Slave-trading and the conquest of the Canaries received some of his attention. Once again, it was the renewal of crusading warfare against the kingdom of Fez in Morocco that took up most of Prince Henry's resources. As Diogo Gomes put it, 'It so happened that for two years [c. 1458–9] no one went back to Guinea because King Afonso was gone, with a fleet of three hundred and fifty-two ships, to Africa, and took the powerful city of Alcacer dalquivi, for which reason the Prince [Henry] being fully occupied, gave no attention to Guinea.'[92] This Portuguese attack on Morocco had its origin in 1453 when the Turkish conquest of Constantinople caused a general interest among the rulers of Western Europe for a crusade against the growing Islamic threat in Eastern Europe. Portugal's King Afonso and his uncle Prince Henry were particularly anxious to participate in such an enterprise. They began raising an army but soon discovered that no other Christian ruler responded with anything more than empty words or grossly inadequate resources. As a result in 1458 the target of Portuguese crusading efforts shifted from the eastern Mediterranean back to Morocco. Initially King Afonso planned an attack on Tangier but his advisors persuaded him to target the smaller settlement of Alcácer Ceguer instead. The expedition sailed on 30 September 1458 and events proceeded briskly with Alcácer Ceguer surrendering on 24 October. Unfortunately for King Afonso, his contemporaries rightly considered it to be a minor victory which aggravated Portuguese–Moroccan relations and interfered with the smooth operation of the African trade. It also revealed that much of the Portuguese political elite opposed conquests in Morocco that were expensive to garrison.[93]

The final two years of Prince Henry's life saw further significant expansion of Portugal's knowledge of the West African coast. Diogo Gomes made a second trading voyage to the area of the Gambia in 1460. There he met two other Portuguese ships under the commands of Gonçalo Ferreira and Antoniotto di Noli. He also learned about a Spanish interloper named de Prado who was illegally trading on the Guinea Coast. Gomes ordered Ferreira to capture de Prado and take him back to Portugal for trial which later resulted in the execution of the Spaniard.[94] Later, while Gomes was sailing back to Portugal in the company of di Noli, the Portuguese ships came upon some islands. Gomes's ship reached them before the others and he insisted on being the first to land. They called that first island Santiago which along with all the others was uninhabited, although the islands were well provided with fish, fowl, forests and grasslands. These islands were the Cape Verdes, whose discovery was claimed by so many. Gomes later stated that he lost credit for his discovery because di Noli returned to Portugal first. Once there di Noli immediately 'begged of the King [Afonso] the captaincy of the Island of Santiago, which I had discovered, and the King gave it to him, and he kept it till his death'.[95] Di Noli undoubtedly told a different story, and apparently a more convincing one since the official documents and the sixteenth-century chronicler João de Barros all credited him with the discovery.[96] Meanwhile, in 1461 or 1462, Pedro de Sintra, a squire of Prince Henry's household, sailed down the coast beyond the Gambia River for some 500 miles noting coastal features and inhabitants until he reached the area of Cape Montserrado. There the Portuguese decided to turn back, taking with them a local Negro who would be trained as an interpreter in Portugal in compliance with instructions from King Afonso. Sintra's journey added a significant length of African coast to the Portuguese store of geographical knowledge. Historians widely consider his voyage to be a final and posthumous achievement of Prince Henry, who had died on 13 November 1460 at the age of sixty-seven.[97]

KING AFONSO AND THE EXPLORATIONS OF FERNÃO GOMES

The death of Prince Henry caused a temporary halt to Portuguese exploration along the African coast although it did not mean that Portugal lost interest in Africa or the

Atlantic islands. Trading for gold and slaves with the inhabitants of the Guinea Coast was very lucrative. Portugal's big problem was with merchants from other European countries trespassing on Portugal's monopoly of the Guinea trade. Many ships sailed to West Africa but none sailed beyond the furthest point reached by Sintra on the coast of Sierra Leone. King Afonso's interest in Africa largely focused on the conquest of Morocco rather than the Guinea business. Various Portuguese expeditions attacked Morocco after the capture of Alcácer Ceguer in 1458. By 1471 they had taken Arzila and Tangier along with other less important towns with the result that King Afonso controlled the northern coast of Morocco and had earned for himself the title of 'the African'.[98] As a consequence, the Portuguese exploration of West Africa languished. As the chronicler João de Barros put it, 'As great men spend most of their lives in works of their preference, King Afonso came to neglect the affairs of discovery, and celebrated much more those of the war in Africa by the seizure of the towns of Alcacer, Arzila, and Tangier.'[99]

Afonso, however, remained well aware of the importance of the African trade, even if he did not want to deal with it personally. In November 1469 Fernão Gomes, a prominent citizen of Lisbon persuaded the King to grant him a monopoly for five years of the Guinea trade from the coast of Sierra Leone onward. The grant forbade Gomes from trading in the already established areas of Arguin Island and the Sene-Gambia region opposite the Cape Verde Islands. It also required him to explore 100 leagues of new coastline each year of the lease. Gomes's efforts bore fruit in 1471 when his captains João de Santarem and Pero de Escober, two knights of King Afonso's household, reached the region of Cape Three Points and the village of Sammá. That area was an important centre of African gold production and a bit over a decade later it would become the site of the great Portuguese fortress/trading post São Jorge de Mina. Further explorations continued under the Gomes grant from 1472 until 1474 with much of the coastline of the Gulf of Guinea being explored including the islands of Fernando Po, São Thome and Principe by the captains Soeiro da Costa, Fernando Po, Lope Gonçalves and Rui de Sequeira. King Afonso was pleased with the work of Gomes and his men and on 1 June 1473 renewed the grant for a sixth year. The next year Rui de Sequeira reached Cape St Catherine, just below the equator, an accomplishment that marked the end of Gomes's voyages of discovery under the grant from King Afonso. It also concluded new exploration during the reign of King Afonso. Gomes achieved great things in locating the Gold or Mina Coast. He gained great wealth for himself from the Guinea trade along with the high regard of his king. Gomes also served in Portugal's Moroccan wars including the capture of Tangier where the King knighted him. In 1474 King Afonso granted Gomes a new coat of arms including the surname of 'da Mina'. The King even went so far in 1478 as to make Gomes a member of his council. Afonso recognized that 'the trade of Guiné and the traffic of Mina were so profitable and assisted the economy of the kingdom so much' and that result was particularly thanks to the labours of Fernão Gomes.[100]

Lisbon, 1553, by an unknown artist. (Heritage Image Partnership)

EXPLORATIONS UNDER KING JOÃO II – CÃO, COVILHÃ AND DIAS

At that point, however, further exploration of the African coast stopped. Past the delta of the Niger River, the African coast turns south and Cape St Catherine lies some 400 miles to the south of that turn. Most ancient geographers (Claudius Ptolemy excepted) considered the circumnavigation of Africa to be feasible. As a result this would take the Portuguese ships to the wealthy land of Prester John in Africa and into the Indian Ocean and its cornucopia of spices. Unfortunately the unremitting southward trend of the African coast past the Niger delta belied that possibility and so discouraged further exploration. Given the ample profits of the Guinea trade in slaves, gold and malagueta pepper, the Portuguese had much to keep them busy and grateful, with no need to mourn too much the inconvenient shape of African geography.

War with Castile from 1474 to 1479 also distracted Portugal's attention and diverted resources from any further explorations of Africa. The Treaty of Alcaçovas ended that conflict in 1479 and left Fernando and Isabel in firm possession of the throne of Castile, despite King Afonso's best efforts. Vicious naval warfare had taken place in the Canary Islands and along the Guinea Coast. While the Portuguese did well in these engagements at sea, they could not dislodge the Castilians from their settlements on the Canaries. The resulting treaty recognized both Castilian ownership of the Canary Islands and Portuguese possession of the African trade. From a national point of view, it was a favourable outcome but the war had proven to be a cruel disappointment for the ageing Afonso V. Accustomed to victories in Africa, he anticipated easily becoming the King of Castile through marriage. The defeat of the Portuguese army at Toro in 1474 and repeated failures to reverse that outcome profoundly discouraged Afonso. He even threatened to abdicate in 1477 although the King remained on his throne until his death on 28 August 1481. During those years the Crown Prince João, soon to be João II, increased Portuguese control over the trade with the Guinea Coast, which the Treaty of Alcaçovas had granted exclusively to Portugal in 1479. On 12 December 1481 the new king João II sent a fleet under the command of Diogo de Azambuja to the Gold Coast of Guinea with orders to establish the great fortress/trading post of São Jorge de Mina.[101] It quickly became the centre of Portuguese trading activity along the West African coast.

Meanwhile, João II prepared an expedition for the purpose of exploring the African coast beyond Cape St Catherine. Diogo Cão, a veteran of the recent war with Castile, commanded the expedition that sailed from Portugal no later than 31 August 1482.[102] Included in his equipment were the stone pillars known as *padrões* which would be used to establish claims of discovery and overlordship. Previously Portuguese explorers had used crosses carved on the trunks of trees to mark the lands they visited. After passing Cape St Catherine, the Portuguese reached the Congo River where they encountered the people of Bakongo. There the Portuguese learned about the great

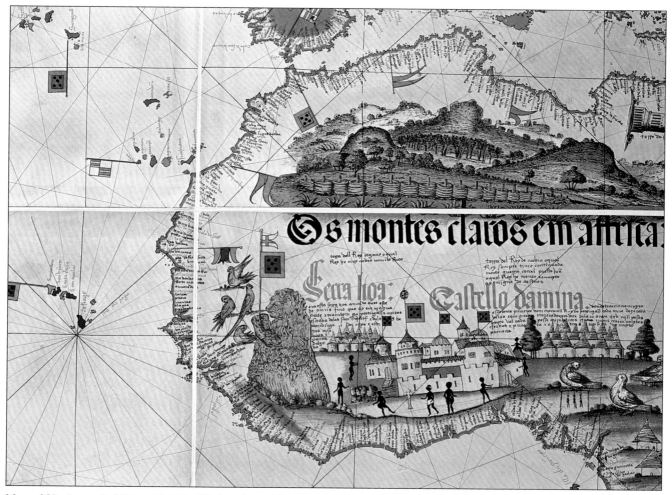

Map of São Jorge da Mina, visited by Christopher Columbus in 1502. (© British Museum/Bridgeman Art Library)

king of Mani-Congo and sent emissaries up the river to meet him. Continuing south Cão passed slightly beyond Cape Santa Maria at 13°S latitude in September 1483 before turning back. On the way home to Portugal, Cão stopped again at Bakongo and took some hostages from the Africans living along the river. He reached Lisbon shortly before 8 April 1484. João II hailed the returning Cão as a hero and rewarded him with a knighthood. It was assumed that Portugal was poised on the verge of circumnavigating Africa.

With the objective of reaching the Indian Ocean, Cão sailed from Portugal in the autumn of 1484. Stopping off at the Congo River, the Portuguese returned their Bakongo hostages to their home and then continued south. They reached as far as Walvis Bay at 22°S latitude. At the point, specific details about Cão's expedition evaporate. Some members of the party definitely managed to get back to Portugal in late 1486 or early 1487, although Cão himself may have died during the return voyage. Others speculate that Cão returned home in disgrace having been unsuccessful in his bid to circumnavigate Africa yet again. It has even been suggested that the impatient and sometimes extremely ill-tempered João II went so far as to have Cão executed for his failure.[103]

Cão's lack of success did not deter João II. In 1487 he began three attempts to explore Africa and to reach the Indian Ocean, one of which was the voyage of Bartolomé Dias.[104] The King assigned some Portuguese explorers to move inland in an attempt to find a way across Africa. Medieval geographical thought postulated various water routes across Africa, including the much-sought but ultimately mythical western branch of the Nile River. All attempts to penetrate the African interior foundered in the face of the vast distances and the hostile environment encountered in travelling through that continent. Another bid to gain information about the world of the Indian Ocean and East Africa consisted of sending Portuguese agents into the area to learn about the region's geography, economy, religion and political structure. These envoys were to learn about India and the navigation of the Indian Ocean and to make contact with the ruler of Ethiopia who was thought to be the legendary Prester John. João II chose two men for this mission – Pero da Covilhã and Afonso de Paiva.[105] Both men spoke Arabic and Covilhã had had extensive experience in diplomacy and espionage.

Departing from Portugal in May 1487, Covilhã and Paiva made their way to Alexandria disguised as merchants. There they both fell ill with a fever that almost killed them and which underscores the all too common perils of travel in that era. Fortunately both men recovered and made their way down the Red Sea to Aden. At that point they separated with Paiva moving on to Ethiopia and Covilhã travelling to India. Their plan was to rendezvous back in Cairo in May 1490. Just what Paiva accomplished on his journey is uncertain. He made his way back to Cairo where he died before Covilhã returned and whatever knowledge he gathered was lost.

Meanwhile, Covilhã, still presenting himself as an Arab merchant, took passage at Aden on a ship bound for Cannanore on India's western coast. From there he travelled south to the port of Calicut, a major mart for exchanging Asian luxury products for goods and money from western markets. Goa was his next stop, which involved backtracking northward. Although Goa was merely a horse-trading centre at that time, Covilhã marked it as a potential site for a Portuguese base in the region. He then visited Hormuz, even further to the north and west. This island port strategically straddled the straits that controlled passage between the Indian Ocean and the Persian Gulf, which was the gateway to the overland trade routes across Mesopotamia, Syria and Central Asia. From Hormuz he sailed over to East Africa and down its coastline until he reached Sofala, which was the southern-most trading city in East Africa. Turning northward he visited other East African posts including Kilwa and Malindi. Throughout his journey Covilhã acquired as much geographical, economic, climatic and navigational information as he could, including the practice of sailing with the monsoon winds.

Covilhã, having completed his assignment from João II, arrived back in Cairo for his rendezvous with Paiva. There he learned that his countryman had died and left no record of his journey to the land of Prester John. Meanwhile, João II had sent two more agents, the Jews Rabbi Abraham of Beja and Joseph of Lamego, with additional instructions for Paiva and Covilhã. They arrived in Cairo and informed Covilhã that he could return home but only if Ethiopia had been visited. João II considered a visit to Prester John and Ethiopia to be essential to Portuguese interests. Joseph of Lamego was there to take the intelligence Covilhã had already gathered back to Portugal. Covilhã also received orders to take Rabbi Abraham to see Hormuz. Travelling back by way of Aden, Covilhã left Rabbi Abraham at Hormuz. Covilhã at that point did not immediately proceed on to Ethiopia but instead he took several side-trips. Reaching Jedda on the Red Sea, he dared fate and made the pilgrimage to Mecca and Media, a journey forbidden to non-Muslims. After successfully posing as a Muslim pilgrim, he next visited the monastery of St Catherine at Sinai where he heard the mass, an extremely rare treat for him given his circumstances.

At this point he finally made his way to the court of the king or negus of Ethiopia. The Ethiopian King Alexander received Covilhã with great hospitality and was anxious to send him home and so open up contact with the Christian kings of Europe. Unfortunately Alexander died before that could occur and his brother and successor Nahum liked Covilhã so much that he refused to let him return home. Instead the Ethiopian ruler set Covilhã up with riches and an Ethiopian wife and he started a family there although he already had a wife back in Portugal. The next Ethiopian ruler David also insisted on Covilhã remaining in Ethiopia. In that position he met and greatly assisted the diplomatic mission of his countryman Rodrigo de Lima that travelled to Ethiopia from Portuguese India in 1520. Covilhã desperately wanted to return home to Portugal. Although he quite liked all the Portuguese, King David refused to change his mind, in spite of pleadings for Covilhã from the Portuguese diplomats. One of Covilhã's sons did secure permission to make the trip to Portugal but Pero da Covilhã had to remain behind, eventually dying in Ethiopia as a bird in a gilded cage sometime after 1526.[106] It was a fate he most certainly never could have imagined would befall him when he began his perilous eastern odyssey. It was also doubtful that João II derived much useful information from the trips his agents made to the East. Although Joseph of Lamego managed to return to Portugal, it is not at all clear that Covilhã's report survived the journey and reached the hands of João II. No real mention of the document was ever made by contemporaries. Some modern scholars suggest that Vasco da Gama's actions on his first voyage show that he possessed accurate intelligence about the trading world of the Indian Ocean, after all he headed straight for Calicut from East Africa. Others claim that exactly the opposite is true. Gama's lack of understanding about the organization of the spice trade, his mistaking of Hinduism as a form of heretical Christianity and his inability to comprehend the monsoonal sailing seasons all point to a general ignorance about conditions in the littoral of the Indian Ocean. If Covilhã's report made it back to Portugal, it would seem that it had little or no impact on the planning or the conduct of Vasco da Gama's first voyage to India.[107]

As Covilhã rambled around the Middle East and the western shores of the Indian Ocean in the guise of a Magribi Arab merchant, João II launched his third effort to reveal the secrets of Prester John, Africa and the Indian spice trade. It was an expedition whose purpose would be to pass the furthest point reached by Diogo Cão and push on until Africa had been rounded and the Indian Ocean attained.[108] João II chose Bartolomé Dias to command. Dias was a knight of the royal household who had engaged in trade along the Guinea Coast in the late 1470s. In 1481 he commanded one of the ships in the fleet of Diogo da Azambuja that founded the fortress of São Jorge de Mina. João II provided Dias with three ships for his expedition, two caravels and a smaller storeship. The crew consisted of sixty Europeans along with six African interpreter/captives whose job was to establish trade along the coast and gather news of Prester John. Dias's fleet sailed from the Tagus River in August 1487. Cruising down the African coast without serious incident, Dias and his ships reached Cape Cross on 4 December 1487, the furthest point reached by Cão. From there Dias pushed southward leaving his supply ship somewhere between Walvis Bay and Elizabeth Bay. Entering Elizabeth Bay on 26 December, Dias's two caravels had come within sight of the Matsikama Mountains by 6 January 1488.[109] At this point the prevailing strong southerly winds had impeded Dias's progress enough for him to decide to strike out for the high seas in the hope of finding a more favourable wind. Further from shore winds and storms drove the Portuguese further south where they encountered cold seas. Fortunately the savage weather moderated and the Portuguese steered east hoping to regain the Africa coast. When they failed to make landfall after a number of days sailing, Dias turned his ships north where on 3 February they finally sighted land. Dias's ships had reached the African coast at Mossel Bay where they spotted Negroes herding cattle. The fearful locals fled when the Europeans approached. More important was the fact that the African coast was trending eastward and northward. Dias and his men realized that they had rounded the long-sought-for southern-most tip of Africa. They were sailing on the waters of the Indian Ocean.[110]

Dias enthused by his achievement sailed his ships up the coast to Algoa Bay where he set up a *padrõ*. At that point Dias's crew began to demand that they turn around and go back to Portugal. The stormy seas south of Africa had claimed lives among the crew and their provisions were running short. The sailors argued that they had discovered enough new coast and now they needed to head back and find the actual southern-most cape which they had passed while far out to sea. Dias managed to persuade them to continue up the coast for three more days in the hope of finding something special. Instead, all they found was the Great Fish River which they named the Rio Infante. Pressure to turn around became impossible to resist and Dias agreed to go back down the coast in a westward direction although, 'he did so with as much grief and sorrow as if he was leaving a son in exile forever'.[111]

Sailing west the Portuguese reached Cape Agulhas in April when vicious storms forced them to take refuge on the coast and repair their damaged vessels. Ready to sail again in May, Dias reached the Cape of Good Hope on 6 June where he set up another *padrõe*. According to the chronicler João de Barros, 'because of the perils and storms they had endured doubling it [Dias], called it the Stormy Cape, but on their return to the kingdom, the king Dom João gave it another more illustrious name, calling it the Cape of Good Hope, because it gave promise of the discovery of India, so long desired and sought for so many years'.[112] Dias continued homeward and on 24 July reached Lüdewitz Bay where he set up a third *padrão* which survived until the end of the eighteenth century. Shortly after that Dias and his two caravels rejoined their supply ship after a nine-month separation. They found six of the nine crew of the supply ship were dead while a seventh, Fernão Colaço, became too excited for his weakened constitution as a result of the reunion with his comrade and he also died. The two remaining survivors reported that the local Negroes had killed the other six Portuguese, 'being covetous of certain things with which they [the Portuguese] traded'.[113] After removing any needed goods, Dias set fire to the supply ship and continued on his return voyage to Portugal.

Upon reaching the island of Principe, Dias's two ships came upon the hapless Portuguese explorer Duarte Pacheco, who had been trying to explore African rivers. His ship had been lost and the surviving crew had taken refuge on Principe where Pacheco had fallen ill. Dias rescued Pacheco and on his advice stopped along the coast to do some trading for gold at the mouths of the Niger River and at São Jorge de Mina before making his final return to Portugal. Dias' arrival in Lisbon took place in December 1488 and marked the end of a historic voyage of sixteen months and seventeen days. King João II greeted Dias's return with enthusiasm but did not go on to reward him with any significant gifts or titles.

Domestic and foreign threats diverted João II's attention from pursuing the implications of Dias's discovery. It is also possible that another aspect of the discoveries of Cão and Dias may have dampened João II's enthusiasm. South-west Africa was a barren and sparsely populated land. As Duarte Pacheco later described that region in his *Esmeraldo*, 'it so happened that in the part [of Africa] discovered by the most serene King John [João II] the country from Cabo de Caterina is mostly deserted or if inhabited has little or no trade'.[114] It was not until 1494, a gap of five years, that João II put Dias in charge of building new ships specifically intended to make the long voyage to India.[115] The sea-road to India had been laid open by Dias but João II did not live to see any of his mariners use it as he died in 1495. Nor did poor Dias ever reach the beckoning shores of India. Neither João II nor his successor Manuel would consider giving him command of the first voyage to India. That honour went to the nobleman Vasco da Gama. Manuel again passed over Dias for command of the second voyage to India in 1500–1 and appointed another nobleman Pedro de Cabral. Dias was made a captain of one of the ships in Cabral's fleet but he and his entire crew drowned when his ship foundered in a violent tempest off the Cape of Good Hope on 23 May 1500. As the Portuguese chronicler Antonio Galvano, looking back from the mid-sixteenth century, poignantly wrote of Dias, 'it may be said that he [Dias] saw the land of India, but, like Moses and the Promised Land, did not enter in'.[116]

CHAPTER FOUR

THE GREAT VOYAGES OF THE 1490s – COLUMBUS, CABOT AND GAMA

The first and principal discoverer, who showed the way to his emulators in our time, was . . . Christopher Columbus. That honour is chiefly his, although the other captains who followed his lead also deserve praise and fame for their accomplishments and their high aspirations, as long as they recognize Columbus as their master from who they took inspiration and guidance and without whom they would never have started.

Gonzalo Fernández de Oviedo (1541)[1]

There is in this Kingdom [England] a man of the people, Messer Zoane Caboto by name, of kindly wit and a most expert mariner. Having observed that the sovereigns first of Portugal and then of Spain had occupied unknown lands, he decided to make a similar acquisition for his Majesty [Henry VII].

Raimondo de Raimondi de Soncino (1497)[2]

We are Portuguese from the West: we seek the lands of the East. We have sailed the seas from the North to the South Pole, skirting the length of Africa and nodding acquaintance with many a land and sky.

Camões (1572)[3]

At the beginning of the 1490s, Europeans, particularly the Portuguese, had been exploring the western coast of Africa and the high seas of the Atlantic Ocean for decades. Bartolomé Dias's successful voyage of 1487–8 around the southern-most tip of Africa and into the Indian Ocean had revealed the indisputable existence of a sea-route to the spice marts of India and the African kingdom of Prester John. Portugal stood poised to harvest the fruits of the many voyages of the sea-captains sponsored by Prince Henry, King Afonso V and King João II. The anticipated success of the Portuguese in developing a sea-road around Africa to India did not deter others, and perhaps even encouraged them to continue seeking an alternative sea-route to Asia. Some continued to argue for the feasibility of a western voyage across the Atlantic as the best way to reach Asia. The Portuguese had been sporadically probing the high seas of the Atlantic beyond the Azores since the 1450s but with no successes. Adverse winds and currents in the latitudes of the Azores thwarted their efforts to sail westward while the route around Africa increasingly appeared to be viable. Ironically, the next big breakthrough in the geographical expansion of Europe was Christopher Columbus's western voyage seeking Asia in 1492. Sailing some five years before the Portuguese finally reached India, he travelled well south of the Azores and had a smooth voyage that took him to unknown lands. Although he did not reach Asia on that historic voyage, it was the beginning of a series of geographical revelations that would profoundly transform the entire world politically, economically, socially and culturally.

CHRISTOPHER COLUMBUS AND HIS 'ENTERPRISE OF THE INDIES'

Christopher Columbus is one of the best-known figures in world history.[4] Many documents survive to illuminate his life and career. Yet in spite of this circumstance, or perhaps because of it, he remains an enigmatic figure and the subject of perennial controversy. While there are numerous theories that espouse other origins, Columbus was definitely born in the territory of Genoa, the eldest of five children.[5] His father Domenico made his living as a weaver and appears to have been a reasonably respectable member of his local community. Growing up happily in Genoa, the young Columbus attended the local grammar school supported by the wool guild. Like other fathers throughout history, Domenico hoped to use a good education to propel his sons into the higher status occupation of overseas merchant. While at school the aspiring Columbus studied mathematics, navigation and accounting, all skills of great potential utility for a merchant engaged in foreign trade.

Starting in about 1470 Columbus began travelling on family business.[6] It was at this same time that his father Domenico moved from Genoa to Savona as a self-imposed exile prompted by the turbulence of Genoese politics. From 1470 to 1472 Columbus participated in a wine-selling voyage. During 1472 he made at least one and possibly two trips to Sicily to sell wool and buy wheat. Some historians have also placed Columbus's first arrival in Portugal sometime between 1471 and 1473. He made his trip to Chios in either 1474 or 1475. The purpose of that journey was to buy gum mastic which was used in medicines and confections. On these voyages, Columbus was engaging in fairly mundane trading of products from around the Mediterranean rather than participating in the fantastically lucrative trade in Asian spices. This is not surprising since the Ottoman Turks had been steadily destroying Genoese spice trading stations in the Black Sea and the eastern Mediterranean from the 1450s onward. This deteriorating situation was forcing Genoese merchants to shift their efforts to the western Mediterranean and the Atlantic in hopes of finding safer markets. Columbus soon became part of that westward shift.

In 1476 Columbus joined a Genoese trading fleet bound for England. On 13 August French pirates ambushed the Genoese off Cape St Vincent and a fierce battle resulted. Columbus ended up in the water and had to swim to shore, losing his trade goods in the process. He soon made his way to Lisbon where the local Genoese merchant community provided hospitality and relief to him and the surviving remnant of the shattered fleet.[7] After several months a second flotilla sailed from Genoa and after stopping at Lisbon to collect the survivors of the ill-fated first voyage, proceeded on to

London. Columbus probably went along with this fleet and while in the northern waters he claimed to have visited Ireland, Iceland and beyond. He possibly even visited Bristol, a hive of vague western voyaging activity. As he described part of his northern voyage to Iceland:

> In the month of February, 1477, I sailed one hundred leagues beyond the island of Tile [Iceland], whose southern part is in latitude 73 degrees N, and not 63 degrees as some affirm; nor does it lie upon the meridian where Ptolemy says the West begins, but much further west. And to this island, which is as big as England, the English come with their wares, especially from Bristol. Where I was there, the sea was not frozen, but the tides were so great that in some places they rose twenty-six fathoms, and fell as much in depth.[8]

Whether Columbus actually made these northern trips and what effect they had on his development as an explorer has been hotly debated by scholars. Some claim that he picked up all sorts of significant information about the Norse voyages to Vinland, castaway Asians (Amerindians?) appearing on the coast of Galway in Ireland and sightings of western isles. As a result, this knowledge inspired him to develop his plan to sail west to reach Asia. The problem is that most of these academic assertions are pure conjecture and not at all firmly based on the contents of Columbus's papers. Furthermore, it is not necessary to attribute special knowledge to Columbus in the development of his plan to travel west to reach Asia.[9] The European Atlantic world of the late fifteenth century existed in a state of ferment concerning geographical knowledge and territorial expansion of trading opportunities. Knowledge of the sphericity of the earth was commonplace among the educated.[10] It was assumed that the Atlantic Ocean was generously littered with islands waiting to be found and which could serve as convenient way-stations to Asia. If Columbus did make these northern voyages, what they gave him was more experience of the tempestuous Atlantic and its ways.

Columbus was back in Lisbon by 1478 and in that year he journeyed to the Madeira Islands to buy sugar for the Centurione Bank of Genoa. Besides giving him additional exposure to the Atlantic Ocean and its winds and currents, Columbus's contact with Madeira apparently set him on the road to marriage. After making his last visit to Genoa in August, he married Dona Felipa Moniz y Perestrelo, the daughter of Bartolomé Perestrelo, the first governor of Porto Santo in Madeira during late 1479.[11] The union gave Columbus some tangible benefits. It conferred Portuguese citizenship on him which improved his opportunities to do business in that country. Furthermore, the two branches of his wife's family the Perestrelos and the Monizs were members of the nobility which gave Columbus access to the highest levels of Portuguese society. Bartolomé Perestrelo appears to have been particularly well connected. Soon Columbus was participating in Portugal's jealously guarded trade with the Guinea Coast of Africa. It has also been speculated that Bartolomé Perestrelo may have planted ideas about western voyaging across the Atlantic to Asia in Columbus's mind.

How Martin Behaim's globe depicted the Atlantic Ocean with the Americas inserted in their proper location. From Justin Winsor, *Narrative and Critical History of America* (Boston, Houghton Mifflin, 1886), vol. 2, p. 105.

Perestrelo's overall career, however, makes such a supposition seem highly unlikely as he demonstrated no ability as a seaman and little talent as a colonizer. Court connections were the secret of his success.

Obviously Columbus's link to the Perestrelos was beneficial to him but how did the Perestrelos benefit from a marriage alliance to a Genoese nobody? It is likely that Perestrelo saw Columbus as a talented young man with future potential and good relations with the Genoese merchant and banking communities in Portugal. Furthermore, Felipa Perestrelo may have played an active role in the courtship and marriage. Contemporary testimony indicates that Columbus was both handsome and charming when it was needed. Unfortunately for Felipa, if she fell in love with Columbus, there is little evidence from his personal papers that he thought very much of her one way or the other. As events unfolded, the marriage turned out to be brief. The next year in 1480 Felipa gave birth to Diego, Columbus's first son, on Porto Santo. Soon after she died leaving Columbus a widower with an infant child.

Columbus had definitely started developing his ideas about a western voyage to Asia by 1481. He had opened a correspondence on that subject with the Florentine scholar Paolo dal Pozzo Toscanelli (1327–1482). During 1474 Toscanelli had discussed the feasibility of sailing west to reach Asia with Canon Fernão Martins at the behest of King Afonso V of Portugal. In Toscanelli's opinion such a voyage was a practical possibility and he told Columbus the same thing six years later.[12]

Meanwhile, Portugal strengthened its trading presence on the Guinea Coast in 1481 by building the fortress of São Jorge de Mina. Sometime between 1482 and 1484 Columbus journeyed to trade with El Mina and during the trip observed the north-east trade winds which would have been ideal to use for sailing west. In this way he gained further experience of both the African trade and the patterns of winds and currents existing on the Atlantic Ocean. Further Portuguese explorations of the African coast and the Atlantic continued at the same

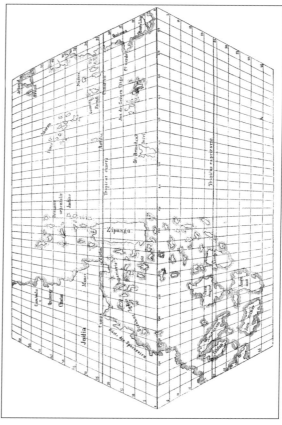

Reconstruction of Toscanelli's map of 1474 which illustrates that fifteenth-century Europeans believed that Asia lay on the western shore of the Atlantic Ocean. From Justin Winsor, *Narrative and Critical History of America* (Boston, Houghton Mifflin, 1886), vol. 2, p. 103.

time. Between 1482 and 1484 Diogo Cão sailed to Cape Santa Maria far below the equator. Another initially exciting but ultimately disappointing development was the claim of Antonio Leme in 1484 to have reached the fabled island of Antillia.

Columbus decided at this time to approach João II of Portugal with his own plan for sailing to Asia. Easily obtaining an audience, probably through the influence of his Perestrelo in-laws, Columbus presented his proposal for a western voyage across the Atlantic Ocean to reach Cathay and its fantastic wealth. Popular history has, thanks to the lasting influence of Washington Irving's biography, viewed Columbus as a lone genius who tried to get fifteenth-century Europeans to abandon their flat-earth world view and adopt his more accurate spherical theory. The fact is that Columbus's idea for a western voyage was based on two widely held but erroneous concepts of fifteenth-century geography. First, many educated people thought that the earth was about 25 per cent smaller in circumference than it really was, i.e., about 18,000 miles around instead of its true 24,000 miles. Second, they thought that the landmass of Asia was significantly larger than it really was and that it stretched much further eastward. The theoretical consequences of these errors was to create a false geography in which a relatively narrow Atlantic Ocean separated Europe from a gigantic Asia. That concept formed the basis for Columbus's plans for a western voyage as it did for similar schemes of Toscanelli and others. Where Columbus differed from his contemporaries was that he had incorporated every calculation, assumption or speculation that would make the earth smaller and Asia bigger eastward. This tactic served to make the Atlantic Ocean narrower and so shortened the distance that a voyage across it would have to make. Whereas Toscanelli's Atlantic was 5,000 miles wide, Columbus's was only 3,200 miles broad. All of Columbus's manipulations of existing geographical theories were single-mindedly designed to make his proposal to sail west to reach Asia seem more feasible.

King João II of Portugal gave Columbus and his plan for a western voyage to Asia an attentive hearing. Intelligent, ambitious and, if need be, ruthless, the Portuguese King wanted his country to develop a usable sea-road to Asia.[13] For some years Portuguese ships had been probing southward along the west coast of Africa searching for the turn that would mean they had circumnavigated that continent and had entered the Indian Ocean. But if Columbus could provide a short-cut to Asia by means of a western route, João II was willing to adopt it instead. It was at this point that Columbus's personality undermined the acceptance of his plans. Like many people of the Renaissance era, Columbus exhibited personal pride and aspirations that crossed the line into arrogance and overweening ambition. He demanded that João II grant him titles of nobility, privileges, shares of profits and offices in exchange for his services, which seemed ludicrous unless his seemingly problematic proposal was entirely successful. Fortunately for Columbus, João II was apparently not put off by Columbus's self-absorbed and almost naive presumptuousness. It was the Portuguese geographical experts who reported negatively on the feasibility of Columbus's idea. They knew the extant geographical writings and theories better than Columbus did and it was obvious to them that Columbus had picked and chosen every concept that bolstered his proposal while ignoring those that did not. In some places he had without warrant improved on existing geographical information to provide even more support for his plan. To the Portuguese experts Columbus's manipulation of geographical knowledge would have appeared self-serving, crass and unrealistic. Their judgement was that Columbus's scheme did not deserve the support of Portugal.[14]

Another problem that Columbus faced with João II was that he was asking the Portuguese King to fund the enterprise but still lavish Columbus with rewards and profits just because he had conceived of the plan and would lead the expedition. But that was not how João II and earlier Portuguese Kings had conducted their exploring business. Their practice was that if the Portuguese crown paid for a voyage, the crown kept the profits and the trading rights that developed. If a private individual or group undertook a journey of exploration at their own expense, the Portuguese monarchs were willing to grant concessions, profits and trading rights to such enterprising people. Columbus was demanding the best of both worlds and more – royal financing for his voyage and privileges and rewards that far exceeded any granted up to that point by João II to anyone who engaged in exploration as a private enterprise. In spite of such audaciousness, Columbus received a polite and interested hearing from the King. In fact it is possible that João II may even have found Columbus to be personally likeable. But with so many negatives associated with what objectively was a relatively dubious plan, royal rejection soon followed.

Interestingly, although João II turned down Columbus's proposal, the idea of a western voyage to Asia appears to have intrigued him. Two caravels were sent from the Azores to look for Antillia and to probe the western Atlantic. Travelling west from the Azores was extremely difficult, if not well nigh impossible, in ships powered only by sails as the prevailing winds blew from the wrong direction. The Portuguese vessels suffered cruelly from the buffeting and turned back without finding anything. As a result, interest in Columbus's ideas at the Portuguese court died. While João II remained friendly, Columbus decided he needed to leave Portugal and seek another sponsor.

Columbus turned his eyes and hopes toward the newly united kingdom of Spain, the realm of Isabel of Castile and Fernando of Aragon.[15] Leaving Lisbon in the middle of 1485 Columbus made his way into Spain.[16] Proceeding down the coast to Cadiz, the Duke of Medinaceli gave Columbus a position in his shipping business, a decision presumably based on an acquaintance with Columbus through the Genoese mercantile network in the Iberian Peninsula. While serving in that post, Columbus discussed his plan for a

Columbus explains his plan for a western voyage to King João II of Portugal. From Washington Irving et al., *The Discovery and Conquest of the New World* (Philadelphia, Syndicate Publishing, 1892), p. 80.

western voyage to Asia with Medinaceli. The Duke proved to be a receptive listener and thought Columbus's scheme was feasible. He also felt that its ultimate importance meant that it rated royal rather than private support. By contacting his uncle, Cardinal Pedro González de Mendoza, the Duke managed to secure Columbus an introduction to the court of Fernando and Isabel, the dual sovereigns of Spain.

Fernando and Isabel found Columbus's proposal for a western voyage to be plausible. By 20 January 1487 he had entered the royal service and had definitely appeared on the payroll by 5 May. The monarchs referred Columbus's idea to a committee of the royal council for closer examination. Hernando de Talavera, the Bishop of Avila, chaired the committee which met during 1486 and 1487. Meanwhile,

Columbus, ever the busy Genoese merchant, engaged in various commercial duties
for Fernando and Isabel. He assisted in the selling of war booty from Granada and
helped with the purchase of gifts for the forthcoming wedding of the Spanish Princess
Isabel to Afonso, the Crown Prince of Portugal. But although he was lucratively
employed by the Spanish monarchs, Columbus continued to dream of the greater
fame, power and riches that a successful western voyage to Asia would bring.
Unfortunately for him, Talavera's committee in January 1487 called for an initial
rejection of his plan. While the committee found the proposal feasible, they also
considered that it threatened the peace between Portugal and Spain and that
Columbus's demands for compensation were overblown.

Meanwhile, events in Columbus's personal life intervened. His wife died back in
Portugal and he needed to return there to get his son. Writing to João II to request
a safe conduct in early 1488, Columbus received a favourable reply on 20 March. By
June he had disappeared from the Spanish royal payroll. Travelling back to
Portugal, Columbus remained there for about two years and it was during that time
that it is commonly thought that he tried to interest João II in his western voyage for
a second time. He was present in Lisbon during December 1488 when Bartolomé

Columbus before the council at Salamanca. From William Cullen Bryant, *A Popular History of the United States* (New York,
Scribners, 1891), vol. 1, p. 109.

Dias returned from having discovered the Cape of Good Hope. That opened the sea-road to India and made Columbus's still highly speculative western voyage even less attractive to João II. Columbus, however, drew somewhat different conclusions from Dias's accomplishment. It revealed that the distance from Portugal to India by sea was great, so great that Columbus astutely and accurately worked out that it would give Portugal little or no cost advantage over the traditional overland spice route through the Middle East. On the other hand, if Columbus was correct in his calculations, his western voyage would open a short and more cost-efficient route to Asia's luxuries.

Columbus returned to Spain in 1490 in a dire financial state and at this point approached Medinaceli once more for assistance and support. By the summer of 1491 he finally brought Diego with him in the hope of placing the boy with his wife's relatives in the Palos region. Discouraged by his failure to secure support from either Portugal or Spain, Columbus contemplated offering his plan to the King of France. Arriving at Palos, he discovered that the family had moved elsewhere. So with no kin to stay with, Columbus and his son sought lodgings at the monastery of La Rabida where he made the acquaintance of Friar Juan Perez, a former official in Queen Isabel's treasury. The two men quickly became friends. Impressed by Columbus's proposal to sail west to Asia, Perez acted as Columbus's agent and contacted the Queen on his behalf, travelled to the court at Santa Fe and secured funds for the destitute Columbus.

With the fall of Muslim Granada imminent, any worries the Spanish monarchs had about offending Portugal by making a western voyage into the Atlantic faded in importance. The approaching end of the war against Granada also eased the pressures on royal finances and allowed Fernando and Isabel the freedom to contemplate giving Columbus's plan modest support. Through the autumn of 1491 Perez busily pushed Columbus's scheme and worked out a tentative arrangement with the Spanish monarchs. Meanwhile, another commission of specialists studied the geographical basis and the details of Columbus's project. Confident of success, Perez summoned Columbus to join him at the siege of Granada and close the deal. He arrived on about 2 January 1492 just as the Spaniards formally took possession of Granada. Unfortunately for Columbus, the royal experts soon after reported unfavourably on his plan. His estimates of the distances involved in a western voyage remained overly optimistic in their minds and, as it turned out, they were correct.

A disappointed Columbus prepared to move on to France and hoped that the French King would provide the support he needed to make his dream of a western voyage to Asia come true. But it never came to that point. Bartolomé Dias's discovery of the Cape of Good Hope and the fall of Granada had changed the atmosphere at the Spanish court. King Fernando recognized that his experts were technically correct, Columbus had exaggerated the ease of such a journey. But even after the distances were changed to more generally accepted numbers, a western voyage remained possible. Given the quite modest cost of such an expedition, compared to the vast potential economic benefits to Spain, Fernando decided to support

An illustration from De Lorgue's *Life of Columbus* showing the monastery of La Rabida that sheltered Columbus when he first arrived in Spain. (Mary Evans Picture Library)

Columbus's plan anyway. A much-relieved Columbus was called back to the Spanish court and from that point onward things began to move more quickly to the accomplishment of Columbus's great enterprise of the Indies.

The Spanish treasury worked to find the least painful way to finance Columbus's voyage. Since the town of Palos owed the Spanish crown the use of two ships, the *Niña* and the *Pinta*, due to a violation of Portuguese territorial waters, they were assigned to Columbus's expedition. A third ship, the *Santa Maria*, and the other costs of the voyage came out of funds of the military organization of the Santa Hermanadad that had been freed up by the defeat of the Moors of Granada. Columbus's understanding with Fernando and Isabel was also formalized. Two sets of agreements were signed on 17 and 30 April 1492, collectively they are known as the Santa Fe Capitulations. These documents granted Columbus rights to profits from his discoveries (one-tenth) and the right to invest further (one-eighth). If his voyage was successful, he would also receive the hereditary title of Admiral of the Ocean Sea. It was a generous contract for the Spanish monarchs to make, especially since it was with a foreigner. The basic assumption was that while Columbus was making his way to Asia he would discover a few small islands and claim them for Spain. He would serve as the governor of these islands in a manner similar to the governorship of his Perestrelo in-laws on the island of Porto Santo. But, as it turned out, Columbus did not merely discover some relatively insignificant islands, rather he revealed the existence of a vast new world of two continents and multitudinous islands. Although all of that potential was largely unsuspected up to the time of Columbus's death, it meant that in the long run his agreement with Fernando and Isabel was unenforceable in a practical sense. Of course, lawsuits followed but ultimately the Columbus family saw their privileges greatly reduced. What the Santa Fe Capitulations show, however, is what Columbus, the Spanish monarchs and everyone else thought would be found as a result of his voyage – a few small islands along a sea-route to the fabled wealth of Cipangu and Cathay.

Preparations for Columbus's voyage began in earnest on 22 May 1492 when he arrived at Palos. Initially reluctant to participate, eventually the people of Palos supplied the *Pinta* and the *Niña*. The ships were captained respectively by the brothers Martín Alonso Pinzón and Vicente Yáñez Pinzón, both respected and popular

Surrender of Granada to Fernando and Isabel in 1492 from the painting by F. Pradilla. From Washington Irving et al., *The Discovery and Conquest of the New World* (Philadelphia, Syndicate Publishing, 1892), p. 109.

residents of Palos. Columbus captained the *Santa Maria*. All three ships were rather small. Both the *Pinta* and the *Niña* were caravels with respective cargo capacities of 65 and 60 tons. The *Santa Maria* was a bulkier nao of about 100 tons capacity. A total of 87 people sailed on the three ships – 39 on the *Santa Maria*, 26 on the *Pinta* and 22 on the *Niña*. Initially efforts to recruit the crews went slowly but some timely help and encouragement from the veteran Atlantic sailor Pedro Velasco assisted Columbus in successfully manning his expedition. The popular idea that Columbus was forced to employ convicts from the local jail to complete the ships' company is not true. Three small ships and eighty-seven men was not a large expedition by fifteenth-century standards but it was typical for how the exploring of unknown routes and regions was carried out by European peoples of that time. Voyages of discovery were risky and the capital invested in them was kept to a minimum.

With the preparations for the western trip completed, Columbus and his little fleet sailed from Palos on 2 August 1492.[17] Their initial destination was the Canary Islands. Various problems impeded their progress. During that leg of the voyage the rudder on the *Pinta* broke and the *Niña*'s lateen sails proved inappropriate and inefficient for use in the prevailing winds of those waters. On 9 August they sighted Grand Canary where the *Pinta* landed to make repairs. Columbus sailed on to the settlement of San Sebastian on the island of Gómera. Altogether the expedition spent three weeks in the Canaries changing the *Niña*'s rigging, replacing the rudder on the *Pinta*, and taking on fresh supplies for the high-seas voyage to come.

Columbus recommenced his western journey on 6 September but only just. Calm conditions stalled the sailing ships within sight of Gómera for three days. It was not until 9 September that the western-most island of Hierro dropped below the horizon. As far as the physical conditions went, Columbus's historic first voyage went smoothly, especially when compared with the travails experienced by some early explorers. The three ships sailed for thirty-three days and except for the winds faltering for a few days on about 20 September, their westward progress was steady and often impressive. It was an almost perfect voyage. No dangerous storms threatened Columbus and his men which was a piece of luck since they were sailing into waters regularly crossed by hurricanes at that time of year.

The problem for Columbus was that his men were nervous from the time of their departure from Gómera. Some even shed tears as Hierro disappeared from view. In an age that depended on wind to propel its ships, some wondered how they would get home if they managed to reach Cathay safely. The secretive Columbus planned on returning by using the westerly winds that blew steadily to the north but he was disinclined to share this information with his crew. At the same time, the unfathomable wealth of the Far East beckoned teasingly in the minds of Columbus and his companions. When would they sight the land that they so anxiously sought to reach? By 18 September a succession of false sightings of land had begun.

Columbus's men were increasingly fearful as they sailed further and further into the western Atlantic. They were plunging into the unknown carried by a steadily eastward wind that could not possibly be used to take them home. To lessen their concerns, Columbus kept a dual record in his log of how far they travelled each day. Some historians have depicted Columbus as keeping both a true but secret record of the distances covered and a false, public record that reported shorter distances than were actually travelled. His motivation was to reduce the anxiety of his crew about the magnitude of their progress into the unknown. In fact, it appears that Columbus was actually keeping his dual set of records in two different units for measuring distance. That would have been easy enough to do in 1492 since there were various standards for measuring distance in use at that time. Columbus's action was the equivalent of a person today keeping a record of distance in miles and kilometres. The suggestion that Columbus could have successfully deceived the whole expedition about how far it was travelling is highly unlikely because several other people on all three ships were duty-bound to keep logs of the distances covered. The discrepancy between their numbers and those of Columbus would have become obvious very quickly. The idea of a false log is simply a misunderstanding of what Columbus was really trying to do.[18]

Many biographers and historians of Columbus have told how he was forced to quell one or more mutinies during his first voyage.[19] According to one account, by 24 September some crew members were contemplating throwing Columbus overboard. Other mutinies supposedly occurred on 6 and 10 October. Some reports credit Martín Pinzón with providing Columbus with crucial support during the crisis. Others accuse Pinzón of siding with the malcontents. The fact is that modern scholars have examined the sources for Columbus's first voyage closely and concluded that tales of mutinies were a later fictional addition, with Columbus's questionable and self-serving hindsight being the ultimate source for all such stories. Given the almost marvellous sailing conditions of the first voyage, the occurrence of mutinies actually seems fairly incongruous.

False sightings of phantom islands continued into October. Various natural phenomena encountered by the little fleet – birds, drifting plants and various sea creatures – were interpreted as signs of an imminent landfall. Columbus had offered a reward of 10,000 *maravedis* to the first person who saw land. That incentive only further encouraged the anxious crew to make more false reports. Then on 11 October at 10.00 p.m. Columbus claimed to have seen a bobbing light, possibly a torch, in the distance. Someone else also noticed it but it disappeared. Finally about 4 hours later at 2.00 a.m. on 12 October, the *Pinta* made a definite sighting of land but since it was night, the first landing did not occur until the next morning. At that point Columbus took formal possession of the new land for Fernando and Isabel which they later learned from the natives was called Guanahani while the Spanish called it San Salvador.

Just where Columbus first made landfall in the Americas is the subject of a long, on-going and ultimately insoluble controversy.[20] Because of the primitive navigational instruments and techniques of that day, the records of Columbus's first voyage lack precision and are full of inaccuracies. Any attempt to locate precisely where Columbus landed in the island-speckled Bahamas using such faulty information is highly problematic. His physical descriptions of Guanahani/San Salvador and the

A painting showing the departure of Christopher Columbus from Palos, Spain, by an unknown artist. (Giraudon/Art Resource, NY)

neighbouring islands also contain contradictions and implausibilities that have confounded modern efforts at identification. Still many have tried. Virtually every island in the entire Bahamas archipelago has been suggested. Watlings Island, renamed San Salvador, has been a perennial favourite but equally credible arguments have been put forward for Cat Island, Samana Cay and Grand Turk among others. The fact is that exactly where Columbus first landed is of minor historical importance since the attention of Columbus and the Spaniards almost immediately shifted to the larger islands of Cuba and Hispaniola. Guanahani was soon forgotten. Over the years the human desire for definitive answers to such questions has kept the landfall controversy alive. Also the answer to the question does possess some modern economic consequences. Any island gaining an indubitable identification as Columbus's Guanahani/San Salvador would become a prime location for resort hotels seeking to combine historical and tropical pleasures all in one site.

Even before they reached the shore, the Spaniards had spotted naked people on the beach. More natives gathered there after the Spaniards had landed and presents were exchanged. The natives received red caps and glass beads and in return they gave the Europeans parrots, cotton thread and javelins. Columbus described the natives of Guanahani in his log, 'It seems to me they were a people poor in everything. All of them go around naked as their mothers bore them.'[21] They also lacked metal

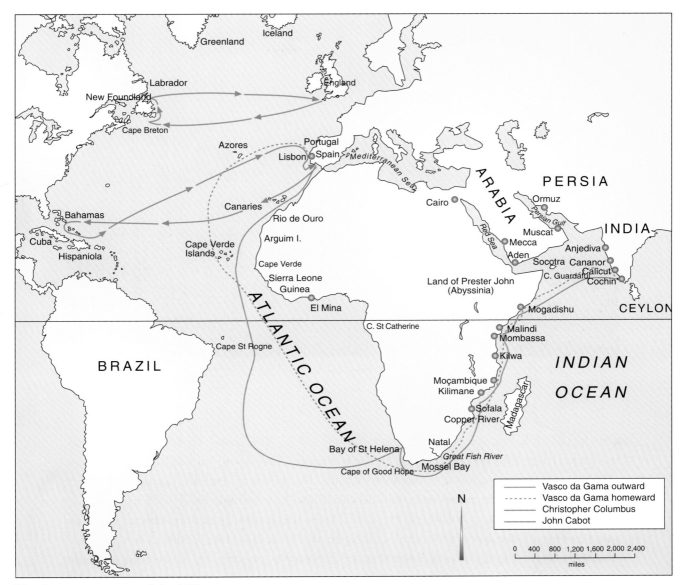

The three great voyages of the 1490s.

tools. He compared them to the Canarians in colour with their thick dark hair and found them to be well formed and healthy. The natives told him that their island was called Guanahani but Columbus renamed it San Salvador. After thirty days at sea any landfall was welcome to Columbus and his crew but they would certainly have preferred to have been met by officials of the Great Khan of Cathay, princes of golden Cipangu or some other sort of Oriental potentate.

Columbus assumed that he had come across some outlying and rather primitive island off the coast of Asia. Thinking that he had reached the edge of the fabled Indies, he called the natives Indians, a name that has been erroneously applied to the

A fanciful painting of the *Niña, Pinta* and *Santa Maria*. From Charles A. McMurray, *Pioneers on Land and Sea* (New York, Macmillan, 1913), p. 136.

aboriginal inhabitants of the Americas ever since. The natives of Guanahani also informed him that more islands, including larger ones with rich rulers, lay to the south. So Columbus's next move was to try and find more civilized territory. As he put it in his log, 'I want to go see if I can find the island of Cipango.'[22]

Turning southward, Columbus departed from Guanahani on 14 October forcibly taking some of the natives along as guides. It was an action that served as a harbinger of future brutal and callous treatment of the native peoples by Columbus and his contemporaries. The next island that he encountered on 15 October was given the name of Santa Maria de la Concepción. From there on 16 October he sailed to an island lying to the west which he named La Ferdandina. A few days later he reached the island which he called La Isabela. Columbus was obviously a man determined to stay on the good side of his royal patrons. On each island he encountered natives who were just like those on San Salvador. He found them to be pleasant people and observed, 'I do not detect in them any religion and I believe that they would become Christians very quickly because they are of very good understanding.'[23] At the same time Columbus was a little perplexed by what he had seen so far and would continue to see during his first voyage through these islands. As an avid student of geography Columbus had acquired the usual late medieval expectations about what types of peoples lived in the Far East and in tropical climates. That meant that he expected to be sighting various specimens of the monstrous races – dog-headed men, headless men, one-footed men, cyclops and a host of others. Medieval scientific thought also required that people living in the glare and heat of the tropical sun should of necessity be dark-skinned. Columbus's Indians did not match those expectations. As he later wrote to Luis Santangel, 'In these islands, I have so far found no human monstrosities, as many expected, but on the contrary the whole population is very well-formed, nor are they negroes as in Guinea, but their hair is flowing.'[24]

By 21 October his native informants had told Columbus about two great and rich islands called Cuba and Bohío that lay to the south. From this information Columbus concluded that Cuba must be Cipangu. Expectations among the company of the little fleet must have been very high and optimistic at that time. As Columbus recorded in his log, 'depending on whether I find a quantity of gold or spices, I will decide what I am to do. But I have already decided to go to the mainland and to the city of Quinsay and to give your Highnesses' letters to the Grand Khan and to ask for, and to come with, a reply.'[25] Continued conversations with the natives had fuelled Columbus's enthusiasm even further by 24 October. Cuba, 'was very large and of great commerce [with] . . . gold and spices and great ships and merchants'. Of course, just how Columbus was learning all of this information from his native informants when they could not speak each other's language makes Columbus's conclusions highly problematic. As he admitted, 'I believe that it [the natives' testimony] is so according to the signs that all the Indians of these islands and those that I have with me make (because I do not understand them through speech).'[26] Wishful thinking probably guided much of Columbus's interpretation of the signs he exchanged with the natives and what he dearly wished for was to locate the riches of the Orient.

So the quest for Cuba/Cipangu continued southward. On 27 October the so-called Islas de Arena were sighted. These are generally thought to be the Ragged Islands located about 50 miles off the north-east coast of Cuba. The next day Columbus made landfall on the north-east coast of Cuba. His guides clearly told him that Cuba was such a huge island that it could not be circled in a canoe in under twenty days. That did not stop him from considering Cuba to be part of the mainland province of Mangi in Cathay by 1 November. Columbus and his men immediately observed signs of human habitation. The shore was sprinkled with little fishing villages but unlike the natives of Guanahani and the other small islands, the Cubans were initially quite shy. It was not until 1 November that the Spanish managed to make direct contact with them. On 2 November Columbus sent Rodrigo de Xierez and Luis de Torres out to reconnoitre in the interior. They returned on 6 November and reported that they had visited a village of about a thousand inhabitants. The people were friendly and even seemed to treat the Spaniards as heavenly creatures. When the Spaniards showed them spices such as pepper and cinnamon, the Indians said that they did not possess any themselves but that to the south-east there was plenty of such goods. Ominously they knew nothing about any large cities. That information must have been worrisome to the expedition since up to that point it appeared that the Indians knew all about the Grand Khan and more importantly how to reach him. Undaunted Columbus continued to cruise the coastline of Cuba looking for signs of the sophisticated civilizations of East and South Asia.

Beginning on 12 November sustained winds made it easiest for Columbus to sail eastward along the northern coast of Cuba. This course was taking the Spanish fleet nearer to Baneque (Great Inagua) and Bohío (Hispaniola), the two other great islands described to them by the guides from Guanahani. Contrary winds had by 20 November thwarted efforts to reach Baneque. Tropical heat also plagued Columbus and his men but in spite of the discomfort, to him it was a hopeful sign since gold was a mineral closely associated with hot climates in the minds of late medieval Europeans. What truly cut Columbus deeply was Martín Pinzón's desertion with the *Pinta* on 21 November. Columbus blamed Pinzón's behaviour on greed for gold and from that point the two men's relationship deteriorated. Meanwhile, the convoluted sailing in the waters between Cuba and Baneque continued for a few more days. Columbus finally returned to the Cuban coast and proceeded eastward. More natives appeared along the way but attempts to communicate with them merely produced confused accounts about cannibals, monstrous humans and supposed references to the Grand Khan.

On 5 December Columbus departed from Cuba for the large island that the Indians called Bohío which he gave the name Española. It is now known as Hispaniola. The beautiful mountains and verdant plant life of Hispaniola so greatly impressed Columbus that he later wrote to Santangel saying, 'Española is a marvel.'[27] Continuing eastward along the coastline, the *Santa Maria* and the *Niña* reached the Bay of Moustique on 12 December. There Columbus set up a great wooden cross, formally claimed the island for Spain and named the place Port Conception. On 14 and 15 December Columbus explored Tortuga Island just off the Hispaniolan coast. Returning to the main island of Hispaniola on 16 December the two ships proceeded eastward until they reached Acul Bay on 20 December. Large numbers of friendly and gift-bearing natives came out to greet Columbus's ships. Their gifts included gold ornaments which aroused the special interest of the Spaniards. The natives also mentioned that their gold came from a place called Cibao which Columbus took to refer to Cipangu. It was also at this place where Columbus first met the great regional ruler or cacique (chief) named Guacanagari. He invited Columbus to visit his village further down the coast. Columbus gladly accepted the invitation particularly since Guacanagari's village was located closer to gold-producing Cibao. So the eastward course of the Spanish fleet continued.

On 25 December, the *Santa Maria* went aground although the accounts of that event are somewhat confused.[28] Columbus's log claimed that the grounding was an accident and blamed it on the dereliction and the cowardice of Juan de la Cosa, the master of the *Santa Maria* who was supposed to have been on watch. Most modern biographers of Columbus claim that all efforts to refloat the ship proved futile and that its hull was soon irreparably breached. Contemporary records are not quite so clear on what actually happened. Alternatively, it has been plausibly suggested that

Columbus scuttled the *Santa Maria* on purpose and with both the connivance of Juan de la Cosa and the complicity of King Fernando. Their motive for that action was to necessitate leaving some of the fleet's company to form a Spanish settlement on Hispaniola, which they assumed was an outlying island off the Asian coast. The result was the founding of Navidad, named for the Christmas season.

Traditionally it has been argued that the loss of the *Santa Maria* forced Columbus to leave some of his men behind.[29] The *Niña* was supposedly not capable of carrying all of the sixty-six men who sailed on the two ships. That assertion is not borne out by practical experience as many ships during the age of discovery were packed tightly with crew and passengers. It is not inconceivable that 66 people could have sailed on the *Niña*; it would carry 127 people on a later occasion. Furthermore, although physical contact with the *Pinta* was not re-established until 6 January, reports received from the natives on 27 December indicated that the ship was in close proximity. So it could have been called upon for assistance with the transportation of the *Santa Maria*'s crew. Such circumstances lend credence to the assertion that Columbus really wanted to establish a settlement.

The building of Navidad was begun, as were preparations for the *Niña* to make its return voyage to Spain. Columbus also became increasingly irritated over Martín Pinzón's failure to rejoin him with the *Pinta*. Suspicions about Pinzón's true intentions grew as the days went by. On the other hand, cordial relations bloomed between Columbus and Guacanagari during those same few days. Columbus went ashore on 2 January 1493 to bid his final farewell to Guacanagari and the thirty-nine men who would stay behind at Navidad. Diego de Arana, the master-at-arms of the fleet, Pedro Gutiérrez, a royal steward, and Rodrigo de Escobedo, secretary of the fleet, were given charge of the settlement in Columbus's absence.

Various matters of rough weather and native passengers delayed the actual departure for Spain until 4 January. Sailing down the coast Columbus sighted a large mountain which he named Monte Cristo and marked it as a good landmark for guiding the next expedition to Navidad. With that Columbus and the *Niña* continued down the coast of Hispaniola when on 6 January they encountered the wayward *Pinta*. An apologetic Martín Pinzón came aboard the *Niña* and made various excuses for his deserting the fleet. Columbus found none of them to be convincing but concealed the extent of his anger and suspicion from Pinzón in order to avoid a possible crisis. He was, after all, on the *Niña*, the ship commanded by Vicente Pinzón, Martín's brother. According to Martín Pinzón, native guides had enticed him with tales of the gold located on various islands. He told of how he searched for that gold but to little avail as it proved elusive and ultimately illusionary. Meanwhile, Columbus began to grow suspicious of Vicente Pinzón who, though he had hitherto loyally remained with Columbus, now seemed to be siding with his arrogant and disobedient brother. By 8 January this situation convinced Columbus that it was time to return to Spain with all due speed. So the two ships continued eastward along the north coast of Hispaniola until they reached Cape Cabron on 13 January. There at Samana Bay a landing party encountered a band of fifty natives armed with bows and arrows. The natives proved hostile but were easily driven off by the superior weapons of the Europeans. Columbus's native informants identified these Indians as the man-eating Caribs that the other natives feared. They warned Columbus to beware of these warlike Caribs. Lingering a few days in the hope of capturing a Carib, Columbus also learned about the existence of an island of women called Matinino. That information was good news because an island of women or Amazons was a sign that Asia was near. Amazons constituted part of the pantheon of monstrous races that inhabited the fringes of the Far East according to traditional geographical lore.

Columbus and the remainder of his fleet finally departed Hispaniola 3 hours before daybreak on 16 January. Although his original intention had been to seek out the land of the Caribs, the direction of the wind and the wishes of the crew convinced him that it was better to head out to the high seas and return to Spain. Sailing in a north-easterly direction, Columbus's plan was to pick up the westerlies in the region of 30° north latitude that he knew would carry him home. It was a good plan and the *Niña* and the *Pinta* made steady progress in reasonably good weather for twenty-eight days. Columbus, in fact, cited the favourable climatic conditions on both the outward and the return voyages as evidence that he had reached the Far East. As he put it, 'venerable theologians and wise philosophers have well said that the terrestrial Paradise is at the end of the Orient because it is the most temperate place'.[30] But Columbus's luck with the weather did not last. One of the most fearsome storms in the memory of the fifteenth-century world blew up on 12 February and lasted for seven days. By 14 February the terrible winds and mountainous seas of the storm had separated the two ships. Conditions became so dire that Columbus and his crew drew lots to determine who would go on a pilgrimage of gratitude to Santa Maria de Guadalupe if God chose to deliver them from the wrath of the storm. Fearful that the *Niña* would founder and that knowledge of his discovery would be lost, Columbus composed an account of his first voyage on parchment and sealed it in a barrel which was thrown overboard. While the *Niña* survived, the letter and the barrel were never seen again.

The storm continued to buffet the hapless *Niña* on 15 February but that day the crew spotted land. Various guesses were put forward as to what land it was – the Portuguese coast near Lisbon, the Castilian coast and Madeira. But Columbus's guess turned out to be closer to the mark; he said it was the Azores and, in fact, it was the island of Santa Maria in that group. Adverse weather made it difficult to approach the island and it was not until 18 February that the *Niña* could attempt a landing. Anchoring at Santa Maria's harbour, the next day Columbus sent half the crew to fulfil their promise to make a pilgrimage in gratitude for their deliverance from the tempest. João de Castañeda, the Portuguese captain of the island, decided to arrest the Spanish visitors. He then proceeded out to the *Niña* in a launch but refused to come aboard in spite of Columbus's invitation. Columbus warned the captain that his seizure of Columbus's crew would not only offend Fernando and Isabel of Spain, it would anger the King of Portugal. When Castañeda replied that he had no fear of the rulers of Castile, Columbus began to wonder if war had broken out between Spain and Portugal during his absence. Continuing foul weather forced Columbus to leave the exposed harbour and head out to sea on 20 February with only three experienced sailors. The next day he returned to the harbour of Santa Maria and this time was able to get his captive crew members released by showing his letters of authority from the sovereigns of Spain. On 23 February he sailed to the south side of Santa Maria to pick up ballast and replenish his supply of wood. Winds became very favourable for a return to Spain on 24 February causing Columbus to abandon his quest for wood and ballast and instead simply set his sails for home. Eight days of sailing brought the *Niña* almost to the coast of Portugal when on 3 March a nasty squall struck and split all of the ship's sails. Once again the crew promised God to make a pilgrimage to Santa Maria de la Cinta in Huelva. This time Columbus drew the lot. Drifting under bare masts, the men of the *Niña* could see that they were close to land which they correctly assumed was in the vicinity of Lisbon.

Terrible weather continued and onlookers at the mouth of the Tagus River despaired for the survival of the *Niña*. Finally on 4 March the *Niña* made its way into the Tagus estuary. Locals immediately informed Columbus that the uncommonly savage weather had already resulted in the sinking of twenty-five ships near Flanders. Columbus quickly wrote to João II asking for an audience and for permission to anchor at Lisbon. He also wrote to the Spanish monarchs reporting his arrival in Lisbon and gave them a preliminary report on his accomplishments. The next day a heavily armed Portuguese ship approached the *Niña*. Its master was Bartolomé Dias and he ordered Columbus to come over and explain himself to the Portuguese officials. But Columbus refused, citing his position and his honour as a Spanish admiral. Fortunately for him, the Portuguese backed down on their demand. During the days that followed, curious throngs of Portuguese came to view Columbus's ship. Finally on 8 March word arrived from João II summoning Columbus into his presence and ordering Portuguese officials to refit the *Niña* at no charge.

Columbus travelled to the Portuguese court at Valparaiso the next day where he was well received. João II expressed great joy at Columbus's successful completion of his western voyage. But he added the ominous comment that Columbus's discoveries in the western seas belonged to Portugal on the basis of the terms of the Treaty of Alcaçovas.[31] Undoubtedly shaken by João II's assertion, Columbus replied that he had never seen the treaty but that he had followed the orders of Fernando and Isabel to stay away from El Mina and any place else in the region of Guinea. João II smoothly replied that he was sure that there would be no need for arbitrators to settle the matter. Meanwhile, the Portuguese court was all in a buzz over the implications of Columbus's discovery. Some sources claim that João II was chagrined that all of Portugal's years of exploration of the African coast would be relegated to a position of insignificance by Columbus's western voyage. Some accounts suggest that some Portuguese nobles contemplated killing Columbus in order to prevent the news of his achievement from getting back to Spain. But the fact is, by the time Columbus met with João II, the news was already on its way to Spain. Killing Columbus would have accomplished nothing except to provoke a war with Spain and it is doubtful that such an action was thought of let alone seriously considered. Another day with the Portuguese King followed and then on 11 March Columbus took his leave of João II and headed back to Lisbon. He declined an offer from João II to provide him with land transport to Castile and arrived back at the faithful *Niña* on the night of 12 March.

Columbus departed from Lisbon on 13 March and sailed down the coast. He crossed the bar at Saltes to enter the harbour of Palos at noon on 15 March. His great voyage was completed after an absence of over seven months. Continuing on, Columbus arrived at Seville on 31 March where he waited for the summons of Fernando and Isabel who were in Barcelona at that time. Meanwhile, Martín Pinzón had been blown by the great storm all the way back to Spain. Arriving on the Galician coast, the *Pinta* took shelter at Bayona. From there Pinzón wrote to Fernando and Isabel reporting his triumphant return and hoping for a royal summons. It was Columbus's worst fear that Pinzón stood poised to usurp credit for the successful completion of the voyage into the western Atlantic. Instead Pinzón's hopes were dashed. The Spanish monarchs refused to see him and instead waited to hear from Columbus who they considered was the legitimate leader of the expedition. That unexpected blow fell heavily on Pinzón's spirits and he had no choice but to sail home to Palos. He arrived a few hours after Columbus but instead of joining Columbus's triumph, he went to his home. His health already severely weakened by the difficult voyage home, the deeply depressed Pinzón died from one of history's many broken hearts.

The summons of Fernando and Isabel for Columbus arrived at Seville on about 7 April. Along with it, they ordered Columbus to begin preparations for another western voyage. Once he made some initial orders to that effect Columbus set out for Barcelona. Accompanying him were six Indians, some parrots and other specimens of plants and animals from the islands that Columbus presented as proof that he had reached the Orient. His journey was a triumphal procession in which large crowds came to see him. Fernando and Isabel greeted his appearance with enthusiasm and even allowed him the rare privilege of sitting in their presence. On 20 May they conferred nobility on Columbus and named him captain-general of the fleet being prepared to return to Navidad and Hispaniola.

Word of Columbus's return spread fast along with the news of his supposed accomplishment of reaching Asia by sailing west. His famous letter to Luis Santangel also circulated quickly and was first published in a Latin version in Rome on 29 April 1493. It spread through Europe in numerous other reprintings, translations and versions over the next few months and years. But while Columbus steadfastly asserted that he had reached Asia, others were not so sure. The Italian humanist Pietro Martire d'Anghiera witnessed the celebrations and ceremonies surrounding Columbus's successful return. But in a letter written on 13 September 1493 to his patrons back in

A nineteenth-century painting showing Columbus appearing before Fernando and Isabel after completing his first western voyage, by Robert Fleury. (Réunion des Musées Nationaux/Art Resource, NY)

Italy, he drew the rather different conclusion that Columbus had stumbled across new and unknown lands.

Meanwhile, Columbus's discoveries and his return generated an intense series of diplomatic negotiations between Spain and Portugal. João II and Portugal stood on the verge of making a sea voyage around Africa to India as a logical follow-up to Bartolomé Dias's discovery of the Cape of Good Hope in 1487. If Columbus had achieved what he claimed – an easier western sea-route to Asia – years of Portuguese explorations down the African coast would have been done largely for nought. Anxious to defend Portugal's substantial investment in an African sea-route to Asia, João II began to gather a fleet to prevent other westward voyages by Spain. War loomed over the Iberian Peninsula.

Fernando and Isabel refused to be intimidated by such bellicose posturing on the part of Portugal. Instead they sought confirmation of their rights to Columbus's western route to Asia from the papacy, a traditional arbiter of disputes between European monarchs. In seeking papal recognition of their rights to Columbus's discovery, Fernando and Isabel possessed a big advantage over João II. The current

Pope was the infamous Alexander VI, a native of Aragon whose original name was Rodrigo Borgia. The Pope was cooperative and responded on 3 May 1493 by issuing the papal bull *Inter Caetera* which granted Spain the right to all discoveries made in the West while preserving the previous concessions made to Portugal in Africa and the East. In the meantime, negotiations between Spain and Portugal continued and Alexander VI issued two more bulls – *Eximae Devotionis* and a second *Inter Caetera*. These documents were issued by 19 July but were backdated to 3 and 4 May. Basically they repeated the first *Inter Caetera* except that the second *Inter Caetera* added the provision for a line of demarcation between Portuguese and Spanish territory to be located 100 leagues west of the Azores and Cape Verde Islands. At that point João II was satisfied. Portugal's lucrative African trade was protected and the African sea-route to India was indubitably placed in Portuguese waters.

In Spain Fernando and Isabel greedily started to let their successes and their special and cordial relationship with the very cooperative Alexander VI go to their heads. They pushed the pontiff for an even more advantageous distribution of the new geographical discoveries. Meanwhile, preparations for Columbus's second voyage continued and on 25 September he departed for Hispaniola with a large fleet and company to solidify Spanish claims and control. The next day on 26 September Alexander VI issued the bull *Dudum Siquidem* which rescinded all previous papal grants to Portugal concerning Africa. It also freed Spain from any obligations incurred under the Treaty of Alcaçovas.[32] It even forbade anyone from sailing the eastern seas without the permission of Fernando and Isabel. In effect, the papacy had given Spain the African trading monopoly and the African sea-route to India that Portugal had spent decades developing.

Dudum Siquidem posed a deadly threat to Portugal's hopes for a lucrative trading empire. João II chose to ignore it rather than reacting with immediate violence. By the beginning of 1494 Fernando and Isabel also realized that *Dudum Siquidem* represented an unsustainable victory over Portugal. Instead of engaging in a rich trade with Asia, both nations would be locked in a vicious death struggle for control of that trade.

Pope Alexander VI. From Washington Irving et al., *The Discovery and Conquest of the New World* (Philadelphia, Syndicate Publishing, 1892), p. 192.

Portugal was too firmly entrenched in Africa and had too much to lose to give up without a long and nasty war. A Spanish victory was by no means certain and victorious or not, the costs to Spain would be a crushing burden. During the spring of 1494 realistic negotiations began between Spain and Portugal. Employing superior diplomats and well-cultivated friends in the Castilian court, the Portuguese managed to negotiate a treaty that was quite favourable to their interests. It was then signed on 7 June 1494 at Tordesillas on the Spanish frontier with Portugal.

The Treaty of Tordesillas included the famous line of demarcation which was placed 370 leagues west of the Cape Verde Islands. This location was at least 600 miles further west than the earlier papal line of demarcation discussed in the second bull of *Inter Caetera*. All lands west of the line were to be Spanish territory while all lands east of the line were to be Portuguese territory. Spanish ships were allowed to sail through Portuguese waters by the most direct route to the Spanish lands in order to take advantage of prevailing winds and currents. An exact interpretation of the Treaty of Tordesillas is impossible. Its provisions were vague because of the fluctuating and inaccurate geographical knowledge of that time and the inability of fifteenth-century Europeans to determine longitude. Furthermore, Spain and Portugal never even sent out the agreed upon demarcation commission to fix the exact location of the line, and this remained under dispute into the eighteenth century. Whether the line went merely from pole to pole or completely circled the globe in a north to south direction was another source of disagreement. Most modern scholars feel that the original intention was simply to divide the Atlantic Ocean from pole to pole. It was only later during the second decade of the sixteenth century when the location of the spice-rich Molucca Islands became an issue that Spain began talking about the line of demarcation extending all the way around the earth.

As a result of the Treaty of Tordesillas, Spain and Portugal remained at peace. The treaty realistically defined their respective spheres of influence. It allowed the two countries to direct their resources toward exploration and the development of their new discoveries rather than into war. Christopher Columbus and Spain were already engaged in establishing an empire all during the time that the Treaty of Tordesillas was being negotiated. Portugal as yet had not made its final move into the Indian Ocean to connect Europe and Asia by the African sea-route but it was only a matter of time. Other European monarchs did not take the Treaty of Tordesillas too seriously. The witty Francis I of France some years later put it best when he quipped, 'I should very much like to see the passage in Adam's will that divides the New World between my brothers, the Emperor Charles V [the grandson and the successor of Fernando and Isabel] and the King of Portugal.'[33]

BRISTOL, JOHN CABOT AND THE REDISCOVERY OF NORTH AMERICA

John Cabot's voyage in 1497 to North America took place between the voyages of Christopher Columbus and Vasco da Gama. Of these three great voyages of the 1490s

Cabot's is the least well documented and it also had considerably less of an immediate and a dramatic impact on European expansion for most of the sixteenth century. At the same time Cabot's voyage and its English context of previous high-seas voyages into the western Atlantic Ocean from the port of Bristol show that Columbus and his ideas about sailing west to reach Asia were not unique. Instead they formed part of the general ferment of geographical ideas about what lay west across the Atlantic that was gaining momentum during the late fifteenth century in Europe.[34]

Little is known about John Cabot, or Zuan Caboto as he was known in Italian, before 1496.[35] He is thought to have been born in Genoa. That information is based on a single reference from 1497 and the archives of Genoa provide no corroboration.[36] In 1472 Cabot became a naturalized citizen of Venice, a process requiring fifteen years of residence which means he began living in that city no later than 1457. It also means that he was born before that date. His father was a merchant named Giulio Caboto. At some time before 1482, John Cabot married a woman named Mattea and by 1484 the couple had at least two sons. According to his own testimony Cabot worked in the Mediterranean spice trade and claimed to have visited Mecca. Between 1490 and 1493 a John Cabot Montecalunya of Venice lived in Valencia and Barcelona in Spain and worked on projects to improve the city's harbour. During this time he would have been well placed to observe Christopher Columbus's triumphant return from his first western voyage. Whether this man is the same person as the explorer John Cabot is a subject of dispute among historians.

Given the general speculation about the geography of the western Atlantic that was prevalent in Europe during the fifteenth century, it is quite possible that Cabot could have developed the idea of sailing west to reach Asia independently of Columbus. John Cabot may even have approached Fernando and Isabel of Spain about sponsoring his own project to sail across the Atlantic Ocean prior to Columbus's departure in 1492. But the Spanish monarchs did not take up his offer because they were already supporting Columbus's similar enterprise. It is also possible that Cabot offered his services to the King of Portugal but was rebuffed. Apparently upon hearing about the results of Columbus's first voyage, Cabot developed the opinion that Columbus had not sailed far enough west and so had not reached Cathay and Cipangu. His unique contribution to the exploration of the western Atlantic was to suggest that an expedition set sail from much further north. Such an expedition would have a considerably shorter voyage across the high seas. Then when it reached the barren north-eastern coast of Asia, it would cruise down the coast following its south-western trend until it reached the realm of the Grand Khan. But if Cabot offered this revised plan to the monarchs of Spain and Portugal, he still did not find a receptive audience. Both countries, after some acrimony during 1493, had divided the eastern and supposed western sea-routes to Asia between them by the Treaty of Tordesillas in 1494. They were not interested in yet another alternative route west to Asia, especially one that the facts of geography left them poorly placed to exploit.

As a consequence, Cabot made his way to England and presented his project for a western voyage to Asia to the prudent King Henry VII, possibly following in the footsteps of Bartholomew Columbus. Arriving in England by or before the end of 1495, he found a more receptive listener in the English King.[37] He engaged in presenting his concept for a voyage to Asia during January and on 5 March 1496 the English King granted Cabot a patent for making such a journey. The patent gave Cabot and his sons permission to sail from Bristol across northern, eastern and western seas with five ships in search of lands unknown to Christians. By excluding southern seas, Henry VII avoided trouble with trespassing on Spanish and Portuguese waters. The parsimonious Henry VII provided no financial support for Cabot's project although he did give Cabot and his English partners an exemption

A painting depicting the departure of John and Sebastian Cabot from Bristol on their first voyage of discovery in 1497, by Ernest Board. (City of Bristol Museum and Art Gallery/Bridgeman Art Library)

from paying customs at Bristol. The King claimed the usual fifth of the future profits. So Cabot had permission to make a western voyage but he still needed financial support.

Cabot had apparently been in contact with merchants in Bristol before seeking the support of Henry VII. Intrepid seamen from Bristol seem to have already anticipated Cabot's project of a western voyage across the North Atlantic and may have already begun exploiting the rich fishing off the Grand Banks of Newfoundland. Prior to Cabot's arrival, the sailors of Bristol appear to have thought of their discovery of western lands across the Atlantic exclusively in terms of the rich fishing. They wanted to keep those fishing grounds a secret from any potential interlopers. Cabot's contribution to this situation was to suggest that English ships proceed further down the barren coastline of what was assumed to be north-eastern Asia until they reached China and the riches of the Far East. Some merchants of Bristol found his plan to be reasonable and provided the needed resources to carry it out, albeit the bare minimum – one ship and a small crew. An abortive voyage took place in 1496 after storms and a fearful crew forced Cabot to turn back.[38]

Cabot and his backers among the Bristol merchants were undaunted by the failure of the first voyage and planned a second one for 1497. It was also a modest affair consisting of a single vessel, the *Matthew*, which was a small bark of about 50 tons.[39] There is reason to believe that it was a fairly new ship and may have been named after Cabot's wife Mattea. The ship's company only consisted of eighteen or twenty men including at least two Bristol merchants. Sebastian Cabot, the famous son of John Cabot, claimed to have accompanied his father on the voyage of 1497 but he is not a particularly reliable informant since he frequently enhanced his curriculum vitae to secure employment from various European goverments. The ship carried enough supplies for a seven- to eight-month voyage.

The *Matthew* departed from Bristol during May. Various accounts say it was 2 May but others say it was 8 May or 20 May.[40] Part of the problem of conflicting dates stems from the peculiar difficulties inherent in starting a sea voyage from Bristol. The city is located some miles up the River Avon. A sailing ship leaving Bristol's docks has to make its way down the river and through the Avon Gorge. That can only be done at certain times by a sailing vessel because tidal conditions reverse the flow of the river. Once a ship has passed out of the mouth of the Avon it enters the River Severn Estuary, which appears to be a large body of water, but is in fact full of shallows and mudflats and these make it treacherous to navigate. Tidal action and contrary winds frequently aggravate the situation and a sailing ship can be stalled in the Severn for days at a time unable to make any headway toward the open sea. Once ships from Bristol cleared the Severn Estuary, they often called in at an Irish port to replenish supplies and do some trading. Cabot and the *Matthew* made such a stop on the west coast of Ireland. So while Cabot's voyage across the Atlantic Ocean is said to have taken thirty-five days, it is not clear when the count of these days began. Was it from the Bristol docks, from the Severn or from Ireland?

Once Cabot left Ireland he headed north. He employed traditional latitudinal sailing techniques and was seeking the favourable easterly winds at about 60°N latitude which the Norse seamen had used for several centuries to reach Greenland. As the *Matthew* neared the coast of North America, the Labrador Current would have nudged its course southward. Finally on 24 June 1497, Cabot sighted land and went ashore and planted a flag to claim it for Henry VII. Where he landed is not known and continues to be the subject of vigorous debate. It was a wooded coastline and the waters around it were full of fish. Signs of human inhabitants were obvious to the explorers. Footpaths and old campsites were observed but no natives made an appearance. Cabot thought he had reached the north-east corner of Asia and some of its outlying islands. It was even suggested that one of the islands was the long-sought-after Island of the Seven Cities. Like other earlier explorers Cabot viewed the unfamiliar landscape optimistically. The fertility of the land and the climate were both described in positive terms. Modern research indicates that the first landfall occurred somewhere between Sandwich Bay in Labrador and White Bay on Newfoundland.[41] Afterwards Cabot cruised the coastline for about a month, travelling some 900 miles, but he and the crew did not go ashore again. In the latter part of July the *Matthew* began its return voyage from Cape Degrat. It was a remarkably swift passage of only fifteen days duration. But once again Cabot and his crew argued over navigational matters. They claimed that he was sailing too far north and compelled him to drop the course southward. As a result, the *Matthew* missed England and first made landfall on the coast of Brittany. As a result, several days were wasted while the ship backtracked its way to Bristol on or before 10 August. From there Cabot made his way to London on 23 August where he received an enthusiastic welcome from Henry VII and the citizens of London. The grateful King immediately gave Cabot a gift of £10 and an annual pension of £20 to be paid out of Bristol's customs.

Perceptions of the significance of Cabot's discovery varied. Cabot thought he had brought England to the threshold of the vast wealth and luxuries of Asia. Others agreed with his assessment and speculation followed that London would displace Alexandria as the greatest spice mart serving the European market. It was a perspective to warm the heart of a thrifty monarch like Henry VII. Others, like most of Cabot's crew, took a more prosaic view of his achievement. The voyage had revealed rich fishing grounds that would free the English from their precarious dependence on the Icelandic sites. Of course, it may be that Cabot's voyage spoiled the fishermen of Bristol's close-kept, secret knowledge of existence of the Newfoundland fishing grounds.

Initially Henry VII talked about organizing a follow-up expedition of between ten and twelve ships to go back across the northern Atlantic. There was even some discussion about establishing a way-station using convicts as settlers. But foreign and domestic political considerations intervened to distract Henry VII's attention and to divert his resources. During 1497 Henry VII found his royal position threatened. Scotland invaded England in support of the pretender Perkin Warbeck while the

Cornish rose in rebellion twice, which included significant battles and sieges. While calm and peace had returned to England by the end of the year, the pressing dangers had strained royal revenues.

When Cabot's third expedition was prepared in 1498 it was a much-reduced enterprise. Sailing in May 1498, his flotilla consisted of only four or five small ships including one royal vessel. The total company of the fleet numbered between 100 and 200 men. This time both Bristol and London merchants contributed to the costs. Just what happened after Cabot's fleet sailed west is a mystery.[42] One storm-battered ship returned to Ireland after the fleet encountered harsh weather on the high seas but the rest of the vessels sailed on. They were never seen again, at least by English eyes. After 1498 Bristol stopped paying Cabot's pension apparently because they considered him to be lost at sea and deceased. It is certainly possible that Cabot died in a tempest on the high seas, a common-enough fate in those days although the loss of four out of five ships was an extremely rare occurrence. Some intriguing bits of evidence indicate the possibility that he or some of his fleet actually made it back to North America. They may even have sailed down the eastern seaboard of North America in search of the Grand Khan and instead reached the Caribbean coast of Columbia. Europeans following Cabot to North America soon after his disappearance found Native Americans in possession of an Italian sword that could have come from Cabot's expedition of 1498. The Juan de la Cosa map of 1500 shows English explorations far down the coast of North America before any English speakers other than Cabot's people could have conceivably visited that area. Spanish sources speak of English intruders west of Cabo de la Vela on the coast of present-day Columbia. If Cabot actually reached that far south, he never managed to get back to England to tell of it personally. Enough information, however, was relayed to England so that from 1500 onward English discussions of the North American discoveries referred to them as a 'new' land rather than as part of Asia as Cabot had originally believed. In contrast Columbus went to his grave convinced he had reached Asia and many people continued to believe that North America was part of Asia for some years.

Unlike his contemporaries Christopher Columbus and Vasco da Gama, John Cabot's accomplishments were quickly forgotten and the lands he found were left unexploited for almost a century. The barren nature of Newfoundland did not promote settlement and Spain's initial difficulties and disappointments in colonizing Hispaniola did not provide any great encouragement to such enterprise among the English. The death of Henry VII in 1509 ended monarchial interest in western explorations for years to come in England. Cabot's personal achievements also quickly dropped out of the public consciousness.[43] By the mid-sixteenth century English writers had merged John Cabot's and his son Sebastian's enterprises and explorations into one single career – that of Sebastian. To enhance his own reputation as a voyager and geographer, Sebastian Cabot appropriated some of his father's achievements. It was not until the late nineteenth century that careful archival research by many historians restored proper credit for the voyage of 1497 to John Cabot. Meanwhile, Cabot's discovery of the North American continent had revealed a massive obstacle lying across the western sea-route to Asia which is where the European sailors really wanted to go. Initially, like Columbus before him, Cabot thought he had reached the mainland of Asia somewhere in the barren regions of Siberia. Later voyages would reveal that Newfoundland was not a part of Asia and that it was a huge mass of land. Eventually it would prove to be an obstacle that confounded all efforts to locate a north-west passage through the unanticipated territory of North America which would allow access to the wealth of the Far East.

Sebastian Cabot. From Justin Winsor, *Narrative and Critical History of America* (Boston, Houghton Mifflin, 1884), vol. 3, p. 5.

VASCO DA GAMA AND THE SEA-ROAD TO INDIA

When Bartolomé Dias returned to Lisbon from his discovery of the Cape of Good Hope in December 1488, he brought news that conclusively proved the existence of a sea-route to India. Many years of Portuguese voyages down the western side of Africa had at last borne fruit. The perplexing aspect of Dias's discovery is that the energetic João II did not immediately follow it up with an expedition to India. Such a trip did not finally take place until 1497 when João II had been dead for several years.

Why did João II delay? Some historians have suggested that between 1488 and 1497, the Portuguese conducted a number of secret voyages into the South Atlantic to determine the pattern of winds and currents.[44] Hugging the coastline of Africa the way the Portuguese had been doing through the voyage of Dias was not the best way for a sailing ship to make its way south in that part of the world. Prevailing winds and currents were against it. A better route was needed. It has even been asserted that Vasco da Gama, the first Portuguese commander to take a fleet to India, participated in some of the secret South Atlantic enterprises. The problem is that no hint of such expeditions has survived in the archives or in contemporary chronicles. Gama did sail boldly out into the high seas of the South Atlantic to take the best advantage of the winds and the currents to carry his ships in a great arc to the Cape of Good Hope. His action is cited as circumstantial evidence that he possessed foreknowledge of the best sailing route which had been acquired as a result of undercover exploratory trips. On the other hand, the fact that he and his ships were out of contact with land for ninety days while sailing the South Atlantic possibly indicates that they did not entirely know what they were doing when they struck out onto the high seas. Seafarers of the age of sail were acute observers of nature. Portuguese explorers cruising the coast of Africa would have noted the winds and currents at various points and in the process gathered sufficient information to speculate about what the pattern of winds and currents further out on the high seas might be. There is no need to imagine that they and Vasco da Gama possessed foreknowledge acquired from secret voyages of the great arc sailing route that the Portuguese eventually came to call the *volta do brasil.*

João II treated Dias coolly upon his return in spite of his successful voyage. Why the King acted this way is unclear. It is possible that João II did not find Dias personally palatable. Although Dias remained active in the Portuguese naval service until his untimely death, he never received another significant command. But the personal relations between sovereign and seaman cannot form an important reason for any delays in João II's programme of exploration. He had plenty of other people to turn to besides Dias if he had been able to continue focusing on the project of an Indian voyage.

It should be remembered that even a forceful ruler like João II had to spend much of his time reacting to events instead of taking the initiative. Circumstances arose in Portugal after 1488 that distracted João II's attention from sailing to India.[45] He did not possess the freedom to ignore his advisors and great nobles on a consistent basis. Portugal was at war with Morocco during the late 1480s and into the 1490s and did not experience uniform success in that conflict. Dynastic tragedy struck in July 1491 when João II's son and heir Afonso was killed in a riding accident. The Avis dynasty's smooth succession was called into question, always a dangerous situation given the ruthless nature of power politics among the Portuguese nobility. João II's legitimate heir was now his cousin Manuel, the Duke of Beja, a circumstance that the King found distasteful enough that he considered legitimizing his bastard son Jorge and making him his successor. His wife Queen Leonor, the sister of Manuel, hotly opposed that plan and the royal couple were at odds virtually until the King's death in 1495. Meanwhile, in 1492 Portugal was faced with a rapid influx of Jewish refugees following Spain's expulsion of its Jews. While the Jews all paid a fee to João II for taking up at least temporary residence in his country, the new population strained resources and demanded royal attention. Some 60,000 Jews entered Portugal in a relatively brief period of time. That was a rather large number for a medieval country of about a million people to absorb.

João II also faced internal opposition to his plan for completing the project of opening a sea-route to India and the spice marts.[46] Some of his advisors and nobles thought that Portugal should concentrate its limited resources on developing its existing trade with Africa. Dias's voyage to the Cape of Good Hope had revealed that a sea-route did exist. But it also showed that the sea-road was difficult and was no obvious improvement, in terms of cost, on the existing routes across the Middle East and the Mediterranean Sea. Furthermore, the opposition argued that because Portugal was a small country, it lacked the resources to engage effectively in the Asian spice trade given the immense distances and vast territories involved. In retrospect, opening a sea-route to Asia has been seen by modern historians as a massively important and unquestionably obvious step in the progress of world history. Not all of João II's contemporaries saw the situation in the same way and he had to take the time to persuade them that he was right and at least make sure he could ignore their wishes with impunity. Even more distracting for João II was Columbus's return from his first western voyage in early 1493. Its success threw all of Portugal's plans for a circum-African voyage to Africa into turmoil. Tense negotiations followed which resulted in the Treaty of Tordesillas in 1494. João II died the next year with the incomplete sea-road to India still beckoning.

Manuel I succeeded his cousin João II as King of Portugal and continued the existing policy of pursuing a sea-route to India in spite of continuing disatisfaction with the scheme. Much of the opposition came from the noble faction that was coalescing around the illegitimate Dom Jorge whom João II had richly endowed with lands and the Grand Mastership of the Order of Santiago. The plans for an expedition to India included giving the command of it to Vasco da Gama (1469–1524). Some contemporary and later sixteenth-century chronicles have claimed that João II completed arrangements for the voyage to India in his last years. Initially he gave the command to the minor courtier Estêvão da Gama who died before the fleet could sail. The office was next offered to Estêvão's son Paulo da Gama who declined on the grounds of poor health. That opened an opportunity for his younger brother Vasco to be given the command. Another account says that King Manuel picked Vasco da Gama to command the Indian voyage simply because he stood out in the crowd at court and he liked his look.[47] Modern historians suggest a somewhat different explanation of how Vasco da Gama came to command the fleet bound for India.

The Gama family were minor nobles from Olivença. A Vasco da Gama, who was the grandfather of the explorer, and Teresa da Silva gave birth to four children. The eldest son Estêvão da Gama became a knight in the household of Fernando, the Duke of Viseu. Estêvão also joined the Order of Santiago and by the 1480s was moving up into the middle ranks of the Order and had developed connections with the town of Sines. Marrying Isabel Sodré, the couple produced many children – Paulo da Gama, João Sodré, the future explorer Vasco, Pedro, Aires and a daughter Teresa. Estêvão also had an illegitimate son who he also named Vasco and who was actually older than his half-brother, the famous voyager Vasco da Gama. In terms of court politics, Estêvão's connection with the Duke of Viseu was a liability as João II hated the Duke and ultimately personally murdered him in 1484. The Gamas, however, managed to weather that political storm. Their link with the Order of Santiago remained intact and several years later involved them in yet another Portuguese noble faction. When João II elevated his illegimate son Dom Jorge to the Grand Mastership of the Order of Santiago, the Gamas became associated with his faction. Dom Jorge's coterie was a thorn in the side of King Manuel from the time he came to the throne onward. Although later Portuguese chroniclers told a somewhat different story, contemporary evidences indicate that the rather beleaguered Manuel I chose Vasco da Gama to command the first fleet to sail to India largely because he was a member of Dom Jorge's grouping.[48] Since the voyage to India was controversial and highly dangerous, Manuel I sought to bring Dom Jorge's party into the venture so that if the worst happened, the odium of failure would be spread around rather than concentrated in the King's party. It also, at least temporarily, deprived Dom Jorge of a follower while not costing Manuel I one of his trusted retainers.

What sort of person was Vasco da Gama?[49] Unfortunately that is a difficult question to answer. Gama left almost no records that provide any insights into his inner personality or thoughts. Large parts of his life are virtually without documentation. His actions, however, do provide a limited means for at least partially assessing his character. All Gama men had a deserved reputation for bravery among their contemporaries. An offshoot of that trait was that, like many members of the fifteenth-century European nobility, they were quarrelsome, unruly and quick to take offence. According to tradition, Vasco da Gama repelled by sheer force of personality the alcade (magistrate) and night watch of Setubel during a nocturnal con-frontation. Gama also possessed immense determination which some-times crossed the line into stubborn-ness. It was the sort of char-acteristic that would help him lead his men and ships to the successful com-pletion of a pioneering voyage of incredible diffi-culty and danger. Frequently Gama showed himself to be ruthless, even to the point of cruelty when it came to dealing with the peoples of the Indian Ocean littoral. Like most fifteenth-century Europeans he disdained any Muslim and regarded them with the deepest suspicion. While his courage and drive brought the first round-trip voyage to India to a successful conclu-sion, Gama's suspicions, ruthlessness and willingness to shoot first and ask questions later may have poisoned the waters of the Indian Ocean trade for the Portuguese who followed. As a commander Gama proved better suited

Vasco da Gama, 1646, by an unknown artist. (Heritage Image Partnership)

for a military rather than a diplomatic mission.[50]

Preparations for the voyage to India proceeded into 1497. Most accounts indicate that King João II began organizing the expedition but that his successor Manuel I completed the task. The fleet consisted of four vessels. Bartolomé Dias supervised the construction of two new vessels built especially for the voyage to India. Instead of caravels, he built larger and sturdier naos which were better suited for high-seas sailing. The new ships were named the *São Gabriel* and the *São Raphael*. They were accompanied by two other ships – the *Berrio*, possibly a caravel, and an unnamed supply ship that was also a nao. Vasco da Gama used the *São Gabriel* as his flagship, while his brother Paulo commanded the *São Raphael* with Nicolau Coelho as the captain of the *Berrio* and Gonçalo Gomes in charge of the supply ship. Several experienced and respected pilots accompanied the fleet. The four

The three ships that Vasco da Gama used during his first voyage to India. This illustration is taken from a manuscript depicting the lives of the Portuguese viceroys and governors in India by Lizuarte de Abreu, Portugal, *c.* 1558. (The Pierpont Morgan Library/Art Resource, NY)

ships were heavily manned with the total company numbering possibly as many as 170 men. A few of the members of the company were convicts, who were sent along to do dangerous or unpleasant tasks as part of their punishment. Provisions were gathered for a long voyage. Only a modest amount of trade goods were included in the cargoes of the ships as Gama's expedition was not considered primarily to be a commercial venture. Even those few trade goods were woefully inadequate for the task as they reflected Portugal's experience trading with West Africa. Beads, rough cloth and iron tools that sold well in Africa were embarrassingly inappropriate for the highly sophisticated markets of cultured India. Basically Vasco da Gama's fleet was going on a voyage of reconnaissance to determine the true feasibility of the sea-route to India and to establish diplomatic relations. Actual trading was a very secondary consideration on this particular voyage; far more important was successfully completing a round trip. And that result was by no means a foregone conclusion.

The fleet of Vasco da Gama sailed for India from Restelo on 8 July 1497 accompanied by a caravel under the command of Bartolomé Dias that was headed for St George of the Mine on the Guinea Coast.[51] On 15 July they sighted the Canary Islands. Proceeding south a dense fog the next day caused the ships to lose sight of each other but undeterred they simply proceeded on to their prearranged rendezvous at the Cape Verde Islands. The scattered ships began to arrive at the Cape Verdes by about 22 July, although the entire fleet was not reunited with Vasco da Gama until 26 July. They finally reached the island of Santiago on 27 July for rest and resupply. It was about this time that Dias's ship parted company with the India-bound fleet and sailed on to Guinea.

Once his fleet was again ready for sea, Vasco da Gama led them east from Santiago on 3 August. Just what course the Portuguese followed is impossible to say. By 18 August they were 200 leagues out of Santiago and heading south. At that point the *São Gabriel*'s main yard broke and it took two days to repair it. The fleet's course had shifted to the south-west by 22 August and sightings of whales began. What the Portuguese were attempting to do was take full advantage of the prevailing winds and currents in that part of the South Atlantic. They followed a course that was a large arc that stretched out toward the coast of South America and then curved back eastward toward Africa. On 1 November the ships' crews began to notice signs of land. Finally sighting land on 4 November, they approached the shore but could not tell where they were. On 7 November the fleet anchored at what is now known as St Helena's Bay. There they made repairs to the ships and took on wood and fresh water.

Vasco da Gama's ships had been out of sight of land from 3 August to 4 November, a period of ninety days which was rather a long time to be at sea at that time. But contemporary sources do not refer to the crew getting nervous or suffering from the usual privations of such a long sea voyage. What Vasco da Gama had done was to let the prevailing winds and currents carry his ships in a vast curve around the South Atlantic and back to the coast of south-eastern Africa. This arc, the *volta do brasil*, was eventually determined to be the optimum route for a sailing vessel to follow when travelling to the Cape of Good Hope. While some modern Portuguese historians and others have suggested that the Portuguese between 1488 and 1497 had secretly explored the South Atlantic and that Gama benefited from that knowledge in choosing his route, it is more likely that Gama made an inspired guess based on earlier observations of wind and currents made by Diogo Cão and Bartolomé Dias. If so, his execution of that conjecture was by no means entirely successful. The Portuguese fleet was out of sight of land for over ninety days. It was a circumstance that would have sorely strained the stores of food and water on most ships. Scurvy would have killed or debilitated many sailors who remained away from land and fresh food for that long. Contemporary accounts, however, are silent about such problems. Gama's crew certainly had one thing in their favour that Columbus's men lacked, they possessed the certain knowledge that Dias's ship had already been to where they were going. Their destination indubitably existed while Columbus's goal was based on unproven speculation.

Gama's fleet stayed at St Helena's Bay for eight days. During that time natives began to appear and some trading took place between them and the Portuguese. Vasco da Gama hopefully questioned the local Hottentots about Asian spices and other luxury items but they knew nothing about such things. On 12 November one of the Portuguese, Fernão Velloso, requested and received permission to visit the Hottentot settlement. His sightseeing tour turned sour for some reason. The Hottentots soon indicated that they wanted him to return to his own people. But when Vasco da Gama and a ship's boat attempted to pick him up on the beach, the natives attacked with spears and wounded Gama and several others. As one Portuguese commented, 'All this happened because we looked upon these people as men of little spirit, quite incapable of violence, and had therefore landed without arming ourselves.'[52] Trusting or underestimating strangers was a mistake that Vasco da Gama would not make again. Ominously for the rest of the voyage he would view foreigners with suspicion and would be ready to resort to violence at the slightest provocation.

Leaving St Helena's Bay on 16 November the Portuguese flotilla reached the Cape of Good Hope two days later. Contrary winds prevented the ships from rounding the Cape until 22 November and on 25 November they landed at Mossel Bay. The Portuguese stayed there for thirteen days. During that time they broke up the unnamed supply ship and distributed its crew and cargo among the three remaining vessels. Once again the local Hottentots appeared and unlike during the previous visit of Bartolomé Dias, they proved to be friendly. Gama, however, was taking no chances and kept his men heavily armed while on shore. After taking on water and food, the Portuguese erected a wooden cross and a pillar (*padrão*) to mark their visit. Apparently the locals took that action amiss for as the Portuguese sailed off on 7 December, a group of natives destroyed both markers even before Gama's ships had sailed out of sight.

Proceeding eastward along the coast, Gama's expedition passed the last pillar erected by Dias's early voyage on 16 December. Besides encountering stormy seas, the ships began to experience difficulty in making headway due to the contrary Agulhas current. Favourable winds finally appeared which allowed them to continue forward. By 25 December the fleet had sailed 70 leagues beyond the furthest point that Dias had reached and was coasting along a land that they appropriately named Natal since it was Christmas time. From 11 to 16 January the Portuguese anchored off a coast that was relatively densely populated but they were received so hospitably that they named it *Terra da Boa Gente*, 'land of the good people'.

Sailing on up the East African coast on 25 January the Portuguese reached a river that they called *Rio dos Bons Signaes*, 'river of the good signs', which was probably the Zambezi. There they spent thirty-two days cleaning and repairing their ships. By this point the rigours of their journey had really started to take their toll – the sailors were exhausted and their vessels were cruelly worn. The crews' inability to secure proper provisions meant that scurvy had become rampant among them. The low-lying and wet nature of the country around the *Rio dos Bons Signaes* also made it unhealthy for the Portuguese. Fortunately the inhabitants were reasonably friendly and there was a supply of fresh fruit to help restore the health of the voyagers.

Departing from the *Rio dos Bons Signaes* on 24 February Vasco da Gama's expedition was at last entering the frontier of Islamic civilization along the east coast of Africa.

Somehow they had already bypassed the trading town of Sofala before ever reaching the *Rio dos Bon Signaes*. Instead, their first contact with the Muslims of the Indian Ocean came on 2 March at the bay of Moçambique. Sailing into Moçambique Bay, Nicolau Coelho's ship wandered out of the channel and went aground on a sandbank. Local boatmen quickly approached to greet the strangers. Moçambique was a Muslim community and its inhabitants jumped to the erroneous conclusion that the white Portuguese were Turks and therefore were fellow Muslims. It was a mistake that the cautious and overly suspicious Vasco da Gama did nothing to dispel. Instead, he used the hospitality and trust of his host to gather information about the lands that lay ahead including the location of the legendary Prester John's supposedly powerful Christian empire. The Portuguese also secured the services of two local pilots. Meanwhile, the local sultan discovered that Vasco da Gama and his men had deceived him and that they were Christians, not Muslims. Hitherto friendly relations quickly degenerated. When on 10 March the Portuguese sent boats to fetch one of their local pilots from the shore, a fight broke out.

The Portuguese attributed the hostility of the Muslims to the discovery that the Portuguese were Christians. However, it is more likely that the locals' ire at the Portuguese stemmed from the Portuguese's dishonesty concerning their true identity. As luck would have it, when the Portuguese first tried to depart from Moçambique, contrary winds blew them back there within a few days. As a result of continuing problems with the wind, the Portuguese remained there until 29 March. The sultan made friendly overtures but the Portuguese continued to be suspicious. Their dwindling supply of fresh water forced them to land on the mainland so that they could restock their supply. But they were unable to find a source and began to face contemptuous resistance from the local Muslims. Vasco da Gama responded by bombarding the town, looting and taking hostages over the course of several days. He also managed to secure a supply of fresh water. But cordial relations with the inhabitants of Moçambique were irreparably ruined. It was a poisoned legacy that would follow Gama and his fleet up the coast of Africa and even across the sea to India.

Sailing north again on 29 March, the Portuguese ships battled against adverse currents. They reached Kilwa on 4 April but uncooperative winds compelled them to sail on to Mombasa. They arrived at that city on 7 April but cautiously did not enter the harbour. It was a wise decision. News of the Portuguese's misbehaviour at Moçambique had reached Mombasa and the Muslims plotted to take them prisoner. Initially the ruler of Mombasa was quite hospitable and invited them into his port. An attempt by a large 'welcoming' party of armed men to come aboard the Portuguese ships was politely refused. On 10 April, the Portuguese ships tried to enter the harbour but became entangled at the mouth. During the confusion one of the over-anxious pilots from Moçambique leaped overboard to make his escape. His ever-present suspicions aroused, Gama questioned some other prisoners under torture and discovered a plan to take the Portuguese fleet captive once it entered Mombasa's harbour. That information ended all thoughts of landing there, although they continued their attempt for two more days to secure the services of a pilot to guide them to Calicut. Finally they departed from Mombasa on 13 April and left behind an implacably hostile Muslim city.

Sailing further up the coast, Gama's fleet headed for the port of Malindi. Along the way the Portuguese stopped two Muslim boats in hope of finding and kidnapping a pilot to guide them to India. Such actions only further besmirched the reputation of the Portuguese among the Muslim peoples of East Africa. Arriving at Malindi on 14 April both the locals and the Portuguese treated each other with a high degree of caution. Luckily for Gama, the Sultan of Malindi was at odds with the ruler of Mombasa. Anxious to secure allies, he was quite willing to overlook the churlish and overly aggressive behaviour of the Portuguese, especially since it had been directed at his enemies. Of particular importance to the Portuguese, he offered them the services of a pilot that they so desperately needed. As a gesture of goodwill on 18 April Gama released his Muslim prisoners. But by 22 April no guide had arrived and an impatient Gama seized one of the Sultan of Malindi's more important servants as a hostage. That action prompted a quick response from the Sultan who sent the Portuguese a Gujarati pilot who they mistook for a Christian.[53] Well pleased with their new navigator and with peace preserved with Malindi, the Portuguese set sail for India on 24 April.

A smooth voyage of twenty-five days followed as the monsoons favoured sailing toward India at that time of year. High mountains appeared on the horizon on 18 May and two days later the Portuguese reached Capocate, a town north of Calicut. Dugout canoes came to meet them. On 21 May, Vasco da Gama sent a convict ashore with some of the locals to reconnoitre the situation. Overall the Portuguese expected a reasonably friendly reception since they assumed that India was a land full of either the Christian subjects of Prester John or Christians descended from the fruits of St Thomas's ancient missionary work. They had no awareness of the existence of Hinduism. Amazingly the first people the scout met upon reaching dry land were two Muslims from Tunis who could speak Castilian and Genoese. Unlike the peoples of East Africa's coastal cities, they immediately recognized who the strangers were. So they exclaimed and asked, 'May the Devil take thee! What brought you hither?' The convict possessing a firm grasp of both the spiritual and temporal goals of the expedition replied, 'Christians and spices.' They then took him to their home and fed him a meal of bread and honey. One of the Moors accompanied the convict back to the ships. Upon boarding he observed, 'A lucky venture, a lucky! Plenty of rubies, plenty of emeralds! You owe great thanks to God for having brought you to a country holding such riches!' He reported more details of India's vast wealth to Vasco da Gama and offered his services. The friendly Moor was named Monçaide and he immediately became a firm ally of the Portuguese. It seems likely that he was a Spanish Christian who had been taken captive as a young boy and raised as a Muslim, although he may simply have been a renegade Tunisian Muslim.[54]

The Portuguese spent several days at Capocate and continued to mistake its inhabitants for Christians. They found the people friendly enough but considered

Calicut. From Washington Irving et al., *The Discovery and Conquest of the New World* (Philadelphia, Syndicate Publishing, 1892), p. 53.

them to be practitioners of many strange customs. Probably most immediately disappointing for the crew, which had largely been at sea for eleven months, the local women were 'ugly and small of stature'. In the meantime Vasco da Gama sent two men along with Monçaide to visit the Zamorin of Calicut, who was the most powerful ruler in that region.[55] They were to inform him that ambassadors from the King of Portugal had arrived. The Zamorin was travelling in the countryside at that time but upon receiving this news, he was initially enthusiastic and sent word back that he would meet them at his chief town of Calicut.

On 27 May the Portuguese ships reached Pandarani, an anchorage close to Calicut. There a large band of natives informed them that the Zamorin awaited them at his palace in Calicut. The next morning on 28 May, Gama sat out with a group of thirteen other men. A friendly greeting awaited them ashore from a large escort party, which included a palanquin to carry Gama. Travelling on the road to Calicut, the men stopped at the town of Capua where a local noble fed the Portuguese. They then embarked on boats that carried them on the Elatur River to Calicut. Upon landing they took the road into the city. All along the way to Calicut large numbers of locals had gathered to gaze in wonder at the strangers.

Once the Portuguese entered Calicut they were taken to a Hindu pagoda which they mistook for a Christian church. Medieval travellers' lore and wishful thinking encouraged the Portuguese to see Christians everywhere. Statues of Hindu deities were erroneously identified as Christian saints. The bewildered Portuguese even thought they heard native priests chanting 'Maria, Maria' in adoration of the Virgin Mary. In fact they were worshipping some Hindu goddess such as Gauri, Maha Maja, Devaki or Mārī. The strangeness of the temple did not put off Vasco da Gama who paused to say prayers with his men. Not everyone among the Portuguese, however, was convinced that they were in a Christian church. As João de Sá knelt down to pray beside Gama, he made the aside, 'If those be devils [the Hindu statues], I worship the true God.' For the most part the Portuguese assumed that they had contacted some long-lost Indian Christians, who were perhaps a bit heretical but were still capable of being saved in terms of theology. Most importantly, they were potential allies against the hated Moors.[56]

Proceeding further into Calicut, the Portuguese found that the roads became so congested with curious onlookers that the way was blocked. At that point the Zamorin sent one of his officials with 2,000 soldiers to finish conducting Gama's party through the crowded streets. Even once they had arrived at and entered the palace they still had to continue forcing their way through the throng and even had to resort to violence. Finally the Portuguese came into the presence of the Zamorin who was reclining in splendour on a couch in a small courtyard surrounded by gold and silver vessels and chewing betel-nuts.

Once Gama and the Zamorin were face to face, a series of polite gestures followed that were intended to satisfy the demands of etiquette. Gama identified himself as the ambassador of the King of Portugal and asked for a private interview. The Zamorin agreed and the two men withdrew to a smaller chamber. There Gama described how the Portuguese had sought to reach India for many years, not for gold or silver but because they desired to be united with their fellow Christians of Asia. He then presented the Zamorin with two letters from King Manuel. In response the Zamorin agreed to send ambassadors back to Manuel in Portugal. By that time it was about 10.00 p.m. and the Portuguese spent the night in Calicut at the house of a Muslim official of the Zamorin.

Vasco da Gama before the Zamorin of Calicut. From Jules Verne, *Famous Travels and Travellers* (New York, Scribners, 1887), p. 174.

On 29 May, the next day, Gama prepared presents for the Zamorin which included hats, strings of coral, sugar and honey. But when the Zamorin's officials saw those gifts they laughed at them and said that the poorest merchant of Calicut could do better. They suggested that gold would have been a more appropriate gift and refused to send what they considered to be a paltry set of gifts onward. Meanwhile, local Moorish merchants joined in the mocking of the Portuguese gifts. Undaunted, Gama insisted on meeting with the Zamorin again which the officials agreed to arrange. Instead they left an increasingly irritated Gama waiting all day for his appointment. It was not until the next day that the officials came to escort Gama to the palace. There the Portuguese waited another 4 hours. At long last orders came for Gama and two others to proceed into the presence of the Zamorin. It was a tense situation and the Portuguese anticipated treachery.

When the three Portuguese saw the Zamorin, he proceeded to interrogate them about his presents and their poor quality. Gama made the excuse that the mission of his expedition had been discovery and not trade. To that the Zamorin somewhat petulantly asked if the Portuguese had come to discover stones or men? Realizing that the Zamorin was rather disappointed by the poor quality of their gifts, Gama promised that subsequent Portuguese visitors would arrive with richer offerings. Then the Zamorin asked for a reported golden statue of the Virgin Mary as a gift. Gama refused saying that the statue was not gold nor was it available as a present. By this juncture the Portuguese began to feel that the local Moors were speaking ill of them to the Zamorin. Still they continued to press the Zamorin for trading rights. Ultimately he agreed to let the Portuguese sell the samples of European merchandise that they had brought with them to the people of Calicut. He also excused them from paying port duties and customs.[57]

Unfortunately for the Portuguese, their relations with the local Muslim merchants and the Zamorin continued to deteriorate. Officials detained the Portuguese party at Pandarani. There were also continual requests for the Portuguese ships to enter the harbour which Gama and his men viewed with suspicion. Once the Portuguese landed their trade goods on the shore the local merchants refused to buy anything and treated the items with contempt. On 24 June at Gama's request the Zamorin had the Portuguese goods moved to Calicut but to no avail. Sales were sluggish and the Portuguese could only sell their merchandise at ruinously low prices. While the common people of the country were friendly to the Portuguese, the Muslim merchants exhibited open hostility. The Zamorin and his officials maintained a cold attitude toward their perplexing and increasingly unwelcome guests.

By early August Gama decided that it was time to return home to Portugal. So he sent Diogo Dias as an envoy to the Zamorin with more presents and a dual request for permission to depart and for the gift of some samples of various spices. Unfortunately on 13 August Dias found the Zamorin in a distinctly unfriendly mood. Instead of giving the Portuguese permission to sail and the requested spices, he demanded a large sum for customs and placed the Portuguese in Calicut under house arrest. Back at the ships, Gama and the rest of his men were appalled by such behaviour from a supposed Christian monarch. Monçaide and other local informants warned the

Portuguese that the Zamorin was plotting to kill the Portuguese captains and take the rest prisoner. Local Muslim merchants were stirring up the Zamorin by threatening a trade boycott against him. They were also spreading all sorts of unfavourable stories about the Portuguese throughout the region.

Determined to get his captive men back safely, Gama dissembled and allowed local traders to continue visiting his ships. But on 19 August he suddenly retaliated by taking six high-born natives hostage along with twelve others. Instead of negotiating, however, Gama abruptly sailed off with his prisoners on 23 August. That caused the Zamorin to rethink his actions and he started treating Diogo Dias with kindness. Contrary winds forced Gama's fleet back to Calicut and discussions for an exchange of captives along with the return of the remaining Portuguese trade goods followed. Officials of Calicut released Dias and the other Portuguese hostages to Gama on 27 August. The next day Monçaide fled to the safety of the Portuguese fleet. His property had been confiscated and his life threatened because the Muslim merchants believed that he was a Portuguese spy. Efforts to exchange the Portuguese goods for Indian prisoners broke down that same day. Finally on 29 August Gama ordered the fleet to sail as 'it appeared impossible to establish cordial relations with the people [of Calicut]'. He hoped that by taking the Indian captives back to Portugal they could learn Portuguese and later be used to establish friendly relations with the Zamorin.[58]

Proceeding north up the coast, the Portuguese viewed any approaching vessel with suspicion as possible pursuers from Calicut. Weak and contrary winds bedevilled their progress and it was not until 20 September that they reached the Anjediva Islands off the west coast of India. They stayed there until 5 October taking on water and wood for the voyage back to East Africa. While on Anjediva various stories reached them via the local fishermen about pursuers from Calicut. Later two galleys full of people approached but the Portuguese drove them off with their bombards. They also foiled a local pirate's plot to take them prisoner. All in all the Portuguese were not finding the coastal waters of western India to be a friendly place, so they decided to set off westward for Africa on 5 October.

Gama's decision to sail from Anjediva at the time he did and without a local pilot was a huge mistake. It was the wrong part of the monsoon cycle to be sailing west. The crossing took from 5 October to 2 January, a voyage of ninety horrible days. Calms and contrary winds rendered forward progress almost impossible. Scurvy appeared and eventually killed thirty crewmen. Each ship was reduced to having only seven or eight seamen who were barely healthy enough to sail it. By about 28 December the captains held a council in which they decided to return to India on the first favourable wind. Fortuitously, right at that time the direction of the monsoons finally shifted and within six days they carried the desperate fleet to Africa. First sighting Africa on 2 January, the next day they passed the Muslim town of Mogadishu. Instead of stopping there, they continued on to friendly Malindi which they reached on 7 January. There the locals treated the Portuguese hospitably once again and helped them to regain their health with supplies of oranges and other fruits.

The Portuguese rested for five days at Malindi and then on 11 January resumed their homeward voyage. By this time Gama's company had been so reduced in number that it was no longer possible to man all three ships. So on 13 January it was decided to scuttle the *São Raphael* at the shoals of São Rafael near Zanzibar. The Portuguese also rested there and spent fifteen days refitting the two remaining ships. Setting sail once more on 27 January, the Portuguese made their way down the East African coast and on 20 March rounded the Cape of Good Hope, where they suffered greatly from the cold. Another twenty-seven days at sea with the wind to their backs carried the Portuguese ships to the neighbourhood of Santiago in the Cape Verde Islands. A storm separated Gama in the *São Gabriel* and Nicolau Coelho in the *Berrio*. Coelho proceeded on to Portugal reaching home on 10 July. Gama at Santiago put João de Sá in command of the *São Gabriel* and sent him on to Portugal. Meanwhile, Gama hired a caravel to carry his ailing brother Paulo to the salubrious climate of Terceira in the Azores in a vain attempt to save his life. Sá arrived in Portugal before 28 August while Gama finally reached Lisbon no earlier than 29 August but no later than 9 September. One of the most significant voyages in human history had been concluded after an interval of a little over two years.

What had Vasco da Gama accomplished? Quite obviously he had completed a round-trip sea journey to India and so had bypassed all the traditional, existing trade routes. That achievement is commonly portrayed as an obvious and indisputable good that represented a manifest improvement over the old trade routes and was the logical and inevitable conclusion to a century of Portuguese exploration in coastal Africa. Nothing could be further from the truth. Gama's voyage clearly proved it was possible to sail to India and back. Whether it was feasible or worthwhile to sail there or not was considerably more problematic. Only two out of four ships in Gama's fleet made it back to Portugal. At least one-third and possibly over half of Gama's men died during the course of the voyage making it a highly dangerous journey as well as a long one. Some accounts claim that Gama's first trip was fantastically profitable thanks to the precious cargo of spices that he brought home. A more sober assessment indicates that the first passage to India was not lucrative nor was it intended to be so. It was a voyage of exploration and diplomacy. The question that remained was whether a commercial journey from Portugal to India could ever be money-making. Manuel I crowed in his letters to Fernando and Isabel of Spain and to the Cardinal-Protector of Portugal in Rome about the potential wealth that had come within Portugal's grasp. Venetian merchants also worried about the possibility of Portugal diverting the spice trade away from them.

Many in Portugal were not so convinced that Gama's voyage had opened up a great and viable opportunity for their little country. The way to India seemed too long, too dangerous and too costly. In fact, the costs of a round trip between Portugal and India were so high that the sea-road was not any more cost-effective than the traditional Indian Ocean and overland routes to the Mediterranean. Furthermore, connoisseurs of Asian spices soon proclaimed that the spices carried to Europe by the sea-route around Africa did not retain their flavour as well as those carried by caravan. In the end King Manuel plunged Portugal into establishing an Asian spice empire in spite of serious domestic opposition. He was motivated by reasons that went beyond mere mercantile considerations into crusading and millennial goals. In establishing the Portuguese presence in the world of the Asian spice trade, King Manuel and the Portuguese had to deal with another legacy left over from Vasco da Gama's first expedition. As a voyage of exploration, it had been successful. He showed that it was definitely possible to sail to India and back. In terms of its other mission – diplomacy – Gama's trip failed. His visceral suspicion of all Muslims and his willingness to resort quickly to violence against the African and Asian peoples meant that Portugal gained few friends. Except for the Sultan of Malindi, the other African and Indian rulers, including the Zamorin, who met Gama came away with a highly negative impression. Gama's high-handed actions were the result of his naturally blunt nature and his lack of knowledge about customs and conditions of trade in the world of the Indian Ocean. His behaviour, if anything, proves that Pero de Covilhã's reports about India never made it back home to Portugal, given Gama's blundering ignorance of Indian ways, particularly the debacle of the presents for the Zamorin.

Although local Muslim merchants regarded the Portuguese as a threat to the status quo of the Indian Ocean's system of trade, at first appearance Gama's fleet could not have appeared to be overly impressive. The arrival of three fairly small ships with only a bit over a hundred men in their total crews did not seem to herald an event of any great future significance to Asian history. However, 60 to 70 years earlier, the arrival of the massive Ming Chinese treasure ships in expeditions consisting of 20,000 soldiers and sailors were obviously more awe-inspiring. Memories of the Chinese fleet still lingered in Calicut at the time of the first visit of the Portuguese. They were bound to suffer in comparison. But it was the Portuguese who came to stay and created a lasting impact, not the Ming Chinese. Superior naval technology and a ruthless willingness to use it allowed the Portuguese quickly to gain control of a big portion of the Indian Ocean trade. It would need other Europeans, particularly the efficient Dutch, to take much of the Portuguese's spice empire away from them during the early seventeenth century. Gama's voyage permanently connected Europe with South and East Asia by sea and began an era of 400 years of European imperialism in Asia. But few people could have envisioned that result as the year 1499 drew to a close.

CHAPTER FIVE

COMPREHENDING THE AMERICAS – OUTLINING THE COASTLINE FOR A WAY TO ASIA

Our modern navigators have already discovered it [the Americas] to be no island, but terra firma, *and continent with the East Indies on the one side, and with the lands under the two poles on the other side, or, if it be separate from them, it is by so narrow a strait and channel, that it none the more deserves the name of an island for that.*

Michel de Montaigne (1580)[1]

America was too big to have been discovered all at one time. It would have been better for the graces if it had been discovered in pieces about the size of France and Germany at a time.

Samuel Butler (1883–7)[2]

During his first voyage of 1492–3, Christopher Columbus discovered islands that he thought were outliers of the Asian mainland. Most of his contemporaries initially agreed with his assessment but all of them were wrong. Two vast continents stood between Europe and Asia with coastlines that stretched interminably for thousands of miles to the north and to the south although no European knew that at that time. As Columbus and other explorers probed the waters around his first discoveries ever more widely, evidences of those two large landmasses accumulated. The new lands proved an unexpected obstacle to reaching Asia. Countless bays, inlets and river mouths were investigated but none proved to be a strait that led to Cathay and the Spice Islands. Several decades of attempts to find a way to the Far East through North and South America only served to reveal the broad outlines of their coasts. Later voyagers tried to pass to the south or to the north of the Americas. The circumnavigations of the earth by Ferdinand Magellan and those who followed him revealed a sea-road to Asia that was impractical due to its extreme difficulty. The northern voyages in search of north-west or north-east passages fared even less well. All ended in failure and some ended in death. The way to Asia did not lie through the Americas although vestiges of that dream continued to entice future explorers of North America into the seventeenth and the eighteenth centuries.

SETTLING HISPANIOLA AND THE DISCOVERY OF SOUTH AMERICA

When Christopher Columbus returned to Palos on 15 March 1493, completing his first western voyage, a wave of euphoria swept across Spain and much of Europe.

A new way to Asia apparently stood revealed. Not everyone, of course, was pleased by this turn of events. João II and the Portuguese muttered threats and grumbled about the way their laborious efforts to circumnavigate Africa to reach India had been suddenly rendered superfluous. The spice merchants of Venice also worried about the looming threat to their eastern trade posed by Columbus's discovery. For Spain and Columbus, the immediate task was to secure and to exploit the wonderful new route to Asia and its limitless riches.

Fernando and Isabel quickly arranged for Columbus to make a second voyage back to Hispaniola and the settlement of Navidad.[3] His new fleet consisted of 17 ships and 1,200 people. Columbus and the Spanish officials readied the expedition to sail in about seven months and it departed from Cadiz on 25 September 1493. As on his first journey, Columbus stopped off at the Canary Islands for rest and resupply from 2 to 12 October. From there he and his ships set out across the Atlantic Ocean, only this time he sailed further south. The voyage went smoothly and on 3 November the fleet sighted the island of Dominica in the Lesser Antilles. Having made landfall south of Hispaniola, the Spanish fleet began to work its way northward through the Leeward Islands of Guadaloupe, St Croix and others.

Based on information he had gathered from the Taino or Arawak Indians of Hispaniola, Columbus knew that he was in the territory of the formidable and reputedly man-eating Caribs. Landing on Guadaloupe, the Spanish sighted some villages. The inhabitants ran off when the Spanish approached, but eventually the sailors managed to capture some of the natives and questioned them. A number turned out to be Arawaks, who were the captives of the dominant Caribs. They were happy to be rescued by the Spanish and denounced the Caribs as warlike cannibals who preyed on their peaceful neighbours. Gruesome accounts accumulated of the Caribs feasting on the flesh of enemy warriors and raising the children of captives to be eventually slaughtered for meat.[4] Such stories, true or not, were just what the Spanish wanted to hear. Cannibals forfeited the normal rights to humane treatment as required by the Christian church. The Spanish could execute and enslave the supposedly man-eating Caribs at will. Reports of cannibals or anthrophagi also indicated that Asia must be near as man-eating people were one of the monstrous races who lived in the eastern-most parts of the region.

The alleged brutality and bestiality of the Caribs brought out the same traits in the Spanish. Whereas during his first voyage, Columbus had viewed the natives as innocents, he and his companions had no hesitation about attacking suspected Caribs, even in the absence of provocation. Near St Croix on 14 October one of Columbus's boats attacked a Carib canoe with four men and two women in it. All six resisted fiercely and shot many arrows at the Spanish.[5] One Carib suffered beheading while another refused to surrender in spite of a horrific abdominal wound and was thrown into the sea. Eventually he succumbed to wounds from Spanish arrows as he trod water while bleeding to death. Columbus gave one of the female captives to Miguel de Cuneo, a fellow Italian, who proceeded noisily to rape her in his ship's cabin.[6] From the point of view of future enterprises in the new western island, the most ominous fact arising out of the encounters with Caribs was their indomitable courage and fighting skills. It appeared that these people would be every bit as difficult to conquer as the natives of the Canaries who doggedly resisted European domination for almost a century. Given these circumstances, bringing these islands under Spanish control might prove to be much more difficult than Columbus had originally thought.[7]

From St Croix, Columbus's fleet sailed on through the Virgin Islands and along Puerto Rico, finally crossing the Mona Passage to reach Hispaniola on 22 November. Cruising along the northern coast of Hispaniola, they reached the site of Navidad on the night of 27 November. The next day a horrified Columbus and his men discovered that Navidad had been destroyed and its settlers had all been killed. The natives also proved to be shy or stand-offish. When some of the friendly Chief Guacanagari's tribe were questioned, they blamed the tragedy on the warriors of Chief Canoabó who had raided the area. At the same time Guacanagari's people complained bitterly about the settlers stealing women and provisions and generally rendering themselves obnoxious. Those complaints and the fact that the local natives possessed loot from Navidad led the Spanish to suspect that Guacanagari's people had also played a role in the destruction of the outpost.[8] Columbus decided to accept Guacanagari's story since the chief's value as a friend and an ally outweighed any satisfaction that might arise from punishing him for the loss of Navidad.

Shifting through the ruins of Navidad, the Spanish came to the conclusion that it was a poor and unhealthy site for a permanent colony. Moving eastward down the coast, the fleet arrived at the location for the new settlement of Isabel on 2 January 1494. The expedition set to work building new dwellings although Isabel would quickly prove to be as unfavourable a site as Navidad had been. At the beginning of February, Antonio Torres, one of Columbus's captains, led twelve ships back to Cadiz in the fantastic time of thirty-five days. Upon arriving at Cadiz, Torres submitted a memorandum suggesting the enslavement of the Caribs, an indication that notions about easy profits from gold and spices were disappearing.

Columbus, back at Isabel, was more anxious to resume his quest for the Asian mainland, rather than seeing to the establishment of a stable colony on Hispaniola. On 24 April he sailed for Cuba, which all previous testimony of the natives had accurately informed him was an island. Columbus, on the contrary, had convinced himself it was actually the Chinese province of Mangi. Sailing along the south coast of Cuba, Columbus also made a side trip and discovered Jamaica on 5 May 1494. Navigating the tricky waters of the southern Cuban coastline, Columbus reach Bahia Cortés on 13 June and, at that point, decided to turn around. Although he failed to find any signs of the great kingdom of Cathay and despite continued native reports to the contrary, Columbus compelled his crew to swear that they had been sailing along the Asian mainland. Those who might dare to say otherwise later were subject to huge fines, whippings and having their tongues cut out.[9] Sailing eastward, adverse winds and currents along the coast forced Columbus to move out to sea again and visit

Jamaica for a second time. After considerable difficulty, Columbus and his three ships finally returned to Isabel on 29 September 1494 after an absence of five months.

Columbus's failure to locate any of the great ports of Cathay, of the Golden Chersonese or of fabled Cipangu constituted merely one of his growing problems. Sickness ravaged the settlers at Isabel, provisions were running short, the supposed spices of Hispaniola proved illusory and the gold mines had yielded only the most paltry amounts of the precious metal. The surviving colonists daily grew more sullen, while revolts against Columbus's authority flared up. Most of the disgruntled longed to leave wretched Isabel and return home to Spain. Meanwhile, they took out their frustrations on the natives through egregious acts of cruelty and the gross exploitation of Indian labour and women. The once-friendly natives grew steadily more hostile even if they managed to avoid enslavement, mutilation or death. A major native uprising led by Chief Guatiguana broke out in March 1495, but Columbus managed to suppress it. The promised opportunities for wealth and missionary work that Columbus's first voyage had unveiled were diminishing rapidly and irrevocably as the true nature of Hispaniola revealed itself. It was not a land of wealth and the growing opinion among other navigators was that Hispaniola and Cuba were nowhere near the Asian mainland, let alone part of it.

Columbus and his brothers Diego and Bartholomew proved to be poor administrators and quickly made themselves widely unpopular among the Spanish colonists. That they were Italians and therefore foreigners only aggravated the growing disdain that the Spanish felt toward them. Finally on 10 March Columbus sailed for Spain in an effort to shore up royal support for his floundering colony. He also left orders with his brother Bartholomew to move the Spanish settlement from Isabel to a new and better-placed location. The new town was called Santo Domingo; it is the oldest European city in the Americas. Columbus's return voyage to Spain turned out to be a slow passage. Instead of sailing directly to Cadiz, he detoured to Guadaloupe to pick up cassava for provisions. That side trip delayed his actual departure until 20 April. Even then Columbus did not reach Cape St Vincent on the Spanish coast until 8 June, arriving at Cadiz on 11 June 1496.

By the completion of Columbus's second voyage, enthusiasm for settling Hispaniola had faded among King Fernando, Queen Isabel and their subjects.[10] They would probably have abandoned the colony as an expensive failure except for two international developments. News of the impending voyages of Vasco da Gama to India and John Cabot westward across the North Atlantic in 1497 served to renew their commitment to Columbus's enterprise for fear they would lose the quest for Asian riches to another country. There were also rumours floating about that João II and the Portuguese suspected that an unknown southern continent existed in the South Atlantic to the west of Africa. Fernando and Isabel wanted to locate that continent before the Portuguese. So on 23 April 1497 they ordered Columbus to begin organizing a third voyage to the west in the hopes of salvaging the deteriorating situation at Hispaniola and of discovering a rich, new, antipodal continent.

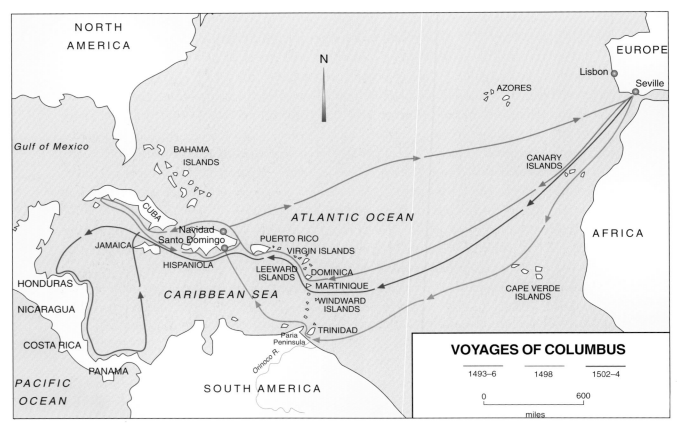

The later voyages of Columbus.

Approximately one month later John Cabot sailed from Bristol and a little over two months later Vasco da Gama commenced his momentous voyage to India.

Preparations for Columbus's third journey proceeded with painful slowness.[11] It was obvious that the monarchs had lost confidence in him. Their instructions for the expedition and its goals were so detailed as to leave him with little discretion. His fleet was also significantly smaller than that of the second voyage – only eight ships, including the faithful *Niña*. Accompanying Columbus were 300 men and 30 women hoping to create a stable, prosperous settlement on Hispaniola.

Columbus and his fleet embarked on his third western voyage from Seville on 30 May 1498, twelve days after Vasco da Gama's arrival on the coast of India, although neither party would have been aware of that synchronicity. The fleet stopped off at the Madeiras and then at the Canaries. There Columbus directed three supply ships on how to sail directly to Hispaniola while he and the remaining ships would continue on a voyage of exploration. Sailing south to the Cape Verde Islands, Columbus's flotilla stayed there for several days replenishing their supplies of wood and water. From the Cape Verdes the ships struck out on to the high seas of the Atlantic Ocean on 4 July. Columbus had definite reasons for sailing so far south. One motivation was that he

Santo Domingo in the sixteenth century. From Washington Irving et al., *The Discovery and Conquest of the New World* (Philadelphia, Syndicate Publishing, 1892), p. 270.

hoped to locate the suspected southern continent. Another factor made that first goal even more desirable. Aristotelian science taught that regions in similar latitudes produced similar people, animals, plants and minerals. Africa in the region of Cape Verde produced gold. If a new southern continent could be found at a similar latitude to the west, it should also possess a rich supply of gold, something that Columbus needed to revive his sinking fortunes with the Spanish monarchs.

The third voyage across the Atlantic Ocean was fairly uneventful. In spite of being becalmed in the stifling heat of the doldrums from 13 to 22 July, the fleet sighted the mountains of Trinidad on 31 July after a voyage of only twenty-seven days. Columbus named the island Trinidad because of the three mountains that he had first seen at sea and as a way to honour the Holy Trinity. The next day the Spanish landed on the island to replenish their supplies of fresh water. On the following day a large canoe carrying twenty-four well-armed natives approached. Although violence was avoided, there was little communication between the parties either.[12]

Columbus could also see other lands in the distance to the south. What he saw was the South American mainland, although he did not realize how big a landmass it really was. Instead, he assumed the distant shorelines were part of another large island like Trinidad. Travelling into the Gulf of Paria, the Spanish ships encountered various dangerous sailing conditions caused by the massive outflow of the Orinoco River and the narrowness of the straits. While in the Gulf of Paria, Columbus also experienced either a tidal bore or a tidal wave that threatened to sink his ships and caused great fear among the crews. After surviving that terrifying experience, the fleet sailed north across the Gulf of Paria where on 5 August a party from the fleet went ashore at Ensenada Yacua, the first European landing on the South American mainland. They laid formal claim to the new territory for Spain, although whether Columbus came ashore and participated in the ceremony in person is unclear. Along the coast of the Gulf of Paria they encountered villages whose inhabitants appeared to possess copious amounts of gold and pearls. Aristotle's science was seemingly vindicated and Columbus developed high hopes that a Spanish settlement in the region eventually would produce wealth on the scale of Portugal's El Mina in Africa.

Relations with the natives, as on the first voyage, remained peaceful. Contrary to another aspect of Aristotle's theory of latitudes, the natives were tawny like those of the islands, not black like their supposed counterparts living on the Guinea Coast of Africa. The unflappable Columbus remained untroubled by that anomalous situation. His spirits rose as he contemplated the lucrative possibilities presented by the new land. He also came to the correct conclusion that he had actually found a new continent. As he later wrote to Fernando and Isabel, 'I believe that this land which Your Highnesses have sent [me] to discover is very extensive and that there are many other lands in the south of which there has never been any report.'[13] Furthermore, he asserted that he was near the location of the early Paradise or the Garden of Eden. The great Orinoco was one of the four rivers of Paradise. This claim was not simply Columbus's attempt to convince his sovereign how wonderful his latest discovery was. It was, however, another way for Columbus to argue that the Asian mainland was near. As he reminded Fernando and Isabel in the course of a rambling geographical argument about the shape of the earth that involved pears and human breasts, 'all the learned theologians agree that the earthly Paradise is in the East'.[14] After several days of exploring the Gulf of Paria, Columbus sailed out of the northern strait and into the Caribbean Sea. He then sailed west along the coastline for a couple more days until on 15 August he turned north and headed for Hispaniola. Sighting Hispaniola on 19 August, Columbus finally brought his fleet into the harbour of Santo Domingo on 31 August 1498.

Columbus's arrival did not prove to be joyous. Santo Domingo seethed with discontent, hatred and cruelty. Fevers and syphilis raged among the colonists. Their diet was poor. The Spanish settlers despised Bartholomew Columbus as a foreigner and considered him to be incompetent and tyrannical. They also bitterly resented the failure of quick and easy wealth in the form of gold to materialize as promised. Renegade Spaniards under the leadership of Francisco Roldán had taken to the countryside in armed bands which terrorized the natives in a greedy quest for gold and women. Meanwhile, some natives of Hispaniola were dragged into the internecine struggles of the Spanish as willing or unwilling allies. Others were forced into the slow-motion death of slavery in the mines. Some native groups plotted rebellion against the foreign oppressors and refused to pay tribute. It was an ugly, volatile situation.[15]

Columbus set about trying to restore order to the Spanish colony on Hispaniola. On 18 October 1498 he sent five ships back to Spain carrying brazilwood, Indian slaves and those disgruntled colonists who had had their fill of Hispaniola and wanted to return home. Various attempts were made to bring Roldán back into obedience. Those efforts culminated in an agreement of September 1499 that restored Roldán to his former office of alcalde and absolved him of his previous misdeeds. But while Roldán transformed himself into a supporter of Columbus, there were plenty of others to take his place as a rebel. Instability, insubordination and conspiracy continued to plague the fledgling colony. Still, Columbus managed to make some noticeable progress during 1500. Unfortunately for him, too many unfavourable reports had reached the ears of Fernando and Isabel back in Spain. Concerned with the chronic strife on Hispaniola and the increasing enslavement of the natives, they sent Francisco Bobadilla to investigate and to restore order. Arriving at Santo Domingo on 23 August 1500, Bobadilla observed the rotting corpses of seven rebels hung by Columbus. That gruesome sight only served to confirm for Bobadilla the truth of the many reports about the cruel tyranny of the government of the Columbus family. Bobadilla immediately arrested Diego Columbus and when Columbus and his brother Bartholomew returned from expeditions into the countryside, he imprisoned them. In October he sent the three Columbus brothers back to Spain in chains.

Columbus was outraged by the injustice of the treatment meted out by Bobadilla. Although the embarrassed captain of the ship carrying him to Spain offered to remove his chains, Columbus refused until the Spanish monarchs had issued a direct order for it to be done. Writing a distraught letter to Fernando and Isabel, he reminded them of his valuable accomplishments and detailed the indignities heaped on him by his enemies. After reading his letter, the royal couple ordered him to be freed and invited him to court as a show of their gratitude for his past service. They did not, however, restore him to a position of authority over the colony on Hispaniola. Columbus had lost their confidence in his leadership and administrative abilities forever. On that low ebb of fortune, Columbus's third voyage ended.

Even before Bobadilla arrested Columbus, the monarchs had decided no longer to rely on Columbus to direct further western explorations. When Columbus's letters arrived at the Spanish court on 11 December 1498, they described the discovery of South America, the great stock of pearls and the continuing troubles on Hispaniola. After reading them, King Fernando quickly concluded that it was time to get others besides the unreliable Columbus involved in trans-Atlantic exploration. The wily King excused his violation of Columbus's privileges by citing Columbus's failure to go ashore at the Gulf of Paria during the ceremony claiming the new land for Spain. The great explorer, his family and supporters would hotly contest that assertion for years to come. It was to no avail at the time as others were quickly brought in to explore the new continent. Their eleven voyages took place between 1499 and 1506 and would collectively come to be known as the Andalusian or the Minor Voyages.[16] These, along with Columbus's fourth trip, would reveal the outline of the eastern coast of much of Central and South America.

Alonso de Ojeda, a captain who had sailed with Columbus on his second expedition, commanded the first voyage to South America. This consisted of four ships and

A nineteenth-century painting showing Columbus returning to Spain in chains at the end of his third voyage, by Lorenzo Delleani. (Galleria d'Arte Moderna, Genova/Art Resource, NY)

included another of Columbus's companions, Juan de la Cosa, as well as Amerigo Vespucci. Departing from near Cadiz on 18 May 1499, the fleet made a stand stop-over at the Canaries before taking to the high seas for an eventual landfall along the Guiana coast near Cape Orange after a period of only twenty-four to twenty-six days. At this point the expedition may have split up with Vespucci taking two ships and sailing south.[17] He claimed to have explored the mouth of the mighty Amazon and to have passed below the equator to a point just beyond the Turiaçu River. He would later rejoin Ojeda and the other two ships. Ojeda, on the other hand, sailed north since his goal was the Gulf of Paria and the rich pearl fisheries previously visited by Columbus on his third voyage. From there, Ojeda explored further down the coast, seeking gold and pearls but obtaining little of either. He discovered the islands of Bonaire, Curaçao and Aruba and sailed into the Gulf of Maracaibo where he observed Indians living over the water in houses built on stilts. It reminded the Spanish of Venice and they named the region Venezuela, i.e., 'little Venice'. Ojeda had reached as far west as Cape de la Vela when he decided to make for Hispaniola in late August

1499. After spending some time fruitlessly harassing Columbus and his people on Hispaniola, he moved on to the Bahamas for some slave-raiding. By late spring or early summer 1500 Ojeda had returned to Spain and managed to obtain a licence for a second voyage one year later. Ojeda's expedition and that of Vespucci revealed a substantial portion of the coastline of northern South America, but failed to make contact with the longed-for Asian mainland. In that respect, it turned out to be a definite disappointment. Ojeda also showed on several occasions a marked tendency to abuse the natives until they turned hostile, at which point he used extreme violence against them. In this unsavoury trait, Ojeda revealed an unpleasant nature that was by no means unique among the early European visitors to the Americas.[18]

Amerigo Vespucci. From Justin Winsor, *Narrative and Critical History of America* (Boston, Houghton Mifflin, 1886), vol. 2, p. 141.

Peralonso Niño, another of Columbus's companions from his first and second voyages, organized the second non-Columbian journey to South America. In early June 1499 he and Cristóbal Guerra sailed from the Rio Tinto in a single caravel. Because they followed the route of Columbus's third trip, they arrived directly at Trinidad and the Gulf of Paria in late July, well before Ojeda, who had departed two weeks before they did. Unlike Ojeda, Niño experienced considerable success in trading with the natives of the Venezuelan coast for their pearls. Sailing back to Spain in mid-February, adverse winds caused their crossing to take sixty-one days before they made landfall in Galicia in northern Spain. They toured no new coastline, but their cargo of pearls generated considerable excitement and stimulated renewed interest in exploration.[19]

Vicente Yañez Pinzón, the captain of the *Niña* on Columbus's first voyage and the brother of Martín Pinzón, was in charge of the third Andalusian journey to South America. Departing from Palos on 18 November 1499 with four caravels, he made his way to the Cape Verdes. After resting and resupplying his ships, he sailed for South America on 6 January 1500. Strong winds pushed his fleet across the Atlantic Ocean in a mere twenty days and on 26 January he arrived at Cape St Roque, which is located at 5°S latitude. If one rejects Amerigo Vespucci's somewhat suspect claims about his separate voyage during the Ojeda expedition in 1499, Pinzón becomes the first European to cross the equator on the American side of the Atlantic. Like his predecessors, Pinzón turned north after making landfall since his destination was Trinidad, Paria and the pearl coast. During this five-month voyage, he encountered the Amazon which he thought must be the River Ganges. Pinzón believed he was coasting along the Asian mainland, rather than some unknown southern continent. Meeting various groups of Indians living along the shore, he found some to be friendly while others were hostile. The basic problem was that none of the cooperative Indians possessed pearls to trade, which turned his expedition into a profitless venture. He then sailed for Santo Domingo on Hispaniola and arrived there on 23 June 1500. While returning to Spain in July, Pinzón's ships encountered a hurricane in the Bahamas with disastrous results. Eventually the flotilla reached Palos on 29 September 1500, although half of the crews and two of the four original ships had been lost.

From the point of view of exploration, Ojeda and Pinzón had revealed the existence of an unbroken coastline from Cape St Roque in the south to Cape de la Vela in the west. While Pinzón thought this landmass was part of Asia, something Columbus was inclined to agree with, others speculated that it was a previously unknown continent that was possibly connected to Asia by some sort of land-bridge.[20] Pinzón also preceded Pedro Cabral in the discovery of Brazil, but the Treaty of Tordesillas in 1494 had given any land in that longitude to Portugal. Instead, credit for revealing the existence of Brazil, which eventually led to a permanent European colony, is given to Cabral who made landfall on the Brazilian coast at Mount Pascoal, well to the south of Cape St Roque, on 22 April 1500.[21]

Diego de Lepe led a fourth Andalusian voyage to South America during December 1499. Apart from making a landfall slightly further south, however, Lepe followed Pinzón's route and made no further geographical discoveries. Of course, to Lepe it was all new since he had no idea that Pinzón had preceded him or what had been accomplished.[22] He also beat Cabral to Brazil for what that was worth given the terms of the Treaty of Tordesillas. Another expedition headed by Alonso Vélez de Mendoza and Luis Guerra sailed from Spain for South America sometime soon after 18 August 1500. Sighting land at Cape St Agostinho, they sailed south to some point between 10° and 20°S latitude before returning to Spain.[23] There were no new findings and the Spanish tried to recoup their expenses by cutting logwood and raiding for slaves among the natives, which provoked fierce resistance by the Tupi tribe who managed to kill some of Mendoza and Guerra's men. Mendoza and Guerra, like Ojeda shortly before them, were setting the dismal general pattern for relations between Native Americans and Europeans in the early period of contact.

Rodrigo de Bastides, a merchant of Seville, obtained a royal licence to sail west on 5 June 1500. More important for the ultimate success of his enterprise, he persuaded the experienced Juan de la Cosa to be his partner on the voyage. Their licence, however, forbade them to land on the pearl coast; they were required to sail further west. Leaving Spain in late February 1501, Bastides and Cosa and their two ships reached South America in early May somewhere in the vicinity of Trinidad. They sailed on westward until they reached Cape de la Vela. From that point onward, the fleet investigated new coasts and traded with the natives, eventually accumulating three chests of gold. Working their way down the coast of present-day Columbia, they continued along the coast of Panama to the Island of the Pines or possibly even as far as the site of Puerto de Escrivanos. If the latter western terminus is correct, Bastides reached the location of Columbus's Puerto de Retrete some eighteen months before the Admiral did. Unlike other Spanish captains, Bastides dealt fairly with the Native Americans, although he did do some slaving. The voyage proved profitable for Bastides despite all of the trouble he experienced from officials at both Hispaniola and Spain when he returned in September 1502. Thanks to his voyage, the existence of a continuous coastline for the great southern landmass had been extended to the southern end of present-day Central America.[24]

As Bastides was expanding the known limits of the great southern continent northward, Amerigo Vespucci sailed for the new land on his second voyage. Vespucci's intention had been to sail again for Spain and partner with Velez de Mendoza or some other individual with a licence to explore. Unfortunately for him, on 18 August 1500 Fernando and Isabel issued an order forbidding Mendoza from taking foreigners on his expedition. Vespucci found himself involuntarily at a loose end in Spain. Rumours that he had developed a practical technique to measure longitude attracted the attention of King Manuel of Portugal who needed to know just how much of the land of Brazil discovered by Pedro Cabral belonged to Portugal. As a result Vespucci and the Portuguese fleet of three ships sailed from Lisbon on 13 May 1501. Stopping off at the Cape Verde Islands to refresh their supplies, the three vessels sailed in a south-westerly direction across the Atlantic. It was a slow passage and, after sixty-four days at sea, they finally made landfall at Cape St Roque. From there they cruised south along the South American coast to possibly as far as 40°S latitude in the region of Patagonia. Along the way Vespucci spent considerable time studying the native tribes. From the safety of his ship he observed one of his luckless companions being killed and eaten by the locals. His researches also revealed the women of Brazil to be a lusty lot not at all adverse to using various mysterious herbal potions to enhance the performance of their flagging male partners.

Like the expeditions before him, Vespucci's voyage revealed nothing but a continuous coastline. He had failed to find a passage through to Asia, although he did add considerably to European knowledge of the east coast of South America. Vespucci's experience convinced him that the mysterious southern continent was not part of Asia. In this opinion Vespucci was by no means alone. Juan de la Cosa had vaguely advanced the same idea in his famous world map of 1500 and others held similar theories. Where Vespucci differed was that when he returned to Portugal in about July 1502 he recorded his adventures and geographical findings in some pamphlets that quickly became very popular. Sex and violence sold books in the early sixteenth century every bit as well as they have in later ages. Vespucci's narrative contained plenty of blood-thirsty cannibals and wanton exotic females. He also unequivocally expressed the opinion that the mysterious southern continent was a new world. In contrast, Columbus went to his grave insisting that Asia was just west of Hispaniola and Cuba, despite mounting evidence that he was wrong.

Columbus was not the self-publicist that Vespucci was. Apart from Columbus's letter of 1493 to Luis Santangel describing his first voyage, little or nothing was known about his later expeditions outside Spain, including his third trip which discovered South America in 1498. Furthermore, Vespucci's popular pamphlet *Quattour Navigationes* (1504) contained the spurious claim that he had made a voyage in 1497 which discovered South America, a year ahead of Columbus. Whether Vespucci or some publisher anxious to sell books concocted this tale is unclear, but its impact on the history of geographical knowledge is abundantly obvious. Given the information available, it is not at all surprising that the cartographer Martin Waldseemuller chose to name the new continent America after Vespucci and entirely ignored Columbus's crucial contributions. As Waldseemuller explained it: 'Since another fourth part [of the world] has been discovered by Americus Vesputius (as will be seen in what follows), I do not see why anyone should object to its being called after Americus the discoverer, a man of natural wisdom, Land of Americus or America, since both Europe and Asia have derived their names from women.' His naming of the new continent America roused the anger of the Spanish from the start. They rejected the appellation and persisted for over a century in calling the new lands the Indies. Among other Europeans the title America caught on even though a chastened Waldseemuller removed it from the maps of the next edition of his world atlas. Vespucci eventually became immortalized in the name of two continents, North America and South America, even though in terms of recognition Columbus possessed the greater historical name by far. Fortunately for the highly strung and touchy Columbus, he died in 1506, the year before Waldseemuller's most famous atlas appeared.[25]

Columbus was able to make one last western voyage between his return in chains and in disgrace to Spain in 1500 and his death in 1506.[26] Ever persistent, Columbus managed during February and March 1502 to persuade Fernando and Isabel to undertake one more enterprise, even if he could not convince them to restore him as governor of Hispaniola. Departing from Seville on 11 May, his fourth expedition roughly followed the same route as his second and made landfall at the end of its Atlantic crossing at Martinique. Sailing for Hispaniola, the alert Columbus tried to warn Nicholas de Ovando, the new governor at Santo Domingo, of an impending hurricane. Ovando contemptuously ignored Columbus's forecast and sent the bulk of his fleet back to Spain. It was a disastrous decision. The hurricane struck on 30 June catching the ships at sea. Most of the vessels foundered and sank and many in the company were drowned, including Columbus's old nemesis Francisco Bobadilla.

Columbus and his ships weathered the tempest and on 14 July he set out from Hispaniola on a new voyage of exploration. He called it his High Voyage and its purpose was to find a passage through the newly discovered southern lands that would lead to the East Indies and their spices. Some people, mainly Columbus, continued to regard Cuba as part of the mainland of China. To the south, the new continent

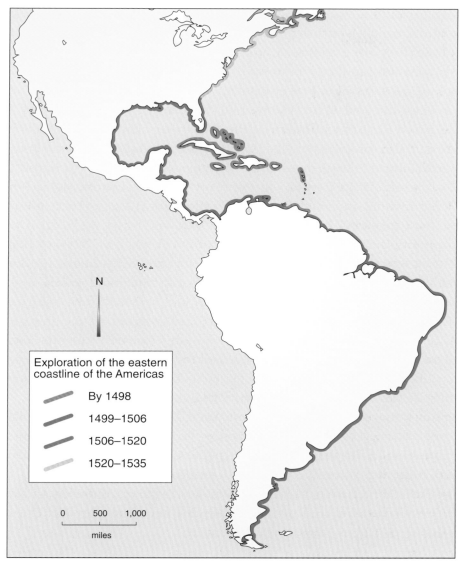

The growth in knowledge about the Americas.

blocked the way to the Spice Islands and India, which were also near, or so people thought. Columbus hoped to find a strait that would take him into the Indian Ocean. On 30 July his fleet reached the coast of Honduras at Bonacca Island. Here the Spanish came upon an extremely large trading canoe that came from the periphery of the Mayan lands to the west and north. Although this encounter was intriguing, Columbus decided to continue pursuing his goal of locating a strait to the Indian Ocean. He sailed east along the Honduran coast to Cape Gracias á Dios. It proved to be a terrible trip through adverse conditions of wind, current and weather that took until 14 September to complete. From Cape Gracias á Dios the coast trended southward and Columbus learned from the natives that he was sailing along a narrow isthmus. But since these communications were conducted in sign language, Columbus also erroneously determined that the Ganges lay some ten days' journey away.[27] He also reached the conclusion that no strait to the Indian Ocean existed and that Asia and the newly discovered southern continent were connected by the isthmus. In addition he believed that the isthmus was the biblical land of Ophir, a region famous for producing gold.[28] Columbus cruised the Panamanian coast, which he called Veragua, looking for gold mines in miserable, wet weather. On 24 January 1503 he established the settlement of Belen at the Rio Belen. During the weeks that the Spanish stayed there, supplies dwindled, gold remained elusive, the local natives grew steadily hostile and it rained incessantly. Meanwhile, teredo worms bored into the hulls of Columbus's ships rendering them increasingly unseaworthy. Finally on 16 April Columbus abandoned Belen and sailed down the coast reaching Cape Tiburon on the Panama/Columbia border on 1 May.

From Cape Tiburon Columbus decided to sail north and head back to Hispaniola. By this time he had already been forced to abandon two of his four ships due to the damage inflicted on their hulls by the teredos. His two remaining vessels were only in slightly better condition. By 12 May Columbus had reached the Cuban coast but contrary winds and currents slowed his eastward progress. Desperate to reach Hispaniola in his leaky ships, Columbus made for Jamaica, but by the time he reached that island on 23 June his two ships had reached the point where they were no longer seaworthy. Columbus and his surviving crew, including his adolescent son Ferdinand, found themselves marooned on Jamaica until 29 June 1504, one year later.

The story of Columbus's long stay on Jamaica is a saga of heroism and villainy. On 8 July Diego Mendez courageously set out across the 100 miles of sea in an open canoe in an attempt to reach Hispaniola. He managed to make it at the cost of considerable danger and suffering. But once he arrived on Hispaniola during August 1503 he found that Governor Ovando had no interest in rescuing Columbus and his men. Ten months elapsed before the persistent Mendez managed to cajole Ovando into sending a ship to pick up the survivors on Jamaica.

Back on Jamaica, Columbus faced mounting problems. Discontent with Columbus's leadership grew as months passed and no rescue ships from Hispaniola arrived. On 2 January 1504 the troublesome Porras brothers led a mutiny. They advocated trying to reach Hispaniola in open canoes like Mendez had done. Their efforts, however, failed. They never even managed to leave the coast of Jamaica. All they accomplished was to increase the alienation of the natives by robbing them of canoes and other resources to no good purpose. As it was, the natives living near the site of Columbus's camp were already growing restless. While inclined to be hospitable, a hundred, non-productive European mouths to feed was severely taxing their food supply. With no end in sight, they felt that their hospitality was definitely being abused. Sensing the native's growing hostility, Columbus cleverly used his knowledge of an impending eclipse of the moon on 29 February to awe the natives and to convince them of the supernatural powers of the Europeans. As a result, the Jamaicans fearfully continued to provide their unwelcome visitors with food. The

Porras brothers proved to be implacable in their opposition to Columbus. In spite of their earlier dismal failure to take charge of the expedition, they remained unchastened. Of course, they were aided by the deepening despair among the Spanish castaways as week after week went by and no rescuers from Hispaniola appeared. By 19 May the Porrases managed to stir up a second mutiny that resulted in a pitched battle in which Columbus and his loyalists emerged victorious.

In the meantime, Mendez finally managed to secure permission to charter a caravel to go and pick up Columbus and his men. It reached Jamaica during late June and loaded everyone on board. The voyage back to Santo Domingo in the lone, over-crowded caravel was perilous but they arrived safely on 13 August. Ever ungracious, Governor Ovando did nothing to make Columbus feel welcome. A month later on 12 September Columbus sailed for Spain and arrived on 7 November 1504 at Sanlucar de Barrameda. Unfortunately for him, slightly more than two weeks later on 26 November, his protector Queen Isabel died ending even the most remote hope for Columbus to regain his control over the explorations and new settlements across the Atlantic Ocean. King Fernando maintained a significantly more sceptical attitude towards Columbus as an explorer, as an administrator and as a man. All Columbus's efforts to get the King to restore him to his governorship came to nothing. Instead, the ageing and bitter adventurer continued to work on his apocalyptic *Book of Prophecies*, which linked his discoveries to a future restoration of Jerusalem to Christian control, and his legalistic *Book of Privileges*, which recorded in tedious and unrealistic detail all his rights over the newly discovered islands and their wealth.[29] Popular history portrays Columbus dying in poverty and obscurity, a lonely genius. In fact, he died rich, possessed of a hereditary title of nobility, and was a well-known, if somewhat eccentric, figure in Spain. Columbus was unpopular in some quarters when his end came on 20 May 1506, but for that he only had his own defects of personality to blame.[30]

Columbus's fourth voyage added greatly to European knowledge about the coastline of the vast southern continent. By the end of 1504 an unbroken shoreline was known to extend from around 40°S latitude on the coast of Argentina northward to the present-day location of Nicaragua. By the middle of the first decade of the sixteenth century, Europeans were aware of the existence and the eastern outline of a previously unsuspected continent which is now known as South America. It marked a revolution in traditional geographical concepts and took less than ten years to accomplish – from Columbus's first landing on South America in 1498 to the conclusion of his fourth voyage in 1504. What lay further to the north was still unclear and would remain rather vague for another quarter of a century or longer. Meanwhile, the predicted strait through South America continued to elude the mariners of Europe.

In 1513 significant progress was made and well documented with Vasco Núñez Balboa's expedition. Balboa and his men cut their way through the savage jungles of Panama and climbed over its rugged terrain between 1 and 29 September. He was the first European to gaze upon the Pacific Ocean from the east and took possession of the great South Sea for Spain. His trek proved conclusively that an ocean leading to

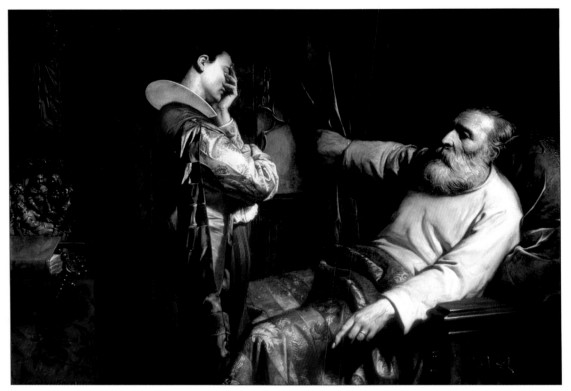

A nineteenth-century painting depicting the death of Columbus, by Claude Jaquand. (Musée des Beaux-Arts André Malraux, Le Havre, France/Bridgeman Art Library)

Asia existed on the other side of Panama, just as the natives had told Columbus ten years before. What was needed was the discovery of a western water route from Europe through to that South Sea or the Pacific Ocean.[31]

Various undocumented or vaguely recorded voyages continued to comb the coastline of South America for a passage to Balboa's South Sea. The Portuguese captain Estéban Froes apparently first discovered the estuary of the Rio de la Plata during a voyage of 1511–12. In the aftermath of Balboa's expedition to the South Sea, the Spanish government decided to locate the strait that linked the South Sea with the Atlantic. The result was Juan de Solis's expedition to the Rio de la Plata in 1515–16.[32] The veteran Solis had made a number of voyages in the Caribbean Sea and the Gulf of Mexico and had gained a sufficient reputation for King Fernando of Spain to appoint him *piloto mayor* as a replacement for Amerigo Vespucci. His mission was to sail through the strait and up the west coast of South America until he reached the Pacific coast of Panama. Solis arrived in the Plata region in February 1516 thinking it was the long-sought strait. Incautiously, he decided to go ashore with a small party to parley with a large group of waiting locals. There he quickly joined that select company of explorers who have been killed and eaten by hostile natives. As soon as the Spanish disembarked, the natives attacked and clubbed all of them to death except one, the lucky Francisco del Puerto who escaped, before the horrified eyes of their companions back on the ship. To add to the agony of the Spanish survivors, the Plata estuary proved not to be a strait leading to the great South Sea.

MAGELLAN AND THE FIRST CIRCUMNAVIGATION OF THE GLOBE

Ferdinand Magellan located the strait that provided a passage from the Atlantic Ocean through South America to Balboa's South Sea. He also conceived of and, for all practical purposes, carried out the first circumnavigation of the earth in human history even though he died in the Philippine Islands. His voyage marked the culmination of the various efforts to find a westward sea-route through the coastlines of Central America and South America in the aftermath of Balboa's expedition. The harsh rigours and difficult sailing conditions of that journey further revealed Magellan to be one of the greater, if not the greatest, of the sea-captains of the early modern age of European exploration.

Ferdinand Magellan (1480?–1521), as he is known to English speakers, was born Fernão de Magalhães the son of a minor Portuguese noble.[33] As he reached his young adulthood, Portugal was engaged in the establishment of its spice empire in the Indian Ocean. In 1505 he joined Francisco de Almeida's expedition to India. While serving in the Indian Ocean, Magellan distinguished himself for his resourcefulness,

Vasco Núñez de Balboa claims the South Sea for Spain as depicted in an illustration from Herrera's *Historia General*. From C.L.G. Anderson, *Old Panama and Castilla del Oro* (Boston, Page, 1914), frontispiece.

bravery and seamanship. He visited many places around the basin of the Indian Ocean and possibly even reached Ambon Island in the East Indies. As a result of his participation in many battles, Magellan was injured several times, including one wound that left him with a permanent limp. He became friends with Francisco Serrão, who in 1511 actually reached the island of Ternate, one of the primary Spice Islands. Serrão wrote Magellan enthusiastic letters about the vast potential profits to be made from direct voyages to the Spice Islands.

It was during his time in the Far East that Magellan began to contemplate the feasibility of making a western voyage to the Spice Islands of the Moluccas through a strait in the South American landmass. He further speculated that the Moluccas were actually located on the Spanish side of the dividing lines established by the Treaty of Tordesillas. That line extended in a great north–south circle all the way around the earth. Before Europeans had reached the Molucca Islands in the East Indies, the exact location of the line did not matter. Now that the Portuguese had reached the Spice Islands, the line's precise position was a matter of crucial importance to both Spain and Portugal. Unfortunately, determining the correct whereabouts of the dividing line was impossible given the state of geographical and navigational technology in the early sixteenth century. Significant differences of opinion existed about the actual size of the earth. Magellan, like Columbus, thought the earth was much smaller than it really was. Furthermore, sixteenth-century navigators and cartographers could not calculate longitude and so possessed no accurate way to determine east–west location. Spanish and Portuguese authorities could not accurately place the location of the dividing line of the Treaty of Tordesillas in the Atlantic Ocean, let alone figure out where it ran in the Pacific Ocean. Such technical considerations did not deter Magellan. He believed that Japan lay no further off the Pacific coast of Panama than Cuba lay from the Caribbean or Gulf Coast of Central America. Although the Moluccas lay further to the west than Japan, they were not that much further west. Magellan reasoned that if he could find a strait leading from the Atlantic to the Pacific Oceans, it would be a straightforward voyage from there to the Moluccas. Such a route would be much easier and quicker than sailing around the Cape of Good Hope and across the Indian Ocean as the Portuguese were doing. Magellan, of course, was wrong. The Pacific Ocean proved much wider than he imagined and that mistake on Magellan's part came close to killing him and his men.

Magellan returned to Portugal in 1513 and hoped to secure King Manuel's backing for an expedition to find a strait through South America to the Pacific Ocean. Before he tried to gain the King's support, Magellan joined the Portuguese forces fighting in Morocco. While in that land he fought bravely but unfortunately he became embroiled in a controversy over his selling captured cattle back to the enemy. Ultimately he cleared himself of the charges but in the process came to the unfavourable notice of King Manuel. The King took an intense dislike to Magellan for some indeterminable reason. When presented with Magellan's idea for a western voyage to Asia, Manuel declined to support it. To add insult to injury, he even refused to increase the faithful Magellan's paltry royal pension by even a pittance. At that point the disappointed Magellan became irate and decided to offer his plan for a western voyage to Charles V, the King of Spain and the Holy Roman Emperor.

Charles V proved to be receptive to Magellan's plan. The terms of Magellan's arrangement with Charles V were similar to those of Columbus's contracts with Fernando and Isabel. The Spanish monarch agreed to support an expedition of five ships with a combined crew of about 250 men and he made Magellan its captain-general. His five ships were named the *Trinidad*, the *San Antonio*, the *Concepción*, the *Victoria* and the *Santiago*. During the preparations for the voyage, Magellan found himself saddled with a spoiled and inexperienced group of minor Spanish aristocrats for three of his ship's captains and other officers. Because he was Portuguese, these men treated him as a despised foreigner to whom they owed little or no obedience, let alone loyalty. The suppliers of the ships' provisions cheated Magellan's expedition at every opportunity. While the canny captain-general frequently caught their tricks, he failed to detect it when they shorted him a year's worth of supplies. That lack of crucial items would later have deadly consequences while the Spanish fleet was crossing the vast Pacific Ocean.

Magellan and his ships departed from Sanlucar de Barrameda on 20 September 1519 with the captain-general leading the way in the *Trinidad*, his flagship. News circulated that King Manuel of Portugal had sent out two fleets to intercept and to destroy the interloping Spanish expedition while it was on its way to the Brazilian coast. Taking this Portuguese threat seriously, Magellan tried a different route across the Atlantic Ocean. After leaving the Canary Islands, he continued further down the African coast to Sierra Leone. From there the Spanish fleet struck out onto the high seas on 18 October in the midst of a furious storm which lit the ship's masts with St Elmo's fire. Unfortunately for Magellan, while he avoided the Portuguese by sailing so far south, his ships entered the doldrums and were becalmed in miserable heat. Eventually they drifted into an area of favourable winds which carried them westward. They sighted Cape St Agostinho on the coast of Brazil on 29 November 1519 after a slow and unpleasant passage of fifty-three days across the narrowest part of the Atlantic outside the arctic.

Magellan wanted to avoid any contact with the Portuguese in Brazil so he did not land. Instead, he moved south to the present-day location of Rio de Janeiro where he stopped to resupply on 13 December. The local natives proved friendly and the Spanish passed a restful and pleasant interlude until 26 December when they departed. On 11 January 1520 the fleet arrived at the Rio de la Plata, previously visited by Juan de Solis, and rested there until 2 February. Moving on further down the coast they arrived at Port St Julian at approximately 49°S latitude on 31 March. With the winter of the southern hemisphere approaching, Magellan decided to stop and settle in until the spring season began.

From the beginning of the expedition Magellan had faced serious problems of insubordination from some of his Spanish captains. They resented that a foreigner was commanding the fleet and they also wanted to divert the expedition from its goal of the Moluccas to raiding Portuguese shipping, slaving among the hapless South American natives and cutting valuable logwood. Animosities that had been festering since the beginning of the Atlantic crossing erupted into mutiny on 2 April 1520. Magellan responded to the threat decisively and courageously. He suppressed the mutineers and was greatly aided in that effort by the loyalty of the common seamen. One leader of the mutiny, Luis de Mendoza, was killed in the fighting while another, Gaspar de Quesada, was tried and executed during the aftermath. Magellan showed mercy to some of the leaders, which turned out to be a misplaced kindness. The incorrigible Juan de Cartegena continued to conspire against Magellan along with a ship's chaplain Pero Sánchez de Reina. A second court-martial followed and it sentenced both men to be marooned at Port St Julian when the fleet departed on 24 August.

During the five-month stay at Port St Julian the Spanish encountered the local inhabitants, many of whom turned out to be extraordinarily tall and big. Impressed by their size, the Spanish named the desolate land Patagonia after the large feet of the natives who also proved to be reasonably friendly. Meanwhile, Magellan sent the *Santiago* south to do some preliminary scouting. That voyage turned out to be a disaster as the ship wrecked on the coast and the survivors had to walk back to Port St Julian through a barren wilderness in wintry conditions.

By 24 August 1520 Magellan decided that winter was waning enough for the fleet to move further south. Arriving at the Rio Santa Cruz just below 50°S latitude on 26 August, he apparently thought better of his decision and decided to hold up again for almost another two months. The fleet remained at the Rio Santa Cruz until 18 October when it started south once more. Within a few days' sailing they sighted what they called Cape Virgins on 21 October, which was the saint's day of St Ursula and the 10,000 seafaring virgins. Beyond lay the strait. Magellan immediately ordered his ships to enter the opening even though many of the officers doubted that it was really a strait. As Antonio Pigafetta, an Italian member of the expedition, remembered it, an insistent Magellan 'said that there was another strait for going out, and said that he knew it well, because he had seen it by a marine chart of the King of Portugal, which map had been made by the great pilot and mariner named Martin of Bohemia [Martin Behaim?]'.[34] From that point onward, Magellan's four ships cautiously proceeded to probe the maze of waterways that is the Strait of Magellan. Once the Spanish reached the section of the strait known as Paso Ancho or Broad Reach, forks began appearing in the waterway and decisions had to be made. The *Trinidad* and the *Victoria* went into the Paso Froward while the *Concepción* and the *San Antonio* entered Bahia Inútil ('Useless') and Admiralty Sound. The latter route proved to be a dead end. Dividing the ships had the unfortunate effect of giving Esteban Gómez, a fellow Portuguese with Magellan, an opportunity to take-over the *San Antonio*, desert the fleet and head back to Spain. The three remaining ships initially thought that the *San Antonio* had become lost and diligently searched the strait for the missing vessel. The

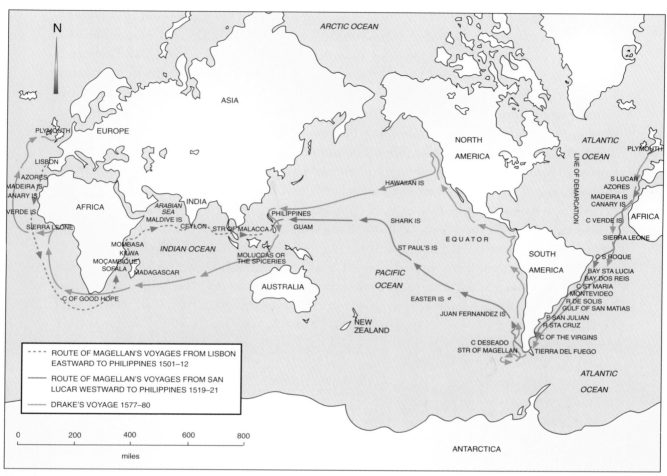

Magellan and Drake circumnavigate the world.

Victoria sailed all the way back to Cape Virgins. Perplexed, Magellan consulted with the chief pilot of the fleet, Andrés de San Martin, who dabbled in astrology. San Martin checked the heavens and reported to Magellan that the *San Antonio* had deserted and was on its way back to Spain. Undaunted by Gómez's treachery, Magellan continued through the strait and emerged into the Pacific Ocean at Cape Pilar on 27 November.

Upon sailing into the open ocean, Magellan found it to be so peaceful that he named it Pacific. Immediately proceeding northward along the west coast of South America until reaching the Isle of Mocha, there he struck out onto the high seas in a north-westerly direction. The Pacific Ocean ultimately proved to be far more vast than Magellan could have imagined. After almost two months without sighting land, the fleet passed the island of Puka Puka in the Tuamotu Group on 24 January 1521, but did not stop. Magellan assumed that other lands were near. He was wrong and six more weeks of suffering followed. Provisions gave out and sailors were reduced to eating leather, rats and sawdust. Scurvy ravaged the crew and one after another they died.[35] By the time the Spanish reached Guam on 6 March 1521, nineteen crewmen had succumbed to scurvy and starvation. The remainder were in a gravely weakened condition after ninety-eight days at sea. The islanders of Guam provided badly needed fruits and other foods to Magellan's men, but they also pilfered everything not bolted down on the Spanish ships. This rather unpleasant trait caused the Spanish to dub Guam the Islas de Ladrones (Islands of Thieves). Once the crew replenished the ships' stores with fresh food and water, Magellan's fleet continued west on 9 March. They sighted Samar in the Philippines on 15 March and a few days later made contact with the civilized inhabitants of Homonhon Island who gave the Spanish a warm welcome. Everything seemed to be proceeding smoothly after the horrendous ordeal of crossing the Pacific Ocean. Other inhabitants of the Philippines, such as Sultan Humabon of Cebu, proved to be equally congenial. Although initially not inclined to show the Spanish any friendship, a Muslim merchant warned him, 'Look well, sire. These men are the same who have conquered Calicut, Malaca, and all India Magiore. If they are treated well, they will give good treatment, but if they are treated evil, evil and worse treatment, as they have done to Calicut and Malaca.'[36] The reputation for ruthlessness gained by the Portuguese in the lands of the Indian Ocean was serving the unwitting Spanish well.

Magellan's ship in the Strait of Magellan. From Henry Eldridge Bourne and Elbert Jay Benton, *Introductory American History* (Boston, D.C. Heath, 1912), p. 165.

Just when things seemed to be going well for the Spanish, Magellan unwisely and unnecessarily involved himself in local power struggles with fatal results for him and near disastrous results for the expedition. On 27 April 1521 Magellan led an ill-conceived attack against Mactan Island which was hostile to Cebu. Magellan hoped to increase his influence with Cebu but instead the ploy ended in his death at the hands of an enraged horde of natives. Duarte Barbosa, one of the surviving officers of the expedition, succeeded Magellan as captain-general of the fleet, but that did not last long. A malicious rumour convinced Sultan Humabon that the Spanish were plotting to kidnap him. He struck first, luring most of the Spanish officers, including Barbosa, to a banquet on 1 May and massacring twenty-eight of them. Only Gómez de Espinosa and João Lopes de Carvalho escaped by leaving early.

The surviving Spanish picked Carvalho as their captain-general and pressed on to the Spice Islands. Before sailing too far they scuttled the *Concepión* as the losses among the crew had reached the point that there were no longer sufficient men to sail all three ships. Carvalho also began engaging in piratical activities, marauding any passing Asian trading vessels, which quickly led to his replacement as captain-general by Espinosa. After six months of sailing the *Trinidad* and the *Victoria* finally sighted the fabled Moluccas on 6 November and entered the harbour of Tidore on 8 November. There they set about trading for cloves and soon filled the holds of both ships with tons of the pungent spice.

Laden with precious cargo, the Spanish prepared to depart for Spain. Fearful of Portuguese attack, the two ships decided to separate and go back by different routes. Sebastian Elcano, an erstwhile mutineer against Magellan and now the captain of the *Victoria*, would return to Spain by sailing around the Cape of Good Hope. Espinosa in the *Trinidad* would go across the Pacific Ocean and try to reach the Spanish settlements in Panama. The *Victoria* sailed out of Tidore on 21 December 1521 and after many vicissitudes arrived at Sanlucar de Barrameda on 6 September 1522. By that time only Elcano and eighteen crew remained alive. A leak delayed the *Trinidad* from leaving Tidore until 6 April 1522. All efforts to cross the Pacific Ocean in an eastward direction failed as the Spanish did not know the patterns of the winds and currents. Eventually forced back to the Indies, Portuguese forces captured the *Trinidad* and imprisoned the crew. Only a few ultimately returned home. Counting the crew of the faithless *San Antonio*, only about 80 of the original 250 men in Magellan's fleet saw Spain again. Only a minority of these survivors actually travelled all the way around the world. Incredibly, the *Victoria*'s cargo of cloves sold for enough money that the whole venture made a profit after all the expenses had been deducted, including the loss of three out of five ships. However, the cost of the expedition in terms of human lives lost was horrific, even by the standards of the age of exploration.

In spite of the awesome difficulties, the Spanish mounted a second trip to the Moluccas.[37] Francisco de Loaysa and Elcano led a fleet through the Strait of Magellan in 1526 after four and a half months of trying to sail through that stormy and unpredictable passage. They reached the Moluccas on 29 December 1526 and became embroiled with the Portuguese in a war to control the source of cloves. Almost all of the Spanish never made it home, except for a few that the Portuguese returned as prisoners of war. Relief expeditions from Mexico also failed to dislodge the Portuguese from the Moluccas. For many years all Spanish efforts to find an eastward route back across the Pacific Ocean were unable to locate the belt of winds needed to carry their ships back to Mexico. That finally changed when Andres de Urdaneta discovered in 1564–5 the North Pacific westerly winds. That led to the establishment, beginning in 1567, of annual voyages of galleons between Manila in the Philippines and Acapulco in Mexico.[38] By that long route the goods of the Far East made their way to Europe via Mexico. A viable trading link between Spain and Asia had been established some seventy-five years after Columbus's first voyage.

Meanwhile, Magellan's route lay unused due to its extreme rigours. The Englishman Sir Francis Drake successfully completed the second voyage of circumnavigation between 1577 and 1580, basically engaging in piracy along the way.[39] Only one of his five ships, the *Golden Hind*, completed the journey. Another Englishman Sir Thomas

Painting of Thomas Cavendish, Francis Drake and John Hawkins, English School, seventeenth century. (© National Maritime Museum)

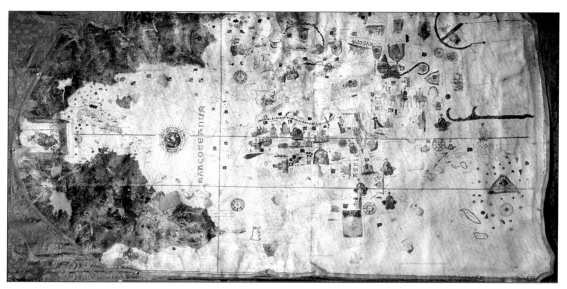

The map of Juan de la Cosa, 1500. (By permission of the Museo Naval, Madrid)

Cavendish followed Drake in 1586–8, but only made a paltry profit for his efforts.[40] At that point the English lost interest in circumnavigation following Magellan's route. Ten years later in 1598, the Dutch, eager to develop a sea-route to the East Indies, attempted the Strait of Magellan.[41] Their efforts also came to nothing. The hard fact remained that the passage pioneered by Magellan was too long, too difficult and too dangerous to serve as a practical trade route with Asia. The eastern coast of South America stood revealed, but the mysteries of the seemingly infinite Pacific Ocean had only been partially plumbed, even by Urdaneta, and would largely remain that way until the great Pacific voyages of the eighteenth century.

VOYAGES TO NORTH AMERICA AFTER CABOT AND THE SEARCH FOR NORTHERN PASSAGES

Early sixteenth-century geographers and explorers had a more difficult time fixing the existence of the continent of North America into their world view. Whereas early maps show a rapid and reasonably accurate evolution of European awareness of South America from the Juan de la Cosa map in 1500 and the Cantino map of 1502 onward, North America from the Yucatan on northwards appeared or disappeared and expanded or contracted on maps for several decades. Europeans appear to have been reluctant to concede the separate existence of North America. They really wanted it to be Asia, but it was not. It was an inconvenience for their plans. It stood in the way of them reaching Asia. The Juan de la Cosa map of 1500 precociously showed a North American coastline that was broadly accurate and may have been the fruit of John Cabot's mysterious third voyage of 1498. Alberto Cantino's world map of 1502 records a vague coastline west of Cuba, while Martin Waldseemuller's map of 1507 appears to depict Florida and the Gulf of Mexico. On later maps, however, North America would disappear, break up into scattered islands or be riven with straits to the Pacific Ocean and Asia. Uncertainty or denial about the extent of an unbroken North American coastline would persist until 1530 and even beyond in some more obstinate quarters.[42]

Just what northern expeditions took place between 1500 and 1530 is a bit obscure.[43] In the far north, European explorations concentrated on the area of Newfoundland and Labrador. John Cabot followed by the Corte-Real brothers of Portugal had established the existence of Newfoundland, which was assumed to be an extreme north-eastern part of Asia. This area's sole attraction for European visitors lay in the abundant fishing in the nearby Grand Banks. Fishermen from Portugal, France, the Basque region and England plied those waters from early on with some historians claiming that such fishing voyages even pre-dated Cabot's trip of 1497. To the south, Spanish explorers fanned out from the islands of Hispaniola and Cuba. For some years it was widely believed that scattered islands lay to the north and to the west of Cuba, a belief that Hernan Cortés's conquest of Mexico in 1519–20 did not entirely end. Vague references and hints indicate the possibility of undocumented voyages to the Yucatan, into the Gulf of Mexico and to Florida, but nothing is certain until Ponce de León's expedition of 1512–13.

On Hispaniola, the destruction of the native population through disease, starvation, over-work and senseless cruelty continued.[44] Columbus's initial promises of rich supplies of spices and gold had proven to be a mirage. The placer mines of Hispaniola's stream beds only produced paltry amounts of gold, wrested from the earth at a great cost in terms of labour and human suffering by the native population. A rapid decline in the Hispaniolan population resulted, while the Spanish need for workers in the mines continued undiminished. As a result, expeditions fanned out across the waters around Hispaniola seeking fresh sources of Indians to enslave and take back to the mines of Hispaniola. Slavers probably made new geographical discoveries that were never recorded. By 1511 both the native population and the gold-producing capabilities of Hispaniola were approaching exhaustion. That circumstance caused Governor Diego Velázquez to move west and to occupy Cuba with its fresh gold mines and healthy population of Indians. The rapaciousness of the Spaniards was so great that it took only ten years for them to use up both the Cuban Indians and the mines.

Into this sordid context stepped Juan Ponce de León, the explorer and conquistador famous for his fruitless quest for a fountain of youth.[45] Ponce had accompanied Columbus on his second voyage and in 1508 commanded a party that conquered Puerto Rico. He established a Spanish settlement there and was appointed its first governor. By 1512 he had become one of the richest men in the Spanish islands, but like so many in that age this achievement did not satisfy him. He wanted to explore new lands and in 1512 King Fernando granted him permission. Some accounts focus on Ponce's quest for a fountain of youth on the islands north of

Hispaniola. Tales circulating among the local Indians told of such a fountain on an island called Bimini. These local fountain of youth stories also dovetailed nicely with pre-existing European beliefs that such a thing existed somewhere in the furthest reaches of East Asia. Since many explorers believed that the Asian mainland lay nearby to the north and west of Hispaniola, the two fountain of youth legends reinforced each other. Most historians, however, agree that Ponce's main motivation for exploring to the north of Hispaniola was to locate new lands and new riches.

Ponce's first expedition departed from Puerto Rico during March 1513 and arrived at a point north of Cape Canaveral on 20 April or Whit Sunday, which in Spanish is Pasqua Florida.

Ponce de León based on an illustration from Herrara's *Historia General*. From Justin Winsor, *Narrative and Critical History of America* (Boston, Houghton Mifflin, 1886), vol. 2, p. 235.

That Christian feast day is the source of Florida's name. As Ponce attempted to sail south down the coast, his ships encountered a strong contrary current that turned out to be the Gulf Stream. That marine phenomenon forced the Spanish ships to hug the coastline in order to make any headway. Eventually they worked their way around the Florida Keys and up the west coast to the region of Charlotte Harbour. Ponce and his men also found the inhabitants of Florida to be quite hostile. Almost everywhere the Spanish landed, the Indians attacked them. It was the first time that a European expedition had found the natives to be aggressive immediately upon their arrival in supposedly unexplored territory. That hostility may have been a product of earlier unrecorded Spanish slaving raids along the Florida coast. It also meant that Ponce did not discover Florida for Spain, someone else had visited there first.

After leaving Charlotte Harbour, Ponce's fleet sailed across the Gulf of Mexico either to Cuba or the northern coast of the Yucatan. Landing on the beach, the Spanish mended their sails. No mention is made of any meetings with the local inhabitants, although they came across some canoes. Initially the Spanish thought that they had landed on Cuba but because they had sailed so far west, some people began to have doubts. They suggested that the Spanish expedition had landed on a separate body of land and they assumed it was an island, which Ponce named Bemini (as opposed to Bimini). Some modern historians have concluded that Ponce and his ships had actually landed on the Yucatan. If so, in this one voyage Ponce had officially discovered Florida and possibly the Yucatan. In 1516 he sailed again into the Gulf of

Initially friendly Native Americans turned distinctly hostile towards all European visitors as a result of widespread slave-raiding as this attack on Amerigo Vespucci's men shows. Based on an engraving by Theodore De Bry. From William Cullen Bryant, *A Popular History of the United States* (New York, Scribners, 1891), vol. 1, p. 123.

Mexico, landed in the region of Vera Cruz and so discovered Mexico. Again he seems to have missed the settled regions with their substantial urban centres that lay sprinkled along the coast.

The completion of the exploration of the Gulf of Mexico took place in 1519 when Alonso Álvarez de Pineda led a fleet up the west coast of Florida and along the northern shores of the Gulf of Mexico.[46] After investigating the mouth of the Mississippi, the Spanish fleet continued around the Gulf to northern Mexico. There they landed among civilized Indians at the Pánuco River. The inhabitants of Pánuco turned out to be very hostile and very effective. They defeated the Spanish in battle, killed and reportedly ate Pineda and some of his men and destroyed all but one of the Spanish ships. But for luck and courage, their miserable fate could have befallen Hernan Cortés and his men to the south during their conquest of Mexico. Ponce also eventually came to a bad end. He returned to Charlotte Harbour in 1521 and attempted to establish a permanent colony. The local Calusa tribe resisted the Spanish encroachment on their land with great ferocity. One of their arrows penetrated Ponce's armour and badly wounded him. His men decided to abandon the settlement and took him back to Havana where he died of his injuries.

As a result of the earlier voyages of Ponce and Pineda, the outline of the Gulf of Mexico had been revealed and no strait to the Pacific Ocean had appeared. That information would be tragically reinforced by the ill-fated and poorly commanded expedition of Pánfilo de Nárvaez.[47] Humiliatingly defeated in 1520 when he attempted to arrest Hernan Cortés for rebelling against Governor Diego Velásquez during the conquest of Mexico, he attempted to recoup his fortunes in 1528 by conquering Florida. After losing contact with his fleet, Nárvaez and his 200 men were forced to build 5 barges which they hoped to sail back to Spanish settlements in Mexico by hugging the coastline. Their plan failed when the current at the mouth of the Mississippi and stormy winds blew the lumbering barges out to sea. None of the vessels made it back to Mexico. All were lost at sea or wrecked on the coastline. In November 1528 ninety men from two barges were wrecked on Galveston Island on the upper Texas coast. Ultimately after years of wandering among the Native American tribes of Texas and northern Mexico only four of these made it back alive to Spanish territory in 1536. One of the survivors was the redoubtable Álvar Núñez Cabeza de Vaca who gained a venerated reputation as a healer among the natives. In turn, he developed a respect and affection for the Native Americans whom he lived among for so many years largely dependent on their hospitality to a stranger. Cabeza de Vaca's reappearance served to confirm that no strait to Asia existed along the Gulf coast from Galveston to Florida. His return also cleared up the mystery of the disappearance of the Narváez expedition and reignited interest in the possibility of hidden empires and rich conquests in the vastness of North America.

By 1520 only the eastern seaboard of the present-day USA remained unexplored, except possibly for John Cabot's fatal voyage of 1498.[48] Further north the areas of Newfoundland, Labrador and Nova Scotia were frequently being visited by ships from England, France and Portugal, although exploration was not an important motivation for these voyages. Fishermen from all three countries worked the rich waters of the seas of Newfoundland. Some of the English vessels also attempted to establish trading relations with the local tribes during the first decade of the sixteenth century. The profits from this proved to be disappointing and the English merchants eventually discontinued that enterprise. Sebastian Cabot, the son of John Cabot, led the first true voyage of exploration to head for North America in the aftermath of his father's expeditions and those of the Corte-Real brothers.[49] Sailing during 1508–9 with English and Dutch financing, he took his ship into the arctic waters of North America. During that voyage he claimed to have located a passage that would lead to Asia, although what he probably saw was the Hudson Strait. At the time, no one else showed any interest in developing any sea-routes to Asia in those frigid waters.

Giovanni da Verrazano. From William Cullen Bryant, *A Popular History of the United States* (New York, Scribners, 1891), vol. 1, p. 176.

Support for exploration languished in England and France until the 1520s. Henry VII had only wanted to pursue western exploration on the cheap, while his son Henry VIII, who became King in 1509, focused his energies almost solely on gaining influence in continental Europe and on domestic affairs.[50] The kings of France also remained largely indifferent to possible opportunities in western exploration through the first two decades of the sixteenth century. As late as 1521 Sebastian Cabot had failed to persuade a group of London merchants to support him on a voyage to explore further what he thought was a north-west passage through the arctic seas to Asia. Interest in investigating the region of what is North America quickly revived in 1522 when Sebastian Elcano arrived back in Spain with the remnants of Magellan's fleet. Despite the appalling losses of men and ships, the Magellan voyage had proved to be profitable. Now people in Spain, France and England reasoned that since a passage existed through South America to Asia, perhaps there was another such passage in the north.

Both Spain and France began to prepare ships to explore the North American coast for the anticipated strait in March 1523. Esteban Gómez, the Portuguese captain who had deserted Magellan during the exploration of the southern strait, was given command of the Spanish expedition. In France, the French King Francis I and his merchants were anxious to secure their share of the beckoning riches of the Asian trade. They placed the Florentine Giovanni de Verrazzano in charge of a fleet of four ships.[51] Sailing in the summer of 1523, storms sank two of the ships and the survivors returned to France. Undeterred, Verrazzano departed for a second time in late 1523 in the caravel *La Dauphine*. On 17 January 1524 he sighted Madeira on his way west. The North American coast came into sight on 20 March at about 34°N latitude in what is now North Carolina. Initially, the French ship sailed further south for a few days at which point Verrazzano turned north again to avoid territory settled by the Spanish. On 25 March at 36°N he sighted what he thought was a very narrow isthmus which he described as 'one mile wide and about two hundred miles long, in which we could see the eastern sea from the ship. . . . This is doubtless the one which goes around the tip of India, China, and Cathay. We sailed along the isthmus, hoping all the time to find some strait or real promontory where land might end to the north, and we could reach the blessed shores of Cathay.'[52] What Verrazzano had actually found was the great barrier island that lies off the North Carolina mainland. Conditions were such that he could not see the mainland and assumed that the apparently open water on the other side of the barrier island extended all the way to China. His error resulted in a non-existent Verrazzanean sea which almost split North America into two parts as it appeared on many sixteenth-century maps. From the supposed isthmus Verrazzano sailed further north, possibly all the way to Cape Breton. Along the way he favourably observed the vast new lands, which he called New France, and met some rather suspicious and rude Indians living on the New England coast. Sailing back to France, he landed at Dieppe on 8 July 1524.

Although interested in developing a sea-route to the Spice Islands, Verrazzano far-sightedly concluded that colonizing North America could be a very worthwhile activity for France to undertake. Unfortunately for those plans, Francis I considered fighting Charles V, the Holy Roman Emperor and the King of Spain, to be his first priority and in the process managed to get himself captured by the Emperor in 1525 at the Battle of Pavia. With royal support unavailable, Verrazzano ventured into the South Atlantic in 1527 and tried unsuccessfully to follow the Portuguese route around Africa to India. He also cut logwood, a highly valued source of dye, on the coasts of Brazil and the Caribbean which generated some handsome profits. Returning to the Caribbean in 1528, an uninformed Verrazzano landed on Guadaloupe where waiting hostile Caribs imme-diately killed him and, if the sixteenth-century reports are to be believed, ate him.[53] That unfortunate incident ended Verrazzano's career in North American exploration, but not France's.

Back in Spain, Esteban Gómez finally sailed from La Coruña on 24 September 1524 to explore the east coast of North America, which was close to three months after Verrazzano's return from his first voyage.[54] Although there is some dispute concerning his route, the best evidence indicates that Gómez sailed first to Santiago de Cuba and from there up the east coast of North America.[55] Along the way he made a detailed study of the Penobscot River in the vain hope that it was a strait to the

Jacques Cartier. From Thomas Joseph Campbell, *Pioneer Laymen of North America* (New York, American Press, 1915), vol. 1, frontispiece.

Pacific Ocean. From there he continued up the coast to Cape Race where he headed back to Spain, arriving on 21 August 1525. Almost two years later on 10 June 1527 John Rut sailed from England to look for a strait through North America.[56] He started out with two ships, but one was lost at sea in a tempest. Rut's surviving vessel continued and he attempted to penetrate the Arctic Sea but was driven back by the cold. Turning south, he explored the east coast of North America from north to south, looking for a strait without success, and eventually ended up in the waters around Hispaniola before returning to England. Verrazzano, Gómez and Rut all failed to find a usable strait through North America for the simple reason that none existed. Gómez's voyage had some geographical impact since its discoveries were recorded on the Diego Ribeiro map. Verrazzano's voyage simply raised the chimera of the non-existent Verrazzanean sea which contributed to confused geographical thinking for decades. Otherwise, Spain lost interest in searching for a northern strait after Gómez's trip, although France and England did not. Their efforts, however, shifted further to the north.

Jacques Cartier continued France's attempts to find a strait to Asia and to investigate the new northern continent.[57] Sailing during 1534 from St Malo with support from Francis I, Cartier explored the Gulf of St Lawrence during his first voyage. Although he was looking for a strait to Asia, he failed to penetrate the mouth of the St Lawrence River, let alone find a strait. During his second voyage of 1535–6, he returned to the same area and sailed up the St Lawrence. An Indian informant told him that it was the

Jacques Cartier discovers the Saint Lawrence River. From Francis Parkman, *Pioneers of France in the New World*, 2 vols (Boston, Little Brown, 1897), vol 2, p. 25.

route to a great kingdom called Saguenay and also described the St Lawrence as a water-route to rich and great lands much further to the west. The eager French took those western lands to be China. Cartier and his ships reached as far as the large Indian village of Hochelaga at the site of present-day Montreal before returning to France. Several years passed before a third voyage could be organized. Francis I and Cartier both hoped to establish a French settlement in North America from which trade, missionary work and the search for a strait to Asia could continue. This time, however, Francis I passed over Cartier and gave command of the expedition to the noble Jean François de la Roque, seigneur de Roberval. As events played out, Cartier left France first on 23 May 1541 with an advanced party of five ships bound for New France. Roberval would follow later with the main expedition. Upon reaching the previously friendly Indian settlements near present-day Quebec, Cartier ordered his men to begin establishing their own settlement. He proceeded on up the St Lawrence River to Hochelaga in the hope of finding the rich kingdom of Saguenay. This achieved nothing and Cartier became distracted by his finding of what he mistakenly thought were rich deposits of gold and precious stones. Anxious to get samples of the new-found riches back to France, Cartier and the French also faced the growing hostility of the Huron Indians of the Quebec region and the disquieting failure of Roberval and the rest of the expedition to arrive from France. Cartier became convinced that the French settlement should be abandoned and that he and his men should return to France.

In early June 1542, Cartier and his ships sailed out of the St Lawrence headed for France. Several weeks later they met up with the tardy Roberval at Newfoundland.

A skirmish with Natives, from Sir Martin Frobisher's second voyage to discover the north-west passage in 1577. (© British Museum/Bridgeman Art Library)

Cartier declined to return back up the St Lawrence with Roberval and continued on his way arriving at St Malo during October 1542. Back on the St Lawrence, Roberval resumed the search for the illusive and chimerical Saguenay, reaching as far as Hochelaga. When his best efforts failed, he too returned to France by September 1543. Cartier's samples of gold and diamonds turned out to be worthless fool's gold and quartz. The St Lawrence River with its rapids at Hochelaga was also obviously no strait to Asia. Fabled Saguenay proved to be just a fable concocted by the Hurons to please and impress their European visitors. At this point, the lack of profitable results from North American exploration combined with continued

Martin Frobisher. From Woodrow Wilson,
A History of the American People (New York,
Harper, 1903), p. 21.

wars with the Spanish and the increasingly violent religious divisions within France itself caused support for further explorations to evaporate. France's search for a north-west passage along with her interest in Canada ended for the remainder of the sixteenth century.

Next the men of Elizabethan England took up the challenge of finding the north-west passage.[58] Sir Humphrey Gilbert (?1539–83) began arguing for the existence of a north-west passage with his *Discourse of a Discoverie for a New Passage to Cataia* which circulated in manuscript form around the English court from 1566 until its publication in 1576. In that year Martin Frobisher led the first English expedition since John Rut's to look for the north-west passage. It discovered Frobisher's Bay and returned to England with an Eskimo captive. Frobisher also came back with a load of fool's gold which only whetted people's appetite for true riches. Investors formed the Cathay Company to find both real gold and the north-west passage. Making two more voyages in 1577 and 1578, Frobisher was unable to achieve either goal although he entered Hudson's Strait in 1578. The Cathay Company went bankrupt as a result of that failure.

Undeterred, John Davis (1550?–1605), the inventor of the Davis Quadrant for calculating latitude, took up the challenge of finding the north-west passage.[59] During his first voyage of 1585 he discovered the Davis Strait. His second trip of 1586 accomplished little more while his third expedition reached 72°N latitude on Greenland and explored the east coast of Baffin Island. Later in the 1590s he tried to locate the north-west passage from the Pacific Ocean side by looking for the Straits of Anian but failed.

Henry Hudson (d. 1611) became in 1610 the first to sail through Hudson's Strait and into Hudson's Bay. Forced to spend the winter at James Bay, his crew mutinied and left him, his son and seven others to die in the arctic wastes. Another Englishman, William Baffin (1584?–1622), conducted three arctic expeditions in search of the north-west passage. In 1612–13 he explored the opening of the Foxe Channel beyond Hudson's Bay and in 1615 made a study of the western coast of Hudson's Bay. During 1616 he explored Greenland, Baffin Bay and Baffin Island. Reaching 78°N on Greenland, he sighted Lancaster Sound which was the way through to Asia. He mistook it for a bay. Even more important, he declared that the floating ice so congested the arctic waters as to make sailing impossibly dangerous. His report served to cool interest in the north-west passage. Luke Foxe's (1586–1633) futile explorations of the Foxe Channel and Foxe Basin only served to confirm Baffin's conclusions. The quest for a north-west passage virtually ended for two centuries.[60]

THE NORTH-EAST PASSAGE

The quest for a north-west passage to Asia was joined by the search for a north-east passage.[61] People desperate to develop any sea-route to Asia speculated that it might be possible to sail along the northern coasts of Europe and Asia to reach China and the Spice Islands. Geographers of the fifteenth and early sixteenth centuries theorized that the seas of the North Pole might be free of ice in midsummer and therefore be navigable. By the early decades of the sixteenth century various unrecorded Norse and Russian seamen had investigated the arctic waters with no success.

The first documented voyage seeking a north-east passage to China was that of Sir Hugh Willoughby and Richard Chancellor of England in 1553–4. Sebastian Cabot organized the Willoughby/Chancellor expedition for the Merchant Adventurers or Muscovy Company. Sailing from London in 1553, Willoughby and Chancellor separated in the Barents Sea. By 14 August 1553 Willoughby discovered Novaya Zemlya and reached 72°N in mid-September. Pack ice forced him back to the Kola Peninsula where Willoughby and his crew became trapped and died from the cold by January 1554. Chancellor experienced better luck and sailed into the White Sea where he established a trading post for the Muscovy Company at Archangel. It proved to be a successful enterprise and more English seamen tested the arctic waters. In 1580

Barents at Nova Zemblya. From William Cullen Bryant, *A Popular History of the United States* (New York, Scribners, 1891), vol. 1, p. 344.

Arthur Pett led an expedition past Novaya Zemlya into the Kara Sea but could go no further. Some unknown foreign merchants, possibly English, reached the Ob River in 1584 but hostile Samoyed tribesmen killed them. It was at about that point that English enthusiasm for finding a north-east passage waned and their efforts shifted to trading with Muscovy and Persia.

The Dutch also became interested in discovering a north-east passage in spite of the lack of success experienced by the English explorers. Oliver Brunel of Enkhuizen was taking ships into the White Sea well before 1584. The most famous Dutch arctic voyager was Willem Barents (c. 1550–97).[62] He first sailed there as part of an expedition in 1594–5. During that journey he took a ship to the northern tip of Novaya Zemlya. Barents's qualities as a seaman insured his inclusion on a subsequent expedition. Leaving the Netherlands in May 1596, the Dutch ships sailed a more westerly course and discovered the Spitzbergen Islands. Unable to penetrate the pack ice which lay beyond Spitzbergen, they headed for Novaya Zemlya. There ice crushed Barents's ship after he rounded its northern-most point. He and his crew were forced to winter there in a makeshift cabin and suffered greatly from scurvy and cold. On 13 June 1594 the survivors put to sea in two open boats and headed for Holland. Barents died at sea seven days later on 20 June. No one else attempted to go beyond the northern end of Novaya Zemlya again until 1871.

The London-based Muscovy Company continued to be interested in a north-east passage in spite of the failure to locate a navigable route. In 1607 and 1608 they hired the famous Henry Hudson to locate it. During the first voyage Hudson attempted to find the supposedly ice-free waters around the North Pole that geographers postulated existed there in the summer. Instead he proved that a permanent ice-pack covered the seas around the North Pole. In 1608 Hudson endeavoured but failed to get past Novaya Zemlya. By that time the Muscovy Company had concluded that no usable north-east passage existed.

Various Russian traders coasted along the Barents Sea and the Kara Sea during the early seventeenth century but they were unable to penetrate past the pack ice that clogged the waters around the Taimyr Peninsula. Wooden sailing ships did not have the power, durability or manoeuvrability to sail safely through the ice-strewn waters. The successful navigation of a north-east passage had to wait until 1878–9 when Baron Nils Nordenskjold of Sweden used a steam-powered metal ship to make his way through the ice-congested waters. His success resulted in the development by 1900 of a profitable arctic sea trade in Siberian goods that used the north-east passage. After centuries of trying by various would-be travellers to China, the north-east passage became a reality. For the people living during the early modern age of discovery, both the north-west and the north-east passages remained beyond their grasp. Meanwhile, by the late 1530s, the broad outline of the eastern coasts of North and South America were known and two new continents had been added to the European world view. The shape of the western coasts of those two continents and what lay in their interiors were still in the process of being revealed.

CHAPTER SIX

CONQUESTS

I have marvelled sometimes at Spain, how they clasp and contain so large dominions with so few natural Spaniards.

Sir Francis Bacon (1612)[1]

I do not much wish well to discoveries, for I am always afraid they will end in conquest and robbery.

Samuel Johnson (1773)[2]

When Christopher Columbus and Vasco da Gama respectively began their great journeys during the 1490s they sought usable sea-roads to Asia. Their goal was to open up direct trade with the spice marts and the other emporiums of Asian luxury goods. Originally they conceived of their voyages leading to a peaceful and profitable business with the merchants of the Indian Ocean and the Far East. Both the Portuguese and the Spanish imagined that they would set up trading factories similar to those of the Portuguese along the West African coast or the funduks (trading posts) operated by Venetian merchants in Alexandria, the great port of Mameluke Egypt or some of the other commercial centres of the eastern Mediterranean Sea. Events, however, conspired to alter these initial plans in radical ways.

Columbus did not reach Asia on his voyage, nor did he ever come close to it. Several decades of further exploration finally and conclusively revealed that what he found was a vast unknown landmass that effectively blocked European vessels from sailing west to Asia. This realization initially proved to be disappointing to Europeans and they continued to seek routes to Asia. New opportunities arose for Spain in the form of the rich Native American civilizations of Mexico and Peru. A combination of luck, courage, biology and superior technology made it possible for Spain to conquer first Mexico and then Peru. Vast riches would flow into Spain as a result of these acquisitions.

Gama successfully reached the spice mart of Calicut. But he was not welcomed with open arms by the existing merchants and many of the local powers involved in the spice trade of the Indian Ocean. The majority of these people regarded the Portuguese newcomers as uninvited interlopers. These enemies of the Portuguese were determined to prevent the Portuguese from gaining a share of the lucrative spice trade and they were in an excellent position to do just that. Faced with such hostility, the Portuguese quickly concluded that the application of military force was the only effective way to break into this area. Their possession of technologically superior ships and naval guns combined with some good fortune and ruthless bravery allowed the

Portuguese to carve out a monopolistic trading empire that dominated the Indian Ocean for much of the sixteenth century.

THE PORTUGUESE CONQUEST OF THE INDIAN OCEAN

When Vasco da Gama returned to Lisbon from his voyage to India on 29 August 1499, he opened a world of potentially infinite wealth to King Manuel and the people of Portugal. The King and his officials had been eagerly awaiting Gama's arrival and had apparently begun organizing a second expedition in anticipation of his successful completion of the journey. With Gama back in Portugal and reporting enthusiastically on the wonders of the Indian Ocean spice trade, the preparations for the second expedition accelerated. By 8 March 1500, 13 ships with a company of 1,200 to 1,500 men stood ready to sail. The new fleet was designed to impress the Indians with Portuguese grandeur and power and its commander Pedro Alvares Cabral and many of his officers came from noble families. During the first voyage, Gama and his men had mistakenly concluded that the Hindus of the Malabar coast of India were some sort of Christians. Cabral's mission was to persuade these supposed Indian co-religionists to start trading with their fellow Christians from Portugal and in this way break the hold of the Muslim merchants over the Asian spice market. At this stage the Portuguese viewed their voyages to India as buying and selling expeditions and military conquests were not part of the plan. They simply hoped to establish a trading factory at Calicut and get rich from the business.[3]

Cabral's fleet sailed on 9 March, passed the Canary Islands five days later and on 22 March sighted the Cape Verde Islands but did not stop. It was at this point that one of Cabral's ships went missing. Two days of fruitless searching followed. Undeterred by the mysterious disappearance, the Portuguese proceeded onward and began the great arc route through the South Atlantic that Gama had used. Cabral's ships sailed deep into the Atlantic along a south-westerly course. In fact, they travelled much further to the west than Gama and on 21 April sighted Mount Pascoul

Pedro Cabral taking possession of Brazil for Portugal. From Jules Verne, *Famous Travels and Travellers* (New York, Scribners, 1887), p. 182.

on the coast of Brazil. Landing on 23 April, they came across some natives who proved to be quite friendly and exploration of the unexpected land, which the Portuguese named Vera Cruz after the constellation of the Southern Cross, continued until 2 May. Although Vera Cruz proved a pleasant interlude during their long sea voyage, numerous queries about the existence of gold there had yielded no positive answers and so rendered the new land relatively worthless in the eyes of the Portuguese. At the time the Portuguese guessed that the new land lay on their side of the dividing line established by the Treaty of Tordesillas. Most scholars also consider Cabral's landing to be the effective discovery of Brazil by European explorers since it ultimately resulted in permanent settlement. The Portuguese, however, did not really understand what they had found. Initially they thought Brazil was a rather large island that could be used as a way-station on the route to India and was good for little else.[4] On 3 May Cabral's fleet resumed its voyage to India although he sent one ship back to Lisbon to bring King Manuel the news of their discovery.[5]

Sailing back into the South Atlantic to the south-east and then the east, Cabral and his ships sought to round the Cape of Good Hope. Instead, on 23 May a ferocious storm fell upon them. It continued for days and four ships were lost to the tempest including the one captained by the intrepid Bartolomé Dias, the discoverer of the Cape of Good Hope. Meanwhile, the great storm scattered the surviving ships and continued to blow them eastward. They passed the Cape of Good Hope and kept going northward up the African coast until the storm finally dissipated around the vicinity of Sofala. Cabral and six of his surviving ships were eventually reunited between 10 and 20 June at Moçambique. The seventh ship of Diogo Dias, a son of Bartolomé, was blown further into the Indian Ocean and in attempting to regain the African coast discovered Madagascar. From there Dias sailed up the coast of East Africa. He never managed to find Cabral and eventually turned around and returned to Portugal empty-handed.[6]

After completing repairs to the storm-damaged ships, Cabral continued up the East African coast where they encountered grudging hospitality from the Muslim cities except Malindi, which had previously proved genuinely hospitable to Gama's fleet. Signs were accumulating that the Muslim merchants of East Africa resented the arrival of Portuguese interlopers and feared the possibly unfavourable future consequences for their commerce. The Portuguese themselves further aggravated the situation by bringing with them and openly displaying their crusading attitudes and their assumptions of superiority. King Manuel had issued instructions that permitted Cabral's fleet to attack Arab ships found on the high seas or outside friendly harbours. Although the Portuguese did not encounter any Arab trading vessels before reaching Calicut, if they had, they would have assaulted them. The situation, with its festering animosities and barely constrained aggressions, did not bode well for the establishment by Portugal of peaceful trading operations in the Indian Ocean.[7]

Departing from Malindi on 2 August, Cabral's fleet finally reached Calicut on 13 September with its numbers sadly reduced from thirteen to a mere six ships. Initially the Zamorin appeared to be friendly and willing to trade. Protracted negotiations took place and the Portuguese secured the right to establish a trading factory in Calicut. At that point, the situation, instead of getting better, deteriorated. Muslim merchants stirred up trouble whenever and wherever they could. Their obstructionism caused the Portuguese efforts at spice dealing to proceed slowly and at a much lower volume than they had hoped for. A Muslim whispering campaign eventually caused the Zamorin's attitude toward the Portuguese to cool. Finally on 17 December the Muslims instigated a riot in Calicut that led to the storming of the Portuguese factory. As a result, fifty Portuguese died in the mayhem while another twenty managed to slash their way to the shore with their swords and escape by swimming to their ships in the harbour. Although angered by the massacre of his compatriots, Cabral delayed retaliating in the hope of receiving a satisfactory apology from the Zamorin. When that did not materialize and instead it appeared that the Zamorin was preparing for war, the Portuguese ships proceeded to attack Indian ships in the harbour and to shell Calicut. Although some attempts took place in later years to repair relations between Calicut and Portugal, the destruction of the Portuguese factory and the bombardment of Calicut created a permanent rift between the two powers.[8]

Cabral and his men had alienated Calicut, the major spice mart on the Malabar coast of India and the dominant power in the region. Portugal's hopes of obtaining a share in the vast profits of the spice trade could have easily been ended. Fortunately for Portuguese interests, the nearby ports of Cochin, Quilon and Cannanore all chafed under the domination of Calicut and were willing to become local allies of the Portuguese. Cabral sailed immediately to Cochin on 19 December and arrived there on 24 December at which point he negotiated a treaty with the local rajah. Emissaries soon arrived from Quilon and Cannanore and asked the Portuguese to come trade with them. After spending two weeks at Cochin, Cabral decided it was time to return to Portugal. He had learned that the Zamorin was preparing a large fleet to attack the Portuguese. Making a stop at Cannanore, Cabral found the local ruler, like the rajah of Cochin, to be anxious for further trade and an alliance with the Portuguese. After loading more spices, on 31 January 1501 the Portuguese fleet started back across the Indian Ocean to East Africa. One of the ships ran aground on the East African coast and had to be abandoned. The five surviving vessels made their way into the Atlantic but became separated, eventually struggling into Lisbon harbour between 23 June and 27 July.[9]

The results of Cabral's journey were momentous for Portugal. Although the voyage was not a tremendous commercial success, the cargoes carried by the five ships proved that the sea-route to India had the potential for tremendous profits. The fact that six ships out of the original thirteen had been lost at sea while only five came home loaded with spices underlined the hazards of the sea-route to India, which became known as the *carreira da India*. Cabral had also revealed the existence of the land of Brazil which lay within the territory assigned to Portugal by the Treaty of Tordesillas. Although the Portuguese were slow to settle in Brazil, it would someday become a very

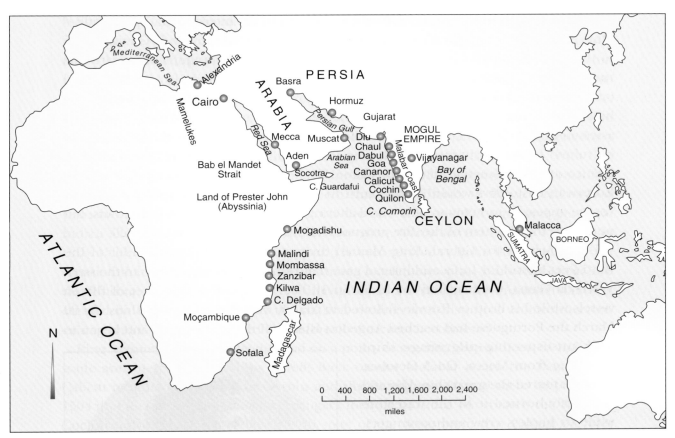

The Indian Ocean in the sixteenth century.

important part of the Portuguese overseas empire. In India, the Portuguese also discovered that Gama had been mistaken about the Hindu Indians being Christians. They were what the Portuguese considered to be idolaters and the Zamorin of Calicut had also proven to be perfidious. Cabral's retaliatory attack on Calicut reinforced the Zamorin's growing feelings of hostility toward the Portuguese newcomers. The ruler of the greatest spice mart in the Indian Ocean was now largely an implacable enemy, but fortunately the Portuguese had also discovered some alternative suppliers and allies.

The home-coming of Cabral's fleet aroused mixed reactions both inside Portugal and out. Upon his return, Cabral advised King Manuel to use force to break into the Indian Ocean spice trade. Some of his councillors were not so sanguine about the supposedly wonderful opportunities in the Indian Ocean. The vast distances and large numbers of entrenched Muslim competitors and enemies caused the more timid among the Portuguese elite to recommend abandoning the newly established link with India. King Manuel, however, was made of more adventuresome stuff. He and his more aggressive councillors saw Portuguese domination of the spice trade as achievable, profitable and, above all, something that would resound to the crusading glory of Manuel and his kingdom. Meanwhile, in the rest of Europe, various powers

Francisco de Almeida, from MS Sloane 197, f. 9.
(British Library)

Asian spice trade and seriously threatened the livelihoods of many powerful groups including the Venetians, the Mamelukes of Egypt, the Gujaratis, various communities of Muslim merchants, the Zamorin of Calicut and later the Ottoman Turks. These groups were bound to resist the Portuguese incursions and did. A decades-long struggle to control the spice trade followed.[17]

Almeida recognized that command of the sea was essential for the continued preservation of Portuguese interests in the Indian Ocean. Fortunately for Portugal, the ships and the cannon of the Europeans proved to be advanced compared with those used by the seafaring powers of the Indian Ocean. From their first appearance on the Indian Ocean, their technological edge allowed small numbers of Portuguese ships to defeat numerically superior Asian and Egyptian fleets. Once the Portuguese gained control of the sea and the trade routes, it was their courage, resourcefulness and ruthlessness that allowed them to maintain their mastery. When it came to such martial virtues, Almeida took second place to no one. His flotillas roamed the Indian Ocean harassing Muslim shipping and in 1505 he fortified the Portuguese position at Quilon. Fresh ships arrived with Afonso de Albuquerque and Tristão de Cunha and together they seized Socotra Island near the mouth of the Red Sea in 1506. The next year Albuquerque captured Hormuz at the entrance of the Persian Gulf but failed to hold it.

Unlike his sovereign, Almeida placed the highest priority on sustaining Portuguese naval supremacy and cautioned against acquiring too many fortresses. His logic was that since Portugal's resources were finite, the costs and the manpower needed to maintain a large number of fortresses would dangerously divide those limited funds. Retaining command of the sea was Portugal's only viable strategy in the Indian Ocean.

Portuguese depredations roused the fury of the Mamelukes of Egypt and the Gujaratis and in 1508 they formed an alliance with Calicut. A Mameluke fleet of twelve western-style ships with 1,500 men under the command of Amir Hussain sailed down the Red Sea and into the Indian Ocean. Their mission was to link up with the forces of Gujarat and Calicut and destroy the troublesome Portuguese. Initially the Portuguese badly underestimated the threat since up to that point their sturdier ships and heavier cannon had thrashed numerically greater Indian fleets with ease. Lourenço de Almeida, the beloved son of the Viceroy, took a fleet of eight vessels up the coast to harass Muslim shipping during March 1508. Their trip remained a routine plundering expedition until the Portuguese put into the harbour at Chaul. Amir Hussain's Mameluke fleet came into sight and initially the Portuguese complacently assumed that it was the ships of Afonso de Albuquerque arriving from Hormuz. One old veteran began to strap on his armour, experienced in warfare with Muslims. When his younger comrades derided him, he pointed out to them that the approaching warships had no crosses on their sails. The ominous truth dawned on Lourenço de Almeida and his men and they quickly beat to quarters. A fierce battle developed between the two fleets which inconclusively lasted until the evening of the next day. At that point Gujarati vessels reinforced Amir Hussain and the Portuguese decided that it would be prudent to withdraw. The next morning seven of their ships escaped but Lourenço's vessel took a cannonball at the waterline and also became entangled in the harbour passage. Hostile boats surrounded it and attempted to board. During the furious fight that ensued, Lourenço died in a hopeless last stand while his ship sank with only nineteen survivors. When the Viceroy Almeida learned of his son's death, he swore revenge.[18]

The Portuguese now faced an extremely grave threat to their survival in India from the Mamelukes and the Gujaratis. They also experienced serious divisions among their leaders at this most inop-portune time. Afonso de Albuquerque had arrived on the Indian coast with royal orders for him to replace Almeida as governor at the expiration of his term of office. Almeida, however, refused to step down until he got his revenge on the Mamelukes and went so far as to shelter some captains who had mutinied against Albuquerque at Hormuz. Fortunately for Portugal's interests, Albuquerque did not push his rights and allowed Almeida to gather a fleet capable of meeting the Mamelukes and their allies in battle. Meanwhile, the twelve Mameluke ships had sailed to the Gujarati port of Diu, where they rested at anchor in the company of over 100 allied ships from Gujarat and Calicut.[19]

By 12 December 1508 Almeida had put together a force of 18 ships and 1,200 men and set off for a showdown

An eighteenth-century painting of one of the many battles fought by the Portuguese for control of the Indian Ocean, by Portuense Vieira. (Nicolas Sapieha/Art Resource, NY)

at Diu. He arrived there on 2 February 1509. Somehow Almeida managed to convince the wily Malik Aiyaz, the governor of Diu, to switch sides or at least remain neutral in the impending struggle. The next day, 3 February, Almeida's fleet sailed into Diu harbour attacking the Mameluke vessels and their remaining allies at anchor. Portugal's enemies suffered a crushing defeat and Almeida had regained command of the sea.[20] Upon returning to Cochin in triumph, Almeida continued to refuse to let Albuquerque assume the governorship until Fernando Coutinho, the Marshal of Portugal, arrived and ordered it. At that point Almeida took the ship back to Portugal but tragically died at Saldanha Bay, in south-west Africa, on 1 March 1510. The Portuguese provoked a disastrous fight with the natives when they tried to rustle some cattle. Later the chronicler João de Barros would lament the irony that Almeida, the victor of Diu, and his men, 'were killed by sticks and stones, hurled not by giants or armed men but by bestial negroes, the most brutal of all that coast, and to these dead and wounded the grandeur of their courage and their prudent industry exercised so often in the illustrious deeds accomplished by them in India and many other places . . . availed them nothing'.[21]

Afonso de Albuquerque belatedly assumed the governorship of Portuguese India in late 1509 at the advanced age of fifty-six.[22] A man of iron determination, who always kept his prodigious energies focused on the good of Portugal and his king, Albuquerque was destined to become the greatest conqueror in the history of Portugal's Asian empire and one of the more successful conquistadors of the age of European exploration. The son of the nobleman Gonçalo de Albuquerque, he first sailed to Asia in 1503 and returned again in 1506, when he and Tristão de Cunha captured Socotra Island. He also carried papers from King Manuel appointing him the next governor of India upon the expiration of Almeida's term. Albuquerque, unlike Almeida, thoroughly believed in the Portuguese government's policy of taking strategic points along the Indian Ocean trade routes and establishing fortresses. In 1507 he proceeded to Hormuz, which was located astride the entrance to the Persian Gulf, and captured it. Dissension broke out among his captains who preferred pursuing short-term plunder for themselves over the long-term benefits of conquests for their king. They abandoned the outraged Albuquerque and sailed to seek the protection of Almeida. Their action forced Albuquerque to abandon Hormuz and also to sail for Cochin. On his arrival, almost two years of tense relations between the outgoing viceroy and the incoming governor commenced. The situation became even more aggravated by Almeida's stubborn refusal to hand power over to Albuquerque even after the emergency created by the marauding Mameluke fleet had ended.[23]

When, thanks to the intervention of Marshal Coutinho, Albuquerque finally gained the office of governor, the Portuguese retained command of the sea and were installed on the islands of Socotra and Angediva, in Cochin and other friendly Indian cities and at Kilwa in East Africa. Otherwise, the most strategic points in the Indian Ocean trading network – Aden, Hormuz and Malacca – remained outside their control while Calicut and the Gujaratis continued to be hostile. Coutinho carried instructions from King Manuel ordering the capture and destruction of Calicut. Strategically, an assault on Calicut was a dubious move but the Portuguese, following royal orders, sailed against the city anyway. Attacking on 3 January 1510, the initial strike went reasonably well. Unfortunately Coutinho decided on a foolhardy assault on the Zamorin's palace. It resulted in Coutinho's death and a repulse of the Portuguese troops with heavy casualties.[24]

This situation enabled Albuquerque to assume undivided control in India. King Manuel's other ill-founded efforts to keep authority diffused in the Indian Ocean through the employment of three regional commanders had also mercifully collapsed. The fortuitous result was that the competent and single-minded Albuquerque could pursue conquests unhampered by rival Portuguese leaders and with all the available resources of men and ships. His keen strategic eye lighted upon Goa as the first target on his list of conquests as governor of India.[25]

Goa was located in the Sultanate of Bijapur on the Indian coast about 300 miles north of Calicut. It possessed a wonderful, sheltered harbour 5 miles up the Mandovi River and was situated on an island that made assaults from the mainland difficult. King Manuel's government had already from afar marked it out as a desirable acquisition. It was also a vulnerable target. Although the rulers of Bijapur followed Islam, the bulk of its population were Hindus and were anxious to free themselves from Muslim rule. Taking advantage of the distraction and instability caused by the death of the Bijapurese monarch Yusuf Adil Shah, Albuquerque struck and easily captured Goa on 4 March 1510. Goa's fortifications had fallen into great disrepair and this fact contributed to the ease with which the Portuguese stormed the city. Unfortunately for the Portuguese, they soon found that those same defences were difficult to repair. Meanwhile, Ismael Adil Shah, the new ruler of Bijapur, counter-attacked with an army of 50,000 and drove Albuquerque back out of Goa and onto his ships. Portuguese fortunes were once again at a low ebb as other intrigues threatened their base in Cochin.[26]

In the face of adversity, Albuquerque proved to be indomitable. Regrouping his troops, after the Adil Shah's main army marched off to face other challenges, he stormed Goa for a second time on 25 November 1510 with a force numbering only a quarter of the size of the Bijapurese garrison. Although the Portuguese at sea possessed far better ships and cannon, on land they faced Asiatic armies whose equipment and tactics were equal or superior to their own. It is a tribute to Albuquerque's leadership and the bravery of his troops that they generally triumphed in their Asian battles even when outnumbered significantly. These qualities allowed the Portuguese to capture Goa for a second time and to keep it permanently. Repairing the fortifications of Goa before the inevitable Bijapurese counter-attack, the Portuguese garrison withstood numerous assaults over the next two years. Thanks to its favourable location and excellent harbour, it soon became the headquarters of Portuguese India. During the course of the sixteenth century it would withstand

Afonso de Albuquerque, 1646, by an unknown artist. (Heritage Image Partnership)

several other protracted sieges. Portugal was now a true imperial power in the Indian Ocean although that status never went unchallenged for long.[27]

Malacca was a rich trading city on the Malay Peninsula, strategically located in the strait leading from the Bay of Bengal in the Indian Ocean into the South China Sea. Its importance in the Indian Ocean trading network had early on earned it a place on King Manuel's list of desired conquests. Although its buildings were made mostly of wood and its defences were weak, a garrison of 20,000 mercenaries with hundreds of top-quality brass cannon protected Malacca. Undaunted, on 1 July 1511 Albuquerque descended upon the rich city with a mere 1,100 troops. The Portuguese assault began on 25 July. Several weeks punctuated by cautious manoeuvring and street fighting followed. At one particularly dramatic point, the Sultan of Malacca even led a charge of his war elephants against the invaders but the doughty Portuguese troops stood their ground and threw the skittish elephants into a panicked rout that resulted in the trampling of the Malaccan troops behind them. The final Portuguese assault came on 24 August and its success was followed by a tightly controlled pillaging of the fantastically wealthy city. For a second time Albuquerque had overcome steep odds to add another gem to the imperial necklace of Portuguese strongholds in Asia. Malacca, like Goa, also proved to be a precarious acquisition as the ousted Sultan kept trying to regain his realm while other local powers attempted to conquer it for themselves over the coming years.[28]

With Malacca under Portuguese control, Albuquerque decided that it was time to reconnoitre the Spice Islands of the Moluccas. He sent António Abreu and Francisco de Serrão to look for them in November 1511. Abreu visited Amboina and the Banda Islands, picked up a rich cargo of spices and returned safely to Malacca. In contrast, Serrão and his crew were shipwrecked but still managed to reach Ternate in the Moluccas in spite of the best efforts of some of the local pirates. There the Portuguese contrived to develop a cordial relationship with the local sultan which would stand their country in good stead. Other Portuguese ships continued to visit the Moluccas periodically from that point onward. Soon the Portuguese had become sufficiently well entrenched that they could withstand the Spanish incursions of the 1520s, which followed in the wake of Magellan's circumnavigations. They were also able to weather those occasions when the natives grew restless and resentful and attempted to throw them out. Much later it would take the Dutch and the English to dislodge them.[29]

In 1513 Albuquerque organized an expedition to conquer Aden, which commanded the strait known as the Bab el Mandab separating the Red Sea from the Indian Ocean. Aden was an independent city-state whose location at the crossroads of the busy trade routes into the Red Sea made it very wealthy. Others coveted Aden's wealth and position but its formidable natural and man-made fortifications protected it from would-be conquerors. Portugal had hoped to cut access to the Red Sea when Albuquerque and Cunha captured Socotra Island in 1506. Socotra's location, however, was not suitable and sea-traffic slipped by it largely unhindered. In light of that fact, King Manuel and Albuquerque had begun planning the seizure of Aden no later than 1510, although it was not until 1513 that the Portuguese finally acted.

Albuquerque gathered his fleet and a force of 2,200 men and departed from Goa on 7 February 1513. Arriving at Aden on 25 March, Albuquerque made a desultory effort to negotiate. The next day the Portuguese attempted to storm the city but their scaling ladders turned out to be too flimsy and broke under the weight of the ascending Portuguese troops. The assault failed miserably and the Portuguese withdrew to their ships. Albuquerque, however, was not finished even if Aden had eluded him. He sailed his fleet into the Red Sea with the goal of harassing Muslims in general and the Mamelukes of Egypt in particular. One of Albuquerque's more unrealistic plans was to dig a canal and divert the Nile River into the Red Sea and so ruin Cairo. Another scheme involved launching a cavalry raid against Medina, taking the Prophet Mohammed's body from its tomb and holding it hostage for the return of Jerusalem. Fortunately for the future of Christian–Muslim relations that project was never implemented. Instead Albuquerque and his fleet became bottled up in the Red Sea by adverse monsoons and was forced to anchor at Qamaran Island for several months. Finally in July 1513 the shifting monsoons allowed Albuquerque to sail out of the Red Sea and back to India.[30] His Red Sea expedition accomplished nothing and was his one great failure. Fortunately for Portugal, political instability in Egypt disrupted the spice trade there during much of the first half of the sixteenth century just about as effectively as any Portuguese blockade at Aden could have done. Portugal never managed to add Aden to its Asian empire. It withstood several other attempts by the Egyptians and the Portuguese to conquer it until 1538 when an Ottoman force finally captured it.[31]

In 1515 Albuquerque turned his attentions to Hormuz for the second time and added it to Portugal's growing network of fortresses in the Indian Ocean. Shortly after that last triumph, the incapable Lopo Soares de Albergaria replaced Albuquerque as governor of India. Depressed by the ingratitude of the Portuguese government, the stern old warrior contracted an illness that rendered him bedridden and ultimately killed him on 15 December at the age of sixty-two. As long as he lived King Manuel would not allow Albuquerque's body to be brought home to Portugal for burial. As the superstitious monarch put it, 'As long as his bones are there, India is safe.'[32]

With the death of Albuquerque, the great era of Portuguese conquest in Asia ended. His immediate successors as governors of India were either incompetent or corrupt, or both. Bits and pieces were added to the Portuguese empire as Albuquerque had created it. A fortress was established on Ceylon in 1518 and eventually Portugal dominated the island's coastal regions. In the Moluccas, Portugal outlasted Spanish competition during the 1520s and retained loose control there until the Dutch superseded them during the early seventeenth century. There were other conquests along the East African coast and at one time Portugal controlled fifty fortresses around the littoral of the Indian Ocean. Various combinations of Portuguese diplomats, missionaries and traders also made their way to China in 1514, Ethiopia in 1515 and Japan in 1543. The little nation of Portugal with its tiny population of between 1 and 2 million had accomplished feats in the Indian Ocean and the Far East that astonished contemporaries and has continued to amaze people in the subsequent years. They overcame ferocious and numerous enemies and treacherous seas and fearsome weather all at vast distances from their homeland.[33]

At the same time, it is important to keep Portugal's achievements in perspective, particularly an Asian or a global one. While Portugal significantly altered the patterns of trade in the Indian Ocean, it never monopolized or totally revolutionized that trade. Furthermore, the development of the international spice trade and the creation of the Portuguese empire in Asia were really only a small part of the overall flow of events in the world of the Indian Ocean and South Asia. From the Portuguese and the Western point of view, the Battle of Diu was one of the more significant engagements in world history. Many contemporary Islamic chronicles failed to mention that it even occurred.[34] That may be an attempt to ignore an ignominious defeat by Muslim historians. But it also reflects the fact that from a Middle Eastern and South Asian perspective, control of the spice trade was not a direct concern to most people, including some of the most powerful rulers.

The population of the Indian subcontinent in 1500 was probably over 100 million but only a minuscule number of those people had a connection with the production and sale of pepper and other spices. None of the major Indian states had important maritime interests, if they had any interests at all. Far more momentous events were occurring within the Indian subcontinent. The Lodi Sultanate of Delhi, the pre-eminent state of India, was in a state of decay at the beginning of the sixteenth century and others sought to supplant it. The ultimate winner of that competition was Babur of Kabul. After probing the Lodi Sultanate with raids for a number of years, he managed to defeat a numerically superior army from Delhi at the Battle of Panipat on 26 April 1526. Six days later he occupied Delhi and thus began the great Mogul Empire of India that would dominate the Indian subcontinent during the sixteenth and seventeenth centuries. In 1565 a coalition of the Muslim sultans of the Deccan would crushingly defeat the army of Vijayanagar and destroy its capital, ending the last great Hindu kingdom in India. Vijayanagar had loomed over the affairs of central and southern India for 200 years and suddenly it was gone. Then from 1576 to 1603 the Mogul Emperor Akbar the Great would conquer the northern Deccan. When he was finished about 110 million of the 140–50 million people living in the Indian subcontinent would be under Mogul rule. In comparison, Portugal and its string of coastal enclaves around the Indian Ocean appeared relatively insignificant.

Unfortunately for Portugal, the golden promise of the Asian spice trade failed to materialize to any great degree. Portugal lacked the business connections and apparatus it needed to gain the full benefit from its spice trade with Asia. As a result, middlemen in Europe soaked up much of the profits from the enterprise. The seaborne spice trade also meant high overheads for the Portuguese crown. The sea-route between Goa and Lisbon became known as the *carreira da India*.[35] It consisted of a round trip of 23,000 miles which took at least eighteen months to complete. Wear and tear on ships and crews was immense and further added to the expense of the voyage. Time and experience also proved the fierce Almeida to be correct about the proliferation of fortresses spreading Portugal's manpower too thin and costing too much to maintain. Ultimately Portugal did not have the military resources to enforce a true monopoly over the trade routes of the Indian Ocean. Much escaped the vigilance of the Portuguese patrols and by 1550 the Red Sea trade route had revived. Even the long-moribund way across the Persian Gulf and overland to Aleppo came back to life as the Ottoman Turks asserted their dominion over the region. Once more spices were flowing to the Mediterranean and Venice again entered the business, which presented Portugal with the spectre of stiff competition from a canny, experienced competitor.[36]

The Portuguese empire also suffered from official corruption which gravely impaired its efficiency. Almeida, Pacheco Pereira, Albuquerque and later Nuno da Cunha in the 1530s and João de Castro in the 1540s provided fearless, capable and dedicated leadership for the tough fighting men of Portugal. Other governors and captains were venal and sought only their own personal enrichment to the detriment of the interests of king and homeland. Officials stationed in the Moluccas were particularly notorious for their corruption but they were not alone.[37]

Portugal's possession of its Asian empire was also frequently and severely contested throughout much of the sixteenth century. Goa, Diu and Cochin all suffered numerous sieges as various Indian powers or the Mamelukes or the Ottomans sought to oust the Portuguese. Calicut and the Gujaratis remained irreconcilable even though they were periodically cowed militarily. From the late 1530s to the early 1580s, the Portuguese had to fend off attacks by formidable Ottoman Turkish armadas who made assaults on Hormuz and Diu.[38] All of this chronic warfare cost the Portuguese government dearly and added to the expensive overheads of maintaining their Asian empire.[39]

Portugal, itself, lacked focus in terms of its goals. A few more resources of soldiers and ships applied early on during the first two decades of the sixteenth century would have greatly strengthened Portugal's long-term position in Asia.[40] Instead the

Portuguese crown remained fixated on the conquest of Morocco, a truly quixotic enterprise. Scarce resources were diverted from the Indian Ocean, where they might have done some good, to Morocco, where they were swallowed up in the maw of see-saw warfare that Portugal was doomed ultimately to lose. Eventually the mirage of conquest in Morocco would result in June 1578 in the death of the unrealistic and irresponsible King Sebastian at the Battle of Ksar-el-Kebir and the death or capture of thousands of Portugal's best warriors. It also set in motion the chain of events that led to Philip II of Spain's succession as King of Portugal in 1580 when the direct line of the Avis dynasty died out. Becoming one of the possessions of the Spanish monarchy had a very negative effect on Portugal's overseas empire by making it a target of Spain's many enemies. When Portugal regained its independence under the Braganza family over half a century later, its worldwide colonies, particularly in Asia, lay prostrate and weakened.[41] Portugal, the nation who had led the way during the age of exploration, found that being in control of a commercial empire was an ultimately disappointing and, even worse, a debilitating experience.

THE DISCOVERY AND CONQUEST OF MEXICO[42]

While the Portuguese were conquering their spice empire in the Indian Ocean during the first decade and a half of the sixteenth century, the Spanish on Hispaniola faced a very different and very disappointing situation. By 1517, in spite of many expeditions, they had failed to locate Asia as Columbus had promised. Instead they had largely revealed the outline of the eastern seaboard of the Americas, a vast and previously unsuspected world. Columbus initially claimed to have found various Asian spices growing on Hispaniola and the neighbouring islands but that 'discovery' soon proved to be illusory. Hispaniola and its natives possessed gold but after the initial accumulated hoard had been wrenched away from its Taino owners, the local gold deposits proved to be paltry. Only the brutal enslavement of the natives to work on placer mines produced appreciable amounts of the precious metal. Compared to Portugal's profits from El Mina and the rest of its West African trade, Hispaniola came in a distant second. The situation on Hispaniola was also worsening.[43]

Back-breaking work, brutality, starvation and disease all caused the native population to go into a rapid decline. The kidnapping of fresh Native American slaves during raids on the surrounding islands did little to arrest the drop in numbers. It did, however, create fear and hostility toward Europeans among the peoples of the surrounding regions. Without sufficient workers, gold production stagnated or sank. The conquests of Puerto Rico in 1508 and Cuba in 1511 proved to be fleeting stopgaps that merely exposed their meagre populations to the insatiable rapacity of the Spanish conquistadors. Declining gold production and the disastrous erosion of the aboriginal population of the islands forced many of the Spanish settlers to take up farming and cattle herding. These enterprises could never produce the levels of

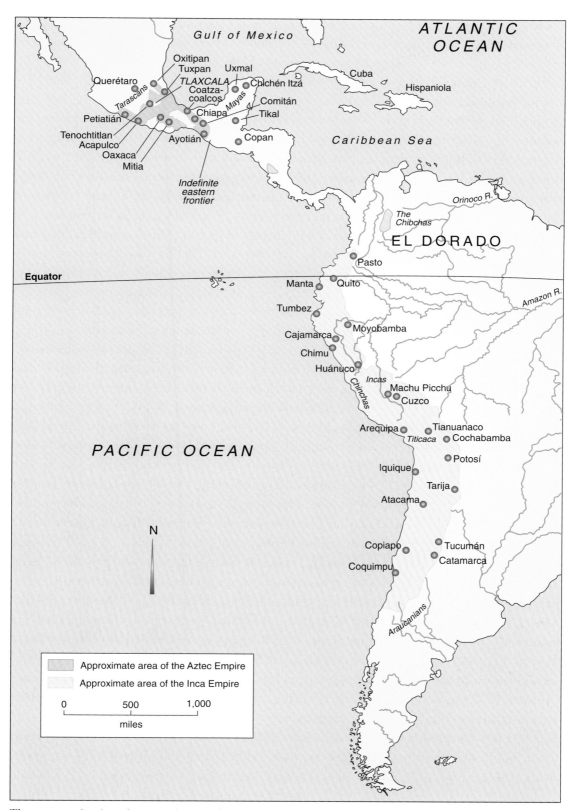

The great native American empires on the eve of the Spanish conquest.

wealth that most of the Spanish on Hispaniola and Cuba were looking for. As a result the Spanish islands housed increasingly discontented communities ready to seek their fortune whenever an opportunity presented itself.

The first intimation that lands with more potential lay to the west occurred in 1514 when Diego Velázquez, the governor of Cuba, reported visits from the natives living to the west of Cuba.[44] At that time the prevailing geographical concept among the Spanish was that various large islands lay to the west along with the long-sought-for passage or strait leading to the wealth of Asia. Such thoughts were more wishful thinking than anything else. Various tentative voyages cruised the coastline but failed to locate any break or gap. Anxious to find unknown, wealthy lands, Velázquez mounted an expedition in 1517. Francisco Hernandez de Córdoba commanded three ships and over a hundred adventurers.[45] Leaving Santiago de Cuba on 8 February, the Spaniards sailed west for six days and reached Cape Catoche on the Yucatan Peninsula. Unlike when Ponce de León visited the Yucatan, Córdoba's men sighted a substantial Maya town with large pyramidal temples. They promptly dubbed it 'Gran Cairo'. Its inhabitants were obviously much more culturally sophisticated than the simple Tainos of the islands. More importantly for the Spanish, they were wealthier.

At first the natives welcomed their Spanish visitors but an attack soon followed. Seeking to avoid trouble, Córdoba moved his fleet further along the coast and reached the Maya city of Champotan. There he encountered even greater hostility from the locals. In spite of warnings, Córdoba landed most of his men and set up a camp away from the beach. That mistake allowed a large body of Maya warriors to surround him and strike. In the fierce fight that followed twenty of the Spaniards died while most of the rest had been wounded by the time they slashed their way back to the shore and to the safety of their ships. Córdoba suffered from thirty-three wounds himself, one of which was quite serious. The expedition needed to replenish its stores of fresh water but the hostile Mayans prevented the Spaniards from landing and doing so. In desperation the Spanish set sail for Florida taking advantage of favourable winds and currents. It was to no avail. Warriors from the local tribe also attacked them using deadly longbows. After withdrawing to their ships, the survivors of Córdoba's battered party limped into Havana where their stricken leader succumbed to his many injuries.

In spite of the heavy casualties and the death of its leader, Velázquez and the Spaniards of Cuba viewed Córdoba's expedition as a success. At long last, Native Americans with a more advanced culture had been located, even if they were unfriendly. Just why the Mayas exhibited such hostility is unclear. They may have heard rumours of the atrocities occurring on Cuba and Hispaniola which put them on their guard. It is possible that roving Spanish slavers had visited the Yucatan earlier and angered the locals with their depredations. Córdoba and his men were seeking fresh water, a precious commodity in the Yucatan. The Maya frequently fought wars over water and they probably did not take kindly to the Spanish helping themselves to such a scarce resource. The prospect of native aggression, however, did not daunt Velázquez in the slightest.

Velázquez organized a second expedition and placed his nephew Juan de Grijalva in command.[46] It consisted of 4 ships and about 200 men but this time the Spanish brought along a couple of cannon. Although he left Santiago de Cuba at the end of January, Grijalva took his time clearing Cuban waters and did not arrive at Cozumel until the beginning of May. Grijalva proved to be a cautious commander and avoided Córdoba's mistake of getting surrounded. The fact that the Spanish force possessed cannon also helped to terrify and to confuse native attackers. Arriving at Champotan on 26 May, the Spanish drove off a Maya attack with relative ease. Grijalva continued along the coast and eventually reached the vicinity of modern Vera Cruz. There on the Isle of Sacrifices, the Spanish came across the grisly evidence of human sacrifice. On the mainland they encountered amiable Totonac Indians. Since it was Grijalva's policy to maintain friendly relations, if at all possible, with the native peoples he met, the two groups got along quite well. Continuing further up the coast, Grijalva reached the Rio Cazones where the local Huaxtecs launched an ineffectual canoe assault on the Spanish ships. After that experience, Grijalva decided to return to Cuba which he reached on 29 September. Throughout the expedition Grijalva sought to treat the natives he met in a calm manner. His peaceful approach would later smooth the way for Cortés. Grijalva also maintained a very cautious attitude about making landings and never contemplated the possibility of establishing a permanent settlement. His

Pre-columbian Mexican city. From William Cullen Bryant, *A Popular History of the United States* (New York, Scribners, 1891), vol. 1, p. 198.

companions found his policy to be lacking in courage and in enterprise and so did his uncle Governor Velázquez.

Even more than Córdoba, Grijalva's expedition revealed a previously unsuspected world of Native American cities and kingdoms to the Spanish. Prior to that, all that the Spanish had found in the Americas were simple tribes living in primitive, little villages and possessing scant material wealth as the Spanish understood it. In comparison, the peoples of the Yucatan and the lower Gulf coast of Mexico were obviously wealthier and more sophisticated.[47] On the Yucatan the Spanish encountered peoples of the Mayan culture while along the Gulf coast there lived Tabascans, Totonacs and Huaxtecs. It was a thrilling discovery for the Spanish but, in fact, they had merely scratched the surface. Further inland lay the rich lands of the Mexica/Aztecs, Tarascans, Cholulans, Tlaxcalans, Mixtecs and many others. All of these cultures practised sedentary agricultures; engaged in sophisticated commerce, arts and crafts; built and lived in urban centres; and followed complex systems of religious beliefs. While these various cultures were distinct in terms of their arts, languages and religions, they were broadly similar in many ways. In terms of metallurgy, they only possessed a stone-age technology although the Tarascans were beginning to produce copper tools and weapons. As for the other peoples of Mexico, their darts, spears and obsidian-edged wooden swords called *macauhuitl* all proved relatively ineffective against the steel weapons and armour of the Spanish. Corn, beans, squash and peppers formed the mainstays of their diets. Their only domesticated animals were dogs and turkeys and they ate both. Otherwise the people of Mexico possessed no large domestic animals for riding, pulling, milking, eating or skinning. Initially the horses of the Spanish were an incomprehensible phenomenon to the natives of Mexico. A cavalry charge by a dozen Spanish cavaliers could throw thousands of normally brave native warriors into a panicked flight. All of the various Mexican cultures practised a gloomy, pes-simistic religion with many gods, some of which demanded human sacrifice by means of cutting out the victim's heart. These offerings were often followed by acts of ritual can-nibalism. While the Mexica/Aztecs appear to have been at the forefront of the practitioners of human sacrifice,

Juan de Grijalva. From Justin Winsor, *A Narrative and Critical History of America* (Boston, Houghton Mifflin, 1886), vol. 2, p. 216.

the gruesome act permeated life throughout Mexico. It certainly influenced the way peoples of pre-Hispanic Mexico engaged in warfare. Instead of focusing on trying to kill their opponents, the armies of Mexico sought to capture as many of their enemies as possible and take them home for sacrifice. Individual fighters sought to wound or to incapacitate their enemies and seldom sought to eradicate them completely. Such attitudes were antithetical to the Spanish approach to warfare as their goal was to kill their enemies rapidly and as many as possible. Small numbers of conquistadors could engage in battles with vastly numerically superior native armies and still emerge victorious.

Diego Velázquez was anxious to follow up on the intriguing discoveries of Córdoba and Grijalva before someone else did. Moving quickly he arranged for a third expedition to explore the western lands which at that time were assumed to be large islands. Because he was not ready to lead the enterprise himself, Velázquez needed to pick a commander he could trust. That person should be more resourceful and adventurous than Grijalva but not so much that he might seize opportunities for wealth and fame that Velázquez wanted to reserve for himself. The governor finally decided to offer the position to Hernan Cortés, a 34-year-old gentleman who had thus far not distinguished himself in Cuba.[48]

Cortés plunged into the work of organizing the new project which rapidly grew in size under his leadership. When the expedition sailed from Cuba, it consisted of 11 ships, over 500 men, 16 horses, 30 crossbows, 12 arquebuses, several cannon and some mastiff dogs. As it increased in size, Velázquez became more alarmed. He feared that Cortés was collecting a force that would be sufficiently large to make significant conquests without the governor being present. Fearing that Cortés would steal his thunder, Velázquez began to contemplate dismissing him from the command. But just when Velázquez had finally decided to remove Cortés, the wily conquistador slipped

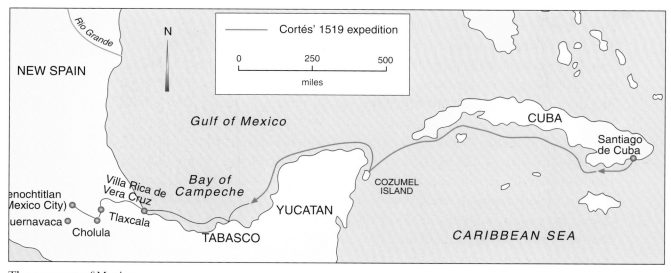

The conquest of Mexico.

out of Santiago harbour on 18 November 1518. He continued to gather supplies along the Cuban coast and did not arrive at Cozumel Island off the Yucatan coast until 13 March 1519. There among the local Maya inhabitants he found the Spanish castaway Geromino de Aguilar. A survivor of the ill-fated Valdivia expedition to Panama, Aguilar had been living among the Maya since 1511. He learned to speak the local language of Chontal and Cortés decided to use him as an interpreter since the existing Maya interpreters were unreliable. Further along the coast at Potonchan, the Spanish easily defeated a large force of Mayas on 24 March which convinced Cortés that native weapons were ineffective against the military technology of the Europeans. In the aftermath the Maya rulers gave the Spanish various presents including young women. Fatefully, among that group of young women was Malinali, better known to history as Doña Marina. She could speak Chontal Maya with Aguilar but also spoke Nahuatl, the language of the Mexica/Aztecs and other peoples of central Mexico. Doña Marina proved completely loyal to Cortés, eventually becoming his mistress and bore him a son. Besides her translating, she also provided the Spaniards with priceless information about Mexican culture, customs and politics.[49]

On 20 April Cortés moved on to the Isle of Sacrifices and soon after reached a place the Spanish named San Juan de Ulúa. There he made contact with the Totonacs, a nation ever anxious to find allies who would support them against their hated Aztec overlords. Emissaries from the Aztec emperor also visited the Spanish several times bearing magnificent gifts which included a disc of gold representing the sun and a disc of silver representing the moon. From the arrival of the Spanish ships at San Juan de Ulloa, the Aztec intelligence network observed the activities of the Spanish strangers. Questions abounded among the wondering natives of Mexico.[50] Who were the Spaniards or even what were they? What did they want? Fortunately for Cortés, Mexican legends predicted the return of the benevolent god Quetzalcoatl from across the eastern sea. Some of the natives thought Cortés was Quetzalcoatl returned. Other legends made it possible to identify the Spaniards with Huitzilopochtli, the blood-thirsty god of the sun and war, or with Tezcatlipoca, the trickster god. Some groups in the Aztec hierarchy considered the Spaniards to be returning gods while others did not. Significantly and eventually fatally, the Aztec Emperor Montezuma believed, at least initially, that the Spanish were gods. This created an uncertainty within Montezuma which inhibited him from acting resolutely in the face of the growing Spanish threat.

The Aztec Empire centred on its capital of Tenochtitlan, a city of possibly 200,000 inhabitants that in consort with its allies ruled a vast empire with millions of subjects that stretched from the Atlantic to the Pacific coasts of central Mexico. Pockets of resistance survived, most notably Tlaxcala, but the Mexica/Aztec were the dominant power of Mesoamerica and that success also made them widely hated. Emperor Montezuma was about fifty years old in 1519 and had ruled since 1502. Spanish observers described him as short with a slight or delicate build. Prior to the arrival of Cortés, Montezuma's subjects would have characterized their emperor as strong, decisive and determined. He had demonstrated great prowess as a warrior. Unfortunately he was excessively superstitious and the arrival of the Spanish as potential gods at an inauspicious time in the light of ancient prophecies and legends rendered him timid and irresolute. The result was a disaster for Montezuma and his people.[51]

Cortés shrewdly detected that many of the subject peoples of the Aztec Empire bitterly resented their overlords. Because Aztec policy left local rulers in place, while Aztec garrisons and officials were often far away, central control was loose. This enabled the Spanish and the Totonacs to cultivate each other as allies unimpeded. Cortés saw vast but obviously vague opportunities in Mexico and decided to pursue them with a calculated recklessness. He provided his self-seeking actions with the comfortable justification of promoting the conversion of the native peoples to Christianity. Everywhere Cortés went he preached Christianity and criticized the local religions as false and idolatrous. On occasion, the Spanish went so far as to destroy idols although Father Bartolomé de Olmedo generally tried to dissuade them from such highly provocative actions. Allies or enemies, none of the Indians welcomed Cortés's interference with their religion but it remained a cornerstone of his approach to subjugating Mexico for Spain.

Colluding with his friends and supporters among the expedition, he established the new settlement of Vera Cruz as a municipality with the purpose of settling Mexico for Spain. In doing this, Cortés effectively declared his independence from the authority of Velázquez back in Cuba. Velázquez's backers among the conquistadors did not like this action nor did the more timid among the expedition who wanted to return to Cuba. Conspiracies to overthrow Cortés started to simmer and periodically they erupted throughout the entire conquest of Mexico. Some were more serious than others but even the best-supported conspirators never managed to overthrow the politically nimble Cortés.[52]

At the end of June, Cortés sent the accumulated Mexican treasures back to King Charles in Spain hoping to curry favour and deflect criticism of his dubiously legal actions. Then after quelling a mutiny, Cortés ordered the scuttling of the ten remaining Spanish ships. That effectively ended any possibility of the expedition returning to Cuba. The only choice left for the Spanish was to march inland and seek their fortune. That is exactly what Cortés did on 8 August. He left the coast for Tenochtitlan, the Aztec capital, with a force that consisted of 300 conquistadors including 40 crossbowmen, 20 arquebuses, 16 horsemen and 3 cannon along with several hundred Cuban Indians and hundreds more Totonacs who mostly served as bearers.

Cortés's first destination was the country of Tlaxcala, whose people maintained a stubborn but precarious independence from the Aztecs. The Spanish hoped to woo the Tlaxcalans as allies but initially that warlike nation doggedly resisted Cortés's entry into their land. Attacks began on 31 August with the Indians managing to kill two Spanish horses. Some Tlaxcalans viewed the Spanish as dangerous barbarian invaders akin to the primitive Chichimecs of northern Mexico. That opinion was

Right: An eighteenth-century Spanish portrait of Hernan Cortés. (Mary Evans Picture Library)

Below: A sixteenth-century Native American codex depicting Cortés meeting with a Mexican delegation, by an unknown artist. Doña Marina, his ubiquitous translator and mistress, stands behind him. (Heritage Image Partnership)

TO
RITR·DI·MOTEZVMA LE
CAVATO·DALL·ORIGINA
VENVTO·DAL·MESSICO
MO
AL·SER·G·D·DI·TOSCA·NA

Montezuma. From Justin Winsor, *A Narrative and Critical History of America* (Boston, Houghton Mifflin, 1886), vol. 2, p. 363.

shared with some of the Mexica/Aztec leadership. Ferocious assaults continued for several days but the Spanish managed to survive. At that point with their armies exhausted, the Tlaxcalan leaders who favoured an alliance with the Spanish came to the fore. They made peace and on 18 September Cortés and his weary troops entered the city of Tlaxcala.[53]

After resting from their struggles, Cortés and his men left Tlaxcala accompanied by a force of Tlaxcalans and headed for the great religious city of Cholula on 12 October. There the local leaders plotted a massacre of the Spanish but warnings reached Cortés and he ordered a pre-emptive strike on the Cholulans. Whether the Cholulans really intended to attack the Spanish is unclear and they may have been framed by the Tlaxcalans. But whichever was the case, Cortés's bloody action thoroughly cowed the Cholulans and many of their neighbours while it increased the anxieties of the pensive Montezuma as the seemingly omniscient and unstoppable strangers continued their advance on Tenochtitlan.[54]

Finally on 1 November the Spanish army departed from Cholula and began the last stage of its journey to Tenochtitlan and the Valley of Mexico.[55] The journey included crossing a rugged range of mountains through a little-used pass between the live volcanoes of Ixtaccihuatl and Popocatepetl. Cortés chose this particular route over the easier and more heavily used passes to lessen the danger of ambush. From the summit of the pass Cortés's force descended into the great Valley of Mexico. In those days the Valley of Mexico contained a large lake or series of lakes divided by causeways and marshes. Some parts of the waters were salty although others were fresh. Substantial sections of the shoreline consisted of marshes. Tenochtitlan, itself, was located on an island and was connected to the mainland by causeways wide enough for four horses to ride abreast. Its population numbered about 200,000 and its skyline bristled with impressive pyramidal temples while rich palaces dotted its various neighbourhoods. To the eyes of the wondering conquistadors, it compared favourably with such great Old World metropolises as Constantinople and Naples. The rest of the lakeshore and valley was sprinkled generously with other rich cities and towns. Some of the Spaniards were so awed by what they saw that they wondered if they were dreaming. As Bernal Diaz, a member of Cortés's army, later wrote,

With such wonderful sights to gaze on we did not know what to say, or if this was real that we saw before our eyes. On the land side there were great cities, and on the lake many more. The lake was crowded with canoes. At intervals along the causeway there were many bridges, and before us was the great city of Mexico [Tenochtitlan]. As for us, we were scarcely four hundred strong, and we well remembered the words and warnings of the people of Huexotzinco and Tlascala and Tlamanalco, and the many other warnings we had received to beware of entering the city of Mexico, since they would kill us as soon as they had us inside. Let the interested reader consider whether there is not much to ponder in this narrative of mine. What men in all the world have shown such daring?[56]

On 8 November 1519 the Spanish army entered a causeway leading to Tenochtitlan and as they neared the city word arrived that Montezuma was approaching. Cortés stopped to wait for him and soon the great emperor appeared clothed in the most splendid garments and transported in a magnificent litter carried by his great nobles. When Montezuma dismounted, other nobles swept the ground before him and laid down their rich cloaks for him to walk upon. No Aztec dared to look him in the eye. Cortés refused to let his awe show and instead waited calmly with Doña Marina at his side to interpret. When Montezuma reached Cortés various pleasantries

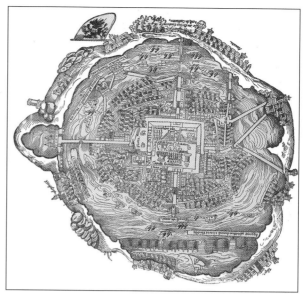

European map of Tenochtitlan first published in 1524. From Justin Winsor, *A Narrative and Critical History of America* (Boston, Houghton Mifflin, 1886), vol. 2, p. 364.

and gifts were exchanged after which the Spanish army was allowed into the city and taken to a large palace where it was to be housed. Cortés and his men had observed much gold and other riches on that day and they fervently desired to make the treasure theirs by any means.[57]

Cortés and his little army had marched into the belly of the beast, the capital of the Mexica/Aztecs and they were becoming increasingly worried. Fierce and numberless enemies surrounded them. Only the most audacious move could bring them, not just survival but victory, and that is exactly the course of action Cortés decided to take. On 14 November the Spanish seized Montezuma as a hostage. Fortunately for the Spanish, the Mexica/Aztec Empire was highly centralized with close control culminating in the emperor. With Montezuma a captive, there was no one to make the momentous decisions or to issue orders. The proud elite of Aztec society seethed in frustration and anger and they longed to strike at the unwelcome Spanish intruders but the commands coming from their hostage emperor ordered them to do nothing.[58]

An uneasy and precarious peace reigned over Tenochtitlan for about five months as Cortés clung tightly to the tail of the Aztec tiger, Montezuma. At this point word reached Cortés that Pánfilo Narváez had arrived at Vera Cruz from Cuba in 18 ships with a force of 900 men. His orders from Governor Velázquez were to arrest Cortés for treason. Cortés now faced an almost intractable dilemma. His army was riddled with Velázquez supporters, the inconstant Totonacs had turned to Narváez as their new deliverer, and Montezuma and the Aztec elite had opened up communication with Narváez in hopes of playing one Spanish faction off against the other. The situation demanded action and Cortés boldly provided it. Leaving Tenochtitlan in early May with the bulk of his army, he marched on Narváez's camp at Cempoallan. Judiciously spreading bribes among Narváez's officers with promises of more riches to follow, Cortés first weakened Narváez's authority and then launched a vigorous attack on the night of 28/9 May. Narváez's army only offered token resistance in spite of outnumbering Cortés's force by three to one. With Narváez and a few faithful officers as captives, the vast majority of the new army enthusiastically joined Cortés and together they all marched back to Tenochtitlan.[59]

Meanwhile, the false calm in Tenochtitlan ended. When he left to confront Narváez, Cortés had left his impetuous captain Pedro Alvarado behind with Doña Marina and slightly more than one hundred troops to guard Montezuma. It was a nerve-racking position to be surrounded by myriad sullen and increasingly hostile Aztecs. To make matters worse, a major Aztec festival took place during that interval of time which involved a large public ceremony. Alvarado jumped to the incorrect conclusion that an attack on the Spanish compound was imminent. Once again, the Spanish response was to strike first and ask questions later. Heavily armed Spanish soldiers waded into an unarmed crowd of native nobles and slaughtered hundreds of them. Alvarado's action brought the Aztec's latent anger to the boil and the small Spanish force found itself besieged within the palace compound in the midst of a hostile city.[60]

Cortés and Montezuma meet for the first time outside of Tenochtitlan. From Charles A. McMurray, *Pioneers on Land and Sea* (New York, Macmillan, 1913), p. 205.

A seventeenth-century painting showing the disastrous retreat of Cortés and his army from Tenochtitlan, 1 July 1520, by Miguel Gonzalez II. (Scala/Art Resource, NY)

Cortés and his reinforced army returned to an ominously quiet Tenochtitlan on 24 June and reached the Spanish compound unopposed. Once the entire Spanish force was trapped in Tenochtitlan, fighting began and steadily increased in intensity. Cortés tried to use Montezuma to quell his people's anger but respect for the emperor's authority had evaporated. His people had come to despise him for his weakness and vacillation toward the hated Spanish intruders. When he appeared before his people from a palace balcony and implored them to stop attacking, they replied with jeers and rained stones and darts on him. Montezuma fell mortally wounded and later died on the morning of 30 June.[61]

One positive consequence, from the Spanish point of view, to come out of Alvarado's ill-considered strike during the Aztec festival was that it resulted in the death of a major portion of the Aztec leadership. The Spanish faced a frenzied but largely leaderless populace. On 29 June Cortés tried to demoralize them further by launching an assault on one of the neighbouring great temples. This succeeded in destroying some idols but did nothing to dampen the Aztec enthusiasm to fight. Recognizing that their position was untenable, Cortés and his army attempted to slip out of Tenochtitlan on the night of 30 June. But they failed to escape undetected or unscathed. Aztec warriors launched onslaughts from rooftops as the retreating Spanish moved through the streets. Once the Spanish reached the causeways they found themselves harassed by Aztec warriors operating from swarms of canoes. The Aztecs had brought down the bridges that formed parts of the causeways which created gaps that now blocked the path of the retreating Spanish until they could be filled up with abandoned baggage and corpses sufficiently to be crossed over. Conquistadors greedily laden with looted gold fell into the lake and drowned. There were hundreds of Tlaxcalan allies killed in the retreat, while some 600 Spanish were lost. A number of these unlucky conquistadors were captured alive and later suffered the grisly fate of having their hearts cut out on the sacrificial altar of some Aztec temple. The indomitable Cortés, however, managed to survive the ghastly experience that the Spanish dubbed 'La Noche Triste', 'The Sad Night'. Stopping to rest by a tree on the mainland at Tacuba, Cortés was already planning how he would return and conquer Tenochtitlan.[62]

The Spanish survivors desperately needed to reach friendly Tlaxcala to rest and to regroup but they were on the wrong side of the lakes. So they set out around the northern side of the lakes and at Otumba on 8 July fought their way through a large Aztec army. Upon reaching Tlaxcala, good luck smiled on Cortés once again when the anti-Spanish faction of Tlaxcalan leaders failed to regain control. Such a development would have resulted in the complete eradication of the Spanish survivors. By 1 August Cortés had recovered sufficiently to begin attacking Aztec outposts. Even more importantly, smallpox had reached Vera Cruz during April 1520 and had spread to the Valley of Mexico by September. The disease indiscriminately killed some 40 per cent of the aboriginal population, both friends and foes of the Spanish, including Montezuma's replacement as emperor, Cuitláhuac. The stalwart Cuauhtémoc took his place. Also, during the latter part of 1520 six small Spanish expeditions arrived at Vera Cruz bringing much needed reinforcements and supplies.[63]

By 27 December 1520, Cortés was ready to depart from Tlaxcala for an assault on Tenochtitlan.[64] The Spanish offensive included the launching of a fleet of brigantine sailing vessels armed with small cannon on 28 April 1521. Their purpose was to wrest control of the lake from the fleets of native canoes. By 10 June the Spanish and their thousands of native allies had re-entered the precincts of Tenochtitlan in spite of dogged Aztec resistance. Fortunately for the Spanish, the Aztecs largely continued to follow their traditional tactics of trying to take enemy soldiers alive for sacrifice rather than killing them on the battlefield. As a result Spanish fatalities were relatively few, although they suffered many wounds and some had some hair-raising escapes. During one attack Bernal Diaz narrowly avoided capture. As he described it, after falling into the lake,

> I was seized by a great number of Indians, but I managed to free my sword-arm and the Lord Jesus Christ gave me strength to deal them a few good thrusts, with which I saved myself, though I had a severe wound in the other arm. Once safely out of the water, I lost all sensation and could not stand on my feet or take breath, so exhausted was I by my efforts to free myself from that rabble, and by copious loss of blood. I declare that when they had me in their claws I was mentally commending myself to our Lord God and Our Lady, His Blessed Mother; and He it was that gave me strength to save myself. Thanks be to God for the mercy He granted me.[65]

All was not unbroken success for the Spanish. On 30 June Aztec forces inflicted a serious defeat on the Spanish and their allies in which twenty conquistadors were killed and another fifty-three were captured and later sacrificed on top of a temple in plain sight of the Spanish force's position. On that occasion Cortés narrowly escaped being seized. Only his bodyguard Cristóbal de Olea's bravery and swordsmanship saved him and that effort cost Olea his life. Many Indian allies also died in the defeat and for a brief period of time Cortés saw the support from his Indian allies dwindle to almost nothing. The assistance of thousands of warriors from Tlaxcala and other allies was essential to the offensive against Tenochtitlan and their withdrawal left the relatively small Spanish forces dangerously exposed to Aztec attack. The crisis passed when some Tlaxcalan troops made an independent and successful sortie into Tenochtitlan which resulted in a restoration of allied morale. After that the native allies rapidly rejoined the Spanish besiegers and the shadow of inevitable defeat fell across Tenochtitlan. The Spanish began to raze captured parts of the city in a systematic manner as a means of reducing the amount of dangerous street fighting and give their cavalry room to manoeuvre. Slowly but surely the population of Tenochtitlan was squeezed into an ever smaller area while supplies of food and drinkable water dwindled and smallpox swept through the beleaguered inhabitants.

Finally on 13 August the Aztec capital surrendered and the Spanish captured its emperor Cuauhtémoc.[66] The beautiful centre of the fearsome Mexica/Aztec Empire had at last fallen and almost nothing was left of the majestic buildings that amazed the conquistadors when they first entered the Valley of Mexico. Writing of the wonders of Tenochtitlan almost fifty years after he had first seen them in 1519, Bernal Diaz wistfully reported, 'today all that I then saw is overthrown and destroyed; nothing is left standing'.[67]

Cortés and his bold conquistadors had overcome the Mexica/Aztecs but they could never have done it without the help of the Tlaxcalans and the other native allies who supplied tens of thousands of troops and bearers. Unfortunately for the native allies, once they had destroyed the hated Mexica/Aztecs, they found that the Spanish newcomers had stepped in to take their place. In the years that followed various expeditions of conquistadors fanned out to take possession of the lands around the Valley of Mexico. Only the Tlaxcalans secured relatively privileged treatment. The other peoples of Mexico soon found the new Spanish overlords to be just as oppressive, if not more so, than the old Aztec tribute collectors. Misery increased as smallpox and other Old World diseases swept through the highly vulnerable Native American peoples, significantly reducing the population.[68]

Cortés and his men had conquered a great and wealthy empire and the resulting loot poured into Spain. Ironically, few of the conquistadors personally became rich. Bernal Diaz died at the age of ninety in about 1580 as poor as he had been born and he was not alone. Others died in battles with the natives or fighting each other as the conquistadors fell out among themselves. Diseases and the rigours of campaigning killed others. For a time Cortés emerged as a hero and a celebrity in the Indies and back in Spain even gaining the title of Marquis of Oaxaca. His success and the manner in which he achieved it also created many enemies for him. Some of them filed lawsuits against him seeking compensation for alleged dishonesty and misdeeds that he committed during the conquest of Mexico. Cortés spent much of his later life combating these lawsuits. When he died in 1547, he had little wealth to show for the great conquests he had made and all the loot he had supposedly stolen from the Aztecs, the Spanish crown and his comrades-in-arms.[69] Cortés did demonstrate to Spain and the rest of Europe that Columbus's discovery contained lands of vast wealth that were well worth exploiting in their own right. Instead of seeking to find a way to Asia around the barrier of the Americas, conquistadors tried to emulate Cortés by finding and controlling other hitherto unknown Native American civilizations and pillaging their treasures.

THE CONQUEST OF PERU AND AFTER

As Cortés was engaged in conquering Old Mexico, the situation down in the Spanish colony of Panama was even worse than that of Hispaniola and Cuba. Gold proved scarce and hard to exploit while the natives retreated into the murky fastness of the area's dense rainforests and showed an implacable hostility to the invading Spanish. Conquered natives quickly died from abuse or disease leaving the Spanish short of workers while the raising of cattle was a very meagre and unsatisfactory option in the environment of Panama. From a Spanish point of view there was little profit in Panama to compensate for the grim living conditions that prevailed there. Still the Spanish spread across the isthmus and founded settlements on the Pacific coast. Soon rumours of a great and rich empire located to the south along the Pacific coast of South America began to trickle into Panama. At about the same time news of Cortés's exploits in Mexico reached the Spanish in Panama who were eager to emulate his success. In 1522 Pascual de Andagoya sailed down the west coast of South America looking for the mysterious empire called 'Biru' or Peru. It was an extremely difficult voyage as treacherous winds and currents impeded any sailing ship trying to make its way south while the inhospitable coast was lined by mangrove swamps and wastelands. The natives living there were poor and possessed no high culture or gold. It was not an encouraging start but the possibility of finding a wealthy southern empire continued to beckon to the Spanish in Panama.[70]

Fatefully in 1524 Francisco Pizarro and his partners Diego de Almagro and Hernando de Luque took over the quest for the land of Peru.[71] A native of Trujillo in Extremadura, Pizarro was born in 1478, the illegitimate son of a Spanish captain and a farmer's daughter. Although he was not legitimate, he was not a loner and as the eldest sibling he became the leader of a close-knit band of brothers and half-brothers.[72] In his youth he herded pigs and never learned to read or write. He became a man possessed of iron determination and courage along with a ruthlessness without pity when needed. All of these qualities helped him to survive the many perils of a conquistador in the Americas. Arriving in Hispaniola in 1502, he moved to Panama in 1509 as a member of the Alonso de Ojeda expedition. During 1513 he accompanied Balboa's trip to the Pacific after which he settled down in Panama and formed his partnership with Almagro and Luque. Their business consisted of cattle-raising, gold-mining and slave-trading and they enjoyed modest success by the early 1520s. Pizarro also managed to become friends with the irascible governor of Panama, Pedrarias Davila.[73]

Compared to his swineherd days in Spain, Pizarro had achieved great success in Panama but Cortés's conquest of Mexico had fired the ambitions, the greed and the imaginations of Spanish swordsmen throughout the Caribbean and Terra Firme, including Pizarro. Rumours of mysterious Peru somewhere on the unexplored Pacific coast of South America further intrigued Pizarro, Almagro and Luque. Securing permission to explore that area from Pedrarias, Pizarro and Almagro sailed from Panama in 1524 with Luque providing the finances. It was a disappointing voyage fraught with danger. All they found was more inhospitable coastland inhabited by even more unwelcoming natives who lived a paltry existence and possessed no wealth as the Spanish understood the term. Returning to Panama with plenty of casualties, including Almagro who had lost an eye fighting the Indians, but

Francisco Pizarro. From William H. Prescott, *The Conquest of Peru* (New York, Lippincott, 1874), vol. 1, frontispiece.

no booty, Pizarro found enthusiasm for financing his Peruvian venture had cooled considerably.[74]

In spite of their setback, Pizarro and Almagro continued to believe that a great empire lay to the south and they managed to scrape together funding for a second voyage, which departed in November 1526. The expedition consisted of 2 ships and 160 men, which was too many for the task of exploring the desolate country they would have to pass through. Pizarro and the bulk of his crew disembarked at the San Juan River with the hope of travelling overland and living off the land. Meanwhile, Almagro took one ship back to Panama to gather supplies and reinforcements. The other ship under the pilot Bartolomé de Ruiz continued southward and crossed the equator. In those waters he encountered a richly laden Peruvian trading raft which served to confirm that a wealthy, civilized area did lay to the south. Ruiz returned with his good news to find Pizarro and his men starving and facing the threat of attack. He moved them to the safety of Gallo Island which is where the relief ship from Panama found them. The new governor Pedro de los Rios had ordered the ship's captain to bring any willing survivors home and not to engage in any further exploration.

Buoyed by Ruiz's report, Pizarro refused to leave Gallo Island. He also managed to persuade twelve or thirteen others to stay with him. According to the historian Garcilaso de la Vega, Pizarro dramatically drew a line in the sand on Gallo Island and challenged his men, saying: 'Gentlemen, this line stands for the labors, hunger, thirst, and toil, wounds and sickness, and all other dangers and trials that must be undergone in this conquest, risking life itself. Those who have the spirit to face them and to prevail in this heroic enterprise, let them cross the line in proof of their courage and in open testimony of their loyalty to me. And let those who feel themselves unworthy of so great a task return to Peru.'[75]

Other versions of this story have Pizarro appealing more to his men's greed than courage by emphasizing the riches to be found in Peru as opposed to the poverty that waited back in Panama.[76] Of course, some chroniclers in their accounts fail to mention the dramatic episode of the line in the sand at all, causing some doubt as to whether it even occurred. What is certain is that Pizarro and about a dozen men were dropped off by the governor's ship at nearby Gorgona Island where they stayed for seven months. While they awaited resupply, they lived on sea turtles, fish, molluscs and rodents. Finally in March 1528, Ruiz returned with fresh supplies procured by Almagro in Panama. Apparently unfazed by his sufferings on Gorgona, the tenacious Pizarro and his small party promptly sailed southward in search of the unknown empire. Entering the Gulf of Guayaquil, they came upon the city of Tumbez in late April. The local inhabitants gave them a friendly reception. From there Pizarro proceeded further down the coast to the Santa River before they turned back to Panama. The great and rich southern civilization of Peru had been found at last and Pizarro intended to make it Spain's and his.[77]

Upon arriving back in Panama, Pizarro headed for Spain as soon as possible. There on 26 July 1529 Queen Isabella granted him the right to explore and to conquer the newly discovered lands with Almagro as his second in command. Armed with that authority, Pizarro returned to Panama and began preparing his third expedition to Peru. By December 1530 he had gathered 180 men and set sail for Tumbez. Almagro and others were recruiting further reinforcements from among the conquistadors of Nicaragua, including Hernando de Soto. They would join Pizarro's original force within a few months. It had taken Pizarro six years to reach this point. His grim

Pizarro draws the line in the sand on Gallo Island based on a painting by F. Lizcano. From Washington Irving et al., *The Discovery and Conquest of the New World* (Philadelphia, Syndicate Publishing, 1892), p. 613.

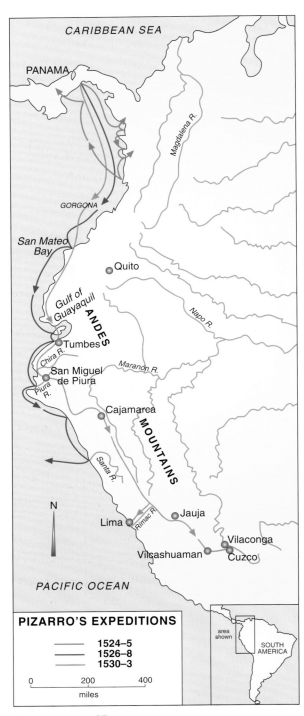

The conquest of Peru.

tenacity had sustained him through many travails. At approximately fifty-five years of age he must have been impatient to get on with the business of seizing the anticipated riches of Peru and winning glory. The fact of the matter, however, was that during the delays that plagued Pizarro's efforts, the situation in Peru had altered in ways that would very much aid the Spanish conquistadors.

The mysterious land of Peru contained a great area of civilization that for all intents had developed indepen-dently of any other culture in the world, including those of Mexico and the Yucatan. The empire of the Incas had recently come to dominate the entire region of Peru. A series of able Inca emperors had vastly expanded their realm from 1438 onward. With the conquest of the formidable kingdom of Quito only a few years before the arrival of the Spanish, Inca territory stretched from north of the city of Quito for thousands of miles down to the Maule River in northern Chile. From the arid coastal valleys over the towering peaks of the Andes Mountains to the borderlands of the vast Amazon rainforest, the Incas controlled the entire civilized world as they knew it. The Inca capital of Cuzco was considered to be the navel of the earth and from it radiated a wondrous system of roads, maintained by an efficient network of imperial officials and guarded by a disciplined army that kept tight control over the populace. It was a marvellous achievement for a society that lacked metal tools and a writing system, while its only domesticated animals were the closely related, camel-like llamas, vicunas and alpacas along with the guinea pig. As was the case with the Aztec realm, many of the conquered peoples of Peru hated their Inca overlords but to little avail. During the first three decades of the sixteenth century the Inca Empire reached its zenith and controlled a population of possibly 8 million people. When Pizarro first arrived at Tumbez in 1528 the highly capable Huayna Capac (1493–1528) ruled the Inca Empire. He would have squashed any Spanish aggression at that time with his overwhelming numerical superiority.[78]

Unfortunately for the peoples of Peru a strange new epidemic swept through their lands in 1528. It appears to have been smallpox which had worked its way through the native peoples of the Caribbean basin and Central America finally to reach isolated Peru. Thousands died including Huayna Capac. Inca emperors had many wives and many children, and it was usual practice for them to name a successor from among their most competent male offspring. Huayna Capac's untimely death prevented him from doing that and left the Inca royal succession undecided. A civil war broke out between the eldest son Huascar and his younger brother Atahualpa. Although Huascar controlled the Inca heartland around Cuzco, Atahualpa possessed the support of the best Inca troops and the recently conquered kingdom of Quito. Plague and internecine strife devastated the Inca Empire for several years with Atahualpa emerging the victor. His troops had captured Huascar and any opposing armies had been utterly defeated. When Pizarro's third expedition returned to Peru in mid-1532, Atahualpa was making his way in a leisurely manner to Cuzco to start putting his shattered realm back into good order.[79]

On 27 December 1530 Pizarro and his men left Panama. Initially his ships made good progress but various problems set in and the Spanish force did not reach Tumbez until May 1532. They found the large and once-lovely city in ruins, a casualty of the Inca civil war. Boldly Pizarro decided to move inland with 170 men and 60 horses and meet the new Inca ruler. The complacent Atahualpa let the Spanish march unopposed. With a battle-hardened army of 40,000 troops guarding him, Atahualpa did not consider a force of less than 200 strangers to be a serious threat. His intelligence network kept him well informed about the progress of the band of conquistadors. It took several months of marching for Pizarro and his men to reach Atahualpa at the town of Cajamarca. Upon arriving there the Spanish could clearly see the vast camp of the Inca army stretching out into the distance. Fear gripped many of the conquistadors when they realized how exposed they were to attack.[80]

Several preliminary meetings took place between Atahualpa and the Spanish. Hernando de Soto dazzled and frightened some of Atahualpa's court with a display of Castilian horsemanship. Atahualpa showed himself to be the stuff of kings and did not flinch when Soto's horse came so close that he could feel its breath on his face. Afterwards he executed any courtiers and soldiers who had displayed fear of the horse. In another meeting Hernando Pizarro, Francisco's brother, offered Atahualpa the services of the Spanish as mercenaries. The Inca ruler, however, showed no interest in this suggestion. Instead he maintained a chilly attitude that exhibited no awe of the strangers. Things looked very grim for the isolated band of Spanish. Still, arrangements were made for the Inca emperor to come and visit Francisco Pizarro at the Spanish quarters in Cajamarca. Pizarro had reached the conclusion that given the desperate circumstances, the only way out was to make Atahualpa his prisoner, just as Cortés had done in Mexico with the Aztec ruler Montezuma. He prepared his troops to carry out the audacious deed.

The next day, 16 November 1532, Atahualpa entered the square of the Spanish compound. He rode in a litter carried by 80 chiefs and was accompanied by 5,000 courtiers. The Incas were unarmed, because 'they thought so little of the Christian army that they expected to capture it with their bare hands'.[81] Once Atahualpa's litter came to a stop in the square, the Dominican friar Vincente Valverde, who accompanied Pizarro's expedition as a missionary, approached the Inca emperor and began to deliver an exposition on the Christian faith for the purpose of converting Atahualpa. Whether Atahualpa actually understood Valverde's sermon as translated or whether it was even accurately translated is not at all clear. Either way, the proud Atahualpa had no interest in becoming a Christian. Instead, he was highly irritated by the way Pizarro's little army had casually stolen and raped its way through his realm. Valverde carried a breviary and a Bible as he referred to them in his sermon. Atahualpa asked to examine the sacred books but coming from a civilization that did not possess even the crudest system of writing, he could have had no concept of their function. After leafing through the breviary and holding it up to his ear without hearing anything, he threw the books to the ground. Some accounts claim that Atahualpa did this deliberately to show his contempt of the Spanish. Others suggest that he simply did not understand the symbolism and the sacred character of the Bible and breviaries among the Spanish. His action gave the waiting Spanish an excuse to attack. Valverde turned and ran to his countrymen calling out, 'At them! At them!'[82] Pizarro then signalled the cannon to fire into the crowded square and the massacre of the Inca royal entourage began. Guns fired, crossbow bolts whirred through the air, horsemen rode down countless victims and Spanish swordsmen hacked and slashed their way into the mass of helpless Inca courtiers. Although the royal litter bearers bravely tried to protect Atahualpa with their lives, they were quickly cut down and Pizarro and his men captured the astonished Inca emperor alive. Some 2,000 Incas died in the massacre while thousands more were captured. Not a single Spaniard died.

Capturing Atahualpa saved Pizarro and his men from death or enslavement. Initially the Inca troops in the area hesitated to mount a counter-offensive. Then Atahualpa, under threat from the Spanish, issued orders explicitly forbidding them to attack. Observing the Spanish greed for gold and silver, he believed that he could buy his freedom from his rapacious captors. Atahualpa took a practical approach. At worst, the Spanish would escape with a king's ransom in gold and silver. At best, once freed, the Inca emperor could track down his enemies, kill them and regain his treasure. So Atahualpa made his legendary offer to have his obedient subjects fill a room with gold as his ransom. Meanwhile, to secure his own position, he ordered his generals to kill his captive brother and rival Huascar.[83]

The capture of Atahualpa could not have occurred at a worse time for the Inca Empire. Some writers have claimed that the imprisonment of Atahualpa left the rigidly hierarchical Inca Empire leaderless. This situation allowed the Spanish to step into the power vacuum and be met with very little resistance. That interpretation is not accurate. The Inca Empire slowly but surely fell apart due to its own internal divisions. Although Atahualpa had won the civil war, he had not had the time to consolidate his victory. The adherents of Huascar hated him and they were centred around Cuzco. The Cuzcans also hated his Quitan allies. Huascar's death left them with no one to rally around in the face of the Spanish threat. With the Inca elite so divided, various subject peoples started to assert their independence. The native social class called the Yanaconas had worked as the traditional servants of the Inca nobles but with the crisis of Atahualpa's captivity they began to switch their allegiances to the Spanish. Later some of the Inca generals, most notably Rumiñavi, tried to set themselves up as kings after the Spaniards executed Atahualpa. As the Inca Empire disintegrated, Pizarro and his conquistadors armed with a vastly superior military technology proceeded to pick up the pieces.[84]

Atahualpa deluded himself when he believed that the Spanish would ever release him. Pizarro wanted Peru's treasure but he also wanted to conquer the land for Spain. That meant that Atahualpa had to die, whether his ransom was paid or not. So on 26 July 1533, after a sham legal proceeding in which they accused the Inca ruler of killing his own brother, the Spanish executed Atahualpa. Sporadic resistance appeared as the Spanish attempted to utilize puppet Inca rulers to control Peru. Eventually, Manco Inca, one of their pawns, rose up in rebellion in 1535 and almost captured Cuzco the next year. For a while the Spanish position in Peru hung in the balance but by 1537 they had reasserted their control over the heartlands of Peru. The defeated Manco fled to the jungle refuge of Vilcabamba to found an Inca kingdom in exile that lasted until 1572.

The Spanish conquest of Peru saw few happy endings. Native peoples suffered from oppression and a succession of deadly Old World diseases. Thousands died working in the incredibly rich silver mines of Potosí, first discovered in 1545. But the conquistadors also fared poorly. In 1537 civil strife broke out between Pizarro and Almagro and their followers. Pizarro executed old Diego de Almagro in 1538 but Almagrists got their revenge in 1541 when they assassinated Francisco Pizarro. Many others close to these men suffered death or imprisonment during the savage struggles for control of Peru. Numerous conquistadors lost the great fortunes that they had accumulated at such great personal risk. Even Father Valverde, reputed by most to be a good man, came to a bad end when the Puná Indians he was trying to convert to Christianity murdered him in 1541. In the end the Spanish viceroys, most notably Francisco de Toledo from 1569 to 1581, established Peru as a profitable and stable colony of Spain.

Pizarro's success in finding and conquering the fantastically rich empire of Peru, like that of Cortés in Mexico, only served to inspire even more conquistadors to seek

Pizarro Seizing the Inca of Peru, 1845, by Sir John Millais. Atahualpa was taken by Pizarro and his men at Cajamarca. (Victoria & Albert Museum, London/Art Resource, NY)

out other wealthy lands to take possession of. The Americas, unfortunately for the Spanish, were running out of unknown wealthy realms. No one would come close to repeating the successes of Cortés and Pizarro. Instead what occurred was a sort of fool's gold rush.

In 1528 Charles V, the Holy Roman Emperor and King of Spain, granted permission for the Welser bankers of Augsburg to explore and to settle the region of present-day Venezuela. The agents of the Welsers arrived on the northern coast of South America and quickly heard native tales of another colossally wealthy Indian empire that was ruled by a king who dressed in gold dust. This legendary monarch came to be known as El Dorado.[85] The story had some basis in fact. There had been a tribe living on the Bogata plateau that annually coated their king in gold dust as part of a ceremony. At the conclusion of the ceremony, the king would dive into a lake to wash off the gold. When the neighbouring Chibchas conquered this tribe some years before the arrival of the Spanish, they suppressed the rite. El Dorado was no more but the legend lived on in the imaginations of the surrounding tribes who passed it on to the Spanish and their Welser allies. In 1529 Welser agents started to look for El Dorado but with no success. Undeterred by the failure of the Welsers, other adventurers joined the quest. In 1536 the Spanish lawyer Gonzalo Jiménez de Quesada began to explore the

Magdalena River of Columbia as a possible route to Peru. Braving floods, rugged mountains, dense jungles and wild animals, Quesada eventually cut his way through to the Bogata plateau where he conquered the Chibchas and other local tribes during 1537 and 1538. Quesada proceeded to loot the Chibcha's hoard of gold which was rather paltry when compared to the troves coming out of Mexico and Peru. It was also not readily renewable. The Chibchas possessed no gold mines. All the gold in their possession had been painstakingly accumulated through trade with various primitive jungle peoples.

When Quesada conquered the Bogata plateau he had also seized the land of El Dorado. But he did not believe he had done any such thing and neither did anyone else. The Chibchas were simply not rich enough to meet Spanish expectations about the wealth of El Dorado. Shortly after Quesada's conquest of the Chibchas, two other Spanish expeditions arrived on the Bogata plateau looking for El Dorado. A fight between the three bands of conquistadors was narrowly averted and all agreed that El Dorado was located somewhere else. So the search continued. In 1541 Gonzalo Pizarro made an ill-fated attempt to explore the Napo River region. His expedition became mired in the jungle and a desperate Pizarro sent Francisco de Orellana down

The King of El Dorado receiving his coating of gold dust, from a print by Theodore de Bry. From J.A. Zahm, *The Quest for El Dorado* (New York, Appleton, 1912), p. 15.

Gonzalo Jimenes de Quesada, conqueror of Columbia. From Justin Winsor, *A Narrative and Critical History of America* (Boston, Houghton Mifflin, 1886), vol. 2, p. 580.

the river in a home-made brigantine to look for food. Swift currents prevented Orellana's return and instead he cruised all the way down the Amazon to its mouth and reached the Atlantic Ocean in August 1542. Along the way he and his men fought their way through various hostile tribes, including some supposed Amazon warriors (hence his name for the great river he was travelling on). They also collected more rumours about El Dorado.[86] For years various Spanish expeditions careened through the interior of South America fruitlessly seeking the elusive golden land. Occasionally they even bumped into each other in that seemingly vast wilderness.

By the end of the sixteenth century the only remaining unexplored region was the land of Guiana near the mouth of the Orinoco River in north-eastern South America. The Spaniard Antonio de Berrio sent six expeditions to look for El Dorado in Guiana between 1581 and 1593. They found nothing but more hearsay. These rumours reached English ears and attracted the attention of the English courtier Sir Walter Ralegh. He looked for El Dorado in both 1595 and 1617 but found nothing because there was nothing to find. All he accomplished was to draw down the fatal ire of his sovereign King James I.[87] The legend of El Dorado helped to encourage the broad exploration of the interior of South America by the end of the sixteenth century. Permanent settlement and detailed examination of the region, however, would not be completed for many years to come.

SPANISH EXPLORATIONS IN NORTH AMERICA

North America was also subject to Spanish expeditions trudging through its vastness vainly searching for other wealthy empires to conquer. The nature of the North American continent was only dimly comprehended at that time and to a certain extent would remain a mystery until the eighteenth and even the early nineteenth century. To the north of Cuba lay the region that the Spanish called *La Florida*. It had repulsed Ponce de León's and Lucas Vásquez de Ayllon's efforts to explore and to settle it. *La Florida* had seemingly swallowed up Panfilo Narváez's expedition without a trace. In spite of these inauspicious circumstances, Spanish

Medieval Arabs and Europeans considered the Atlantic Ocean to be a 'Sea of Darkness' full of ferocious monsters, terrible storms and other terrors. From William Cullen Bryant, *A Popular History of the United States* (New York, Scribners, 1891), vol. 1, p. 64.

interest in *La Florida* remained high in the late 1530s. Many thought that the lost Christian realm of Antillia or the Land of the Seven Cities was supposedly located there. Because it remained unexplored, it was an excellent place to look for undiscovered kingdoms rich in gold and silver.[88]

In 1537 the Emperor Charles V granted to Hernando de Soto, one of Francisco Pizarro's captains from the conquest of Peru, the concession to take control of and govern *La Florida*. Soto with his Peruvian loot had recently returned to a hero's welcome in Spain but being a restless spirit he longed for a new world to appropriate rather than settling down to enjoy the luxuries his new wealth could buy him. Just after Soto received his royal commission, the mystery of the disappearance of the Narváez expedition was solved by the reappearance of one of its survivors Álvar Núñez Cabeza de Vaca. After eight years of wandering among the tribes living in the lands that now comprise Texas, New Mexico, Arizona and northern Mexico, Cabeza de Vaca finally found his way back to European settlements. He returned to Spain with tales about the riches that lay in *La Florida* and hinted that he was not even telling the whole story. Cabeza de Vaca's stories drove the ever-present gold fever of the conquistadors to new heights both in Cuba and in Mexico as well as in Spain which helped Soto's recruitment for his expedition.[89]

On Cuba, Soto organized a fleet and 600 soldiers, a more impressive force than either Cortés or Pizarro had initially commanded. On 18 May 1539 the expedition

PROGENIES·DIVVM·QVINTVS·SIC·CAROLVS·ILLE
IMPERII·CAESAR·LVMINA·ET·ORA·TVLIT
AET   SVAE   ·   XXXI
ANN · M · D · XXXI

Emperor Charles V, a ruler who benefited from the new discoveries but little understood their significance. From Washington Irving et al., *The Discovery and Conquest of the New World* (Philadelphia, Syndicate Publishing, 1892), p. 465.

departed and landed on the western coast of Florida, probably near Tampa Bay. Soto marched his soldiers northward seeking a gold-drenched realm similar to those of the Aztecs and the Incas. Instead what he found was a series of petty kingdoms of the Mississippian culture consisting of small towns surrounded by maize fields and largely bereft of gold and silver. The Mississippians were no match for the Spanish in terms of military might so they opted for cooperation as a way to avoid destruction. They also learned that telling the Spanish tales about large, prosperous cities with lots of gold that lay further off was the best way to get their unwelcome guests to move on quickly. Soto and his conquistadors moved through what is now Georgia, South Carolina, Tennessee, Alabama and Mississippi severely disrupting the hapless Mississippian culture as they went. The rigours of the journey and occasional battles with the more warlike of the Native American tribes gradually wore down the Spanish army. Finally, on 8 May 1541, the Spanish reached the great Mississippi River which gave Soto the distinction of discovering it as an inland waterway. Crossing the mile-wide river into Arkansas, they failed once more to locate a kingdom of gold. At that point Soto decided to head back to the Gulf of Mexico and return to Cuba but fever struck him down and he died on 21 May 1542, just over three years after beginning his fruitless quest. His lieutenant Luis de Moscoso managed to lead the 311 survivors of the expedition back to Panuco, Mexico, on 10 September 1543. They had nothing to show for all their hardships and substantial losses of life.[90]

As Soto began his exploration of the south-eastern region of North America, enthusiasm was building in Mexico for a trip into the south-western region. Cabeza de Vaca's return to civilization had aroused the curiosity of Antonio de Mendoza, the viceroy of New Spain, about the lands to the north. In 1539 he sent the priest Marcos de Niza to the region that now comprises Arizona and New Mexico. There he picked up rumours about the seven wealthy cities of the land of Cibola. The Spanish concluded that Cibola and its cities were the same place as their own legendary seven cities of the refugees fleeing the Moorish conquest of Iberia. Marcos even claimed to

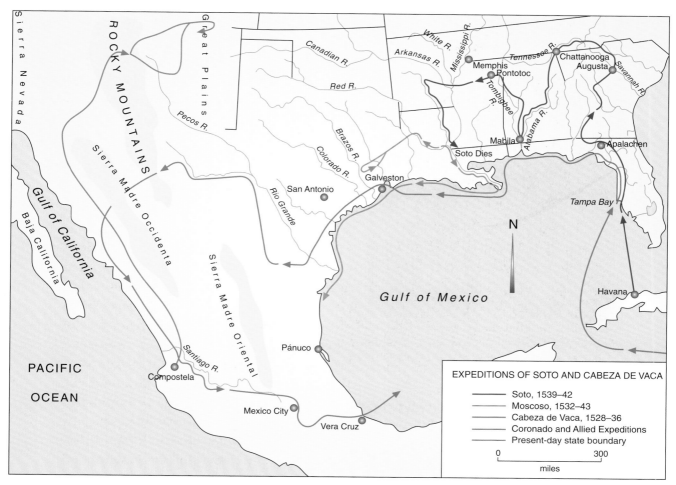

Spanish explorations of North America.

have viewed one of the golden cities from afar. Upon his return, Viceroy Mendoza organized a major expedition under the command of Francisco Vásquez de Coronado. It got under way on 23 February 1540. Some 340 Spaniards along with 300 allied Indian warriors and 1,000 native and African slaves made their way northward along the west coast of Mexico. Reaching the Sonora River, they marched inland along its banks and into what is now Arizona. They were seeking wealthy cities like Tenochtitlan and Cuzco but none existed to be found. Several side expeditions were sent out, one of which discovered the Grand Canyon. Cibola, however, never materialized. Instead what the disappointed conquistadors found were the modest pueblos of the Zunis or simple Hopi villages. At that point a plains Indian nicknamed 'the Turk' enticed Coronado's expedition to march eastward into the prairie with tales of a rich land called Quivira. Moving into the largely empty grasslands of the Texas panhandle the Spanish discovered 'the Turk' had not been telling the truth and they executed him by strangulation. Local Indians, however, also claimed that Quivira

Hernando de Soto. From Edward Gaylord Bourne, *Narratives of the Career of Hernando De Soto* (New York, Allerton Book Co., 1922), frontispiece.

existed somewhere to the north. Not wanting to miss what might be a truly golden opportunity, Coronado led a small band of cavalry across the grassy plains of Oklahoma and deep into Kansas. There all that they found were more poor villages of Native Americans. A deeply discouraged Coronado began the long march back to Mexico in April 1542. By the time the survivors reached Mexico City less than a hundred conquistadors remained alive.[91]

Soto's and Coronado's expeditions thoroughly explored the southern half of what is now the United States. At one point the two leaders unknowingly came within less than 200 miles of each other. Juan Rodriquez Cabrillo conducted an almost contemporary enterprise up the west coast of North America at the behest of Viceroy Mendoza. Leaving Mexico on 24 June 1542, Cabrillo systematically examined the various bays and inlets beyond Baja California and contributed many of present-day California's placenames. He also established friendly relations with many of the coastal tribes but not all. During an Indian attack at San Miguel Island he broke his leg and died on 3 January 1543 as a result of complications from the injury. His expedition continued to investigate the coastline up into Oregon before returning to Mexico on 14 April 1543.[92] None of these three projects found a rich empire to conquer and their failure greatly diminished Spanish enthusiasm for further exploring and settling of North America for many years to come. It would not be until the last years of the sixteenth century that Spain would resume the establishment of permanent colonies outside the core areas of its American empire in Mexico and Peru, the Florida peninsula being a notable exception.

FRENCH, ENGLISH AND DUTCH EXPLORATIONS AND SETTLEMENTS, *c.* 1550–*c.* 1600

Where did the fantastic successes of Portugal and Spain in Asia and the Americas leave the other countries of Western Europe? It left them jealous and with a burning desire to imitate those achievements. When French privateers captured a Spanish vessel returning home with Mexican treasure in 1522, King Francis I justified their actions by quipping, 'I would like to see the clause in Adam's will which excludes France from the division of the world.'[93] Emulation of the Iberian successes, however, did not come quickly or easily. The Dutch, who were rebel subjects of Spain from the late 1560s until 1648, did not get started on the path of overseas empire until the late sixteenth century. When they did, they quickly became a pre-eminent world trading power during the seventeenth century.[94] Both England and France attempted to rival Spain and Portugal during the sixteenth century but only with extremely limited success. Like the Dutch, they would not establish permanent colonies in the Americas and in Asia until the seventeenth century.

From the beginning of the sixteenth century both France and England sought to interfere with any Portuguese or Spanish territories overseas that they could reach. Portugal faced persistent problems with French, English and even Spanish merchants trespassing on her Guinea trade in West Africa.[95] French and English ships also quickly appeared in the Americas to do business with the West Indies and Brazil. During the 1550s the French even threatened to take over the fledgling Portuguese settlements in Brazil. Even earlier, during the first decade of the sixteenth century, French privateers had begun attacking Spanish vessels returning from the Americas as they approached Europe. They gradually moved their operations across the Atlantic Ocean to the West Indies. French corsairs came to pose a significant hazard to Spanish shipping, particularly the treasure fleets that carried American gold and silver back to

Jean Ribaut's men building Fort Caroline, from a Theodore de Bry print. From Justin Winsor, *Narrative and Critical History of America* (Boston, Houghton Mifflin, 1886), vol. 2, p. 268.

Spain.[96] That threat became even more irksome when French Protestants, known as Huguenots, began engaging in privateering. One group of Huguenots led by Jean Ribaut even tried to found a settlement at Port Royal Sound on the coast of present-day South Carolina. This colony was intended to serve as a forward base for attacking Spanish shipping, particularly the treasure fleets. Spanish officials in the area quickly discovered what the French were up to and proceeded to assault the trespassers without mercy. Their efforts were greatly assisted by a passing hurricane that devastated the French fleet. Scattered and demoralized the Huguenots were easy prey for the Spanish who massacred most of them.[97] That bloody episode ended French attempts to settle the Americas until the beginning of the seventeenth century and the era of Samuel de Champlain.

Spanish hostility was only part of the explanation for the cessation of French attempts to establish colonies. The biggest reason for France's failure to challenge Spain and Portugal overseas was the outbreak of the savage French civil wars of religion which bitterly divided that unfortunate country and sapped its strength from the late 1560s through the 1590s. These conflicts, however, did not stop French corsairs from raiding the West Indies, French fishermen from visiting Newfoundland or French traders from buying furs on the Canadian coast. During that troubled time the French government simply lacked the energy and the resources to think about permanent foreign colonies. By 1600 relative religious peace had returned to France and a policy of overseas expansion soon followed.

The situation in England was somewhat different. During the sixteenth century England was a relatively weak power but, like everyone else in Northern and Western Europe, it desired cheaper spices and greater wealth, hence the impetus for the Cabot voyages of 1497 and 1498. English sailors and merchants, like their French counterparts, visited West Africa, Brazil and the West Indies.[98] In 1562 John Hawkins of Plymouth pioneered the first English trading expedition to the Spanish West Indies. The outcome was favourable and Hawkins returned to do business again in 1564 with equal success. Unfortunately for Hawkins, Spanish officials were extremely irritated by his illegal trading in the West Indies, while at the same time back in Europe peaceful relations between England and Spain were deteriorating. When Hawkins attempted a third voyage in 1567 with six boats, the venture turned into a disaster. The trading went well but when a hurricane badly damaged the English fleet, they were forced to sail into the Spanish port of San Juan de Ulloa on the Mexican coast to make repairs. Soon after the new viceroy of New Spain or Mexico arrived there with the annual treasure fleet. A stand-off developed which degenerated into a nasty fight from which only two of the English ships managed to escape. The English seafaring community was greatly angered by what they considered to be Spanish perfidy. Tales of the enslavement and torture of the captured English sailors that began to flow into England only added to the swelling animosity.[99] More provocations followed. Hawkins's kinsman and fellow survivor of San Juan de Ulloa, Francis Drake made several raids in the West Indies and Central America in search of Spanish treasure between 1570 and 1573. Soon after, Drake conceived of the bold enterprise of sailing around South America to attack the Spanish along the Pacific coast of South America. He successfully carried out his daring plan and managed to circumnavigate the world between 1577 and 1580.[100]

Meanwhile, other Englishmen besides Drake preyed upon Spanish America and the treasure fleets. Some also continued to seek a north-west passage to Asia. In 1576 Martin Frobisher and Michael Lok sailed past Greenland into the Hudson Strait looking for the elusive passage. During the voyages of 1577 and 1578 the phantom of arctic gold mines distracted them from their original goal and they attempted to establish a mining colony. It failed in the face of a harsh climate and the absence of gold.[101] Sir Humphrey Gilbert also sought to locate the north-west passage and strived to establish a settlement in 1578 and again in 1583 in the region of New England and Newfoundland. His hope was that his colony would provide England with a base for

The Boyhood of Ralegh, 1870, by Sir John Millais. According to legend, the fascinating tales of an old Portuguese sailor inspired the young Sir Walter Ralegh to take up a career as an explorer and colonizer. (Tate Gallery, London/Art Resource, NY)

Sir Humphrey Gilbert. From Woodrow Wilson, *A History of the American People* (New York, Harper, 1903), p. 26.

attacking the Spanish treasure fleets. His efforts failed and he was lost at sea during his second try in 1583. His half-brother Sir Walter Ralegh attempted to found his own permanent colony in North America at Roanoke Island, North Carolina, between 1584 and 1590. The settlers, however, were never seen again after August 1587 and a relief expedition in 1590 found that Roanoke had been abandoned with the fate of the colonists a mystery.[102] Meanwhile, in 1588 war had broken out between England and Spain and this was to last until 1604. Interest in further colonization projects was largely subsumed by the need to fight the conflict. Plenty of voyages to raid Spanish and Portuguese shipping took place during that war but it was not until several years after peace returned that the English were able to establish their first permanent settlement of Jamestown in Virginia in 1607. It survived and other colonies followed along the eastern seaboard of North America as the seventeenth century progressed. In Asia the English had also entered the competition for mastery of the spice trade. In 1599 they formed the infant East India Company largely out of concern over Dutch efforts to wrest control of the spice trade from the Portuguese.[103] These events mark the true beginnings of the future British Empire. Seventeenth-century overseas expansion by Europeans would be dominated by the great trading companies formed by the Dutch, the English and, to a lesser extent, the French.[104] These firms would thrust aside the Portuguese and encroach on Spanish trade and force them to share some of the riches of Asia, Africa and the Americas. This change marked a new phase in European overseas commercial expansion and the end of the first great age of exploration.

CONCLUSION

The discovery of America, and that of a passage to the East Indies by the Cape of Good Hope, are the two greatest and most important events recorded in the history of mankind. Their consequences have already been very great, but, in the short period of between two and three centuries which has elapsed since these discoveries were made, it is impossible that the whole extent of their consequences can have been seen. What benefits or what misfortunes to mankind may hereafter result from those great events, no human wisdom can foresee.

Adam Smith (1776)[1]

The discovery of gold and silver in America, the extirpation, enslavement, and entombment in mines of the aboriginal population, the beginning of the conquest and looting of the East Indies, the turning of Africa into a warren for the commercial hunting of negroes, signalize the rosy dawn of the era of capitalist production.

Karl Marx (1867)[2]

From the early decades of the sixteenth century to the present, people have recognized that the European expansion into Africa, Asia and the Americas represented a historical change of immense proportions. No aspect of life was left untouched by the consequences of those discoveries and the conquests that followed. Trade, agriculture, eating habits, population growth and decline, public health and pre-existing world views were all transformed. Even for the people who lived through these events the monumental transformations that were occurring seemed obvious.

People of sixteenth-century Europe probably considered the influxes of spices from Asia and the gold and silver from the Americas to be the most dramatic manifestations of direct contact with the distant lands. Portuguese ships carried pepper and other spices around Africa and home to the markets of Europe. Some connoisseurs claimed that the pepper brought to Europe along the traditional spice route through Egypt tasted better than the pepper that travelled around the Cape of Good Hope. One suspects that these culinary aesthetes may have been Venetians anxious to protect their city's livelihood. Whether their judgements were objectively true or not, as the supplies of spices increased so did the demand. Initially prices fell in Portugal and other areas close by as the inventory of spices mounted. But that situation was only temporary. For most of Europe the general trend was for the cost to rise. Between 1500 and 1600 pepper prices doubled and even quadrupled in absolute terms. Basically the amount paid for spices followed the same pattern as the increases for other commodities.[3] In 1600 spices still remained luxuries although more and more people could afford to enjoy them.

Unfortunately for the Portuguese, their spice empire in Asia did not make them a wealthy nation or a great power in Europe. The Portuguese territories in the Indian

Ocean generated great wealth but also necessitated high maintenance costs. Back in Europe, merchants from Antwerp and other European trading cities along with various Italian financiers quickly proved adept at shoving the Portuguese merchants aside and taking over the marketing and the distribution of Portuguese spices. They ended up profiting more than the Portuguese crown or people ever did since the foreign merchants had to bear none of the enormous costs of the Asian empire.[4] Portugal remained a poor nation in spite of its intrepid explorers and its overseas provinces. All that empire ultimately ended up doing was to make Portugal a target for other more powerful, greedy and ambitious European nations.

American gold and silver began to arrive in Europe in significant quantities after 1520. Initially the gold and silver reaching Spain consisted of the pillaged hoards of the Aztecs, the Incas and some of the lesser Native American civilizations. Those treasures fascinated people from all over Europe when they saw or heard about the fabulous booty of the Americas. The volume of precious metals flowing to Europe increased dramatically as the sixteenth century progressed when wealthy new mines were brought into production in Peru and Mexico. The Spanish discovered the great mine of silver at San Luis Potosí in 1545. Smelting the silver deposits to refine them into flawless silver ore was a problem that slowed production for a number of years. Later, in 1559, mercury was discovered in Peru and by 1571 it was being used to purify silver ore more efficiently. Both the silver and mercury mines proved to be hellish places for native miners to work and thousands upon thousands perished in them.[5] Other equally horrendous mines opened in late sixteenth-century Mexico and quickly became just as lethal and almost as rich as the legendary mine at Potosí. Between 1500 and 1650, the Spanish treasure fleets delivered 181 tons of gold and 16,000 tons of silver to Europe. During that time they tripled the supply of precious metals in Europe.[6] Observers at the time thought that the massive influx of Spanish treasure triggered the price revolution that occurred in sixteenth-century Europe – enriching some and impoverishing others. Modern historians have rejected the American gold and silver as the prime cause for the inflation. Instead they credit the growing population of Europe as the chief reason with the increased supply of American precious metals as a very slight secondary cause.[7] Slight, that is, except in the case of Spain. There American treasure tarried in the Spanish economy just long enough to inflate prices and tempt Spanish monarchs to engage in fruitless and expensive wars but not long enough to make any positive changes. After that the precious metals quickly flowed out of an increasingly penurious Spain and into the hands of others. Spain had discovered some of the earth's greatest troves of precious metals but by 1650 had ended up poorer than when it started on its course of overseas expansion in 1492.

Contact with Europeans did not prove to be all that traumatic for the peoples of Asia. The Portuguese conquered a few minor states but barely came to the notice of the great powers – the Moghul Empire, Vijayangar, the Mings of China and the Safavids of Persia. In the sixteenth century Europeans lacked the manpower and the

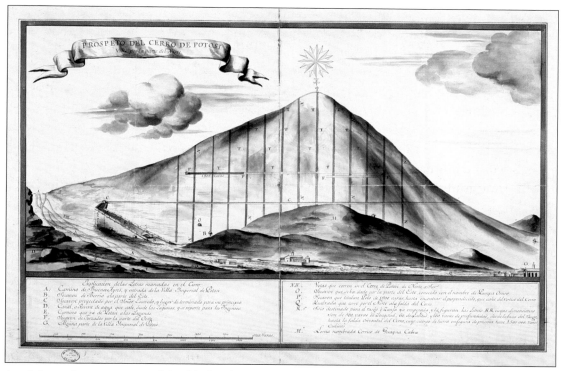

An eighteenth-century map of the fabulously wealthy silver mines at Potosí. (Scala/Art Resource, NY)

more advanced weapons needed to conquer the sophisticated civilizations of Asia. It was only at sea that Europeans possessed the technological advantages that allowed them to dominate the Indian Ocean.[8]

In comparison, European contact with the Americas proved incredibly destabilizing and deadly for the native peoples and states. Vastly superior weapons helped the Spanish to make dramatic conquests of huge and powerful land empires in Mexico and Peru. Far more important to Spanish victory was the devastation visited upon the Native Americans by Old World diseases. Smallpox swept through Mexico during Cortés's conquest. While it indiscriminately struck down both the foes and the allies of the Spanish among the Mexican peoples, it is certain that the ravages of pestilence hastened the fall of Tenochtitlan. Smallpox reached Peru in 1528 and included among its many victims the Inca emperor Huayna Capac. His untimely death precipitated the civil war between Atahualpa and Huascar that fatally divided the Inca Empire in the face of the Spanish invasion.[9]

The Native American peoples had been isolated from Old World diseases for thousands of years. Periodic visitations of contagious illnesses had not hardened their natural resistance and their populations contained no adults who had survived the childhood complaints that still afflicted Europeans. As a result smallpox, influenza, measles, dysentery and other Old World diseases swept through Native American populations causing high levels of mortality among all age groups. Just how high is a matter of intense debate and controversy among historians and obviously depends on how many people lived in various parts of the pre-European contact, disease-free Americas. Surviving sources reliably indicate that Spanish Mexico had a population of between 2 and 3 million people in 1558. But what were the numbers in 1519? Scholarly estimates made during the twentieth century have ranged from 4.5 million to 30 million for the Mexican population at contact. Estimates of the contact population of Hispaniola have shown an even wider variance from a low of 55,000 to a high of 7–8 million. Although in the absence of a census it is impossible to produce a reasonably accurate estimate, the most sensible academic studies place the population of the Tainos on Hispaniola at between 100,000 and 300,000 in 1492. By 1540 the Tainos were extinct, mostly dead from disease or overwork with the few survivors having been assimilated into the population of the European settlers. On the mainlands of the Americas, the native peoples managed to survive the onslaught of Old World diseases much better. Estimates that 90 per cent declines occurred during the sixteenth century among the populations of Native Americans are too high but still shattering losses of half or more of the population appear to be quite reasonable guesses. Even the more modest figures mean that the Native Americans experienced a demographic disaster that was significantly more severe than the Black Death of the fourteenth century that swept through Asia and Europe. The losses among the Native American population opened the way for the occupation of the Americas by Spanish settlers and later by other Europeans. As the Europeans advanced into the interiors of North and South America they carried the Old World diseases with them as unwitting allies in the process of fatally weakening the structures of many Native American societies.[10]

Europeans and the peoples of the Old World did not escape unscathed in the exchange of diseases with the Americas. Syphilis existed in the pre-Columbian Americas and Columbus, somehow, took the disease back to Spain with him in 1493 when he returned from his first voyage. The carrier may have been one or more of his sailors or it may have been one of the Native Americans taken back to Spain. The fact that syphilis appeared almost immediately among some of the ladies of the court of Fernando and Isabel speaks volumes about the state of aristocratic morals. Initially the new disease was highly contagious and extremely virulent. Victims died painfully and often hideously within months of contracting syphilis and it killed people of all social ranks, even kings such as Francis I of France. Because it was spread venereally, the onslaught of the disease brought about a cooling of sexual freedoms and led to the shutting down of bathhouses as dangers to public health. By 1600 the syphilis pathogen had burned through its most vicious and lethal strains and evolved into the less severe but still deadly and ugly version of the disease that exists today. That less virulent affliction still managed to maintain a significant chronic level of infection of 5–10 per cent among Europe's urban population until the appearance of antibiotics capable of controlling the pathogen in the human body. Europeans paid a heavy price

Indians of Hispaniola killed their children and committed suicide rather than be the slaves of the Spanish. From Girolamo Benzoni, *History of the New World* (London, Hakluyt Society, 1857), p. 77.

for their successful expansion throughout the globe in the form of syphilis, although not as heavy as the price paid by the Native Americans.[11]

The drastic decline of Native American populations also had an impact on Africa. Prince Henry the Navigator's captains had begun slave-raiding on the West African coast but quickly found that trading for slaves was far safer and just as profitable given the formidable military capabilities of the black African states and tribes along the tropical coast. Portuguese traders acquired slaves to provide labourers on the plantations of the Madeiras, the Azores, the Cape Verde Islands and for the Portuguese homeland. Demand remained limited. With the settling of the West Indies and the mainland of Spanish America and Portuguese Brazil along with the declines in the Native American populations, the need for slaves increased dramatically. It remained high well into the nineteenth century. African rulers waged war on each other to obtain prisoners for slaves and condemned minor criminals to slavery to obtain additional bodies to sell to the eager European slave traders. During

As native populations dwindled, Spain began bringing African slaves to the Americas, from a Theodore de Bry print. From Jules Verne, *Famous Travels and Travellers* (New York, Scribners, 1887), p. 155.

the era of the Atlantic slave trade millions of Africans were carried to the Americas. Many died en route. Others died of the harsh conditions on the plantations. Replacements were needed constantly. Slaves became Africas foremost commodity in the market of international trade to the shame and the detriment of all involved.

On the positive side, the greatest gift that the Americas bestowed on the Old World was its vast array of useful plants, although animal husbandry never developed to a significant level among the peoples of the Americas. Apart from the ubiquitous dog the peoples of Mexico had domesticated turkeys while the Incas tamed the camel-like llamas and their smaller cousins the vicunas and alpacas. They also raised guinea pigs for food. Llamas were the only pre-Columbian pack animals in the Americas and their utility was limited by an absolute and stubborn refusal to carry loads of much more than 70 pounds. There were no large draught or riding animals in the Americas which is why Spanish cavalry initially intimidated the Native Americans. The Native Americans also possessed no dogs of war and found the fierce mastiffs of the Europeans to be frightful opponents. In the post-conquest era, however, surviving Native Americans rapidly adopted European animals. The horse even became the centrepiece of the Plains tribes of North America's nomadic-hunter way of life.[12]

Native Americans equalled or surpassed the horticultural achievements of any Old World society. Many familiar and important plants were originally domesticated in the Americas. Maize corn, sweet potatoes, white potatoes, common beans, peanuts, squash, tomatoes, pineapples, cacao for chocolate and tobacco are all native to the Americas. Maize spread rapidly through the Old World and reached China so quickly that some scholars have suggested that maize actually reached there prior to 1492 by means of undocumented pre-Columbian Chinese voyages to the Americas. That theory, however, cannot stand up under a close examination of all the evidence. What is indisputably true is that maize became an important food crop throughout the Old World, whether for human consumption or animal fodder. It was a highly adaptable plant that could successfully grow in a variety of climatic conditions. The process of adoption was also a slow one that took centuries as humans are relatively conservative about changes in their food supply. The same observation applies to other American plants that migrated to the Old World. Europeans took many years to accept the potato although it and maize both proved to be prodigiously efficient producers of calories per acre when compared to most Old World plants. They have been credited with stimulating or at least sustaining the population boom that began in the eighteenth century. Common beans also achieved importance as a new source of food through its provision of needed vegetable protein. Diets in many parts of the Old World were greatly enriched. Cacao, the fundamental ingredient of chocolate, mixed with sugar and milk became a popular beverage throughout seventeenth-century Europe and

A Mochican jar from pre-Incan Peru depicting three fertility gods as corn cobs. It illustrates the importance of maize corn in the diets of all Native Americans. Following contact with Europeans, its presence in other diets around the world became widespread. (© British Museum/Art Resource, NY)

remained popular in that form well into the nineteenth century. Solid chocolate candy did not make its appearance until the 1840s. Tomatoes were accepted more slowly in Europe and were long considered a decorative plant that was also poisonous, which is true of the green parts of the plant. When its nutritional value and many culinary applications were finally appreciated, the tomato figured prominently in recipes and on dinner tables. Many other American plants had influences on the world, especially the massive impact of tobacco for better or for worse. American

New food plants from the Americas – maize, squash, potatoes and tomatoes. From Washington Irving et al., *The Discovery and Conquest of the New World* (Philadelphia, Syndicate Publishing, 1892), p. 366.

plants created huge alterations in the lifestyles of people at all levels of society and in all parts of the world but it is important to keep in mind that these changes occurred slowly.[13]

Europe's expansion throughout the globe in the fifteenth and the sixteenth centuries profoundly changed the continent's world view. As with the introduction of American plants, this transformation took place slowly and was not a sudden revolution. Europeans had been

Tobacco, one of the Americas' more dubious contributions to the world. From William Cullen Bryant, *A Popular History of the United States* (New York, Scribners, 1891), vol. 1, p. 250.

exposed to other parts of the world before although on a smaller scale and on a temporary basis. The Roman Empire had enjoyed wide contacts with India. Crusaders opened up large parts of the Middle East to Europeans while the Pax Mongolica allowed European merchants like Marco Polo to travel to China and to India. But all of these contacts were eventually broken off because of political changes and instability. Connections were renewed and expanded thanks to the voyages of Christopher Columbus and Vasco da Gama. As the sixteenth century arrived and progressed, more Europeans travelled further and visited more places than ever before. They reached the previously unknown Americas, the furthest southern portions of Africa and fabled Japan or Cipangu. In the early stages there was a very real danger that their achievements might be abandoned but that passed and the contacts they established have remained seemingly permanent. The world has been one ever since. The age of European exploration and overseas expansion was the first manifestation of globalization.

Europeans had developed ideas about the unknown parts of the world based on partial or faulty information or even complete fantastical speculation as the legends about monstrous races and Prester John clearly demonstrate. In many ways the reality of Africa, the Americas and Asia turned out to be stranger than the myths and legends and far more complex. The vast populations of India, China and Japan with their alien cultures astounded European visitors. Vasco da Gama and his men initially mistook the Hindus of Calicut for heretical Christians because they had no inkling that Hinduism existed or what constituted it. The peoples of the Americas proved even harder to absorb into the European world view. At first Columbus and other early explorers thought that Hispaniola and the neighbouring islands were outliers of Asia. During the first decades of the sixteenth century, Europeans gradually came to the realization that the Americas were previously unknown lands that were far removed from Asia. That awareness created the problem of fitting the Native Americans into the traditional Christian cosmology and anthropology. In a sense the European encounter with the Native Americans was the equivalent of modern human society coming into contact with intelligent life from another planet and what such an event would do to existing ideas about religion, the nature of humanity or intelligent life and culture. How were the Native Americans to be assimilated into the relatively tidy medieval view of cosmology and anthropology? Were they descended from Noah and his sons and if so, how was that possible? Some people postulated that various Old World peoples migrated to America by sea in the distant past. The Jesuit missionary José de Acosta correctly suggested the existence of a land-bridge between Asia and North America in prehistoric times which allowed people to pass from Asia into the Americas. Others asserted that the Native Americans represented a separate creation from that of Adam. The Native Americans were supposedly pre-Adamitic or co-Adamitic humans which raised the ominous possibility that they were not created in God's image, i.e., possessed of a soul. Such a condition meant that Native Americans were simply intelligent animals but animals nonetheless and so could be

Bernardino de Sahagún, missionary and proto-ethnographer of sixteenth-century Mexico. From Justin Winsor, *Narrative and Critical History of America* (Boston, Houghton Mifflin, 1889), vol. 1, p. 156.

exploited accordingly. High-minded people like Bartolomé de Las Casas vociferously rejected such an approach and argued persuasively that the Native Americans were as fully human as Old World peoples.[14]

Direct contact with the peoples of Africa, the Americas and Asia provided Europeans with an eye-opening experience. In some ways the new, the different and the strange was so overwhelming that many Europeans worked hard at ignoring or minimizing the effects. Initially the only measure Europeans had to judge Africans, Asians and Native Americans by was comparison with European culture. For most Europeans, other peoples suffered in the juxtaposition. A few people were more open-minded. Alvise da Cadamosto developed a very positive opinion of the natives of West Africa that he visited. The same observation applies to Cabeza de Vaca as his respect and affection for the tribes of Texas, the south-west and northern Mexico grew during his many years of wandering. Saint Francis Xavier dearly loved his Japanese flock while the castaway conquistador Gonzalo Guerrero went completely native and became a respected and intensely loyal member of the Maya community that adopted him. Slowly but surely Europeans developed a sense of cultural relativism and a greater appreciation that foreign peoples could be different but not necessarily bad. That realization did not stop them from exploiting, enslaving, conquering or slaughtering peoples from other cultures on frequent occasions but Europeans were by no means unique in engaging in such practices. Ultimately Europeans emerged more open-minded and less prone to assume automatically that their way was the only right and true way.[15]

The age of exploration opened up great sources of wealth and vast new lands to Europeans. Valuable plants entered the world's diet. Spices became more common commodities. Much good came out of the age of exploration as did much bad. The slave trade blighted Africa and poisoned racial relations in many parts of the Americas. Its ills remain manifestly present as the world has entered the twenty-first century. Native American cultures and civilizations suffered conquest and destruction with many tribes becoming extinct. On the other hand, the Americas eventually provided a new home and a better life for millions of immigrants from Europe.

One of the great ironies of the age of exploration is that few of its direct participants, the explorers and the conquistadors, came out of their adventures happy and rich. Many lost their lives in the course of their exploits. Columbus died in bed of old age, consumed by bitterness because he did not receive what he considered was his fair share of the riches or sufficient recognition of his achievements. Vasco da Gama lived for many years after his second voyage to India but was ignored by the Portuguese crown. When King João III relented and made him viceroy of India, Gama returned in triumph to Asia only to sicken and die from living in the harsh tropical climate. Hernan Cortés accumulated great wealth through violence and shady dealings and acquired the title of marquis but he also made many enemies. After his moment of fame had passed, he found himself plagued by numerous lawsuits and his estate dissipated by legal costs while the memory and gratitude of the Spanish crown proved woefully short. Others suffered far more than Columbus and Cortés. Francisco Pizarro died at the hands of assassins and obtained little joy from his triumph in Peru and the stupendous loot that it generated. The brave and relatively pleasant Balboa was beheaded on the

Bartolomé de Las Casas, defender of the Native Americans in Spanish America. From Justin Winsor, *Narrative and Critical History of America* (Boston, Houghton Mifflin, 1886), vol. 2, p. 332.

orders of the ruthless and corrupt Governor Pedrarias of Panama. Enraged natives killed the meddling Magellan in the Philippines, Caribs slaughtered Verazanno in the West Indies and Hottentots stove in Francisco de Almeida's head on some obscure South African beach. John Cabot, Bartolomé Dias and Humphrey Gilbert belong to that large fraternity of voyagers who were lost at sea. Hernando de Soto could have stayed in Spain enjoying his celebrity and his Peruvian booty but instead he returned to America for more conquests and died in madness at some forlorn spot in Arkansas along the Mississippi which then served as his grave.

The histories of Spain and Portugal read at the national level like the lives of so many of the individual explorers and conquistadors. They led the way to Africa, the Americas and Asia but the rewards of national strength and wealth proved elusive.

Philip II, King of Spain (1556–98), 1578, by an unknown artist. American silver made Philip the richest monarch in late sixteenth-century Europe. However, this wealth eventually resulted in the bankruptcy of his realm and encouraged the King to pursue an overly aggressive foreign policy. (Heritage Image Partnership)

Portugal never achieved true great power status. Its population was too small, its commitments too many and its new-found overseas wealth flowed too quickly into foreign hands. Then in 1580 the Avis dynasty died out and Portugal came under the rule of Philip II of Spain and national independence was lost. That situation continued until 1640 and the revolt of the Braganzas although Spain did not formally recognize Portugal's regaining of its independence until 1668. Spain did come to dominate Western Europe and the western Mediterranean. It was truly a great power during its so-called Golden Age in the second half of the sixteenth century and the early seventeenth century. Much of that political and military weight was created by the financial liquidity that access to and possession of the precious metals of the Americas provided the Spanish crown. It was also an ephemeral foundation for national power. Inflation racked the fragile Spanish economy. Ready supplies of treasure tempted Spain to over-commit itself. Symptoms of serious decline appeared even as Spain reached the zenith of its power and progressed rapidly. By 1648 and the end of the Thirty Years' War, Spain had been transformed from the foremost player in the arena of international competition to a mere pawn. Some might be tempted to compare Spain, Portugal and all the explorers and conquistadors of the early modern age of exploration with the fictional character of Don Quixote – futile, foolish and even a bit threadbare. But they would be making the mistake of focusing on one aspect of this chapter of human history. Spain and Portugal with a bit of help from the English, the French and the Dutch collectively opened up the world and made it one permanently. They accomplished that task by means of tenacity, courage and intrepidity frequently mixed with greed, ruthlessness and cruelty. Perhaps Bernal Díaz's assessment of his own personal profits from his role in the conquest of Mexico applies equally well as an epithet for most of those who participated in the age of exploration. Writing about 1576, he stated with a certain justifiable pride, 'I am now an old man, over eighty-four years of age, and have lost both sight and hearing; and unfortunately I have gained no wealth to leave my children and descendants, except this true story, which is a most remarkable one.'[16]

NOTES

OPENING QUOTATIONS

1. E.G. Ravenstein (ed.), *A Journal of the First Voyage of Vasco da Gama 1497–1499* (London, Hakluyt Society, 1898), p. 114.
2. From *The General and Natural History of the Indies* (1541) in Jesús Carillo (ed.), *Oviedo on Columbus*, vol. IX of *Repertorium Columbianum* (Turnhout, Belgium, Berpols, 2000), p. 54.
3. From *Fifty Stanzas on the Nobility of Spain* (*c.* 1535–52) in Carillo, *Oviedo on Columbus*, p. 98.
4. Bartolomé de Las Casas, *A Short Account of the Destruction of the Indies* (1542), Penguin Classics edn (Harmondsworth, Penguin, 1992), p. 3.
5. Luis Vaz de Camões, *The Lusiads* (1572), Penguin Classics edn (Harmondsworth, Penguin, 1973), p. 167.
6. From *Anatomy of Melancholy* (1621) (New York, Tudor Publishing Company, 1955), pt 2, sec. 2, p. 430.
7. Thomas Paine, *Common Sense* (1776) in *Collected Writings*, ed. Eric Foner (New York, Library of America, 1995), p. 25.
8. Karl Marx and Joseph Engels, *The Communist Manifesto* (1848) (Chicago, Brittanica Great Books, 1952), ch. 1, p. 420.
9. From 'Geography and Some Explorers' in *Last Essays*, vol. 23 of *Collected Works of Joseph Conrad, Memorial Edition*, ed. Ford Maddox Ford (New York, Doubleday, Page & Company, 1926).

PREFACE

1. Sebastian Brant, *Ship of Fools* (New York, Dover Publications, 1962), p. 221.
2. Stephen J. Summerhill and John Alexander Williams, *Sinking Columbus: Contested History, Cultural Politics, and Mythmaking during the Quincentenary* (Gainesville, University Press of Florida, 2000). This is an interesting account of the trials, tribulations and occasional triumphs connected with the quincentenary of Columbus.

ACKNOWLEDGEMENTS

1. Edward Gibbon, *Autobiography* (Oxford, Oxford University Press, 1978).

CHAPTER ONE

1. Joseph Conrad, 'Geography and Some Explorers' in *Last Essays*, vol. 23 of *Collected Works of Joseph Conrad: Memorial Edition* (New York, Doubleday, Page & Company, 1926), p. 4.
2. Jeffrey Burton Russell, *Inventing the Flat Earth: Columbus and Modern Historians* (New York, Praeger, 1991) is an excellent study of how erroneous ideas about Columbus and the flat earth have developed and persisted. The book chronicles the tenacity with which a highly

inaccurate concept about the past has continued in academic and popular culture for well over a century.

3. J.R.S. Phillips, *The Medieval Expansion of Europe*, 2nd edn (Oxford, Oxford University Press, 1998), pp. 4–13 for a discussion of the sphericity of the earth and the size of the earth. Also see F.S. Betten, 'The Knowledge of the Sphericity of the Earth during the Earlier Middle Ages', *Catholic Historical Review*, New Series, 3 (1923–4) and C.W. Jones, 'The Flat Earth', *Thought*, 9 (1934). Besides Phillips, some useful older works dealing with medieval geographical and cosmographical knowledge are Charles Raymond Beazley, *The Dawn of Modern Geography* (3 vols, 1897–1906, rprt. New York, Peter Smith, 1942) and John Kirtland Wright, *Geographical Lore of the Time of the Crusades* (New York, American Geographical Society, 1925).

4. *The Christian Topography of Cosmas, an Egyptian Monk*, tr., ed. and intro. J.W. McCrindle, First Series (London, Hakluyt Society, 1897), vol. 98, makes the curious book available to English readers.

5. Besides Phillips, *Medieval Expansion*, fuller accounts of the history of ancient geography are E.H. Bunbury, *A History of Ancient Geography*, 2 vols (1883, rprt. New York, Dover, 1959) and H.F. Tozzer, *A History of Ancient Geography* (1897, rprt. New York, Biblio and Tanner, 1964).

6. John K. Wright, *Geographical Lore*, pp. 155–65.

7. José de Acosta, *The Natural and Moral History of the Indies*, tr. Edward Grimston and ed. Clements R. Markham (2 vols, London, Hakluyt Society, 1880), I, p. 90.

8. James S. Romm, *The Edges of the Earth in Ancient Thought: Geography, Exploration, and Fiction* (Princeton, NJ, Princeton University Press, 1992), pp. 130–1; W.G.L. Randles, 'Classical Models of World Geography and Their Transfer Following the Discovery of America' in *The Classical Tradition and the Americas*, ed. Wolfgang Haase and Reinhold Meyer (Berlin, W. de Gruyter, 1994), vol. 1; and Boies Penrose, *Travel and Discovery in the Renaissance 1420–1620* (Cambridge, MA, Harvard University Press, 1960), pp. 3 and 6.

9. G. Duchet-Suchaux and M. Pastoreau, *The Bible and the Saints* (Paris, Flammarion, 1994), pp. 222–4 and Richard C. Trexler, *The Journey of the Magi* (Princeton, NJ, Princeton University Press, 1997).

10. O.A.W. Dilke, 'Marinus of Tyre' and 'Ptolemy' in *The Columbus Encyclopedia*, ed. Silvio A. Bedini (2 vols, New York, Simon & Schuster, 1992).

11. A seminal article on this topic is Rudolf Wittkower, 'Marvels of the East', *Journal of the Warburg and Courtauld Institutes*, 5 (1942), 159–97. More recent helpful discussions include Valerie I.J. Flint, *The Imaginative Landscape of Christopher Columbus* (Princeton, NJ, Princeton University Press, 1992), esp. ch. 4, and James S. Romm, *The Edges of the Earth in Ancient Thought*, esp. ch. 3. The following paragraphs are based on these works.

12. M. Cary and E.H. Warmington, *The Ancient Explorers* (1929, rprt. Baltimore, MD, Penguin, 1963), p. 73–109 and 194–8 and Donald F. Lach, *Asia and the Making of Europe* (Chicago, University of Chicago Press, 1965), vol. 1: *The Century of Discovery*, p. 17.

13. See the introduction to *The Greek Alexander Romance*, tr. and intro. Richard Stoneman (London, Penguin Books, 1991) and the more detailed studies of George David Cary, *The Medieval Alexander* (1956, rprt. Cambridge, Cambridge University Press, 1963) and David J.A. Ross, *Alexander Historiatus* (London, Warburg Institute, 1963).

14. John Larner, *Marco Polo and the Discovery of the World* (New Haven, CT, Yale University Press, 1999), p. 13.

15. Several works provide detailed studies of the lore of the monstrous races: Rudolf Wittkower, 'Marvels of the East', *Journal of the Warburg and Courtauld Institutes* 5 (1942), 159–97; John Block Friedman, *The Monstrous Races in Medieval Art and Thought* (Cambridge, MA, Harvard University Press, 1981); and Valeria I.J. Flint, 'Monsters and Antipodes in the Early Middle Ages and the Enlightenment', *Viator* 15 (1984), 65–80.

16. William Arens, *The Man-Eating Myth: Anthropology and Anthrophagy* (Oxford, Oxford University Press, 1979) is an insightful study which argues that the existence of cannibalism is a myth. For the opposite perspective see Peggy Reeves Sanday, *Divine Hunger: Cannibalism as a Cultural System* (Cambridge, Cambridge University Press, 1986).

17. For a study focusing exclusively on Cynocephali see David Gordon White, *Myths of the Dog-Man* (Chicago, University of Chicago Press, 1991).

18. *The Vinland Sagas: The Norse Discovery of America: Graenlendinga Saga and Eirik's Saga*, tr. and intro. Magnus Magnusson and Hermann Palsson (New York, New York University Press, 1966), pp. 101–3. For a discussion of Norse geographical concepts see Gwyn Jones, *The Norse Atlantic Saga: Being the Norse Voyages of Discovery and Settlement to Iceland, Greenland, and North America*, 2nd edn (Oxford, Oxford University Press, 1986), pp. 16–24.

19. A useful study of the idea of the Terrestrial Paradise is Jean Delumeau, *History of Paradise: The Garden of Eden in Myth and Tradition* (New York, Continuum, 1995). Other useful sources are Valerie I.J. Flint, *The Imaginative Landscape of Christopher Columbus*, ch. 5; Leonardo Olschki, 'Ponce de León's Fountain of Youth: History of a Geographical Myth', *Hispanic American Historical Review* 22 (Aug. 1941), 361–85; and Alessandro Scafi, 'Mapping Eden: Cartographies of the Early Paradise', in Denis Cosgrove (ed.), *Mappings* (London, Reaktion Books, 1999), pp. 50–70.

20. For a useful discussion of the place of the Islamic world in the international trade of the later Middle Ages see David Abulafia, 'Asia, Africa, and the Trade of Medieval Europe', *The Cambridge Economic History of Europe*, ed. M.M. Postan and Edward Miller, 2nd edn (Cambridge, Cambridge University Press, 1987), vol. 2, pp. 402–11 and 472–3 and J.R.S. Phillips, *The Medieval Expansion of Europe*, 2nd edn (Oxford, Oxford University Press, 1998), chs 3 and 6.

21. David Abulafia, 'Asia, Africa, and the Trade of Medieval Europe', pp. 462–70.

22. Edward William Bovill, *The Golden Trade of the Moors*, 2nd edn (1968, rprt. Princeton, NJ, M. Weiner, 1995); Richard W. Bulliett, *The Camel and the Wheel* (Cambridge, MA, Harvard University Press, 1975); and Roland Oliver (ed.), *The Cambridge History of Africa* (Cambridge, Cambridge University Press, 1977), vol. 3: *From c. 1050–c. 1600*.

23. Herodotus, *The History*, bk 4, ch. 42; Rhys Carpender, *Beyond the Pillars of Heracles: The Classical World Seen Through the Eyes of Its Discoverers* (New York, Delacorte Press, 1966); and Cary and Warmington, *Ancient Explorers*, pp. 110–31.

24. Phillips, *Medieval Expansion*, pp. 201–4 and 218.

25. For a good overview of the Norse Atlantic voyages and explorations see Gwyn Jones, *The Norse Atlantic Saga* and William W. Fitzhugh and Elisabeth I. Ward (eds), *Vikings: The North Atlantic Saga* (Washington, DC, Smithsonian Institution Press, 2000).

26. David B. Quinn, *North America from Earliest Discovery to First Settlements: The Norse Voyages to 1612* (New York, Harper & Row, 1977), pp. 43–6.

27. For an English translation of the *Navigatio* see ed. and tr. D.H. Farmer and tr. J.F. Webb *The Age of Bede* (Harmondsworth, Penguin Books, 1983). Also see Geoffrey Ashe, *Land to the West: St. Brendan's Voyage to America* (New York, Viking, 1962).

28. William H. Babcock, *Legendary Islands of the Atlantic: A Study in Medieval Geography* (New York, American Geographical Society, 1922) and George E. Buker, 'The Seven Cities: The Role of Myth in the Exploration of the Atlantic', *American Neptune* 30 (1970), 249–59.

29. D.B. Quinn, *North America from Earliest Discovery*, p. 42.

CHAPTER TWO

1. Marco Polo, *The Travels of Marco Polo: The Complete Yule-Cordier Edition*, 2 vols (1929, rprt. New York, Dover, 1993), II, p. 264.

2. Mark Twain, *The Innocents Abroad* (New York, Library of America, 1984), p. 170.

3. For a good overview of cultural and economic exchanges in ancient and medieval times see Jerry H. Bentley, *Old World Encounters: Cross-Cultural Contacts and Exchanges in Pre-Modern Times* (New York, Oxford University Press, 1993).

4. Stephen Neill, *A History of Christian Missions*, 2nd edn (Harmondsworth, Penguin, 1986) and Samuel Hugh Moffat, *A History of Christianity in Asia* (San Francisco, HarperCollins, 1992), vol. 1: *Beginnings to 1500*.

5. Ira M. Lapidus, *A History of Islamic Societies* (Cambridge, Cambridge University Press, 1988), pp. 15–80 and Hugh Kennedy, *The Prophet and the Age of the Caliphates: The Islamic Near East from the Sixth to the Eleventh Century* (London, Longman, 1986).

6. David Abulafia, 'Asia, Africa, and the Trade of Medieval Europe', *The Cambridge Economic History of Europe*, 2nd edn, ed. M.M. Postan and Edward Miller (Cambridge, Cambridge University Press, 1997), vol. 2, pp. 451–2.

7. Lionel Casson, *Ancient Mariners: Seafarers and Sea Fighters of the Mediterranean in Ancient Times*, 2nd edn (Princeton, NJ, Princeton University Press, 1991), pp. 8–9 and George F. Hourani, *Arab Seafaring in the Indian Ocean in Ancient and Early Medieval Times*, expanded edn (1951, rprt. Princeton, Princeton University Press, 1995), pp. 10–11.

8. Casson, *Ancient Mariners*, pp. 9–10 and Hourani, *Arab Seafaring*, pp. 7–9.

9. Casson, *Ancient Mariners*, pp. 62 and 64.

10. Casson, *Ancient Mariners*, pp. 160–1 and Lach, *Asia*, vol. I, bk 1, p. 11.

11. Liu Xinru, *The Silk Road: Overland Trade and Cultural Interactions in Eurasia* (Washington, DC, American Historical Association, 1998), pp. 1–8.

12. Donald F. Lach, *Asia in the Making of Europe* (2 vols, Chicago, University of Chicago Press, 1965), vol. I: *The Century of Discovery*, bk 1, pp. 15–16.

13. Bentley, *Old World Encounters*, pp. 29–33 and 65–6.

14. Lach, *Asia*, vol. I, bk 1, p. 21.

15. Abulafia, 'Asia, Africa, and the Trade of Medieval Europe', p. 402.

16. Abulafia, 'Asia, Africa, and the Trade of Medieval Europe', p. 421.

17. Abulafia, 'Asia, Africa, and the Trade of Medieval Europe', pp. 412–13 and Lach, *Asia*, vol. I, bk 1, p. 44.

18. Abulafia, 'Asia, Africa, and the Trade of Medieval Europe', pp. 404, 407 and 408.

19. Abulafia, 'Asia, Africa, and the Trade of Medieval Europe', p. 433.

20. Lach, *Asia*, vol. I, bk 1, p. 47.

21. J.R.S. Phillips, *The Medieval Expansion of Europe*, 2nd edn (Oxford, Clarendon Press, 1998), pp. 68–77 and 115–16 provides an excellent account of the various diplomats who visited Mongol leaders in the mid-thirteenth century. The introduction in Christopher Dawson (ed.), *Mission to Asia* (1955, rprt. Toronto, University of Toronto Press, 1980) provides a good overview. The volume also presents a fine translation of the narratives of Carpini and William of Rubruck.

22. Christopher Dawson (ed.) *Mission to Asia*, p. 3.

23. John Larner, *Marco Polo and the Discovery of the World* (New Haven, CT, Yale University Press, 1999), pp. 20–1.

24. Morris Rossabi, *Voyager from Xanadu: Rabban Sauma and the First Journey from China to the West* (Tokyo, Kondasha, 1992), pp. 99–180.

25. Phillips, *Medieval Expansion*, pp. 78–95 and Moffatt, *Christianity in Asia*, pp. 442–75.

26. Lach, *Asia*, vol. I, bk 1, p. 47.

27. Abulafia, 'Asia, Africa, and the Trade of Medieval Europe', pp. 404–6.

28. Lach, *Asia*, vol. I, bk 1, pp. 44–6.

29. James D. Ryan, 'European Travellers before Columbus: The Fourteenth Century's Discovery of India', *Catholic Historical Review*, 79 (1993), 648–70.

30. Lach, *Asia*, vol. I, bk 1, pp. 43–5.

31. Larner, *Marco Polo*, p. 97.

32. Abulafia, 'Asia, Africa, and the Trade of Medieval Europe', p. 407.

33. Abulafia, 'Asia, Africa, and the Trade of Medieval Europe', pp. 437–43.

34. Edward William Bovill, *The Golden Trade of the Moors: West African Kingdoms in the Fourteenth Century* (1958, rprt. Princeton, NJ, Markus Wiener Publishers, 1995), pp. 119–23.

35. G.R. Crone (ed.), *The Voyages of Cadamosto and Other Documents on Western Africa in the Second Half of the Fifteenth Century* (London, Hakluyt Society 1937), pp. 21–5.

36. Bovill, *The Golden Trade of the Moors*, pp. 85–7.

37. Bovill, *The Golden Trade of the Moors*, p. 87.

38. Bovill, *The Golden Trade of the Moors*, p. 90.

39. Abulafia, 'Asia, Africa, and the Trade of Medieval Europe', p. 470.

40. Richard W. Bulliett, *The Camel and the Wheel* (Cambridge, MA, Harvard University Press, 1975), pp. 115–40 and Bovill, *The Golden Trade of the Moors*, pp. 16–17 and 36–8.

41. Abulafia, 'Asia, Africa, and the Trade of Medieval Europe', pp. 469–70.

42. Abulafia, 'Asia, Africa, and the Trade of Medieval Europe', p. 468.

43. Abulafia, 'Asia, Africa, and the Trade of Medieval Europe', pp. 462–3.

44. Abulafia, 'Asia, Africa, and the Trade of Medieval Europe', p. 467.

45. Bovill, *The Golden Trade of the Moors*, pp. 110–12.

CHAPTER THREE

1. Damião de Goes, 'Chronicle of the Most Fortunate King Dom Emmaneul' in *Records of South-Eastern Africa*, ed. George McCall Theal (Cape Town, Government of the Cape Colony, 1899), vol. 3, p. 67.

2. Jerry H. Bentley, *Old World Encounters: Cross-Cultural Contacts and Exchanges in Pre-Modern Times* (New York, Oxford University Press, 1993), p. 177.

3. Henry Hobhouse, *Seeds of Change: Five Plants that Transformed Mankind* (New York, Harper & Row, 1985), pp. 44–5 and Sidney W. Mintz, *Sweetness and Power: The Place of Sugar in Modern History* (New York, Viking Penguin Inc., 1985).

4. Bailey W. Diffie and George D. Winius, *Foundations of the Portuguese Empire 1415–1580* (Minneapolis, MN, University of Minnesota Press, 1977), pp. 35–6.

5. Felipe Fernández-Armesto, *Before Columbus: Exploration and Colonisation from the Mediterranean to the Atlantic, 1229–1492* (Basingstoke, Macmillan, 1987), pp. 152–3 and Francis M. Rogers, 'The Vivaldi Expedition', *Seventy-Third Annual Report of the Dante Society* (1955), 31–45.

6. Diffie and Winius, *Foundations*, pp. 25–6.

7. J.R.S. Phillips, *The Medieval Expansion of Europe*, 2nd edn (Oxford, Oxford University Press, 1998), p. 149; Bailey W. Diffie, *Prelude to Empire: Portugal Overseas Before Henry the Navigator* (Lincoln, University of Nebraska Press, 1960), p. 58; Diffie and Winius, *Foundations*, pp. 27–9 and 31; Fernández-Armesto, *Before Columbus*, pp. 153–6; and Eduardo Aznar Vallejo, 'The Conquests of the Canary Islands' in *Implicit Understandings*, ed. Stuart B. Schwartz (Cambridge, Cambridge University Press, 1994), pp. 134–56.

8. Diffie and Winius, *Foundations*, p. 31; Fernández-Armesto, *Before Columbus*, pp. 156–9; and Diffie, *Prelude to Empire*, p. 59.

9. Fernández-Armesto, *Before Columbus*, p. 174.

10. Ibid., pp. 180–1.

11. Ibid., pp. 175–9; Diffie and Winius, *Foundations*, pp. 42–4; and Charles Verlinden, 'Canary Islands and Bethencourt' in *Dictionary of the Middle Ages*, ed. Joseph R. Strayer (New York, Charles Scribner's Sons, 1983), vol. 3, pp. 61–3.

12. Fernández-Armesto, *Before Columbus*, pp. 181–3.

13. Ibid., pp. 179–81 and Diffie and Winius, *Foundations*, pp. 43–4.

14. Diffie and Winius, *Foundations*, p. 37.

15. Ibid., pp. 39–40.

16. P.E, Russell, *Prince Henry 'the Navigator' a Life* (New Haven, CT, Yale University Press, 2000), pp. 39–42.

17. Ibid., pp. 30–1 and Diffie and Winius, *Foundations*, pp. 53–4.

18. Ibid., pp. 53–4.

19. Russell, *Henry*, pp. 51–4.

20. Diffie and Winius, *Foundations*, pp. 54–5.

21. Russell, *Henry*, pp. 64–8.

22. Samuel Eliot Morison, *The European Discovery of America: The Southern Voyages A.D. 1492–1616* (New York, Oxford University Press, 1974), pp. 4–5; Diffie and Winius, *Foundations*, pp. 113–18; and Russell, *Henry*, pp. 6–7. For the myth of the school at Sagres see W.G.L. Randles, 'The Alleged Nautical School Founded in the Fifteenth Century at Sagres by Prince Henry of Portugal, called the "Navigator"', *Imago Mundi* 45 (1993), 20–8 and Russell, *Henry*, p. xx.

23. Russell, *Henry*, pp. 19–26.

24. Gomes Eannes de Azurara, *The Chronicle of the Discovery and Conquest of Guinea*, ed. Charles Raymond Beazley and Edgar Prestage (2 vols, London, Hakluyt Society, 1896 and 1899), vol. I, pp. 12–13; Russell, *Henry*, pp. 75–6; and Diffie and Winius, *Foundations*, pp. 121–2.

25. Azurara, *The Chronicle*, vol. I, p. 15.

26. Ibid., pp. 14–15 and Duarte Pacheco Pereira, *Esmeraldo de Situ Orbis*, ed. George H.T. Kimble (London, Hakluyt Society, 1937), p. 61.

27. Azurara, *The Chronicle*, vol. I, pp. 27–9.

28. Azurara, *The Chronicle*, vol. I, p. 30.

29. Russell, *Henry*, pp. 14–19.

30. Pacheco, *Esmeraldo*, p. 62.

31. Russell, *Henry*, pp. 76 and 78.

32. Diffie and Winius, *Foundations*, pp. 55–6.

33. J.H. Parry, *The Age of Reconnaissance: Discovery, Exploration and Settlement 1450 to 1650* (Berkeley, CA, University of California Press, 1981), p. 83.

34. Russell, *Henry*, pp. 236–8.

35. G.R. Crone (ed.), *The Voyages of Cadamosto and Other Documents on Western Africa in the Second Half of the Fifteenth Century* (London, Hakluyt Society, 1937, hereafter cited as Cadamosto, *voyages.*), pp. 101–2, from the section of 'The Voyages of Diogo Gomes', and W.G.L. Randles, 'The Emergence of Nautical Astronomy in Portugal in the Xvth Century', *Journal of Navigation* 51 (1998), 46–57 *passim* but for Gomes see specifically p. 47.

36. Alfredo Pinheiro Marques, *Portugal and the Discovery of the Atlantic* (Casa de Moeda, Imprensa Nacional, 1990), pp. 61–80.

37. Parry, *Reconnaissance*, pp. 87–8.

38. W.G.L. Randles, 'The Emergence of Nautical Astronomy in Portugal in the XVth century', 46–57.

39. Charles Raymond Beazley, *The Dawn of Modern Geography*, 3 vols (1897–1906) (rprt. New York, Peter Smith, 1942); David Woodward, 'Medieval Mappaemundi' in *The History of Cartography*, vol. 1: *Cartography in Prehistoric, Ancient, and Medieval Europe and the Mediterranean*, ed. J.B. Harley and David Woodward (Chicago, IL, University of Chicago Press, 1987); and John Kirtland Wright, *Geographical Lore of the Time of the Crusades* (New York, American Geographical Society, 1925).

40. Tony Campbell, 'Portolan Charts from the Late Thirteenth Century to 1500' in *The History of Cartography*, vol. 1: *Cartography in Prehistoric, Ancient, and Medieval Europe and the Mediterranean*, ed. J.B. Harley and David Woodward, and Parry, *Reconnaissance*.

41. G.R. Crone (ed.), *The Voyages of Cadamosto and other Documents on Western Africa in the Second Half of the Fifteenth Century* (London, Hakluyt Society, 1937), p. 2. Hereafter cited as Cadamosto, *Voyages*.

42. Roger C. Smith, *Vanguard of Empire: Ships of Exploration in the Age of Columbus* (New York, Oxford University Press, 1993), pp. 46–8.

43. Carlo M. Cipolla, *Guns, Sails, and Empires: Technological Innovation and the Early Phases of European Expansion, 1400–1700* (New York, Pantheon, 1961), pp. 101–2 and 138–43 and W.G.L. Randles, 'The Artilleries and Land Fortifications of the Portuguese and of Their Adversaries in the Early Period of the Discoveries' in *Geography, Cartography and Nautical Science in the Renaissance: The Impact of the Great Discoveries* (Aldershot, Variorum, 2000), item XVII, pp. 1–16 *passim*.

44. K.M. Panikkar, *Asia and Western Dominance* (London, George Allen & Unwin, 1959).

45. Fernández-Armesto, *Before Columbus*, p. 185.

46. Russell, *Henry*, p. 107.

47. Alfredo Pinheiro Marques, *Portugal and the Discovery of the Atlantic*, pp. 21–8 is a good, brief overview of Portugal's efforts to conquer and settle the Canary Islands.

48. Russell, *Henry*, pp. 264–76.

49. Ibid., pp. 278–81.

50. Ibid., pp. 82–3 and 288–90.

51. Diffie and Winius, *Foundations*, pp. 150–2.

52. Marques, *Portugal and the Discovery of the Atlantic*, pp. 31–40.

53. Fernández-Armesto, *Before Columbus*, pp. 195–7.

54. Edgar Prestage, *The Portuguese Pioneers* (London, A. & C. Black, 1933), pp. 39–40 and Cadamosto, *Voyages*, pp. 8–9.

55. Russell, *Henry*, pp. 86 and 90–4.

56. Fernández-Armesto, *Before Columbus*, p. 199; Prestage, *Portuguese Pioneers*, pp. 40–1; Cadamosto, *Voyages*, pp. 9–10; and Alfred W. Crosby, *Ecological Imperialism: The Biological Expansion of Europe*, 900–1900 (Cambridge, Cambridge University Press, 1986), pp. 74–9.

57. Azurara, *The Chronicle*, vol. I, pp. 245–7.

58. Marques, *Portugal and the Discovery of the Atlantic*, pp. 43–55.

59. Diffie and Winius, *Foundations*, pp. 61–2 and Fernández-Armesto, *Before Columbus*, p. 197.

60. Crosby, *Ecological Imperialism*, pp. 73–4.

61. Diffie and Winius, *Foundations*, p. 62.

62. Ibid., p. 62.

63. Fernández-Armesto, *Before Columbus*, pp. 200–2.

64. Prestage, *Portuguese Pioneers*, pp. 227–32 and Marques, *Portugal and the Discovery of the Atlantic*, pp. 55–8.

65. Samuel Eliot Morison, *Portuguese Voyages to America in the Fifteenth Century* (Cambridge, MA, Harvard University Press, 1940), p. 21.

66. Ibid., pp. 33–41.

67. Ibid., p. 32.

68. Samuel Eliot Morison, *The European Discovery of America: The Northern Voyages A.D. 500–1600* (New York, Oxford University Press, 1974), pp. 211–13 and Morison, *Portuguese Voyages*, pp. 59–68.

69. Morison, *Northern Voyages*, pp. 213–17 and Morison, *Portuguese Voyages*, pp. 68–72.

70. Cadamosto, *Voyages*, p. 2.

71. Azurara, *The Chronicle*, vol. I, p. 31.

72. Russell, *Henry*, p. 112.

73. Azurara, *The Chronicle*, vol. I, pp. 30–4; Diffie and Winius, *Foundations*, p. 68; and Pacheco, *Esmeraldo*, pp. 65–6.

74. Cadamosto, *Voyages*, pp. 2–3; Russell, *Henry*, pp. 127–8; and Diffie and Winius, *Foundations*, p. 59.

75. Azurara, *The Chronicle*, vol. I, p. 34.

76. Ibid., vol. I, pp. 35–7.

77. Russell, *Henry*, p. 130.

78. Azurara, *The Chronicle*, vol. I, pp. 35–6 and Diffie and Winius, *Foundations*, p. 69.

79. Azurara, *The Chronicle*, vol. I, pp. 38–9 and Diffie and Winius, *Foundations*, p. 72.

80. Azurara, *The Chronicle*, vol. I., pp. 39–43 and Russell, *Henry*, pp. 195–7.

81. Azurara, *The Chronicle*, vol. I, pp. 44–5 and Diffie and Winius, *Foundations*, pp. 77–9.

82. Azurara, *The Chronicle*, vol. I, pp. 50–1.

83. Ibid., vol. I, pp. 98–100.

84. Ibid., vol. II, pp. 253–7.

85. Ibid., vol II, pp. 288–9; Russell, *Henry*, pp. 200–1 and 212–13; and Diffie and Winius, *Foundations*, pp. 79–90.

86. John William Blake, *West Africa: Quest for God and Gold, 1454–1578: A Survey of the First Century of White Enterprise in West Africa, with Particular Reference to the Achievements of the Portuguese and Their Rivalries with Other European Powers* (London, Curzon Press, 1977), pp. 16–17.

87. Cadamosto, *Voyages*, p. 60.

88. Russell, *Henry*, p. 309 and Cadamosto, *Voyages*, pp. xxiii–xxv.

89. Russell, *Henry*, p. 106.

90. Diffie and Winius, *Foundations*, pp. 106–7 and 111.

91. Cadamosto, *Voyages*, pp. xiii–xv and 93–8. For a brief study dealing with Portuguese speculations about a West African location for Prester John see Charles Beckingham, 'Prester John in West Africa' in Charles F. Beckingham and Bernard Hamilton (eds), *Prester John, the Mongols and the Ten Lost Tribes* (Aldershot, Variorum, 1996), item XI, pp. 20–211.

92. Cadamosto, *Voyages*, p. 98, narrative of Diogo Gomes.

93. Russell, *Henry*, ch. 13, *passim*.

94. Blake, *West Africa*, pp. 23 and 197 and Cadamosto, *Voyages*, pp. xxvi–xxvii and 98–101.

95. Cadamosto, *Voyages*, p. 102, narrative of Diogo Gomes.

96. Cadamosto, *Voyages*, p. 106, excerpt from João de Barros's *Décadas da Ásia*.

97. Russell, *Henry*, pp. 334–41 and Cadamosto, *Voyages*, pp. 78–84.

98. Diffie and Winius, *Foundations*, pp. 144–5.

99. Cadamosto, *Voyages*, p. 112, excerpt from João de Barros's *Décadas da Ásia*.

100. Diffie and Winius, *Foundations*, pp. 146–7; Cadamosto, *Voyages*, pp. 107–12; and John Williams Blake (ed.), *Europeans in West Africa, 1450–1560*, 2 vols (London, Hakluyt Society, 1942), I, pp. 68–9.

101. Blake, *West Africa*, pp. 98–100; Blake, *Europeans in West Africa*, I, pp. 70–8 prints an English translation of the relevant section of Ruy de Pina's *Chronica del Rey Dom João II*; Crone, *Voyages of Cadamosto*, pp. 114–23 prints an English translation of the relevant section of João de Barros's *Décadas da Ásia*; and Christopher R. DeCorse, *An Archaeology of Elmina: Africans and Europeans on the Gold Coast, 1400–1900* (Washington, DC, Smithsonian Institution Press, 2001) presents a detailed study of the history and nature of Elmina as a trading town.

102. E.G. Ravenstein, 'The Voyages of Diego Cão and Bartholomeu Dias, 1482–88', *Geographical Journal* (1900), 625–38 and Eric Axelson, *Congo to Cape: Early Portuguese Explorers* (New York, Barnes & Noble, 1973), p. xx.

103. Diffie and Winius, *Foundations*, pp. 154–6 and Prestage, *Portuguese Pioneers*, pp. 206–11.

104. Diffie and Winius, *Foundations*, p. 159.

105. Prestage, *Portuguese Pioneers*, pp. 216–22 and Diffie and Winius, *Foundations*, pp. 163–4.

106. Francisco Alvares, *The Prester John of the Indies*, 2 vols (Cambridge, Cambridge University Press, 1961), pp. 369–76.

107. Diffie and Winius, *Foundations*, pp. 164–5.

108. W.G.L. Randles, 'Bartolomeu Dias and the Discovery of the South-east Passage Linking the Atlantic to the Indian Ocean' in W.G.L. Randles, *Geography, Cartography and Nautical Science in the Renaissance*, item VII, 19–28 *passim*.

109. For a detailed study of the placenames of the Dias voyage see Eric Axelson, 'The Dias Voyage, 1487–1488: Toponymy and Padrões', *Revista da Universidade de Coimbra* 34 (1998), 29–55.

110. E.G. Ravenstein, 'The Voyages of Diogo Cão and Bartolomeu Dias, 1482–1488', *Geographical Journal* (1900), 638–49; Prestage, *Portuguese Pioneers*, pp. 222–4; and Axelson, *Congo to Cape*, pp. 97–108.

111. Barros, *Décadas da Ásia*, I, bk 3, ch. 4 in *Records of South-Eastern Africa*, ed. George McCall Theal (Cape Town, Government of the Cape Colony, 1899), vol. 6, p. 152; Axelson, *Congo to Cape*, p. 108–14; and Prestage, *Portuguese Pioneers*, pp. 224–5.

112. Barros, *Décadas da Ásia* in Theal (ed.), *Records*, vol. 6, p. 152.

113. Barros, *Décadas da Ásia* in Theal(ed.), *Records*, vol. 6, p. 153; Axelson, *Congo to Cape*, pp. 156–76.

114. Pacheco, *Esmeraldo*, p. 141.

115. Axelson, *Congo to Cape*, pp. 177–96 and Diffie and Winius, *Foundations*, pp. 160–2.

116. Antonio Galvano, *The Discoveries of the World from Their First Original unto the Year of Our Lord 1555*, ed. C.R.D. Bethune (London, Hakluyt Society, 1862), p. 77.

CHAPTER FOUR

1. Jesús Carillo (ed.), *Oviedo on Columbus*, vol. IX of *Repertorium Columbianum* (Turnhout, Belgium, Berpols, 2000), p. 91.

2. James A. Williamson, *The Cabot Voyages and Bristol Discovery under Henry VII* (London, Hakluyt Society, 1962), p. 209.

3. Luis Vaz de Camões, *The Lusiads* (Harmondsworth, Penguin Books, 1952), p. 47.

4. There are numerous biographies or biographical studies of Columbus. A good although somewhat dated guide to the literature about Columbus is Foster Provost, *Columbus: An Annotated Guide to the Scholarship on His Life and Writings, 1750–1988* (Detroit, MI, Omnigraphics, 1991). The fount of many popular misconceptions about Columbus is Washington Irving, *A History of the Life and Voyages of Christopher Columbus*, 4 vols (New York, Carvill, 1828). Still worth reading are Justin Winsor, *Christopher Columbus and How He Received and Imparted the Spirit of Discovery* (Boston, Houghton Mifflin, 1891) and John Boyd Thacher, *Christopher Columbus: His Life, His Work, His Remains . . .*, 3 vols (New York, Knickerbocke, 1903). The standard biography for many years has been Samuel Eliot Morison, *Admiral of the Ocean Sea: A Life of Christopher Columbus*, 2 vols (Boston, Little, Brown, 1942) although it is more commonly encountered and read in its Pulitzer Prize-winning, single-volume abridgement which omits, among other things, all scholarly documentation. More recent biographies include Felipe Fernández-Armesto, *Columbus* (Oxford, Oxford University Press, 1991); Gianni Granzotto, *Christopher Columbus: The Dream and the Obsession* (New York, Doubleday, 1985); William D. Phillips Jr and Carla Rahn Phillips, *The Worlds of Christopher Columbus* (Cambridge, Cambridge University Press, 1992); Paolo Emilio Taviani, *Columbus the Great Adventure: His Life, His Times, and His*

Voyages (New York, Orion Books, 1991); and John Noble Wilford, *The Mysterious History of Columbus: An Exploration of the Man, the Myth, the Legacy* (New York, Alfred W. Knopf, 1991). For a biographical study that also critiques the common fallacies of Columbus biographies there is Miles H. Davidson, *Columbus Then and Now: A Life Re-examined* (Norman, OK, University of Oklahoma Press, 1997).

5. For an excellent brief account of Columbus's birth and youth see the first-rate entries by Paolo Emilio Taviani, 'Birth and Origins' and Helen Nader, 'Adolescence and Youth' under 'Columbus, Christopher' in Silvio A. Bendini (ed.), *The Christopher Columbus Encyclopedia*, 2 vols (New York, Simon & Schuster, 1992); John Dotson and Aldo Agosto (eds), *Christopher Columbus and His Family: The Genoese and Ligurian Documents*, vol. IV of *Repertorium Columbianum* (Turnhout, Belgium, Berpols, 1998) gathers together the large number of documents that clearly prove Columbus's Genoese origins. In spite of these documents numerous theories suggesting alternate ethnic origins for Columbus abound. Probably the most common idea claims that Columbus was Jewish. Among the many works espousing this theory are Salvador de Madariaga, *Christopher Columbus: Being the Life of the Very Magnificent Lord Don Cristóbal Colón* (New York, Macmillan, 1940); Simon Wiesenthal, *Sails of Hope: The Secret Mission of Christopher Columbus* (New York, Macmillan, 1973); and there are many others. For Columbus as a Portuguese spy see Mascarenhas Barreto, *The Portuguese Columbus: Secret Agent of King John II* (New York, St Martins, 1992). One particularly exotic concept claims that Columbus was a castaway Native American just trying to get home.

6. For a succinct account of Columbus's early years in maritime and commercial activities see Helen Nader, 'Early Maritime Experience' under 'Columbus, Christopher' in Bendini (ed.), *The Christopher Columbus Encyclopedia*.

7. Rebecca Catz, 'Columbus in Portugal' under 'Columbus, Christopher' in Bendini (ed.), *The Christopher Columbus Encyclopedia*.

8. Benjamin Keen (ed.), *The Life of the Admiral Christopher Columbus by his Son Ferdinand* (New Brunswick, NJ, Rutgers University Press, 1959), p. 11.

9. For a good discussion of this problem see John Larner, 'The Certainty of Columbus: Some Recent Studies', *History* 73 (Feb. 1988), 3–23.

10. Jeffrey Burton Russell, *Inventing the Flat Earth: Columbus and Modern Historians* (New York, Praeger, 1991) is an excellent account of both medieval ideas and the history of the popular misconception that Columbus was one of the few people of his time to believe that the earth was round.

11. For a somewhat different look at the Columbus–Perestrello marriage see Peter W. Dickson, 'Colon the Younger, the House of Braganza, and the Columbus–Perestrello Marriage of 1479', *Terrae Incognitae* 31 (1999), 12–24.

12. Although early in the twentieth century some scholars questioned the authenticity of the Toscanelli correspondence and map, e.g., Henry Vignaud, *Toscanelli and Columbus: the Letter and the Chart of Toscanelli . . .* (London, Sands, 1902), subsequent scholarship has accepted these documents as genuine. See Frederick A. Kirkpatrick, 'Toscanelli', *Hispanic American Historical Review* 15 (1935), 493–5; Charles E. Nowell, 'The Toscanelli Letters and Columbus', *Hispanic American Historical Review* 17 (1937), 346–8; and Thomas Goldstein, *Dawn of Modern Science from the Arabs to Leonardo Da Vinci* (Boston, Houghton Mifflin, 1980).

13. Elaine Sanceau, *The Perfect Prince: Dom João II* (Oporto, Livraria Civilização, 1959), for a biography in English.

14. W.G.L. Randles, 'The Evaluation of Columbus's "India" Project by Cosmographers in the Light of the Geographical Science of the Period', *Imago Mundi* 42 (1990), 50–64.

15. Although they are popularly known as Ferdinand and Isabella, to their contemporaries they were Fernando and Isabel. The use of the name Isabella has no contemporary warrant. For a modern biography see Peggy K. Liss, *Isabel the Queen* (Oxford, Oxford University Press, 1992). For a good fairly recent dual biography but using the old-style nomenclature see Felipe Fernández-Armesto, *Ferdinand and Isabella* (1975, rprt. New York, Dorset Press, 1991). William H. Prescott's *History of the Reign of Ferdinand and Isabella* (1838, many edns) is a classic account in the romantic style of the early nineteenth century and is worth reading in spite of its New England Protestant prejudices.

16. Helen Nader, 'Columbus in Spain' under 'Columbus, Christopher' in Bendini (ed.), *The Christopher Columbus Encyclopedia* is a useful brief account. Davidson's *Columbus Then and Now* corrects various misconceptions about Columbus's years in Spain.

17. Columbus's first voyage is reasonably well documented when compared to most of the voyages of exploration during the fifteenth and sixteenth centuries. The outstanding but frequently misrepresented source is the transcription of Columbus's log made by Bartolomé de Las Casas which is known as the *Diario*. The best English translation that preserves its true nature and its strengths and weaknesses as a primary document is Oliver Dunn and James E. Kelley Jr (eds and trans), *The Diario of Christopher Columbus's First Voyage to America 1492–1493* (Norman, OK, University of Oklahoma Press, 1989). The famous 'Columbus Letter' in which he describes his first voyage and discoveries is printed in English translation in Cecil Jane (ed.), *The Four Voyages of Columbus*, 2 vols (London, Hakluyt Society, 1930 and 1933; rprt. slightly corrected as a single volume by Dover Books, 1988). For a useful overview and critique of these and other sources see David Henige, *In Search of Columbus: The Sources for the First Voyage* (Tuscon, AZ, University of Arizona Press, 1991). The following narrative is based largely on the *Diario*.

18. Davidson, *Columbus Then and Now*, pp. 210–12.

19. Ibid., pp. 213–22 and David Henige, 'The Mutinies on Columbus's First Voyage: Fact or Fiction?', *Terrae Incognitae* 23 (1991), 29–37.

20. For a useful overview of the landfall controversy see Wilcomb E. Washburn, 'Landfall Controversy' in Bendini (ed.), *The Christopher Columbus Encyclopedia*. Also informative is the collection of essays in Louis De Vorsey Jr and John Parker, *In the Wake of Columbus: Islands and Controversy* (Detroit, MI, Wayne State University Press, 1985) which reprints vol. 15 of *Terrae Incognitae*.

21. Dunn and Kelley (eds and trans), *Diario*, p. 65.

22. Ibid., p. 73.

23. Ibid., p. 89.

24. Jane, *Four Voyages of Columbus*, vol. I, p. 14.

25. Dunn and Kelley (eds and trans), *Diario*, p. 109.

26. Ibid., p. 113.

27. Jane, *Four Voyages of Columbus*, vol. I, p. 6.

28. Davidson, *Columbus Then and Now*, pp. 237–45 provides the sensible explanation of the existing evidence and is the basis for this narrative.

29. Ibid., pp. 246–51.

30. Dunn and Kelley (eds and trans), *Diario*, p. 383.

31. See above, p. 75.

32. Charles Edward Nowell, 'The Treaty of Tordesillas and the Diplomatic Background of American History' in *Greater America: Essays in Honor of Herbert Eugene Bolton* (Berkeley, CA, University of California Press, 1995), pp. 1–18.

33. Hugh Thomas, *Conquest: Montezuma, Cortés, and the Fall of Old Mexico* (New York, Simon & Schuster, 1993), pp. 564 and 569.

34. Two excellent works that place John Cabot's voyages in the context of both what occurred before and what followed are David Beers Quinn, *England and the Discovery of America, 1481–1620* (New York, Alfred W. Knopf, 1974) which summarizes the large but scattered research concerning pre-1494 voyages from Bristol to North America, and Kenneth R. Andrews, *Trade, Plunder, and Settlement: Maritime Enterprise and the Genesis of the British Empire, 1480–1630* (Cambridge, Cambridge University Press, 1984). A recent book that is a tie-in to the BBC television programme produced to commemorate the 500th anniversary of Cabot's voyage is Peter Firstbrook, *The Voyage of the Matthew: John Cabot and the Discovery of North America* (Toronto, McClelland & Stewart, 1997).

35. Peter E. Pope, *The Many Landfalls of John Cabot* (Toronto, University of Toronto Press, 1997), p. 13. Most reference works refer to Cabot's Italian name as Giovanni Caboto, an error that Pope corrects. Pope's book is not a biography of John Cabot. Instead it is a history of historical writing about John Cabot and his voyage. It describes the landfall controversy connected to Cabot's voyage of 1497 and how it related to internal Canadian nationalism and the history of how Sebastian Cabot appropriated credit for his father's achievements and how historians uncovered his deception. It also begins with an excellent chapter on the sources for John Cabot's career and constructs a minimalist biographical sketch that tends to reject most previous speculations about Cabot's achievements.

36. This Genoese reference comes from a letter written from London by Pedro de Ayala to Fernando and Isabel of Spain on 25 July 1498. An excerpt of the letter is printed in James A. Williamson, *The Cabot Voyages*, pp. 228–9. Williamson's book includes an extensive introduction which discusses the pre-1494 Bristol voyages, Cabot's background, Cabot's voyages for Henry VII and the career of Sebastian Cabot. It also prints in whole or excerpts all extant documentary references to these topics.

37. Some scholars assert that John Cabot made a voyage from Bristol to the North American coast without a landing in 1494. If true he would have been resident in England by or prior to 1494. Evidence for this claim is based on a caption from a map by Sebastian Cabot mentioning a voyage of 1494. Assumed by some historians to be a transcription error for 1497, others claim that 1494 was the intended reading. For an interpretation that accepts the 1494 reading see Harry Kelsey, 'The Planispheres of Sebastian Cabot and Sancho Gutiérrez', *Terrae Incognitae* 19 (1987), 41–58, esp. pp. 48–51.

38. Knowledge of Cabot's unsuccessful voyage of 1496 is based solely on a reference in the John Day letter to the Lord Grand Admiral of Spain (Christopher Columbus?) written in 1497 and reporting on John Cabot's voyage of 1497. The relevant passage reads, 'Since your lordship wants information relating to the first voyage, here is what happened: he went with one ship, his crew confused him, he was short of supplies and ran into bad weather, and he decided to turn back.' Day's letter remained unknown until 1956 when

L.A. Vigneras published the Spanish text. He published an English translation in his article 'The Cape Breton Landfall: 1494–1497', *Canadian Historical Review* 38 (1957), 219–28. The letter also appears in Williamson, *Cabot Voyages*, pp. 211–14.

39. Firstbrook, *Voyage of the Matthew*, pp. 55–85 *passim*, contains considerable material about the ships of the late fifteenth century and modern efforts to build a replica of the *Matthew* as part of the commemoration of the 500th anniversary of his voyage. An attractive booklet by Steve Martin and Colin Sanger, *Matthew: A Voyage from the Past into the Future* (Bristol, Godrevy Publications, 1996) describes the *Matthew* Project and includes many photographs of the replica of the *Matthew* that sailed from Bristol to Newfoundland during 1997.

40. Discussion of the problem of the date of Cabot's departure can be found in Williamson, *Cabot Voyages*, pp. 61–2; Firstbrook, *Voyage of the Matthew*, p. 118; Quinn, *England and the Discovery of America*, p. 94; and Samuel Eliot Morison, *The European Discovery of America: The Northern Voyages* (Oxford, Oxford University Press, 1971), pp. 168–9 which also includes a good map of Bristol, the River Avon and the Severn Estuary on pp. 162–3.

41. The most up-to-date discussion of the Cabot landfall controversy is Pope, *Many Landfalls of John Cabot*, pp. 69–89 *passim*.

42. Both Williamson, *Cabot Voyages*, pp. 104–13, and Firstbrook, *Voyage of the Matthew*, pp. 136–45, speculate about Cabot or some of his fleet of 1498 reaching South America. Morison, *Northern Voyages*, pp. 191–2 is highly sceptical.

43. Pope, *Many Landfalls of John Cabot*, pp. 43–68, details how John Cabot's role in the exploration of the Americas was lost and found from about 1500 to the early twentieth century.

44. Armando Cortesão, *The Mystery of Vasco da Gama* (Coimbra, Portugal, Junta de Investgacoes do Ultramar, 1973) is a good example of such scholarship and asserts that secret voyages took place and that Gama commanded at least one of them.

45. For the background of Portuguese history during the fifteenth century see H.V. Livermore, *A New History of Portugal*, 2nd edn (Cambridge, Cambridge University Press, 1976); Charles E. Nowell, *A History of Portugal* (New York, D. Van Nostrand Co., 1952); A.H. de Oliveira Marques, *History of Portugal*, 2nd edn (New York, Columbia University Press, 1976); Bailey W. Diffie and George D. Winius, *Foundations of the Portuguese Empire 1415–1580* (Minneapolis, MN, University of Minnesota Press, 1977); and Sanceau, *The Perfect Prince*.

46. Sanjay Subrahmanyam, *The Career and Legend of Vasco da Gama* (Cambridge, Cambridge University Press, 1997), pp. 64–75.

47. Gaspar Correa, *The Three Voyages of Vasco da Gama and his Viceroyalty from the Lendas da India*, trans. and intro. by Henry E.J. Stanley (London, Hakluyt Society, 1869), pp. 28–30 tells the story of King Manuel being so very impressed with Vasco's appearance and deciding on that basis to make him commander of the voyage to India.

48. Subrahmanyam, *Vasco da Gama*, pp. 66–8.

49. Vasco da Gama is a hard subject for a biographer due to the lack of or poor quality of the documentation. Sanjay Subrahmanyam's *Vasco da Gama* is the best and most up-to-date biography. It includes considerable material about internal Portuguese politics. Other useful biographical works are Luc Cuyvers, *Into the Rising Sun: Vasco da Gama and the Search for a Sea Route to the East* (New York, TV Books, 1999); Henry H. Hart, *Sea Road to the Indies:*

An Account of the Voyages and Exploits of the Portuguese Navigators, Together with the Life and Times of Dome Vasco da Gama, Capitão-Mor, Viceroy of India, and Count of Vidigueira (New York, Macmillan, 1950); Kingsley Garland Jayne, *Vasco da Gama and his Successors, 1460–1580* (1910, rprt. New York, Barnes & Noble, 1970); Charles E. Nowell, 'Vasco da Gama – First Count of Vidigueira', *Hispanic American Historical Review* 20 (Aug. 1940), 342–58; and Elaine Sanceau, *Good Hope: The Voyage of Vasco da Gama* (Lisbon, Academia International de Cultura Portuguesa, 1967).

50. Sanjay Subrahmanyam's *Vasco da Gama* consistently points out manifestations of Gama's aggressive and suspicious behaviour towards various peoples in Africa and India and its corrosive effects on Portuguese relations with the peoples of the Indian Ocean.

51. The best account of Vasco da Gama's first voyage is provided by the unknown author of the *roteiro* or journal for that voyage. The author was a member of the expedition and accompanied Gama to Calicut for his meetings with the Zamorin. Some scholars identify the author as Alvaro Velho. An English translation of the *roteiro* by E.G. Ravenstein was published as *A Journal of the First Voyage of Vasco da Gama, 1497–1499* (London, Hakluyt Society, 1898). Ravenstein doubts that Velho was the author. This edition also prints other documents relevant to Gama's voyage. Gaspar Correa's (d. *c.* 1563) *Lendas da Índia* has been partially translated into English as *The Three Voyages of Vasco da Gama, and his Viceroyalty. From the Lendas da India of Gaspar Correa*, ed. Henry E.J. Stanley (London, Hakluyt Society, 1869). It adds many details to the story but modern historians consider most details found only in Correa to be suspect as unfounded embellishments. A far better history of the Portuguese in Asia was composed by João de Barros (*c.* 1496–1570) as *Asia: Dos feitos que os Portugueses fizeram no descobrimento e conquista dos Mares E Terras do Oriente*. It is more commonly known as *Décadas da Ásia* and was first published in 1552–3 and was a typically renaissance history with an emphasis on rhetorical and moral considerations. Although never translated into English, excerpts are included in *The Three Voyages of Vasco da Gama*. The great Luis Vaz de Camões (*c.* 1524–80) composed an epic poem commemorating Gama's exploits. It was titled *Os Lusíadas* (the Lusiads, that is the sons of Lusus referring to Lusus, the ancient founder of Portugal) and modelled on the *Aeneid* of Virgil. Published in 1572, any historical details that it provides should be treated with the utmost caution. There is a prose English translation *The Lusiads*, ed. and trans. William C. Atkinson (London, Penguin Books, 1952). Excerpts translated as verse can be found in *The Three Voyages of Vasco da Gama*.

52. Ravenstein (trans.), *First Voyage of Vasco da Gama*, p. 8.

53. It has been frequently suggested in older accounts that Gama's pilot was the famous Arab pilot Ahmad ibn Majid but Subrahmanyam's *Vasco da Gama*, pp. 121–8, has conclusively demonstrated that this was not the case.

54. Ravenstein (trans.), *First Voyage of Vasco da Gama*, pp. 48–9 and 180–1.

55. Ibid., pp. 49 and 61, n. 2. The title Zamorin is thought by most to be a corruption of *Samudriya Rajah*, which translates as 'king of the coast' and underlines the importance of maritime trade for the rulers and people of Calicut.

56. Ibid., pp. 52–4. The quote from Sá comes from the Portuguese chronicler Lopez de Castenheda.

57. Ibid., p. 62.

58. Ibid., p. 76.

CHAPTER FIVE

1. Michel de Montaigne, 'Of Cannibals' in *Essays*, ed. W. Carow Hazlitt (Chicago, Britannica Great Books, 1952), p. 92.

2. Samuel Butler, *Further Extracts from the Notebooks of Samuel Butler*, ed. A.T. Bartholomew (London, Jonathan Cape, 1934), p. 158.

3. Samuel Eliot Morison, *Admiral of the Ocean Sea: A Life of Christopher Columbus*, 2 vols (Boston, Little, Brown, 1942), pp. 389–502 is a detailed account of the second voyage. There is a briefer, more recent narrative in Morison's *The European Discovery of America: The Southern Voyages A.D. 1492–1616* (New York, Oxford University Press, 1974), pp. 92–139. Other accounts of the second voyage can be found in Felipe Fernández-Armesto, *Columbus* (Oxford, Oxford University Press, 1991), pp. 95–114 and William D. Phillips Jr and Carla Rahn Phillips, *The Worlds of Christopher Columbus* (Cambridge, Cambridge University Press, 1992), pp. 193–211. For critical commentary on all, see Miles H. Davidson, *Columbus Then and Now: A Life Re-examined* (Norman, OK, University of Oklahoma Press, 1997), pp. 311–34.

4. Cecil Jane (ed.), *The Four Voyages of Columbus*, 2 vols (London, Hakluyt Society, 1930 and 1933), vol. 1, pp. 26–34.

5. Ibid., pp. 36–8.

6. Davidson, *Columbus Then and Now*, p. 333; Phillips and Phillips, *The Worlds of Christopher Columbus*, p. 198; and Morison, *Admiral*, p. 417.

7. Fernández-Armesto, *Columbus*, p. 103 and Morison, *Admiral*, pp. 417–18.

8. Jane, *Four Voyages*, vol. 1, pp. 48–52 and Morison, *Admiral*, pp. 424–8.

9. Morison, *Admiral*, pp. 465–7; Fernández-Armesto, *Columbus*, pp. 109–10; and Davidson, *Columbus Then and Now*, pp. 380–2.

10. Phillips and Phillips, *The Worlds of Christopher Columbus*, pp. 207–11.

11. More detailed accounts of Columbus's third voyage and its context can be found in Morison, *Admiral*, pp. 505–72; Morison, *Southern Voyages*, pp. 141–61; Fernández-Armesto, *Columbus*, pp. 115–32; Phillips and Phillips, *The Worlds of Christopher Columbus*, pp. 212–27; and Davidson, *Columbus Then and Now*, pp. 407–47.

12. Jane, *Four Voyages*, vol. 2, pp. 14–16.

13. Ibid., pp. 36–8.

14. Ibid., pp. 32–8, with quote at p. 36.

15. For a good modern account of the first years of the Spanish colony on Hispaniola see Fernández-Armesto, *Columbus*, pp. 132–51.

16. Louis-André Vigneras, *The Discovery of South America and the Andalusian Voyages* (Chicago, University of Chicago Press, 1976), pp. 19–20.

17. Frederick J. Pohl, *Amerigo Vespucci: Pilot Major* (New York, Columbia University Press, 1944) is a good overview of Vespucci's career.

18. Morison, *Southern Voyages*, pp. 184–90 and Vigneras, *Discovery*, pp. 47–57.

19. Morison, *Southern Voyages*, pp. 63–9 and Vigneras, *Discovery*, pp. 194–8.

20. Morison, *Southern Voyages*, pp. 210–14 and Vigneras, *Discovery*, pp. 69–76.

21. Morison, *Southern Voyages*, pp. 217–29.

22. Vigneras, *Discovery*, pp. 76–82.

23. Ibid., pp. 83–94 and Morison, *Southern Voyages*, pp. 214–16.

24. Vigneras, *Discovery*, pp. 99–109 and Morison, *Southern Voyages*, pp. 198–200.

25. Franz Laubenberger, 'The Naming of America', *The Sixteenth Century Journal* 13 (no. 4, 1982), 91–113.

26. More detailed accounts of Columbus's fourth voyage can be found in Morison, *Admiral*, pp. 575–659; Morison, *Southern Voyages*, pp. 236–71; Fernández-Armesto, *Columbus*, pp. 153–75; Phillips and Phillips, *The Worlds of Christopher Columbus*, pp. 230–40; and Davidson, *Columbus Then and Now*, pp. 448–66.

27. Jane, *Four Voyages*, vol. 2, p. 82.

28. Jane, *Four Voyages*, vol. 2, pp. 102–4.

29. For modern editions of these documents with excellent introductions see Helen Nader and Luciano Formisano (eds), *The Book of Privileges Issued to Christopher Columbus by King Fernando and Queen Isabel 1492–1502* (Berkeley, University of California Press, 1996) and Delno C. West and August Kling (eds), *The Libro de las Profecías of Christopher Columbus: An en face edition* (Gainesville, University of Florida Press, 1991).

30. For more details on Columbus's last years see Morison, *Admiral*, pp. 659–71 and Fernández-Armesto, *Columbus*, pp. 177–94.

31. Morison, *Southern Voyages*, pp. 200–4.

32. Ibid., pp. 297–303 and Francis Augustus MacNutt (ed. and trans.), *De Orbe Novo: The Eight Decades of Peter Martyr D'Anghera* (1912, rprt. New York, Burt Franklin, 1970), I, p. 402.

33. The best biography of Magellan in English is over 100 years old, F.H.H. Guillemard, *The Life of Ferdinand Magellan and the First Circumnavigation of the Globe* (London, G. Philip and Son, 1890). Morison, *Southern Voyages*, pp. 313–473 provides an excellent record. Charles McKew Parr, *So Noble a Captain: The Life and Times of Ferdinand Magellan* (New York, Thomas Y. Crowell, 1953) is a popular biography. There is also a good account in Robert Silverberg, *The Longest Voyage: Circumnavigation in the Age of Discovery* (1972, rprt. Athens, OH, Ohio University Press, 1997), pp. 65–233. There are several editions of the primary sources for Magellan's voyage: Henry E.J. Stanley (ed.), *The First Voyage Round the World by Magellan: Translated from the Accounts of Pigafetta and Other Contemporary Writers* (London, Hakluyt Society, 1874); Charles E. Nowell (ed.), *Magellan's Voyage Around the World: Three Contemporary Accounts* (Evanston, IL, Northwestern University Press, 1962); and Antonio Pigafetta, *Magellan's Voyage: A Narrative Account of the First Circumnavigation* (1969, rprt. New York, Dover Publications, 1994).

34. Stanley (ed.), *The First Voyage Round the World*, p. 58.

35. Pigafetta, *Magellan's Voyage*, p. 57.

36. Nowell (ed.), *Magellan's Voyage Around the World*, p. 149.

37. Morison, *Southern Voyages*, pp. 474–92 and O.H.K. Spate, *The Spanish Lake* (Minneapolis, MN, University of Minnesota Press, 1979), pp. 90–4.

38. Spate, *Spanish Lake*, *passim* is a good detailed overview of Spanish ventures in the Pacific Ocean during the sixteenth century. For the history of the trade between Manila and Acapulco see William Lytle Schurz, *The Manila Galleon* (New York, E.P. Dutton, 1939).

39. Harry Kelsey, *Sir Francis Drake: The Queen's Pirate* (New Haven, CT, Yale University Press, 1998), pp. 93–204.

40. Silverberg, *The Longest Voyage*, pp. 333–82 and Derek Wilson, *The Circumnavigators* (New York, M. Evans and Company, 1989), pp. 51–65.

41. Silverberg, *The Longest Voyage*, pp. 383–491.

42. For a detailed study of this whole question see Eviatar Zerubavel, *Terra Cognita: The Mental Discovery of America* (New Brunswick, NJ, Rutgers University Press, 1992).

43. David B. Quinn, *North America from Earliest Discovery to First Settlements: The Norse Voyages to 1612* (New York, Harper & Row, 1977), pp. 121–36.

44. Carl Ortwin Sauer, *The Early Spanish Main* (Berkeley, CA, University of California Press, 1969), pp. 147–60 and 178–89 and Carl Ortwin Sauer, *Sixteenth Century North America: The Land and the People as Seen by the Europeans* (Berkeley, CA, University of California Press, 1971), p. 26.

45. Morison, *Southern Voyages*, pp. 502–16; Quinn, *North America*, pp. 137–43; Sauer, *Sixteenth Century North America*, pp. 26–8; and Hugh Thomas, *Conquest: Montezuma, Cortés, and the Fall of Old Mexico* (New York, Simon & Schuster, 1993), p. 57. For some insight into the historiography of the thesis that Ponce discovered Yucatan and Mexico see Clinton R. Edwards, 'The Discoveries of Mexico and the Meaning of Discovery', *Terrae Incognitae* 17 (1985), 61–7. An interesting recent study is Robert H. Fuson, *Juan Ponce de León and the Spanish Discovery of Puerto Rico and Florida* (Blackburg, VA, McDonald & Woodward Publishing, 2000). He does not credit Ponce with discovering the Yucatan.

46. Morison, *Southern Voyages*, p. 517 and Quinn, *North America*, pp. 138 and 142.

47. There is a large body of historical writing dealing with Cabeza de Vaca. A good, recent and brief account is in Michael Wood, *Conquistadors* (Berkeley, CA, University of California Press, 2000), ch. 6. There is also Edward G. Bourne, *Spain in America* (New York, Harpers, 1904), pp. 158–69; Quinn, *North America*, pp. 148–51 and 192–4; and Sauer, *Sixteenth Century North America*, pp. 107–25. Sauer provides considerable detail about the adventures of Cabeza de Vaca's three other companions who are often neglected by historians.

48. Quinn, *North America*, pp. 152–68 and Sauer, *Sixteenth Century North America*, pp. 47–76.

49. David B. Quinn, *England and the Discovery of America, 1481–1620* (New York, Alfred W. Knopf, 1974), pp. 131–59.

50. Ibid., pp. 161–91.

51. The most detailed modern study of Verrazzano in English is Lawrence C. Wroth, *The Voyages of Giovanni da Verrazzano 1524–1528* (New Haven, CT, Yale University Press, 1970), which includes a translation of Verrazzano's letter to Francis I describing his voyage of 1524. Also worth reading are the accounts of Samuel Eliot Morison, *The European Discovery of America: The Northern Voyages, A.D. 500–1600* (New York, Oxford University Press, 1971), pp. 277–325; Quinn, *North America*, pp. 153–9; and Sauer, *Sixteenth Century North America*, pp. 52–62.

52. Wroth, *Voyages of Verrazzano*, p. 136.

53. For the disputes regarding the manner of Verrazzano's death see Wroth, *Voyages of Verrazzano*, pp. 255–62.

54. The most recent collection of essays that include scattered insights about the Esteban Gómez voyage is Emerson W. Baker et al. (eds), *American Beginnings: Exploration, Culture, and Cartography in the Land of Norumbega* (Lincoln, NB, University of Nebraska Press, 1994). Other good accounts can be found in Morison, *Northern Voyages*, pp. 328–31; Quinn, *North America*, pp. 153 and 160–3; and Sauer, *Sixteenth Century North America*, pp. 62–9.

55. Louis-André Vigneras, 'The Voyage of Esteban Gómez from Florida to the Baccalaos', *Terrae Incognitae* 2 (1970), 25–8 presents a convincing argument for a south to north

voyage. Compare the accounts of Quinn, who follows Vigneras, with Morison, who wrote before the publication of Vigneras's article.

56. Morison, *Northern Voyages*, pp. 233–7; Quinn, *North America*, pp. 164–6; and David B. Quinn, *England and the Discovery of America 1481–1620*, pp. 171–82.

57. The primary sources for the voyages of Cartier can be found in H.P. Biggar, *The Voyages of Jacques Cartier* (Ottawa, Public Archives of Canada, 1924); H.P. Biggar, *Collection of Documents Relating to Jacques Cartier and the Sieur de Roberval* (Ottawa, Public Archives of Canada, 1930); and Ramsay Cook, *The Voyages of Jacques Cartier* (Toronto, University of Toronto Press, 1993). Good accounts of the Cartier voyages can be found in Morison, *Northern Voyages*, pp. 339–463; Quinn, *North America*, pp. 169–90; and Sauer, *Sixteenth Century North America*, pp. 77–103.

58. James McDermott, *Martin Frobisher: Elizabethan Privateer* (New Haven, CT, Yale University Press, 2001), pp. 95–256; Morison, *Northern Voyages*, pp. 494–616; Quinn, *North America*, pp. 369–84; and Kenneth R. Andrews, *Trade, Plunder, and Settlement: Maritime Enterprise and the Genesis of the British Empire 1480–1630* (Cambridge, Cambridge University Press, 1984), pp. 167–82. The primary sources for Frobisher's voyage have been collected and edited in Richard Collinson (ed.), *The Three Voyages of Martin Frobisher, in Search of a Passage to Cathaia and India by the North-West, A.D. 1576–8* (London, Hakluyt Society, 1867) and V. Stefansson and E. McCaskill (eds), *The Three Voyages of Martin Frobisher*, 2 vols (1938, rprt. London, Argonaut Press, 1971).

59. The primary sources for John Davis's voyages are printed in Albert Hastings Markham (ed.), *The Voyages and Works of John Davis, the Navigator* (London, Hakluyt Society, 1880).

60. The relevant primary sources for these voyages are printed in G.M. Asher (ed.), *Henry Hudson the Navigator: The Original Documents in which His Career is Recorded* (London, Hakluyt Society, 1860); Clements R. Markham (ed.), *The Voyages of William Baffin, 1612–1622* (London, Hakluyt Society, 1881); and Miller Christy (ed.), *The Voyages of Captain Luke Foxe, of Hull, and Captain Thomas James, of Bristol, in Search of a North-West Passage . . .* (London, Hakluyt Society, 1894).

61. Good accounts of the attempts to find a north-east passage can be found in Andrews, *Trade, Plunder, and Settlement*, pp. 64–75; Boies Penrose, *Travel and Discovery in the Renaissance 1420–1620* (Cambridge, MA, Harvard University Press, 1960), pp. 171–4; J.H. Parry, *The Age of Reconnaissance: Discovery, Exploration and Settlement 1450 to 1650* (1963, rprt. Berkeley, CA, University of California Press, 1981), pp. 204–6; and William Foster, *England's Quest of Eastern Trade* (London, A. & C. Black, 1933), pp. 3–13.

62. The primary sources for Barents's career can be found in Charles T. Beke (ed.), *A True Description of Three Voyages by the North-East Toward Cathay and China, Undertaken by the Dutch in the Years 1594, 1595, and 1596* (London, Hakluyt Society, 1853) and Koolemans Beynen (ed.), *The Three Voyages of William Barents to the Arctic Regions, 1594, 1595, and 1596* (London, Hakluyt Society, 1876).

CHAPTER SIX

1. Francis Bacon, 'Of the True Greatness of Kingdoms and Estates' in *Essays*, ed. Gordon S. Haight (Rosyn, New York, Walter C. Black/Classics Club, n.d.), p. 127.

2. Samuel Johnson, *The Letters of Samuel Johnson*, ed. R.W. Chapman, 3 vols (Oxford, Clarendon Press, 1952). Letter of Dr Samuel Johnson to William Samuel Johnson of Stratford, Connecticut, written on 4 March 1773.

3. Bailey W. Diffie and George D. Winius, *Foundations of the Portuguese Empire 1415–1580* (Minneapolis, MN, University of Minnesota Press, 1977), pp. 187–9 and 220–2; R.S. Whiteway, *The Rise of Portuguese Power in India 1497–1550* (1899, rprt. New York, Augustus M. Kelley, 1969), p. 83; William Brooks Greenlee (ed.), *The Voyage of Pedro Alvares Cabral to Brazil and India* (London, Hakluyt Society, 1938), pp. xvi–xix; and Sanjay Subrahmanyam, *The Career and Legend of Vasco da Gama* (Cambridge, Cambridge University Press, 1997), pp. 174–84. Other writings that provide an up-to-date overview of the Portuguese in Asia are Sanjay Subrahmanyam and Luís Filipe F.R. Thomaz, 'Evolution of Empire: The Portuguese in the Indian Ocean During the Sixteenth Century' in *The Political Economy of Merchant Empires*, ed. James D. Tracy (Cambridge, Cambridge University Press, 1991), pp. 298–331 and Sanjay Subrahmanyam, *The Portuguese Empire in Asia 1500–1700: A Political and Economic History* (London, Longman, 1993), esp. ch. 3.

4. Greenlee (ed.), *The Voyage of Pedro Alvares Cabral*, pp. 32–3.

5. Diffie and Winius, *Foundations*, pp. 189–94 and Greenlee (ed.), *The Voyage of Pedro Alvares Cabral*, pp. xix–xx.

6. Whiteway, *Portuguese Power*, pp. 83–4.

7. Greenlee (ed.), *The Voyage of Pedro Alvares Cabral*, pp. xx–xxii.

8. Whiteway, *Portuguese Power*, pp. 84–7 and Greenlee (ed.), *The Voyage of Pedro Alvares Cabral*, pp. xxii–xxvii.

9. Whiteway, *Portuguese Power*, pp. 87–9; Diffie and Winius, *Foundations*, pp. 221–2; Greenlee (ed.), *The Voyage of Pedro Alvares Cabral*, pp. xxvii–xxviii; and Frederick Charles Danvers, *The Portuguese in India: Being a History of the Rise and Decline of their Eastern Empire*, 2 vols (1894, rprt. New York, Octagon Books, 1966), I, pp. 71–4.

10. Diffie and Winius, *Foundations*, pp. 206–8.

11. Greenlee (ed.), *The Voyage of Pedro Alvares Cabral*, pp. 132 and 134.

12. Greenlee (ed.), *The Voyage of Pedro Alvares Cabral*, pp. 133 and 137.

13. Diffie and Winius, *Foundations*, pp. 222–3 and M.N. Pearson, *The Portuguese in India*, vol. I, pt 1 of *The New Cambridge History of India*, ed. Gordon Johnson (Cambridge, Cambridge University Press, 1987), pp. 13–14.

14. Subrahmanyam, *Vasco da Gama*, pp. 184–210.

15. Diffie and Winius, *Foundations*, pp. 222–5 and Subrahmanyam, *Vasco da Gama*, pp. 210–34.

16. Diffie and Winius, *Foundations*, pp. 225–6; Whiteway, *Portuguese Power*, pp. 96–8; and Danvers, *Portuguese in India*, I, 93–109.

17. Diffie and Winius, *Foundations*, pp. 227–30 and Whiteway, *Portuguese Power*, pp. 104–15.

18. Diffie and Winius, *Foundations*, pp. 230–9 and Whiteway, *Portuguese Power*, pp. 115–18. Islamic chronicles gleefully reported the victory of the Mameluke fleet at Chaul and the death of Lourenço Almeida. One source even claimed that the Mamelukes killed 10,000 Portuguese soldiers and sailors, an obvious exaggeration. See E. Denison Ross, 'The Portuguese in India and Arabia between 1507 and 1517', *Journal of the Royal Asiatic Society* (1921), 550–3.

19. Whiteway, *Portuguese Power*, pp. 118–24; M. Longworth Dames, 'The Portuguese and Turks in the Indian Ocean in the Sixteenth Century', *Journal of the Royal Asiatic Society* (Jan. 1921), 6–10; and Ross, 'The Portuguese in India and Arabia', 549–53.

20. Diffie and Winius, *Foundations*, pp. 240–2; Whiteway, *Portuguese Power*, pp. 124–6; Dames, 'Portuguese and Turks', 10; and Ross, 'The Portuguese in India and Arabia', pp. 547–8.

21. George McCall Theal (ed.), *Records of South-Eastern Africa* (Cape Town, Government of the Cape Colony, 1899), vol. 6, p. 302.

22. Elaine Sanceau, *Indies Adventure: The Amazing Career of Afonso de Albuquerque* (London, Blackie & Son, 1936) is a good, detailed account of his life. Albuquerque's son Braz wrote a valuable account of his father that is available in English as *The Commentaries of the Great Afonso D'Alboquerque, Second Viceroy of India*, trans. and ed. Walter de Gray Birch, 4 vols (London, Hakluyt Society, 1875–84).

23. Sanceau, *Indies Adventure*, chs 5–9.

24. Diffie and Winius, *Foundations*, pp. 243–8 and Sanceau, *Indies Adventure*, chs 10 and 11.

25. Diffie and Winius, *Foundations*, pp. 248–54 and Whiteway, *Portuguese Power*, pp. 133–41.

26. Sanceau, *Indies Adventure*, chs 12 and 13.

27. Ibid., chs 14 and 15.

28. Diffie and Winius, *Foundations*, pp. 254–60; Whiteway, *Portuguese Power*, pp. 141–4; and Sanceau, *Indies Adventure*, ch. 17.

29. Diffie and Winius, *Foundations*, pp. 360–79.

30. F.E. Peters, *Mecca: A Literary History of the Muslim Holy Land* (Princeton, NJ, Princeton University Press, 1994), pp. 173–93 provides a good account of Albuquerque at Aden and in the Red Sea through excerpts from various primary sources.

31. Diffie and Winius, *Foundations*, pp. 263–8 and Sanceau, *Indies Adventure*, ch. 20.

32. Diffie and Winius, *Foundations*, pp. 268–71; Whiteway, *Portuguese Power*, pp. 160–7; and Sanceau, *Indies Adventure*, chs 23–5 and Epilogue.

33. Diffie and Winius, *Foundations*, chs 17 and 19–21.

34. Ross, 'The Portuguese in India and Arabia', 547–9.

35. C.R. Boxer, 'The Carreira da India (Ships, Men, Cargoes, Voyages)' in *O centro de estudoes historicos ultramarinos e as comemoracoes Henriquinas* (Lisbon, CEHU, 1961), pp. 33–82.

36. Pearson, *Portuguese in India*, pp. 40–51; Diffie and Winius, *Foundations*, pp. 407–26; and C.R. Boxer, *The Portuguese Seaborne Empire 1415–1825* (1969, rprt. London, Hutchinson, 1977), pp. 39–64. An important study of the shifting nature of the international spice trade can be found in Niels Steengaard, *The Asian Trade Revolution of the Seventeenth Century: The East India Companies and the Decline of the Caravan Trade* (Chicago, IL, University of Chicago Press, 1974).

37. Pearson, *Portuguese in India*, pp. 65–8 and Diffie and Winius, *Foundations*, pp. 418–20.

38. Salih Özbaran, 'The Ottoman Turks and the Portuguese in the Persian Gulf, 1534–1581', *Journal of Asian History* 6 (no. 1, 1972), 45–87.

39. Pearson, *Portuguese in India*, pp. 40–60.

40. Diffie and Winius, *Foundations*, pp. 278–80.

41. Ibid., pp. 427–30; E.W. Bovill, *The Battle of Alcazar* (London, Batchworth Press, 1952); and A.R. Disney, *Twilight of the Pepper Empire: Portuguese Trade in Southwest India in the early Seventeenth Century* (Cambridge, MA, Harvard University Press, 1978).

42. The classic account of the conquest of Mexico is William H. Prescott's *History of the Conquest of Mexico*, which was first published in 1843. It is available in many editions. The modern, definitive account is Hugh Thomas, *Conquest: Montezuma, Cortés, and the Fall of Old Mexico* (New York, Simon & Schuster, 1993). Michael Wood, *Conquistadors* (Berkeley,

CA, University of California Press, 2000) contains two chapters on Cortés which provide a brief and insightful overview. Other accounts well worth reading are R.C. Padden, *The Hummingbird and the Hawk: Conquest and Sovereignty in the Valley of Mexico, 1503–1541* (Columbus, OH, Ohio State University Press, 1967); Jon Manchip White, *Cortés and the Downfall of the Aztec Empire* (New York, St Martin's Press, 1971); and Ross Hassig, *Mexico and the Spanish Conquest* (London, Longman, 1994). Hassig contributed an essay to *What If? The World's Foremost Military Historians Imagine What Might Have Been*, ed. Robert Cowley (New York, Putnam, 1999) titled 'The Immolation of Hernán Cortés' which speculates about the various points at which Cortés could have lost and what the consequences would have been.

43. Carl Ortwin Sauer, *The Early Spanish Main* (Berkeley, University of California Press, 1969), chs 7, 9 and 10 and Thomas, *Conquest*, chs 5 and 6.

44. Thomas, *Conquest*, p. 85.

45. Thomas, *Conquest*, ch. 7. Bernal Díaz participated in the Córdoba expedition and included an account of it in his famous history of the conquest of Mexico. A good English translation of Díaz's history is *The Conquest of New Spain*, ed. J.M. Cohen (Harmondsworth, Penguin Books, 1963). The account of Córdoba is found on pp. 15–26. Another collection of primary sources for the Córdoba expedition is Henry R. Wagner, *The Discovery of the Yucatan by Francisco Hernández de Córdoba* (Berkeley, CA, Cortés Society, 1942). Besides Bernal Díaz's history, other useful and convenient Spanish sources for the conquest of Mexico are Patrica de Fuentes (ed.), *The Conquistadors: First-Person Accounts of the Conquest of Mexico* (1963, rprt. Norman, OK, University of Oklahoma Press, 1993); Anthony Pagden (ed.), *Hernan Cortés: Letters from Mexico* (1971, rprt. New Haven, CT, Yale University Press, 1986); and Francisco López de Gómara, *Cortés: The Life of the Conqueror by his Secretary*, ed. Lesley Byrd Simpson (Berkeley, CA, University of California Press, 1966). Mexica/Aztec accounts of the conquest were collected during the post-conquest years by the Franciscan missionary Bernardino de Sahagún. The most convenient edition of the native accounts is Miguel Leon-Portilla (ed.), *The Broken Spears: The Aztec Account of the Conquest of Mexico* (1962, rprt. Boston, Beacon Press, 1992), although a more scholarly edition is James Lockhart (ed.), *We People Here: Nahuatl Accounts of the Conquest of Mexico*, vol. I of the *Repertorium Columbianum* (Berkeley, CA, University of California Press, 1993).

46. Thomas, *Conquest*, ch. 8. For primary sources see Henry R. Wagner (ed.), *The Discovery of New Spain in 1518 by Juan de Grijalva* (Berkeley, CA, Cortés Society, 1942) and Bernal Díaz, *The Conquest of New Spain*, pp. 27–43. Díaz also participated in the Grijalva expedition.

47. For a good, brief overview of the native peoples of the pre-Columbian Americas see John E. Kicza, *The Peoples and Civilizations of the Americas before Contact* (Washington, DC, American Historical Association, 1998). A good recent account of the Aztecs is Inga Clendinnen, *The Aztecs* (Cambridge, Cambridge University Press, 1991). See Miguel León-Portilla, 'Men of Maize' in Alvin M. Joséphy, Jr (ed.), *America in 1492: The World of the Indian Peoples Before the Arrival of Columbus* (New York, Alfred W. Knopf, 1992), pp. 147–75. This essay discusses both the natives of the Caribbean islands and of Mesoamerica.

48. Thomas, *Conquest*, chs 9 and 10.

49. Ibid., pp. 171–3 and Bernal Díaz, *The Conquest of New Spain*, pp. 85–7. For an interesting comparative study of guides and interpreters that contains a large section on Doña Marina see Frances Karttunen, *Between Worlds: Interpreters, Guides, and Survivors* (New Brunswick, NJ, Rutgers University Press, 1994).

50. Thomas, *Conquest*, pp. 180–7; Padden, *Hummingbird and the Hawk*, pp. 116–31; and Davíd Carrasco, *Quetzalcoatl and the Irony of Empire: Myths and Prophecies in the Aztec Tradition* (Chicago, IL, University of Chicago Press, 1992).

51. Both Thomas, *Conquest*, and Prescott, *Conquest of Mexico* include extensive discussions of the background of Mexica/Aztec history and Montezuma's character. Additional insightful studies of Montezuma can be found in Padden, *Hummingbird and the Hawk*, chs 5–7 and White, *Cortés and the Downfall of the Aztec Empire*, pp. 81–155.

52. Thomas, *Conquest*, pp. 199–204 and 215–23.

53. Ibid., ch. 17 and Díaz, *Conquest of New Spain*, pp. 140–88.

54. Thomas, *Conquest*, ch. 18; Prescott, *Conquest of Mexico*, bk 3, chs 6 and 7; and Díaz, *Conquest of New Spain*, pp. 189–204.

55. Thomas, *Conquest*, ch. 19; Prescott, *Conquest of Mexico*, bk 3, chs 8 and 9; and Díaz, *Conquest of New Spain*, pp. 207–15.

56. Díaz, *Conquest of New Spain*, p. 216.

57. For an interesting assessment of the significance of the meeting between Cortés and Montezuma see Hugh Thomas, *The Real Discovery of America: Mexico November 8, 1519* (Mount Kisco, New York, Moyer Bell Limited, 1992).

58. Thomas, *Conquest*, pp. 304–10; Prescott, *Conquest of Mexico*, bk 4, ch. 3; and Francis J. Brooks, 'Montecuzoma Xocoyotl, Hernán Cortés, and Bernal Díaz del Castillo: The Construction of an Arrest', *Hispanic American Historical Review* 75 (no. 2, 1995), 149–83.

59. Thomas, *Conquest*, chs 24 and 25 and Prescott, *Conquest of Mexico*, bk 4, chs 6 and 7.

60. Thomas, *Conquest*, ch. 26.

61. Ibid., ch. 27; Prescott, *Conquest of Mexico*, bk 5, chs 1 and 2; and Díaz, *Conquest of New Spain*, pp. 284–96.

62. Thomas, *Conquest*, ch. 28; Prescott, *Conquest of Mexico*, bk 5, ch. 3; and Díaz, *Conquest of New Spain*, pp. 296–302.

63. Thomas, *Conquest*, chs 30 and 31; Prescott, *Conquest of Mexico*, bk 5, chs 5 and 6.

64. Thomas, *Conquest*, ch. 33 and Hassig, *Mexico and the Spanish Conquest*, ch. 8.

65. Díaz, *Conquest of New Spain*, p. 371.

66. Thomas, *Conquest*, chs 34 and 35 and Hassig, *Mexico and the Spanish Conquest*, ch. 9.

67. Díaz, *Conquest of New Spain*, p. 215.

68. Thomas, *Conquest*, pp. 592–3 and 601.

69. Ibid., pp. 595–600; Prescott, *Conquest of Mexico*, bk 7, chs 4 and 5; and White, *Cortés and the Downfall of the Aztec Empire*, pp. 283–97.

70. J.H. Parry, *The Discovery of South America* (New York, London, Taplinger, 1979), pp. 174–8.

71. Two excellent narratives of the conquest of Peru by Francisco Pizarro are William H. Prescott, *History of the Conquest of Peru*, first published in 1847, with many editions issued since that date, and John Hemming, *The Conquest of the Incas* (New York, Harcourt, Brace, Jovanovich, 1970). A brief, more recent account can be found in chs 3 and 4 of Michael Wood, *Conquistadors* (Berkeley, CA, University of California Press, 2000). References to Prescott's *History of the Conquest of Peru* will be to the Modern Library edition (New York, Random House, n.d.) which combines the complete *History of the Conquest of Mexico* and the complete *History of the Conquest of Peru* into one volume.

72. For a good study of the Pizarro family see Rafael Varon, *Francisco Pizarro and His Brothers* (Norman, OK, University of Oklahoma Press, 1997).

73. Prescott, *Conquest of Peru*, pp. 834–6.

74. Parry, *Discovery of South America*, p. 178 and Prescott, *Conquest of Peru*, pp. 834–47. For a detailed sixteenth-century account of this first voyage see Pedro de Cieza de Leon, *The Discovery and Conquest of Peru* trans. and ed. Alexandra Parma Cook and Noble David Cook (Durham, NC, Duke University Press, 1998), pp. 42–73.

75. Garcilaso de la Vega, El Inca, *Royal Commentaries of the Incas and General History of Peru*, 2 vols, trans. and ed. Harold V. Livermore (Austin, TX, University of Texas Press, 1966), II, p. 651.

76. Prescott, *Conquest of Peru*, p. 864.

77. Parry, *Discovery of South America*, pp. 178–80; Prescott, *Conquest of Peru*, pp. 848–82; and Cieza, *Discovery and Conquest of Peru*, pp. 71–140.

78. For good, brief accounts of the Incas on the eve of the Spanish conquest see Alan Kolata, 'In the Realm of the Four Quarters', in *America in 1492*, ed. Alvin M. Josephy, Jr (New York, Alfred W. Knopf, 1991), pp. 215–47 and John E. Kicza, *The Peoples and Civilizations of the Americas before Contact* (Washington, DC, American Historical Association, 1998), pp. 31–6.

79. Wood, *Conquistadors*, pp. 122–4 and Prescott, *Conquest of Peru*, pp. 898–907.

80. The events relating Pizarro's march to Cajamarca and the subsequent capture of Atahualpa are described in detail by Prescott, *Conquest of Peru*, pp. 908–51 and Hemming, *Conquest of the Incas*, pp. 23–45.

81. Augustin de Zárate, *The Discovery and Conquest of Peru* (Harmondsworth, Penguin Books, 1968), p. 100.

82. Ibid., p. 104; Hemming, *Conquest of the Incas*, p. 41; and Cieza, *Discovery and Conquest of Peru*, pp. 211–12.

83. Hemming, *Conquest of the Incas*, pp. 46–70. On the death of Huascar see Prescott, *Conquest of Peru*, pp. 949–51 and Cieza, *Discovery and Conquest of Peru*, pp. 223–7.

84. Hemming, *Conquest of the Incas* is an excellent detailed account of how the Spanish conquered the Incas through to the fall of Vilcabamba in 1572. Prescott, *Conquest of Peru* goes into more detail concerning the civil wars of the Spaniards. Cieza chronicles the events of the civil wars and they have been translated into English by C.R. Markham in the Hakluyt Society volumes *The War of Las Salinas* (1923), *The War of Chupas* (1918) and *The War of Quito* (1913).

85. The search for El Dorado is well served by three studies: Walker Chapman, *The Golden Dream: Seekers of El Dorado* (Indianapolis, IN, Bobbs-Merrill, 1967); John Hemming, *The Search for El Dorado* (London, Michael Joseph, 1978); and Victor W. von Hagen, *The Golden Man: The Quest for El Dorado* (London, Book Club Associates, 1974).

86. Anthony Smith, *Explorers of the Amazon* (New York, Viking, 1990) and Wood, *Conquistadors* have good chapters on Orellana, as do Chapman, *The Golden Dream* and Hemming, *The Search for El Dorado*. Primary sources dealing with Orellana's journey down the Amazon can be found in José Toribio Medina (ed.), *The Discovery of the Amazon* (1935, rprt. New York, Dover, 1988).

87. Charles Nicholl, *The Creature in the Map: A Journey to El Dorado* (New York, William Morrow, 1995) is an excellent account of Ralegh's expedition. For Ralegh's own words see Sir Walter Ralegh, *The Discoverie of the Large, Rich, and Bewtiful Empyre of Guiana*, transcribed, annotated and introduced by Neil L. Whitehead (Norman, OK, University of Oklahoma Press, 1997).

88. Edward Gaylord Bourne, *Spain in America, 1450–1580* (New York, Harper, 1904), pp. 149–74 and David B. Quinn, *North America from Earliest Discovery to First Settlements: The Norse Voyages to 1612* (New York, Harper & Row, 1977), pp. 148–51.

89. Wood, *Conquistadors*, ch. 6 and David Ewing Duncan, *Hernando de Soto: A Savage Quest in the Americas* (New York, Crown, 1996), pp. 215–19.

90. Duncan, *Hernando de Soto*, pp. 215–425 and Lawrence A. Clayton, Vernon James Knight, Jr and Edward C. Moore (eds), *The De Soto Chronicles: The Expedition of Hernando de Soto to North America in 1539–1543*, 2 vols (Tuscaloosa, AL, University of Alabama Press, 1993) which is a very large collection of the chronicles relating to the Soto expedition.

91. Quinn, *North America from Earliest Discovery to First Settlements*, pp. 194–206; Bourne, *Spain in America*, pp. 169–74; and Pedro de Castañeda et al., *The Journey of Coronado*, trans. and ed. George Parker Winship (1933, rprt. New York, Dover, 1990) for a collection of primary sources about Coronado's expedition.

92. Quinn, *North America from Earliest Discovery to First Settlements*, pp. 223–5 and Carl Ortwin Sauer, *Sixteenth Century North America: The Land and the People as Seen by the Europeans* (Berkeley, CA, University of California Press, 1971), pp. 154–6.

93. Thomas, *Conquest*, p. 569.

94. Charles R. Boxer, *The Dutch Seaborne Empire: 1600–1800* (New York, Alfred W. Knopf, 1970) and George Masselman, *The Cradle of Colonialism* (New Haven, CT, Yale University Press, 1963) are good surveys of the rise of the Dutch trading empire.

95. John W. Blake, *West Africa: Quest for God and Gold, 1454–1578*, 2nd edn, 1937 (Totowa, NJ, Rowman and Littlefield, 1977) tells the story of Portugal's trade with West Africa and its competition from Spain, France and England.

96. Lyle N. McAlister, *Spain and Portugal in the New World, 1492–1700* (Minneapolis, MN, University of Minnesota Press, 1984), pp. 199–203, 233–5 and 258–66.

97. Bourne, *Spain in America*, pp. 175–89 and Quinn, *North America from Earliest Discovery to First Settlements*, pp. 240–61.

98. English overseas activities in the sixteenth century are usefully surveyed in David B. Quinn, *England and the Discovery of America, 1481–1620* (New York, Alfred W. Knopf, 1974) and Kenneth R. Andrews, *Trade, Plunder, and Settlement: Maritime Enterprise and the Genesis of the British Empire 1480–1630* (Cambridge, Cambridge University Press, 1984). For a more recent work that also covers the seventeenth century see Nicholas Canny (ed.), *The Origins of Empire: British Overseas Enterprise to the Close of the Seventeenth Century*, vol. 1 of the *Oxford History of the British Empire*, ed. William Roger Louis (Oxford, Oxford University Press, 1998).

99. Rayner Unwin, *The Defeat of John Hawkins: A Biography of His Third Slaving Voyage* (London, George Allen & Unwin, 1960) is a detailed and well-written account of Hawkins's fateful third voyage.

100. Harry Kelsey, *Sir Francis Drake: The Queen's Pirate* (New Haven, CT, Yale University Press, 1998) is the most recent of the many biographies of Drake. It is very good for his privateering voyages.

101. James McDermott, *Martin Frobisher: Elizabethan Privateer* (New Haven, CT, Yale University Press, 2001), chs 6–13.

102. Quinn, *North America from Earliest Discovery to First Settlements*, chs 13–15; David B. Quinn (ed.), *The Voyages and Colonising Enterprises of Sir Humphrey Gilbert*, 2 vols (London, Hakluyt Society, 1940); and David B. Quinn (ed.), *The Roanoke Voyages, 1584–1590. Documents to Illustrate the English Voyages to North America under the Patent Granted to Walter Raleigh in 1584*, 2 vols (London, Hakluyt Society, 1955).

103. John Keay, *The Honorable Company: A History of the English East India Company* (New York, Macmillan, 1991) is a good, readable survey.

104. Holden Furber, *Rival Empires of Trade in the Orient, 1600–1800* (Minneapolis, MN, University of Minnesota Press, 1976) provides an excellent overview.

CONCLUSION

1. Adam Smith, *Wealth of Nations* (Chicago, IL, Britannica Great Books, 1952), p. 271.

2. Karl Marx, *Capital* (Chicago, IL, Britannica Great Books, 1952), p. 372.

3. Donald Lach, *Asia in the Making of Europe*, vol. I of *The Century of Discovery*, ed. Lach, bk 1 (Chicago, IL, University of Chicago Press, 1965), pp. 143–7.

4. C.R. Boxer, *The Portuguese Seaborne Empire 1415–1825* (1969, rprt. London, Hutchinson, 1977), pp. 39–64; Bailey W. Diffie and George D. Winius, *Foundations of the Portuguese Empire, 1415–1580* (Minneapolis, MN, University of Minnesota Press, 1977), pp. 301–7; Herman van der Wee, 'Structural changes in European long-distance trade, and particularly in the re-export trade from south to north, 1350–1750' in *The Rise of Merchants Empires: Long-Distance Trade in the Early Modern World, 1350–1750*, ed. James D. Tracy (Cambridge, Cambridge University Press, 1990), pp. 27–33; and Lach, *Asia*, vol. I, bk 1, pp. 119–26. Also see A.R. Disney, *Twilight of the Pepper Empire: Portuguese Trade in Southwest India in the Early Seventeenth Century* (Cambridge, MA, Harvard University Press, 1978) and Donald Lach and Edwin J. Van Kley, *Asia in the Making of Europe*, vol. 3, *A Century of Advance* (Chicago, IL, University of Chicago Press, 1993), bk 1, pp. 10–40.

5. John Hemming, *The Conquest of the Incas* (New York, Harcourt, Brace, Jovanovich, 1970), pp. 223 and 368–72.

6. Roger Schlesinger, *In the Wake of Columbus: The Impact of the New World on Europe, 1492–1650* (Wheeling, IL, Harlan Davidson, 1996), p. 4 and Ward Barrett, 'World Bullion Flows, 1450–1800' in *Rise of Merchant Empires*, ed. Tracy, pp. 224–45.

7. Schlesinger, *Wake of Columbus*, pp. 1–10; Fernand Braudel, *The Mediterranean and the Mediterranean World in the Age of Philip II*, 2 vols (New York, Harper & Row, 1972), I, pp. 476–542; and the classic article by Earl J. Hamilton, 'American Treasure and Andalusian Prices, 1503–1660: A Study in the Spanish Price Revolution' in *The Price Revolution in Sixteenth-Century England*, ed. Peter H. Ramsey (London, Methuen, 1971), pp. 147–81, but first appearing in the *Journal of Economic and Business History*, vol. I (no. 1, Nov. 1928), and his excellent monograph, *American Treasure and the Price Revolution in Spain, 1501–1650* (Cambridge, MA, Harvard University Press, 1934).

8. Carlo M. Cipolla, *Guns, Sails, and Empires: Technological Innovation and the Early Phases of European Expansion, 1400–1700* (1965, rprt. Manhattan, KS, Sunflower University Press, 1985).

9. Alfred W. Crosby, *The Columbian Exchange: Biological and Cultural Consequences of 1492* (Westport, CT, Greenwood Press, 1972), pp. 35–63.

10. The historiography and conclusions concerning the pre-contact population of the Americas is briefly and sensibly summarized in Hugh Thomas, *Conquest: Montezuma, Cortés, and the Fall of Old Mexico* (New York, Simon & Schuster, 1993) in Appendix I, 'The Population of Old Mexico', pp. 609–14 along with other information about population scattered throughout the text of the book. Another brief but useful survey of the state of knowledge is Tamar Stieber, 'Consequences of Contact', *American Archaeology*, vol. 5 (no. 3, Fall 2001), 33–9. The maximalist view of pre-contact population and the role of disease is usefully summarized by Noble David Cook, *Born to Die: Disease and New World Conquest, 1492–1650* (Cambridge, Cambridge University Press, 1998). A trenchant critique of the inflated estimates of Native American populations and disease victims is provided

by David Henige, *Numbers from Nowhere: The American Indian Contact Population Debate* (Norman, OK, University of Oklahoma Press, 1998) which is nicely summarized in David Henige, 'De-Population Myths: How Many People Really Lived in the Americas Before the European Conquest', *Skeptic*, vol. 7 (no. 2, 1999), pp. 42–7. Also see his 'On the Contact Population of Hispaniola: History as Higher Mathematics', *Hispanic American Historical Review*, vol. 58 (no. 2 , May 1978), 217–37 and 709–12.

11. Brenda J. Baker and George J. Armelagos, 'The Origin and Antiquity of Syphilis: Paleopathological Diagnosis and Interpretation', *Current Anthropology*, 29 (1988), 703–37; Crosby, *Columbian Exchange*, ch. 4; Claude Quétel, *History of Syphilis* (Baltimore, MD, Johns Hopkins University Press, 1990); and Schlesinger, *Wake of Columbus*, pp. 100–5.

12. Crosby, *Columbian Exchange*, pp. 75–85 and 100–6 and Deb Bennett and Robert S. Hoffman, 'Ranching in the New World' in *Seeds of Change: A Quincentennial Commemoration*, ed. Herman J, Viola and Carolyn Margolis (Washington, DC, Smithsonian Institution Press, 1991), pp. 106–10.

13. Crosby, *Columbian Exchange*, ch. 5; William H. McNeill, 'American Food Crops in the Old World' in *Seeds of Change*, pp. 43–59; Sophie D. Coe and Michael D. Coe, *The True History of Chocolate* (London, Thames & Hudson, 1996); and Redcliffe Salaman, *The History and Social Influence of the Potato* (1949, rev. edn Cambridge, Cambridge University Press, 1985).

14. Lee Eldridge Huddleston, *Origins of the American Indians: European Concepts, 1492–1729* (Austin, TX, University of Texas, 1967) and Ronald H. Fritze, *Legend and Lore of the Americas before 1492: An Encyclopedia of Visitors, Explorers, and Immigrants* (Santa Barbara, CA, ABC-Clio, 1993).

15. Margaret T. Hodgen, *Early Anthropology in the Sixteenth and Seventeenth Centuries* (Philadelphia, PA, University of Pennsylvania Press, 1964) is a classic overview that discusses the impact of the age of exploration on early modern anthropology which can be supplemented by the essays in Stuart B. Schwartz (ed.), *Implicit Understandings: Observing, Reporting, and Reflecting on the Encounters between Europeans and Other Peoples in the Early Modern Era* (Cambridge, Cambridge University Press, 1994). For the Americas see Schlesinger, *Wake of Columbus*, ch. 3; J.H. Elliott, *The Old World and the New 1492–1650* (Cambridge, Cambridge University Press, 1970); and Fredi Chiappelli (ed.), *First Images of America: The Impact of the New World on the Old*, 2 vols (Berkeley, CA, University of California Press). For Asia there is the massive study of Donald Lach, *Asia in the Making of Europe*.

16. Bernal Díaz, *The Conquest of New Spain* (Harmondsworth, Penguin Books, 1963), p. 14.

BIBLIOGRAPHY

Abulafia, David. 'Asia, Africa, and the Trade of Medieval Europe' in *The Cambridge Economic History of Europe*, vol. II: *Trade and Industry in the Middle Ages*, ed. M.M. Postan and Edward Miller, 2nd edn, Cambridge, Cambridge University Press, 1987

Acosta, José de. *The Natural and Moral History of the Indies*, 2 vols, London, Hakluyt Society, 1880

Andrews, Kenneth R. *Trade, Plunder and Settlement: Maritime Enterprise and the Genesis of the British Empire 1480–1630*, Cambridge, Cambridge University Press, 1984

Arens, W. *The Man-Eating Myth: Anthropology & Anthropophagy*, Oxford, Oxford University Press, 1979

Ashe, Geoffrey. *Land to the West: St. Brendan's Voyage to America*, New York, Viking, 1962

Axelson, Eric. *Congo to Cape: Early Portuguese Explorers*, New York, Barnes & Noble, 1973

Azurara, Gomes Eannes de. *The Chronicle of the Discovery and Conquest of Guinea*, ed. and trans. Charles Raymond Beazley and Edgar Prestage, 2 vols, London, Hakluyt Society, 1896 and 1899

Babcock, William H. *Legendary Islands of the Atlantic: A Study in Medieval Geography*, New York, American Geographical Society, 1922

Baker, Emerson W. et al. (eds). *American Beginnings: Exploration, Culture, and Cartography in the Land of Norumbega*, Lincoln, NB, University of Nebraska Press, 1994

Barreto, Mascarenhas. *The Portuguese Columbus: Secret Agent of King John II*, New York, St Martin's Press, 1992; first pub. in Portuguese in 1988

Beazley, C. Raymond. *The Dawn of Modern Geography*, 3 vols, 1897–1906, rprt. New York, Peter Smith, 1942

——. *Prince Henry the Navigator: The Hero of Portugal and of Modern Discovery 1394–1460 A.D.*, 1901, rprt. London, Frank Cass, 1968

Beckingham, C.F. *Between Islam and Christendom: Travellers, Facts and Legends in the Middle Ages and the Renaissance*, London, Variorum Reprints, 1983

Bedini, Silvio A. (ed.). *The Christopher Columbus Encyclopedia*, 2 vols, New York, Simon & Schuster, 1992

Bentley, Jerry H. *Old World Encounters: Cross-Cultural Contacts and Exchanges in Pre-Modern Times*, Oxford, Oxford University Press, 1993

Betten, F.S. 'The Knowledge of the Sphericity of the Earth during the Earlier Middle Ages', *Catholic Historical Review*, New Series, 3 (April, 1923), pp. 74–90

Biggar, H.P. (ed.). *The Precursors of Jacques Cartier 1497–1534: A Collection of Documents Relating to the Early History of the Dominion of Canada*, Ottawa, Government Printing Bureau, 1911

—— (ed.). *The Voyages of Jacques Cartier; Published From the Originals with Translations, Notes, and Appendices*, Ottawa, Public Archives of Canada, 1924

—— (ed.). *A Collection of Documents Relating to Jacques Cartier and the Sieur de Roberval*, Ottawa, Public Archives of Canada, 1930

Blake, John William (ed.). *Europeans in West Africa, 1450–1560*, 2 vols, London, Hakluyt Society, 1942

——. *West Africa: Quest for God and Gold, 1454–1578: A Survey of the First Century of White Enterprise in West Africa, with Particular Reference to the Achievements of the Portuguese and Their Rivalries with Other European Powers*, London, Curzon Press, 1977

Bodmer, Beatriz Pastor. *The Armature of Conquest: Spanish Accounts of the Discovery of America, 1492–1589*, trans. Lydia Longstreth Hunt, first pub. in 1983, rprt. and trans., Stanford, CA, Stanford University Press, 1992

Bourne, Edward Gaylord. *Spain in America, 1450–1580*, New York, Harpers, 1904

Bovill, Edward William. *The Golden Trade of the Moors: West African Kingdoms in the Fourteenth Century*, 1958, rprt. Princeton, NJ, Markus Wiener Publishers, 1995

Boxer, C.R. *The Dutch Seaborne Empire: 1600–1800*, New York, Alfred W. Knopf, 1965

——. *The Portuguese Seaborne Empire, 1415–1825*, 1969, rprt. London, Hutchinson, 1977

Brooks, Francis J. 'Motecuzoma Xocoyotl, Hernán Cortés, and Bernal Díaz del Castillo: The Construction of an Arrest', *Hispanic American Historical Review* 72 (no. 2, 1995), 149–83

Buker, George H. 'The Seven Cities: The Role of Myth in the Exploration of the Atlantic', *American Neptune* 30 (1970), 249–59

Bulliett, Richard W. *The Camel and the Wheel*, Cambridge, MA, Harvard University Press, 1975

Bunbury, E.H. *A History of Ancient Geography*, 2 vols, 1883, rprt. New York, Dover, 1959

Carillo, Jesús (ed.). *Oviedo on Columbus*, vol. IX of *Repertorium Columbianum*, Turnhout, Belgium, Brepols, 2000

Carpender, Rhys. *Beyond the Pillars of Heracles: The Classical World Seen Through the Eyes of Its Discovers*, New York, Delacorte Press, 1966

Carrasco, Davíd. *Quetzalcoatl and the Irony of Empire: Myths and Prophecies in the Aztec Tradition*, Chicago, IL, University of Chicago Press, 1982, rprt. with a new preface 1992

——. *Religions of Mesoamerica: Cosmovision and Ceremonial Centers*, San Francisco, CA, Harper & Row, 1990

Cary, George David. *The Medieval Alexander*, 1956, rprt. Cambridge, Cambridge University Press, 1963

Cary, M. and Warmington, E.H. *The Ancient Explorers*, 1929, rprt. Harmondsworth, Penguin, 1963

Casson, Lionel. *The Ancient Mariners: Seafarers and Sea Fighters of the Mediterranean in Ancient Times*, 2nd edn, Princeton, NJ, Princeton University Press, 1991

Cieza de Leon, Pedro de. *The Discovery and Conquest of Peru*, ed. and trans. Alexandra Parma Cook and Noble David Cook, Durham, NC, Duke University Press, 1998

——. *The Incas*, ed. Victor Wolfgan von Hagen, Norman, OK, University of Oklahoma Press, 1959

Cipolla, Carlo M. *Guns, Sails, and Empires: Technological Innovation and the Early Phases of European Expansion, 1400–1700*, 1965, rprt. Manhattan, KS, Sunflower University Press, 1985

Columbus, Christopher. *Select Documents Illustrating the Four Voyages of Columbus*, ed. and trans. Cecil Jane, 2 vols, London, Hakluyt Society, 1930 and 1933

Columbus, Ferdinand. *The Life of the Admiral Christopher Columbus by his Son Ferdinand*, trans. and ed. Benjamin Keen, New Brunswick, NJ, Rutgers University Press, 1959, rprt. with a new introduction 1992

Cook, Noble David. *Born to Die: Disease and New World Conquest, 1492–1650*, Cambridge, Cambridge University Press, 1998

Cook, Ramsay (ed.). *The Voyages of Jacques Cartier*, Toronto, University of Toronto Press, 1993

Crone, G.R. (ed.). *The Voyages of Cadamosto and Other Documents on Western Africa in the Second Half of the Fifteenth Century*, London, Hakluyt Society, 1937

Crosby, Alfred W. *The Columbian Exchange: Biological and Cultural Consequences of 1492*, Westport, CT, Greenwood Press, 1972

——. *Ecological Imperialism: The Biological Expansion of Europe, 900–1900*, Cambridge, Cambridge University Press, 1986

Cuyvers, Luc. *Into the Rising Sun: Vasco da Gama and the Search for the Sea Route to the East*, New York, TV Books, 1999

Dames, M. Longworth. 'The Portuguese and the Turks in the Indian Ocean in the Sixteenth Century', *Journal of the Royal Asiatic Society* (Jan. 1921), 1–28

Danvers, Frederick Charles. *The Portuguese in India: Being a History of the Rise and Decline of Their Eastern Empire*, 2 vols, 1894, rprt. New York, Octagon Books, 1966

Davidson, Miles H. *Columbus Then and Now: A Life Re-examined*, Norman, OK, University of Oklahoma Press, 1997

Dawson, Christopher (ed.). *Mission to Asia*, 1955, rprt. Toronto, University of Toronto Press, 1980

DeCorse, Christopher R. *The Archaeology of Elmina: Africans and Europeans on the Gold Coast, 1400–1900*, Washington, DC, Smithsonian Institution Press, 2001

Delgado-Gomez, Angel. *Spanish Historical Writing about the New World 1493–1700*, Providence, R.I., The John Carter Brown Library, 1992

Delumeau, Jean. *History of Paradise: The Garden of Eden in Myth and Tradition*, New York, Continuum, 1995

Díaz, Bernal. *The Conquest of New Spain*, trans. and ed. J.M. Cohen, Harmondsworth, Penguin, 1963

Diffie, Bailey W. *Prelude to Empire: Portugal Overseas before Henry the Navigator*, Lincoln, NB, University of Nebraska Press, 1960

Diffie, Bailey W. and Winius, George D. *Foundations of the Portuguese Empire 1415–1580*, Minneapolis, MN, University of Minnesota Press, 1977

Disney, A.R. *Twilight of the Pepper Empire: Portuguese Trade in Southwest India in the Early Seventeenth Century*, Cambridge, MA, Harvard University Press, 1978

Disney, A.R. and Booth, Emily (eds). *Vasco da Gama and the Linking of Europe and Asia*, New Dehli, Oxford University Press, 2000

Dor-Ner, Zvi. *Columbus and the Age of Discovery*, New York, William Morrow, 1991

Dotson, John (ed. and trans.). *Christopher Columbus and his Family: The Genoese and Ligurian Documents*, vol. IV of *Repertorium Columbianum*, Turnhout, Belgium, Brepols, 1998

Duchet-Suchaux, G. and Pastoreau, M. *The Bible and the Saints*, Paris, Flammarion, 1994

Duncan, David Ewing. *Hernando de Soto: A Savage Quest in the Americas*, New York, Crown, 1996

Dunn, Oliver and Kelley, Jr, James E. (eds and trans.). *The Diario of Christopher Columbus's First Voyage to America 1492–1493: Abstracted by Fray Bartolomé de Las Casas*, Norman, OK, University of Oklahoma Press, 1989

Durán, Diego. *The History of the Indies of New Spain*, trans. and ed. Doris Heyden, Norman, OK, University of Oklahoma Press, 1994

Eatough, Geoffrey (ed.). *Selections from Peter Martyr*, vol. V of *Repertorium Columbianum*, Turnhout, Belgium, Brepols, 1998

Edwards, Clinton R. 'The Discoveries of Mexico and the Meaning of Discovery', *Terrae Incognitae* 17 (1985), 61–7

Elliott, J.H. *The Old World and the New, 1491–1650*, Cambridge, Cambridge University Press, 1972

Estensen, Miriam. *Discovery: The Quest for the Great South Land*, New York, St Martin's Press, 1998

Farmer, D.H. (trans. and ed.). *The Age of Bede*, Harmondsworth, Penguin, 1983

Fernández-Armesto, Felipe. *Before Columbus: Exploration and Colonisation from the Mediterranean to the Atlantic, 1229–1492*, Basingstoke, Macmillan, 1987

——. *Columbus*, Oxford, Oxford University Press, 1991

——. *Ferdinand and Isabella*, 1975, rprt. New York, Dorset Press, 1991

——. *The Times Atlas of World Exploration: 3000 Years of Exploring, Explorers, and Mapmaking*, New York, HarperCollins, 1991

Fitzhugh, William W. and Ward, Elisabeth I. (eds). *Vikings: The North Atlantic Saga*, Washington, DC, Smithsonian Institution Press, 2000

Flint, Valerie I.J. *The Imaginative Landscape of Christopher Columbus*, Princeton, NJ, Princeton University Press, 1992

——. 'Monsters and Antipodes in the Early Middle Ages and the Enlightenment', *Viator* 15 (1984), 65–80

Foster, William. *England's Quest of Eastern Trade*, London, A. & C. Black, 1933

Friedman, John Block. *The Monstrous Races in Medieval Art and Thought*, Cambridge, MA, Harvard University Press, 1981

Furber, Holden. *Rival Empires of Trade in the Orient, 1600–1800*, Minneapolis, MN, University of Minnesota Press, 1976

Fuson, Robert H. *Juan Ponce de León and the Spanish Discovery of Puerto Rico and Florida*, Blackburg, VA, McDonald & Woodward Publishing, 2000

Galvano, Antonio. *The Discoveries of the World, from Their First Original unto the Year of Our Lord, 1555*, ed. C.R.D. Bethune, London, Hakluyt Society, 1862

Garcilaso de la Vega, El Inca. *Royal Commentaries of the Incas and General History of Peru*, trans. Harold V. Livermore, 2 vols, Austin, TX, University of Texas Press, 1966

Granzotto, Gianni. *Christopher Columbus: The Dream and the Obsession*, London, Collins, 1986

Greenlee, William Brooks (trans. and ed.). *The Voyage of Pedro Alvares Cabral to Brazil and India: From Contemporary Documents and Narratives*, London, Hakluyt Society, 1938

Griffin, Nigel (ed. and trans.). *Las Casas on Columbus: Background and the Second and Fourth Voyages*, vol. VII of *Repertorium Columbianum*, Turnhout, Belgium, Brepols, 1999

Haase, Wolfgang and Reinhold, Meyer (eds). *The Classical Tradition and the Americas*, vol. 1: *European Images of the Americas and the Classical Tradition, Part 1*, Berlin, Walter de Gruyter, 1994

Hagen, Victor W. von. *The Golden Man: The Quest for El Dorado*, London, Book Club Associates, 1974

Hassig, Ross. *Mexico and the Spanish Conquest*, London, Longman, 1994

Hemming, John. *The Conquest of the Incas*, New York, Harcourt, Brace, Jovanivich, 1970

——. *The Search for El Dorado*, London, Michael Joseph, 1978

Henige, David. *In Search of Columbus: The Sources for the First Voyage*, Tucson, AZ, University of Arizona Press, 1991

——. *Numbers from Nowhere: The American Indian Contact Population Debate*, Norman, OK, University of Oklahoma Press, 1998

Hobhouse, Henry. *Seeds of Change: Five Plants that Transformed Mankind*, New York, Harper & Row, 1985

Hodgen, Margaret T. *Early Anthropology in the Sixteenth and Seventeenth Centuries*, Philadelphia, PA, University of Pennsylvania Press, 1964

Hourani, George F. *Arab Seafaring in the Indian Ocean in Ancient and Early Medieval Times*, 1951, rprt. in an expanded edn Princeton, NJ, Princeton University Press, 1995

Jones, C.W. 'The Flat Earth', *Thought* 9 (1934), 296–307

Jones, Gwyn. *The North Atlantic Saga: Being the Norse Voyages of Discovery and Settlement to Iceland, Greenland, and North America*, rev. edn Oxford, Oxford University Press, 1986

Kennedy, Hugh. *The Prophet and the Age of the Caliphates: The Islamic Near East from the Sixth to the Eleventh Century*, London, Longman, 1986

Lach, Donald F. *Asia in the Making of Europe*, vol. 1: *The Century of Discovery*, in 2 vols, Chicago, IL, University of Chicago Press, 1965

Lapidus, Ira M. *A History of Islamic Societies*, Cambridge, Cambridge University Press, 1988

Larner, John. 'The Certainty of Columbus: Some Recent Studies', *History* 73 (Feb. 1988), 3–23

——. *Marco Polo and the Discovery of the World*, New Haven, CT, Yale University Press, 1999

Laubenberger, Franz. 'The Naming of America', *Sixteenth Century Journal* 13 (no. 4, 1982), 91–113

Leon-Portilla, Miguel (ed.). *The Broken Spears: The Aztec Account of the Conquest of Mexico*, expanded and updated edn, Boston, MA, Beacon Press, 1992

Lestringant, Frank. *Mapping the Renaissance World: The Geographical Imagination in the Age of Discovery*, Berkeley, CA, University of California Press, 1994

Levathes, Louise. *When China Ruled the Seas: The Treasure Fleet of the Dragon Throen, 1400–1433*, New York, Simon & Schuster, 1994

Liss, Peggy K. *Isabel the Queen: Life and Times*, Oxford, Oxford University Press, 1992

Litvinoff, Barnet. *Fourteen Ninety Two: The Decline of Medievalism and the Rise of the Modern Age*, New York, Scribners, 1991

Liu, Xinru. *The Silk Road: Overland Trade and Cultural Interactions in Eurasia*, Washington, DC, American Historical Association, 1998

Lockhart, James (ed. and trans.). *We People Here: Nahuatl Accounts of the Conquest of Mexico*, vol. 1 of *Repertorium Columbianum*, Berkeley, CA, University of California Press, 1993

McAlister, Lyle N. *Spain and Portugal in the New World 1492–1700*, Minneapolis, MN, University of Minnesota Press, 1984

McCrindle, J.W. (ed.). *The Christian Cosmography of Cosmas, An Egyptian Monk*, London, Hakluyt Society, 1897

MacNutt, Francis Augustus (ed. and trans.). *De Orbe Novo: The Eight Decades of Peter Martyr D'Anghera*, 2 vols, 1912, rprt. New York, Burt Franklin, 1970

Madariaga, Salvador de. *Christopher Columbus: Being the Life of the Very Magnificent Lord Don Cristóbal Colón*, New York, Macmillan, 1940

Magnusson, Magnus and Hermann Palsson (trans.). *The Norse Discovery of America: Graenlendinga Saga and Eirik's Saga*, New York, New York University Press, 1966

Major, Richard Henry (trans. and ed.). *India in the Fifteenth Century Being a Collection of Voyages to India in the Century Preceding the Portuguese Discovery of the Cape of Good Hope*, London, Hakluyt Society, 1857

—— (trans. and ed.). *The Canarian, or, Book of the Conquest and Conversion of the Canarians in the Year 1402*, London, Hakluyt Society, 1872

Marques, Alfredo Pinheiro. *Portugal and the Discovery of the Atlantic*, Casa da Moeda, Portugal, Imprensa Nacional, 1990

Masselman, George. *The Cradle of Colonialism*, New Haven, CT, Yale University Press, 1963

Means, Philip Ainsworth (ed.). *Relation of the Discovery and Conquest of the Kingdoms of Peru by Pedro Pizarro*, 2 vols, New York, Cortés Society, 1921

Mintz, Sidney W. *Sweetness and Power: The Place of Sugar in Modern History*, New York, Viking Penguin Inc., 1985

Moffat, Samuel Hugh. *A History of Christianity in Asia*, vol. I: *Beginnings to 1500*, San Francisco, CA, HarperCollins, 1992

Morison, Samuel Eliot. *Portuguese Voyages to America in the Fifteenth Century*, Cambridge, MA, Harvard University Press, 1940

——. *The European Discovery of America: The Northern Voyages A.D. 500–1600*, New York, Oxford University Press, 1971

——. *The European Discovery of America: The Southern Voyages A.D. 1492–1616*, New York, Oxford University Press, 1974

Murray, James C. *Spanish Chronicles of the Indies: Sixteenth Century*, New York, Twayne Publishers, 1994

Nader, Helen (ed. and trans.). *The Book of Privileges Issued to Christopher Columbus by King Fernando and Queen Isabel 1492–1502*, vol. II of *Repertorium Columbianum*, Berkeley, CA, University of California Press, 1996

Nebenzahl, Kenneth. *Atlas of Columbus and the Great Discoveries*, Chicago, IL, Rand McNally, 1990

Neill, Stephen. *A History of Christian Missions*, Harmondsworth, Penguin, 1986

Nicholl, Charles. *The Creature in the Map: A Journey to El Dorado*, New York, William Morrow, 1995

Nordenskiöld, A.E. *Facsimile-Atlas to the Early History of Cartography with Reproductions of the Most Important Maps Printed in the XV and XVI Centuries*, 1899, rprt. New York, Dover Publications, 1973

Nowell, Charles E. *The Great Discoveries and the First Colonial Empires*, Ithaca, NY, Cornell University Press, 1954

——. *Magellan's Voyage Around the World: Three Contemporary Accounts*, Evanston, IL, Northwestern University Press, 1962

Nunn, George E. *The Geographical Conceptions of Columbus: A Critical Consideration of Four Problems*, 1924, rprt. Milwaukee, WI, The American Geographical Society Collection of the Golda Meir Library, 1992

Oliver, Roland (ed.). *The Cambridge History of Africa*, vol. 3: *From c. 1050–c. 1600*, Cambridge, Cambridge University Press, 1977

Olschki, Leonardo. 'Ponce de León's Fountain of Youth: History of a Geographical Myth', *Hispanic American Historical Review* 22 (Aug. 1941), 361–85

Panikkar, K.M. *Malabar and the Portuguese: Being a History of the Relations of the Portuguese with Malabar from 1500–1663*, Bombay, D.B. Tarporevala Sons & Co., 1929

——. *India and the Indian Ocean: An Essay on the Influence of Sea Power on Indian History*, New York, Macmillan, 1945

Parry, J.H. *The Establishment of the European Hegemony: 1415–1715, Trade and Exploration in the Age of the Renaissance*, New York, Harper & Row, 1966

——. *The Spanish Seaborne Empire*, Berkeley, CA, University of California Press, 1966

——. *The Discovery of South America*, New York, Taplinger Publishing Company, 1979

——. *The Age of Reconnaissance: Discovery, Exploration and Settlement 1450 to 1650*, 1963, rprt. Berkeley, CA, University of California Press, 1981

——. *The Discovery of the Sea*, 1974, rprt. Berkeley, CA, University of California Press, 1981

Pearson, M.N. *The Portuguese in India*, vol. I, pt 1 of *The New Cambridge History of India*, ed. Gordon Johnson, Cambridge, Cambridge University Press, 1987

Penrose, Boies. *Travel and Discovery in the Renaissance 1420–1620*, Cambridge, MA, Harvard University Press, 1960

Peters, F.E. *Mecca: A Literary History of the Muslim Holy Land*, Princeton, NJ, Princeton University Press, 1994

Phillips, J.R.S. *The Medieval Expansion of Europe*, 2nd edn, Oxford, Oxford University Press, 1998; first pub. in 1988

Phillips, Jr, William D. and Phillips, Carla Rahn. *The Worlds of Christopher Columbus*, Cambridge, Cambridge University Press, 1992

Pigafetta, Antonio. *Magellan's Voyage: A Narrative Account of the First Circumnavigation*, 1969, rprt. New York, Dover Publications, 1994

Pinto, Ferão Mendes. *The Travels of Mendes Pinto*, ed. and trans. Rebecca D. Catz, Chicago, IL, University of Chicago Press, 1989

Pohl, Frederick J. *Amerigo Vespucci: Pilot Major*, New York, Columbia University Press, 1944

Polo, Marco. *The Travels of Marco Polo: The Complete Yule-Cordier Edition*, 2 vols, 1871, 1875 and 1920, rprt. New York, Dover Books, 1993

Poma de Ayala, Don Felipe Huamán. *Letter to a King: A Peruvian Chief's Account of Life under the Incas and under Spanish Rule*, New York, Dutton, 1978

Pope, Peter E. *The Many Landfalls of John Cabot*, Toronto, University of Toronto Press, 1997

Prescott, William H. *History of the Conquest of Mexico and History of the Conquest of Peru*, New York, The Modern Library, n.d.

Prestage, Edgar. *The Portuguese Pioneers*, London, A. & C. Black, 1933

Quinn, David B. (ed.). *The Voyages and Colonising Enterprises of Sir Humphrey Gilbert*, 2 vols, London, Hakluyt Society, 1940

—— (ed.). *The Roanoke Voyages, 1584–1590. Documents to Illustrate the English Voyages to North America under the Patent Granted to Walter Raleigh in 1584*, 2 vols, London, Hakluyt Society, 1955

—— *England and the Discovery of America 1481–1620*, New York, Alfred W. Knopf, 1974

——. *North America from Earliest Discovery to First Settlements: The Norse Voyages to 1612*, New York, Harper & Row, 1977

Randles, W.G.L. 'Classical Models of World Geography and Their Transfer Following the Discovery of America' in *The Classical Tradition and the Americas*, ed. Wolfgang Haase and Reinhold Meyer, Berlin, Walter de Gruyter, 1994, pp. 5–76

Ravenstein, E.G. (ed. and trans.). *A Journal of the First Voyage of Vasco da Gama, 1497–1499*, London, Hakluyt Society, 1898

Romm, James S. *The Edges of the Earth in Ancient Thought: Geography, Exploration, and Fiction*, Princeton, NJ, Princeton University Press, 1992

Ross, David J.A. *Alexander Historiatus*, London, Warburg Institute, 1963

Ross, E. Denison. 'The Portuguese in India and Arabia between 1507 and 1517', *Journal of the Royal Asiatic Society* (Oct. 1921), 545–62

——. 'The Portuguese in India and Arabia, 1517–1538', *Journal of the Royal Asiatic Society* (Jan. 1922), 1–18

Rossabi, Morris. *Voyager from Xanadu: Rabban Sauma and the First Journey from China to the West*, Tokyo, Kodansha International, 1992

Russell, Jeffrey Burton. *Inventing the Flat Earth: Columbus and Modern Historians*, New York, Praeger, 1991

Russell, P.E. 'Prince Henry the Navigator', *Diamente* 11 (London, 1960), 3–30

——. 'Prince Henry the Navigator: The Rise and Fall of a Culture Hero', Taylorian Special Lecture 10, Oxford, 1984, rprt. in Russell, *Portugal, Spain and the African Atlantic 1343–1490*

——. *Portugal, Spain and the African Atlantic, 1343–1490: Chivalry and Crusade from John of Gaunt to Henry the Navigator*, Aldershot, Variorum Reprints, 1995

——. *Prince Henry 'the Navigator' a Life*, New Haven, CT, Yale University Press, 2000

Russell-Wood, A.J.R. *The Portuguese Empire, 1415–1808: A World on the Move*, 1992, rprt. Baltimore, MD, Johns Hopkins University Press, 1998

Ryan, James D. 'European Travelers before Columbus: The Fourteenth Century's Discovery of India', *Catholic Historical Review* 79 (1993), 648–70

Sale, Kirkpatrick. *The Conquest of Paradise: Christopher Columbus and the Columbian Legacy*, New York, Alfred W. Knopf, 1990

Sanceau, Elaine. *Indies Adventure: The Amazing Career of Afonso de Albuquerque*, London, Blackie, 1936

Sanday, Peggy Reeves. *Divine Hunger: Cannibalism as a Cultural System*, Cambridge, Cambridge University Press, 1986

Sauer, Carl Ortwin. *The Early Spanish Main*, Berkeley, CA, University of California Press, 1969

——. *Sixteenth Century North America: The Land and the People as Seen by the Europeans*, Berkeley, CA, University of California Press, 1971

Scafi, Alessandro. 'Mapping Eden: Cartographies of the Early Paradise' in *Mappings*, ed. Denis Cosgrove, London, Reaktion Books, 1999

Scammell, G.V. *The World Encompassed: The First European Maritime Empires, c. 800–1650*, London, Methuen, 1981

Schlesinger, Roger. *In the Wake of Columbus: The Impact of the New World on Europe, 1492–1650*, Wheeling, IL, Harland Davidson, 1996

Schurz, William Lytle. *The Manila Galleon*, New York, E.P. Dutton, 1939

Silverberg, Robert (as Walker Chapman). *The Golden Dream: Seekers of El Dorado*, Indianapolis, IN, Bobbs-Merrill, 1967

——. *The Longest Voyage: Circumnavigators in the Age of Discovery*, 1972, rprt. Athens, OH, Ohio University Press, 1997

Smith, Anthony. *Explorers of the Amazon*, New York, Viking, 1990

Smith, Roger C. *Vanguard of Empire: Ships of Exploration in the Age of Columbus*, New York, Oxford University Press, 1993

Spate, O.H.K. *The Spanish Lake*, Minneapolis, MN, University of Minnesota Press, 1979

Stanley, Henry E.J. (ed. and trans.). *The First Voyage Round the World by Magellan, Translated from the Accounts of Pigafetta and Other Contemporary Writers*, London, Hakluyt Society, 1874

—— (ed. and trans.). *The Three Voyages of Vasco da Gama, and his Viceroyalty: From the Lendas da India of Gaspar Correa; Accompanied by Original Documents*, London, Hakluyt Society, 1869

Stannard, David E. *American Holocaust: Columbus and the Conquest of the New World*, Oxford, Oxford University Press, 1992

Steengaard, Niels. *The Asian Trade Revolution of the Seventeenth Century: The East India Companies and the Decline of the Caravan Trade*, Chicago, IL, University of Chicago Press, 1974

Stoneman, Richard (ed.). *The Great Alexander Romance*, London, Penguin, 1991

Subrahmanyam, Sanjay. *The Career and Legend of Vasco da Gama*, Cambridge, Cambridge University Press, 1997

———. *The Portuguese Empire in Asia 1500–1700: A Political and Economic History*, London, Longman, 1993

Taviani, Paolo Emilio. *Columbus the Great Adventure: His Life, His Times, and His Voyages*, New York, Orion Books, 1991

Thomas, Hugh. *The Real Discovery of America: Mexico November 8, 1519*, Mount Kisco, New York, Moyer Bell, 1992

———. *Conquest: Montezuma, Cortés, and the Fall of Old Mexico*, New York, Simon & Schuster, 1993

Tozzer, H.F. *A History of Ancient Geography*, 1897, rprt. New York, Biblio and Tanner, 1964

Trexler, Richard C. *The Journey of the Magi*, Princeton, NJ, Princeton University Press, 1997

Vignaud, Henry. *Toscanelli and Columbus: The Letter and Chart of Toscanelli*, 1902, rprt. Freeport, NY, Books for Libraries, 1971

Vigneras, Louis-André. *The Discovery of South America and the Andalusian Voyages*, Chicago, IL, University of Chicago Press, 1976

Viola, Herman J. and Margolis, Carolyn (eds). *Seeds of Change: A Quincentennial Commemoration*, Washington, DC, Smithsonian Institution Press, 1991

Wagner, Henry R. (ed.). *The Discovery of New Spain in 1518 by Juan de Grijalva*, Berkeley, CA, Cortés Society, 1942

——— (ed.). *The Discovery of the Yucatan by Francisco Hernández de Córdoba*, Berkeley, CA, Cortés Society, 1942

Watts, Pauline Moffitt. 'Prophecy and Discovery: On the Spiritual Origins of Christopher Columbus's "Enterprise of the Indies"', *American Historical Review* 90 (Feb. 1985), 73–102

West, Delno C. and Kling, August (eds and trans.). *The Libro de las profecías of Christopher Columbus*, Gainesville, FL, University of Florida Press, 1991

White, David Gordon. *Myths of the Dog-Man*, Chicago, IL, University of Chicago Press, 1991

Whitehead, Neil L. *The Discoverie of the Large, Rich and Bewtiful Empyre of Guiana by Sir Walter Ralegh*, Norman, OK, University of Oklahoma Press, 1997

Wilford, John Noble. *The Mysterious History of Columbus: An Exploration of the Man, the Myth, the Legacy*, New York, Alfred W. Knopf, 1991

Wilson, Derek. *The Circumnavigators*, New York, M. Evans & Company, 1989

Winsor, Justin. *Christopher Columbus and How He Received and Imparted the Spirit of Discovery*, 1890, rprt. Stanford, CT, Longmeadow Press, 1991

Wittkower, Rudolf. 'Marvels of the East', *Journal of the Warburg and Courtauld Institutes* 5 (1942), 159–97

Wood, Michael. *Conquistadors*, Berkeley, CA, University of California Press, 2000

Wright, John Kirtland. *Geographical Lore of the Time of the Crusades*, New York, American Geographical Society, 1925

Wroth, Lawrence C. *The Voyages of Giovanni da Verrazzano, 1524–1528*, New Haven, CT, Yale University Press, 1970

Zárate, Augustin. *The Discovery and Conquest of Peru*, ed. and trans. J.M. Cohen, Harmondsworth, Penguin, 1968

Zerubavel, Eviatar. *Terra Cognita: The Mental Discovery of Amerca*, New Brunswick, NJ, Rutgers University Press, 1992

INDEX